MASTERING
THE POWER OF
GRIT

STRATEGIES, TACTICS, AND TOOLS FROM THE HEROES OF TENACITY, RESILIENCE, AND GUTS

*Timeless Lessons from the Legends
of Making Things Happen and
Getting Things Done*

John C. Welch IV, Ed.D., M.T.S., M.B.A.
By the People Books, San Diego, CA

Get Your Free
Companion Poster Guide
for *Mastering the Power of Grit* here:

www.ClassicInfluence.com/grit

By the People Books
Copyright © 2016 | All Rights Reserved

ISBN-13: 978-0692749371
ISBN-10: 0692749373

For Stella, Dad, Mom, Sandy and Chris—
You guys mean the world to me.

In memory of Theodore Roosevelt (1858—1919),
who taught us all about the importance of grit.

A portion of the proceeds of this book will
go toward helping to launch the new
Progressive Bull Moose Party

www.ProgressiveBullMoose.Party

"Lives of great men oft remind us
We can make our lives sublime,
And departing, leave behind us
Footprints on the sands of time."
—Longfellow, "Psalm of Life"

TABLE OF CONTENTS

CONTENT SUMMARIES

MASTER THE POWER OF GRIT

Grit is the great game changer on the road to excellence and success. All of the great hustlers and heroes of history have been marked by grit. Virtually every one of them has had to persevere through countless setbacks, crushing rejection, distressing attacks and sometimes even devastating defeat in pursuit of their dreams. Develop an inner core of fortitude, perseverance and guts; steel yourself for criticism, opposition, and resistance; equip yourself for an onslaught of obstacles, rejection, and adversity in advance and you will begin to understand that grit was their secret weapon of success. Rather than spending inordinate time trying to avoid failure and rejection, seek to exploit it when it comes. Learn from it. Build on it. Leverage it. Turn it around and bounce back. Rather than letting your emotions control your reactions, adopt an optimistic outlook, and the mindset of learning and growth. Be oblivious to rejection. Become a master of resilience. Foster a spirit of fearlessness. Give yourself permission to fail again and again, faster and faster, all the way to the summit of success.

| 1 |
SUCCEED BY STICKING IT OUT

The will to persevere is the ultimate power. "Will makes men giants," wrote Ik Marvel. Your ability to persevere is directly dependent on the depth of your interest in and enthusiasm for your vision and goals. Desire is what incites the will to work hard and persevere. The more you want something, the harder you will work, the more pain you can and will endure to get it. Create a clear and compelling vision of what exactly it is you want, a purpose that truly inspires, a dream that will get you up early, with goals that will keep you up late. Then resolve in advance that you will persevere. Make up your mind that you will do whatever it takes to achieve your dreams and goals, that you will pay the price to make it happen, then turn your mind away from any other possibility. Expect challenges and temporary defeats along the way, but never expect ultimate defeat. Instead, get the leverage you need to greatly amplify your odds of success.

| 2 |
FOSTER A SPIRIT OF FEARLESSNESS,
FORGE A SPINE OF STEEL

Cowardice and fear have no part to play in your success. Whatever your greatest dreams, there will always be moments where courage will be vital to your advance. Whatever apprehensions and insecurities you may now possess, however they may have ruled you in the past, your task is to face your fears, control them, exploit them, acknowledge and dismiss them, but never allow them to define your future or dictate your next steps. Never let your imagination get the best of you. Rather than accepting ideas that don't serve your purpose and goals, your task is to discover and discard your limiting beliefs. Take the time to identify and challenge the beliefs behind the fears that are holding you back, then replace those perceptions and beliefs with more resourceful alternatives, ideas that lead to greater self-assurance and guts. Use action as a tool for overcoming fear. "Get action" said Theodore Roosevelt. Just begin it. "Act just as if" you are not afraid, he said, and the fear will gradually disappear.

| 3 |
FOCUS ON THE POSITIVE,
CULTIVATE AN OPTIMISTIC OUTLOOK

Never underestimate the power of your thoughts, or your ability to facilitate the achievement of your goals by thinking big, positive possibilities. Your success depends on your frame of mind, and the way you see and interpret the world. Regardless of what challenges you face, a subtle shift of perspective from the negative to the positive can transform virtually everything in your life. Understand: The intent is not simply to see things differently (though that is precisely where change most often begins). A shift in perspective will change what you see; it will change the way you think, what you say, and how you act in the world. No matter what your situation, optimism is genuinely a matter of choice. It is not enough to decide to be optimistic. You must train your brain to think optimistically. This means cultivating mindfulness. Learning to observe your thoughts, and manage your internal dialogue. But don't just manage or maintain it. Integrate optimism into your plans. Beware: Maintaining a relentless optimism does not mean denying reality. Delusional thinking is as deadly to your goals as distorted facts. It is a sober optimism—backed by practical and effective action—that wins.

| 4 |
FAIL YOUR WAY TO THE TOP

The most successful people are, inevitably, also the people who fail the most. This frame of mind is sewn into the psychology of all great hustlers. If you, from this point forward, would never undertake anything without first resolving to accept failure over and over again, and be prepared to continue failing until you succeed, the likelihood of your eventual success will increase exponentially. It may not be precisely where or how you thought you'd succeed, but you will find success as long as you steel yourself for repeated failure first. Recognize that your failures are revealing important lessons you must learn on your path to ultimate victory. Find ways to use failure to your advantage—the value is in the learning—then look for ways to pick up the speed. Stop fearing failure, and start going after your biggest dreams—and when you fail, pick yourself up and go after it again. Find the seed of advantage in adversity, and use it for your success.

| 5 |
STEEL YOURSELF FOR CRITICISM, OPPOSITION AND RESISTANCE

Giving yourself over to your emotions is never the path to personal power and success. Whatever criticism, resistance, or opposition you face, it is how you see it—your perspective, paradigm, or frame—that matters most. Learn how to win the inner game, and stay cool under fire. Your success depends on your ability to reframe opposition and resistance so that your options are increased and your position or power is strengthened. Build capacity to detach and you will gain the advantage of your greatest and most powerful asset: Your mind. Keep your mission at the top of your mind, and recognize that there are always numerous options for how to respond to the attacks of an opponent, many of which will actually enhance your position or strengthen your power.

| 6 |
BE OBLIVIOUS
TO REJECTION AND DEFEAT

History's heroes of hustle and grit all learned to become increasingly immune to rejection and defeat. At first, you may have to rely on small victories, or successes in other areas of your life to neutralize or counteract rejection and defeat. Even without any real significant triumphs, you can use your creative imagination to construct experiences that serve the same end. Over time, as you begin to stockpile your victories and successes, you will build a shield of resistance and develop a kind of hardiness that makes you essentially oblivious to future rejection and defeat. Rather than instinctively falling back on your automatic programming, deliberately decide how you will respond to rejection and defeat. Resolve to make choices aligned with your purpose and goals, rather than your emotions and moods or, worse still, the moods and emotions of others. Steal a play from the champions and focus your mind on the long game, several moves ahead. Never dwell on the mistakes of the past. Never obsess over rejection or defeat. Take full responsibility for learning what you can, then shut the door and move on.

BOUNCE BACK,
REBUILD, BEGIN ANEW

There is nothing more important to regaining your initiative, and seizing responsibility for your comeback than believing that you have what it takes. The record of human history is clear: We are all capable of far more than most anyone imagines. We have far more power over our individual lives than most people are willing to admit. And we have complete responsibility for how we choose to respond to our lives' individual events. The winners of the world know this and, as a result, they own their decisions and the results of their mistakes and failures—not in a prideful or sacrificial way, but in a way that maximizes their ability to learn and grow from these experiences and move on. Take the necessary time to recover and regroup, then rise to fight again. Never see failure as final, or defeat as a dead end, instead imagine a new beginning. Understand: It is often impossible to stage a great comeback without learning. There can be no comeback if you only rise to repeat the same costly mistakes. In fact, it may be that learning is the best kept secret of resilience. Do not respond without thinking. The setback you suffered may have changed your situation or position and, therefore, to achieve your dreams and goals, be prepared to recalibrate based on where you are now, or find an alternative route to the top.

COUNTERPUNCH:
BE PREPARED TO PIVOT,
KNOW WHEN TO QUIT

The heroes of history recognize the power of fortitude, consistency and grit. And, yet, they also have the courage and confidence to change, pivot, or adjust when they must. It is your ability to recognize what you are up against, and your willingness and flexibility to adapt that will ensure the success of your greater purpose. A willingness to adapt to a given set of circumstances is often a critical factor of success. Rather than remaining intractable, hustlers adjust to the reality at hand. Understand: The objective is not to be flexible about everything, adapting the moment there's a shift in the wind. True champions remain committed to their purpose and principles, their vision and values, but remain flexible on strategy, tactics, and objectives, adapting as needed to the environment, the landscape, or emerging opportunities and threats. Sometimes quitting is the best, most practical way to move forward with your broader ambitions and goals. In fact, when what you are doing is no longer bringing you closer to your dreams and goals, then it's time to quit. To be clear: The point is not to do whatever you feel like doing whenever you feel like doing it. Your life must be guided by your dreams and goals, not society's rules, cultural standards, or the expectations of your family and friends. Quit when your dreams demand it. Persistence, resilience and grit have little value if they are not geared toward achieving your life's greater purpose and goals.

GRIT BLUEPRINT:
Peering Below the Surface

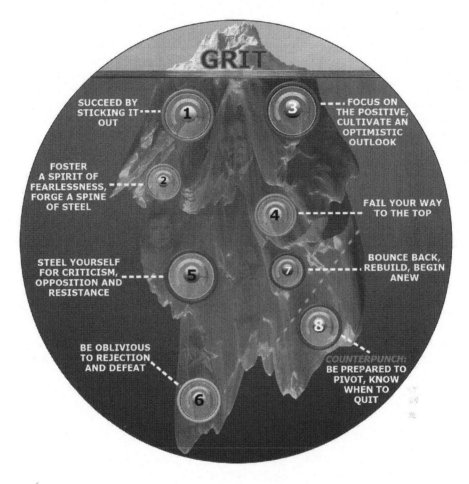

Grit is not a solitary trait, but rather a rich combination of characteristics, competencies, and skills which are frequently found in varying degrees, but which essentially fuse to form a kind of synergistic organizing principle of success.

PREFACE

"If the mind is willing, the flesh could go on and on without many things."
–Sun Tzu (544—496 B.C.)

On October 14, 1912, Theodore Roosevelt was scheduled to give a presidential campaign speech at the Gilpatrick Hotel in Milwaukee, Wisconsin. Roosevelt was running for an unprecedented third term, and he was on a whirlwind speaking tour, frequently making more than two dozen speeches a day. By the time his campaign reached Milwaukee, Roosevelt was physically exhausted, his voice was fading fast, and he was often reduced to delivering his speeches in a near whisper. Nevertheless, "I want to be a good Indian,"[1] Roosevelt said, and so he soldiered on. But on this particular night the celebrated war hero found himself in a battle not for campaign contributions or votes, but for his life.

At the scheduled time, Roosevelt and his entourage proceeded to walk out of the Gilpatrick Hotel to their large, topless automobile. At the first sight of Colonel Roosevelt, the patiently waiting crowd roared with approval. Suddenly, just as Roosevelt stood up from the car to bow to the cheering throng, a lone gunman, John Flammang Schrank, a delusional German immigrant who had been stalking Roosevelt for weeks, standing less than seven feet away, pulled out a .38 revolver and shot Roosevelt square in the chest.[2]

As Roosevelt fell, several men quickly tackled and disarmed Schrank. The crowd was immediately whipped into a frantic rabble. One of Roosevelt's aides held Schrank in a head lock, tightening as if struggling to break the man's neck. Others were kicking Schrank, while still others began to shout, "Kill him! Kill him!"[3]

Roosevelt regained his footing. He was, in the words of one witness, "the coolest and least excited of anyone in the frenzied mob."[4] Appearing to have miraculously escaped harm, he quickly intervened to save Schrank. "Don't hurt him. Bring him here," Roosevelt shouted, "I want to see him."[5] He wanted to know why Schrank shot him, but the would-be assassin offered only the blank stare of a madman's demented mind. "Oh, what's the use?" Roosevelt said, "Turn him over to the police."[6]

"For the moment, nobody but he realized he had stopped a bullet."[7] Roosevelt reached under his heavy army overcoat to examine the wound. Surprised to see his fingertips covered in blood, Roosevelt turned to his aide, "He pinked me, Harry."[8] The would-be assassin's bullet penetrated the thick speech papers and the metal glasses case in his pocket and was lodged in Roosevelt's thick, muscular chest, "less than a quarter of an inch from his heart."[9] "It was a ragged, dime-sized hole, bleeding slowly...The bullet was nowhere to be seen or [felt]."[10]

Suddenly Harry and the others were scrambling to rush Roosevelt to the nearest hospital. But Roosevelt, still calm, drew on his experience as a big game hunter and war veteran. He intentionally coughed a few times, raised his hand to his lips to check for blood, and concluded that the bullet had not pierced his lungs. It was unlikely to be fatal, he thought. And, thus, to the utter disbelief of all concerned, Roosevelt insisted on proceeding with the program as planned. Knowing that nearly ten thousand people were waiting to hear him speak, Roosevelt demanded adamantly, "You get me to that speech," and then, he added dramatically, "it may be the last I shall deliver, but I am going to deliver this one."[11]

Model the Masters

"The search after the great man is the dream of youth and the most serious occupation of manhood. We travel into foreign parts to find his works, if possible, to get a glimpse of him."
—Ralph Waldo Emerson (1803—1882), Representative Man (1850)

"If I have seen further it is only by standing on the shoulders of giants."
–Isaac Newton (1642—1727)

Theodore Roosevelt continues to stand as an exemplary role model, a premier American illustration of the indispensable characteristics of fortitude and success. Indeed, throughout the world and across the political spectrum, men and women continue to look to the life, leadership and example of TR for ideas, insight and inspiration.

Arnold Schwarzenegger tells the story of the time he broke his leg in a skiing accident in Sun Valley, Idaho, two days before Christmas in 2006. The Governator began to question his ability to deliver his impending inaugural address, scheduled for January 5, less than two weeks after his bunny slope mishap.[12] Schwarzenegger later said that he, "had prepared landmark statements of what I wanted to accomplish in the next four years. But if I was distracted by pain or doped up on painkillers, it was hard to see how I'd deliver them."[13] But Schwarzenegger soon remembered how the Bull Moose took a bullet mere minutes before his own speech. "Teddy Roosevelt, of course, once got shot by a would-be assassin..." Arnold wrote, "...and calmly finished his remarks before seeing a doctor. I wondered how he'd pulled that off."[14]

When Arnold agreed with his wife, Maria, to cancel the inauguration, he said, "I felt like a total wimp."[15] The next morning, however, remembering Roosevelt and the brave men and women of America's military who were determined to "get back to the battlefield, and continue the fight," Schwarzenegger knew he had to go ahead with his inaugural address, "even," he said, "if I had to crawl on all fours up the steps of the capitol."[16]

Nearly a century after his death, Roosevelt's example continues to inspire. The wisdom, understanding and insight we can glean from the stories of his life are practical, applicable, and deep. This itself is an important lesson: The wisdom of life is found in the stories of our heroes. Thus, in your endeavor to live the ideal life you've imagined, learning from the legends is key. Indeed, the legends themselves learn from the legends. Only a fool would fail to tap into this vast storehouse of wisdom and insight.[17] In fact, Roosevelt himself made excellent use of the history and biographical records of the great men and women of the world. Adopting men like Lincoln and Washington as his heroic role models (to emulate, not imitate), Roosevelt quickly emerged as a great leader in his own right.[18] But this is the key: He never stopped learning, he never stopped analyzing and scrutinizing the lives of other great leaders.

Roosevelt, of course, is just one brick in a great wall of champions and heroes. Indeed, the history of America alone is teeming with stories of these titans of fortitude and grit, stories which continue to offer lessons and insights, principles and practices, strategies and tactics that you can use today. Abraham Lincoln, for example, is another great American icon of dogged determination, resilience and grit. While many of the world's great leaders were born into positions of power and privilege, Lincoln had no such advantages. He was born in a one-room log cabin. He had less than a year of formal education. His father lost all of their property when Lincoln was five. His mother died when he was only nine. He failed in business. His first true love died when he was twenty-five. He suffered from depression. His wife was mentally unstable, and abusive.[19] He endured several electoral defeats. And yet through it all he rose to become

President of the United States. Lincoln faced an incredible number of obstacles and setbacks that would have licked a weaker man. But Lincoln possessed something else, this indispensable quality: Willpower—strength of mind. It was this will, this determination in the face of seemingly insurmountable odds that allowed Lincoln to persevere, to bounce back, to fall and get up again and again. The lesson from Lincoln, in his own words? "Always bear in mind that your own resolution to succeed is more important than any other one thing."[20] "Hold on," he said, "with a bulldog grip, and chew and choke as much as possible."[21]

But Arnold's question remains: How did TR pull it off? How was he able to so boldly and calmly face down the prospect of imminent death? Even from this single incident—looking carefully at Roosevelt's words and actions, both during and afterwards—there are lessons and insights that we can take away, as we can with scores of other great men and women (many of which will be revealed in the pages ahead) about how to attain and sustain this kind of indomitable spirit, this relentless resilience and stamina and guts.

Push Beyond Perceived Limits

"We have not journeyed all this way across the centuries, across the oceans, across the mountains, across the prairies, because we are made of sugar candy."
—Winston Churchill (1874—1965)

When Roosevelt reached the auditorium where he was scheduled to speak, his condition appeared to have worsened. His aides continued to protest, begging him to go to the hospital. Once he settled in the holding room behind the stage, Roosevelt allowed his traveling physician (Dr. Scurry Terrell, a throat specialist), to take a quick look. When he saw that, "the whole right side of his body had turned black," he insisted that Roosevelt get immediate medical attention.[22]

Clearly, Roosevelt was pushing up against a perceived limit, a limit bluntly identified by the insistent orders of his own physician. Nevertheless, with a lifetime of his own relevant experience, Roosevelt understood the risks, perhaps better than his throat doctor, and so he calmly assessed the situation with a level head, and decided to push on. "It's all right, Doctor," Roosevelt said as he took a deep breath.[23] "I don't get any pain from this breathing."[24] Roosevelt then stood up and headed for the stage.

The story of the assassination attempt on Teddy Roosevelt stands, in American politics, as one of the foremost examples of courage under fire, of guts and grit in the face of mortal danger. And though no illustration captures Roosevelt's unflinching, undaunted, determination and grit better, this was no rare, or uncharacteristic response from Roosevelt. This incident merely helped to further reveal Roosevelt for who he was: A man of tenacity and stamina, a man of purpose and valor in the face of danger, even death. This after all was Roosevelt "The Rough Rider," "The Lion," "The Bull Moose," "The Hero of San Juan Hill," and the 26th President of the United States. But it was not just that Roosevelt remained calm and clear headed, despite taking a bullet to his chest. Roosevelt also had the strength of character and presence of mind to stay true to his purpose, and the audacity and sheer tenacity to carry on with his campaign.

Roosevelt's example here is, no doubt, exceptional. It is unlikely that your ambitions will ever be momentarily blocked by the bullet of a mad gunman. Roosevelt, nonetheless, serves as a vivid reminder of the characteristics of success, of the power of human endurance and grit, of what is possible for you when you push yourself beyond your own perceived limits. Master the art of tapping into your own rich inner reservoirs of strength and power and you will soon find yourself achieving what may now seem to be entirely out of reach. Learn to continuously push beyond your perceived limits and you may find yourself making miraculous things happen, getting greater and greater things done.

This is not to suggest that natural boundaries do not exist. "Of course there are limits," writes the great Harvard psychologist William James, in his fantastic essay *The Energies of Men*, "the trees don't grow into the sky."[25] Pushing yourself beyond your perceived limits and fighting to more fully unleash your prodigious potential is not about reckless endangerment or driving yourself beyond the breaking point—though it may look that way to others, including many experts, but especially the fearful, the lazy, the foolish, and uninformed. No matter how hard you are prepared to drive yourself, no matter how many new layers of unearthed capacity that you discover within yourself, sound judgment and wisdom must always prevail. But this is the key: Wisdom teaches us that we are all capable of far more than we imagine. Utterly false are the vast majority of limits we impose on ourselves; entirely bogus are most all of the boundaries we draw in our minds. In the words of William James, "We habitually live inside our limits of power."[26] We habitually underestimate our true potential. "What we face may look insurmountable. But," writes Arnold Schwarzenegger, "I learned something from all those years of training and competing. I learned something from all those sets and reps when I didn't think I could lift another ounce of weight. What I learned is that we are always stronger than we know."[27]

But how do you push beyond your own perceived limits? How can you more fully tap your true potential? How can you unleash the untapped power within?

Tap Your Prodigious Potential

Roosevelt believed deeply in the potential greatness in people, and he went on to live this creed and carry this message to the world, becoming in time the very symbol of fortitude, determination and grit. It was these characteristics that he believed would lead to success, and it was this philosophy that he so resolutely recommended to others with his gospel on The Strenuous Life. "I wish to preach," Roosevelt said to an audience in Chicago in 1899, "not the doctrine of ignoble ease, but the doctrine of the strenuous life, the life of toil and effort, of labor and strife; to preach that highest form of success which comes, not to the man who desires mere easy peace, but to the man who does not shrink from danger, from hardship, or from bitter toil, and who out of these wins the splendid ultimate triumph."[28]

At its core, this is a book about tapping the extraordinary potential that TR knew was within us. It is about personal power, determination, optimism, resilience and guts. Your ability to adopt the applicable paradigms, principles and practices, and master the relevant strategies, tactics and skills is one of the most critical factors in your success. Whether you are an entrepreneur or an executive, a politician or a preacher, a soldier or a diplomat, or whether you just want to tap more of your potential and find greater success, your ability to master the power of grit is indispensable to getting the outcomes you desire. The purpose of this book is to arm you with the tools you need to shape your world, to achieve more, to earn more, to attract the right people and have greater success. You can have more power and influence—much more. You can have more of all of the things you want in life, and you can avoid more of the things you don't want—simply by learning, internalizing and mastering the lessons in this book, lessons grounded in the wisdom and insights of the leaders and legends of making things happen, and getting things done.

If you work to allow it, the stories of these great men and women can transform your life. Let their stories, the wisdom and insight from their hard-won experience, guide and illuminate your path as you take hold of your life. "Seize the day," wrote Horace.

> *"There is a tide in the affairs of men,*
> *Which taken at the flood, leads on to fortune;*
> *Omitted, all the voyage of their life*
> *Is bound in shallows and in miseries.*
> *On such a full sea are we now afloat,*
> *And we must take the current when it serves,*
> *Or lose our ventures."*
>
> —William Shakespeare, *The Tragedy of Julius Caesar* (1599)[29]

Hold Fast with an Iron Grip

"To think we are able is almost to be so; to determine upon attainment is frequently attainment itself. Thus earnest resolution has often seemed to have about it almost a savor of omnipotence."
—Samuel Smiles (1812—1904)

Imagine the splendid triumphs of the world's unconquerable spirits. Imagine how grit transformed setbacks and obstacles and debilitating defeat into ultimate success. Indeed, grit is one of the master keys of success.

It was grit that enabled George Washington and his ill-fed, ill-clad and poorly equipped band of unruly civilian soldiers to persist through several brutally cold winters, physical hardship and disease and yet, in the end, to triumph over the greatest military machine on Earth.

It was grit that sustained Edison through thousands of failed experiments to create the first commercially viable incandescent light bulb.

It was grit that enabled Lincoln to persevere through a lifetime of failed political campaigns, until at last he was elected and re-elected President of the United States.

It was grit that allowed Sandra Day O'Connor—who finished third in her class at Stanford Law School—to persevere in the face of continuous rejection and discrimination as a woman—in a profession dominated by men—until she, ultimately, in 1981, was nominated by President Reagan, and unanimously confirmed by the U.S. Senate, as the first woman of the United States Supreme Court.

Despite being repeatedly ridiculed and dismissed by his colleagues in Parliament as an alarmist, spewing forth the ravings of a restless rabble rouser, it was this same indispensable characteristic that compelled Churchill to warn the world over and over again of the rising Nazi threat.

Again it was grit that enabled Martin Luther King to continue to lead the civil rights movement after his body was beaten and jailed and, remarkably, even after the home that held his precious wife and daughter was bombed.

And what allowed Sonia Sotomayor to rise up from humble beginnings in a New York City housing project with an alcoholic father, who she lost when she was only nine, to become the first Hispanic justice of the United States Supreme Court? It was grit.

It was grit that enabled Oprah Winfrey to endure countless obstacles and setbacks on the road to becoming the "Queen of All Media."[30]

It was grit that let Donald Trump come back from the greatest financial downfall in the history of the world.

And it was again grit that enabled Walt Disney to survive multiple nervous breakdowns and endure the rejection of countless banks and decades on the brink of bankruptcy only to emerge as one of the great American legends.

14

Whether you look to the example of Roosevelt or Lincoln, Thomas Edison or FDR, Eleanor Roosevelt, Oprah Winfrey, Arnold Schwarzenegger, or Martin Luther King, what you will see over and over again, what the stories of each one of these great men and women illustrates in their own way is the irrefutable and preeminent power of grit. It is grit that rules the human race. "It is grit, it is perseverance, it is moral stamina and courage that govern the world."[31] The story of human history is the story of the triumph of perseverance. The great men and women of the world all endured considerable setbacks and defeats on the road to high achievement and eventual success. It was their drive, their diligence, their fortitude and determination that set them apart and ensured their "splendid ultimate triumph."

Unleash the Power of Grit

"Pure grit is that element of character which enables a man to clutch his aim with an iron grip, and keep the needle of his purpose pointing to the star of his hope. Through sunshine and storm, through hurricane and tempest, through sleet and rain, with a leaky ship, with a crew in mutiny, it perseveres; in fact, nothing but death can subdue it, and it dies still struggling."[32]
—Orison Swett Marden (1850—1924), Founder of *Success Magazine*

Grit is the great game changer. It is difficult to exaggerate the power and importance of grit. Indeed, among the most celebrated characteristics of high achievement, grit is now understood as an indisputable rival to both talent *and* intelligence.[33] But what is it and why is it so important to high achievement?

Grit can be defined as stamina and resolve in the pursuit of one's purpose and goals; the ability to persevere in the face of resistance and adversity, the capacity to carry on, overcome obstacles, and bounce back in the face of defeat. And, to be sure, new studies in psychology and education are establishing an increasingly compelling case for grit as a core component of personal growth, human achievement and success.[34]

Nor is grit limited to a narrow world of applications. Psychologists have now studied this concept in a variety of different domains—from sports and academics to sales and business, and, as University of Pennsylvania's Angela Duckworth reports, "In all those very different contexts, one characteristic emerged as a significant predictor of success—and it wasn't social intelligence, and it wasn't good looks, physical health, and it wasn't IQ. It was grit."[35] According to Duckworth, there is "one personal quality [which] is shared by the most prominent leaders in every field: grit"[36]

While our understanding of its significance continues to advance, belief in the power and importance of grit is not new. In fact, it is as old as ancient Greece. Aristotle, more than two millennia ago, argued that *endurance* was perceived as one of the key virtues of the heroic and godlike, writing that those who are able to unite the virtues of *self-control* and *endurance* together are seen as men and women of "perfect self-mastery." Long considered a virtue tightly bound up with the culture and character of America, it was the premier American hustler, Benjamin Franklin, writing more than two centuries ago, who included grit (resolution) as one of his twelve virtues and, thus, considered it a key part of his system for success. "Resolve," he said, "to perform what you ought. Perform without fail what you resolve."[37] Indeed, grit is a persistent theme in Ben Franklin's *Poor Richard's Almanac*, Aesop's fables, both the Old and New Testament, and the stories we pass on to our kids. "Tis a lesson you should heed," parents often repeat, "Try, try, try again. If at first you don't succeed; try, try, try again."[38]

English polymath Sir Francis Galton's research in the late 1800s, on the preeminent people of his era, likewise pointed to the importance of grit in their success.[39] Working from the biographies of leading politicians, scientists, artists and others led Galton to conclude that it was not ability alone that led to success.[40] "Rather he believed high achievers to be triply blessed by 'ability combined with zeal and with capacity for hard labor.'"[41]

More recently, William James, professor of philosophy and psychology at Harvard, highlighted the importance of endurance in his writings and lectures in Cambridge. James believed that the vast majority of human beings—purely out of poor habit ("the habit of inferiority to our full self"[42])—live far within our limits, and that if we would only learn to push ourselves beyond our perceived limits, to persevere through whatever pain, adversity or resistance we may be facing, we will find, on the other side of that push, vast resources of mental and physical energy that we did not yet know we possessed. These resources, James contends, remain masked from where we now sit, yet they *will* come, "gradually or suddenly," once we pass that indefinite critical point.[43] "There may be layer after layer of this experience," James writes.[44] "A third and fourth "wind" may supervene."[45]

Whether in pursuit of a mental or physical goal, the will to persist and endure will take you further than you are now in the habit of imagining. "Mental activity shows the phenomenon as well as physical," James adds, "and in exceptional cases we may find, beyond the very extremity of fatigue-distress, amounts of ease and power that we never dreamed ourselves to own—sources of strength habitually not taxed at all, because habitually we never push through the obstruction, never pass those early critical points."[46]

James' insight here is crucial. To achieve our most remarkable dreams we must continue to explore and push beyond what we *think* we are capable of. Our habitually limited thoughts put false constraints on our ability to achieve our goals and desires. "Compared with what we ought to be, we are only half awake. Our fires are damped, our drafts are checked. We are making use of only a small part of our possible mental resources."[47] Achieving our *greatest* dreams demands that we push ourselves to our *uppermost* limits. "The plain fact remains that men the world over possess amounts of resource, which only exceptional individuals push to their extremes of use."[48] And, yet, as these resources are available to us all, there is nothing stopping anyone. It is fundamentally a choice to strive for these uppermost limits. "It is not eminent talent that is required to ensure success in any pursuit, so much as purpose," wrote Samuel Smiles (1812—1904), the Scottish political reformer, and author of *Self-Help* (1859), "not merely the power to achieve, but the will to labor energetically and perseveringly. Hence energy of will may be defined to be the very central power of character in a man—in a word, it is the Man himself."[49]

Strive to *Apply* Each Lesson Learned

"I have been impressed with the urgency of doing. Knowing is not enough;
we must apply. Being willing is not enough; we must do."
—Leonardo da Vinci (1452—1519)

As our understanding of grit continues to expand so too does the recognition of its constituent parts. As research and investigations into the heroes and champions of grit repeatedly reveals, grit is not a solitary trait, but rather a rich combination of characteristics, competencies, and skills which are frequently found in varying degrees, but which essentially fuse to form a kind of organizing principle of success. After years of rigorous research, reading through hundreds of articles and books—from biography, history, and social science to business, politics, sports, warfare, and the arts—a number of critical themes surface in relation to the construct of grit again and again. In the pages ahead, you will discover the most critical factors in developing the grit you need to succeed. In fact, if you resolve to read and study and absorb the stories of the great heroes and champions and hustlers of history, laid out in the pages ahead, and you work to *apply* their wisdom and insight, implementing and mobilizing their strategies, tactics and tools for success, your life will never be the same. That is the promise of this book.

Imagine *Mastering the Power of Grit* as a kind of guidebook for tapping your true potential. Each of the eight chapters of this book are based on the eight key themes that repeatedly surface in the research of the men and women who have mastered the power of grit. The premise of this book is that there are tremendously important lessons that can be learned from the stories of the men and women who have gone before us, men and women like Theodore Roosevelt, Benjamin Franklin, Abraham Lincoln, Eleanor Roosevelt, Martin Luther King, Walt Disney, Harriet Tubman, JFK, LBJ, Thomas Edison, FDR and so many more. More than a few of these figures remain controversial (e.g., Napoleon Bonaparte, Huey Long, P. T. Barnum, Arnold Schwarzenegger, Bill Clinton, Donald Trump, et cetera). And, yet, there are nonetheless countless *constructive* lessons that can be learned from their stories and experience as well. This, of course, is not to suggest that *any* of the great hustlers or heroes of history are exemplars of moral rectitude. Clearly, some people are more virtuous than others. And though these people may all be heroes on some level, none are perfect saints. They all had flaws. They all made mistakes. In fact, many of the great champions of grit have stories of epic failure and defeat—stories which are equally instructive to those who are determined to master the power of grit.

As a guidebook, *Mastering the Power of Grit* can be used in a few different ways. You can read the book straight through to gain a general understanding of the power of grit and its' constituent parts. It is unlikely that each of the many themes will apply directly to your particular circumstances or situation at this time, but by absorbing the subject at once you will gain an understanding that will enable you to more effectively deal with whatever relevant situation arises when the time comes. This approach will also enable you to examine your past experience through a new lens, and, thus, it will allow you to gain insight and wisdom into your previous failures and successes. This, of course, will enable you to make wiser, more resourceful decisions, adjust course as needed going forward, and improve the likelihood and increase the speed of achieving your most cherished dreams and goals.

This book (and the Companion Poster Guide) has also been created in a way that facilitates focusing strictly on the subtopic most applicable to you given your current state of affairs. Simply browse the initial overviews included in the Content Summaries section of this book, and you can identify the relevant theme before you deep dive into the corresponding chapter—each of which is filled with applicable stories and anecdotes, as well as the wisdom and insights gained, and the strategies, tactics and tools learned from the legends of tenacity, resilience and grit.

1

SUCCEED BY STICKING IT OUT

"Most people never run far enough on the first wind to find out they've got a second. Give your
dreams all you've got, and you'll be amazed at the energy that comes out of you."
—William James (1842—1910), American Philosopher and Psychologist

Tap the Power of Focused Persistence:
The Wright Brothers Flying Above the Pack

"Energy and persistence conquer all things."
–Benjamin Franklin (1705—1790)

On December 17, 1903, over the beaches of North Carolina's Outer Banks, two bicycle mechanics achieved their dream of flying. It was the first successful piloted, powered airplane flight in history and the world was forever changed. One of the oldest of dreams, flying had long mystified some of the most imaginative of minds—including Thomas Edison and Leonardo da Vinci.[50] And, yet, after a lifetime of fascination with flying and several years of experimentation, innovation and courageous risks, it was Orville and Wilbur Wright who first realized the dream of flight.

The Wright Brothers were not the only people actively pursuing the dream. Indeed, there were others, including Samuel Pierpont Langley, who were better schooled and better supported. In fact, Langley, "one of the most prominent names in aviation at the time,"[51] had received a $50,000 grant from the U.S. War Department.[52] But it was the Wright Brothers, with an investment of only a thousand dollars, who achieved the dream first.

So, what *was* the difference? What allowed the Wright brothers to succeed where so many others had failed? Above all, it was perseverance. The Wright brothers were men of grit. Where many others had fallen and given up, Orville and Wilbur Wright carried on the fight.

The Wright brothers faced countless obstacles and setbacks, including wing design challenges, broken propeller shafts, adverse weather conditions, and a number of accidents, including one that left Wilbur with his head split open. Unable to find a suitable manufacturer, they even had to build their own lightweight engine to power their plane. Their challenges were further exacerbated when they were unknowingly using flawed data and lift tables, which had been published by Langley. Knowing that other aviation pioneers died in pursuit of their dream, the Wright Brothers also had to overcome their own fears of mid-flight mishaps and other troubles in the sky. Meanwhile, the world laughed at the Wright Brothers and their impossible pursuit. They were ridiculed by their critics. "Leave flying to the birds," they were repeatedly told. But the two bicycle mechanics refused to give in to their fears, they refused to listen to the naysayers, they refused to back down. They never stopped working toward their dream, and their success on that cold, winter day catapulted them into the history books and the hearts of people everywhere.

The Wright Brothers were not necessarily more intelligent or talented than the other aviation pioneers. As did some others, they too looked to learn from the birds. But they were persistent. They watched different birds fly hour after hour, day after day, until they eventually learned that the birds controlled their flights by changing the angle of the tips of their wings. Adapting this insight to their Flyer, they were able to design an aircraft that gave the pilot total control, and thereby solved the third part of "the flying problem."

The will to persevere is the ultimate power. "Will makes men giants," wrote Ik Marvel. And this power is equally available to you. By staying with the problem longer you will discover subtle differences, develop a more nuanced understanding, and gain insights that may be in plain view but are nonetheless invisible to those with an undeveloped eye. As Einstein once said, "It's not that I'm so smart. It's just that I stay with problems longer." In the words of President Woodrow Wilson, who served as professor and later as president of Princeton University, "Genius I cannot claim nor even extra brightness, but perseverance *all* can have."[53] Henry Austin put it this way, "Genius, that power which dazzles mortal eyes, is oft but perseverance in disguise."[54]

Perseverance is often what separates the history makers from the masses. Henry Ford was not the only one working on the "horseless carriage." But it was Ford who never gave up on his dream to build an automobile that *every* American could afford, including his own employees. "Despite his boss and his father thinking it a crazy idea, he persevered, hearing only the voice inside him that said, 'Do it.'"[55]

Mary Kay Ash was not the only woman selling cosmetics when she started in 1963. But it was Ash who, after facing years of unfair business practices, transformed a few ideas about women, empowerment and direct sales, along with some products created at her dining room table, into a global empire, employing hundreds of thousands of women around the world.

Thomas Edison was not the only inventor working on the light bulb, but he was the only one who worked tirelessly without ceasing to find the proper filament to make the bulb burn through the night. It was Ford, Ash and Edison's *determination* to follow their dreams, to provide value to the masses that made the difference, and ensured that they would take their place among some of the richest entrepreneurs of their day. The truth is, Seth Godin writes in *The Dip*, "Extraordinary benefits accrue to the tiny minority of people who are able to push just a tiny bit longer than most."[56] In the words of Mary Kay Ash, "Don't limit yourself. Many people limit themselves to what they think they can do. You can go as far as your mind lets you. What you believe, remember, you can achieve."[57]

Perseverance is underrated. "I do not think that there is any other quality so essential to success of any kind as the quality of perseverance," declared John D. Rockefeller, another American business titan. "It overcomes almost everything, even nature."[58] The power to persist and persevere is a distinguishing feature of all great men and women; regardless of whatever other strengths and weaknesses, common or peculiar characteristics, their ability to stick it out is never lacking.[59] Those who achieve greatness either find a way or make one. "No matter what opposition he meets or what discouragement overtakes him," writes Orison Swett Marden in *An Iron Will* "drudgery cannot disgust him, obstacles cannot discourage him, labor cannot weary him; misfortune, sorrow, and reverses cannot harm him." [60]Never doubt whether you have what you need to succeed. "It is not so much brilliancy of intellect, or fertility of resource, as persistency of effort, constancy of purpose, that makes a great man..." and a great woman.[61] "Those who succeed in life are the men and women who keep everlastingly at it, who do not believe themselves geniuses, but who know that if they ever accomplish anything they must do it by determined and persistent industry."[62]

It is of course easy to acknowledge the importance of perseverance. And understanding its significance is certainly a good first step. But what else does it take? What is it about those who persevere? What are their secrets to sticking it out?

Make Up Your Mind:
Theodore Roosevelt's Mental Makeover

"Nothing great will ever be achieved without great men,
and men are great only if they are determined to be so."
—Charles De Gaulle (1890—1970)

A man worthy of his place on Mount Rushmore, Theodore Roosevelt was a true American hustler. There are scarce few who better exemplify his fierce spirit of unshakable grit, of an indomitable will, of resolve in the face of great challenges, bitter setbacks, and marked defeat. But there is yet another important reason Roosevelt remains as an enduring exemplar: He didn't *start out* as a determined and tenacious hustler with excess reserves of resolve and grit. *He willed it.*

Despite an upbringing of privilege and comfort, despite a frail frame and extreme nearsightedness, despite being, in his own words, "a sickly and timid boy . . . a wretched mite,"[63] (which often required his *younger* brother to fight off bullies for him), despite his "weak" heart and warnings from his doctor to live a subdued life; in spite of all of this Roosevelt would eventually determine to live his life, as he put it, "up to the hilt."[64] With a solemn word of encouragement from his father when he was young, Theodore Roosevelt simply *decided* that he would face down his fears and man up to his potential. *He made up his mind* to make maximum use of his mind and body, pushing himself with strenuous workouts, including boxing and lifting weights, long hours of reading and study, and near constant adventure and exploration.

To succeed at anything significant, the first step is to resolve *in advance* that you *will* persevere. *Make up your mind* that you will do *whatever it takes* to achieve your dreams and goals, then turn your mind away from any other possibility. Roosevelt very much wanted to be great and, therefore, he made up his mind to make it so.

When TR's nephew Franklin Roosevelt ascended to the presidency he was grounded in this same set of beliefs. In fact, rather than letting it defeat him, his experience with paralysis served only to strengthen his resolve. As President, Roosevelt maintained this mindset throughout the Great Depression and World War II, one of America's most tumultuous periods. According to historian William E. Leuchtenburg, a prominent scholar on the life and leadership of FDR, "He believed that the country could lift itself out of the depression by sheer will power."[65] During one of his fireside chats, Roosevelt said to the nation, "When Andrew Jackson, "Old Hickory," died, someone asked, 'Will he go to Heaven?' and the answer was, 'He will if he wants to.' If I am asked," Roosevelt said, "whether the American people will pull themselves out of this depression, I answer, 'They will if they want to.'"[66] "I have no sympathy," he said, "with the professional economists who insist that things must run their course and that human agencies can have no influence on economic ills."[67]

Most people, Zig Ziglar often used to say, "are about as committed as a Kamikaze pilot on his thirty-ninth mission—they just aren't serious…"[68] And, yet, commitment is key. Your will plays a critical role in your success. If you have not made up your mind to succeed in advance, when the inevitable obstacles and setbacks come, you will immediately begin looking for a way out. If, on the other hand, you *have* made up your mind in advance, when the inevitable obstacles and setbacks come, you will immediately begin looking for a way to stick it out. And, whichever it is, you will inevitably find what you are looking for.[69] To succeed you must make up your mind, never wavering from your ultimate purpose, always pursuing your goals with energy, enthusiasm, and grit. Only then can you hope to overcome the obstacles that stand in your way, and achieve what may now seem impossible. As Niccolò Machiavelli wrote in *The Prince*, "Where the will is great, the difficulties cannot be great."[70]

Persist with Your Purpose and Plan:
The Bull Moose, Bloody On Point

"I have brought myself by long meditation to the conviction that a human being with a settled purpose must accomplish it, and that nothing can resist a will which will stake even existence upon its fulfillment."
—Benjamin Disraeli (1804—1881), British Prime Minister

"The goddess of fame or of fortune has been won by many a poor boy who had no friends, no backing, or anything but pure grit and invincible purpose."
—Orison Swett Marden (1848—1924), *Pushing to the Front*

When Theodore Roosevelt began to walk out on the stage in Milwaukee, just after he was shot, the emcee was stupefied. He abruptly introduced Roosevelt, awkwardly explaining to the audience that someone just attempted to kill the former President. As Roosevelt made his way to the podium someone in the audience shouted, "Fake! Fake!"[71]

"It is true," Roosevelt said, backing up the emcee's hurried explanation, as he took over the rostrum.[72]

"I have just been shot."[73] "But it takes more than that to kill a bull moose."[74]

As nervous laughter trickled up from the audience, Roosevelt reached into his coat and pulled out his thick, bloodied, bullet-holed speech. He then unbuttoned his vest, exposing his shirt and the slowly spreading blood-soaked spot, now the size of a large hand. Shrieks of horror erupted as the crowd collectively gasped. Others shouted, "Turn this way! Turn this way!"[75]

By this time, as he began to speak, his face was pale. He felt weak and spoke softly. "Friends, I shall ask you to be as quiet as possible. Fortunately," he said, "I had my manuscript, so you see I was going to make a long speech, and there is a bullet—there is where the bullet went through—and it probably saved me from it going into my heart. The bullet is in me now, so that I cannot make a very long speech, but I will try my best."[76]

Roosevelt then proceeded to take full advantage of the situation. A seasoned politician and speaker, he knew he now had his audience in his hand. No amount of money could be spent or political talent exploited to create a situation that would match the intensity with which his listeners were now engaged, or the credence they would now give to his words. "I cannot speak to you insincerely within five minutes of being shot," Roosevelt said. "I am telling you the literal truth when I say that my concern is for many other things. It is not in the least for my own life."[77]

Shrewdly alluding to his heroism in the Spanish-American War, Roosevelt went on to depict his greater purpose as a sacrifice and a moral duty. "It was just as when I was colonel of my regiment," he said. "I always felt that a private was to be excused for feeling at times some pangs of anxiety about his personal safety, but I cannot understand a man fit to be a colonel who can pay any heed to his personal safety when he is occupied as he ought to be with the absorbing desire to do his duty."[78]

With that, Roosevelt had set his audience up for what he urgently wanted them to take away: An understanding of, and belief in, the urgency and importance of the Progressive cause. He wanted to dispel the idea that the election was all about him, or winning a third term (which his opponents—including his would-be assassin—had charged). "I can tell you with absolute truthfulness that I am very much uninterested in whether I am shot or not. [...] I am in this cause with my whole heart and soul," he said.[79] "I believe that the Progressive movement is making life a little easier for all our people; a movement to try to take the burdens off the men and especially the women and children of this country. I am absorbed in the success of that movement." [80]

Effectively connecting his courage to continue with the importance of his cause, the apostle of the strenuous life carried on; sometimes swaying, losing blood and strength, yet continuing to speak for a full hour and a half, finishing his speech at last. Finally, he was persuaded to go to the hospital. And as for the bullet? It remained lodged in Roosevelt's chest until he died, over six years later.

Exploit the Power of a Passionate Purpose.

Given the circumstances, it is easy to take TR at his word: He persevered with this speech, despite the pain and risks, because he believed in the importance of his purpose. As the German philosopher Nietzsche once put it, "He who has a strong enough *why* can bear almost any *how*."[81] In Roosevelt's mind, the significance of the message was greater than the messenger; the work went beyond the worker. "Far and away the best prize that life offers," he once said, "is the chance to work hard at work worth doing."[82] For Roosevelt, this was work worth doing—indeed, at that moment, no other work was more important. "It has always seemed to me," Roosevelt said, "that the best way to die would be in doing something that ought to be done..."[83] This powerful sense of purpose gave him the strength to persevere.

Only the naïve and fanciful dispute the importance of hard work and perseverance. The question is not *whether*, but *how* to elicit these characteristics of success. And, as Roosevelt's story reveals, the first secret is to begin with a passionate purpose. Your ability to persevere is directly dependent on the depth of your interest in and enthusiasm for your vision and goals. *Desire* is what incites the will to work hard and persevere. The more you want something, the harder you will work, the more pain you can and will endure to get it. "Real success goes to those who obsess."[84]

When President Bill Clinton was asked how he dealt with the relentless, brutal attacks he faced as President, how he survived the travails that would have, according to one interviewer, sent weaker men running from office, or to an early grave, Clinton said this: "I think by far the most important thing is...I never thought the political office was primarily about personal attainment or ego or validation or even being thought well of. I always thought it was a job designed to achieve larger purposes for the people you were representing."[85] Clinton believed that his personal experience as a political leader had clearly demonstrated that having a larger purpose can enable you to survive personal adversity. "If you have good ideas," Clinton said, "and they relate to people and their lives and their future, [then] you can survive personal adversity, because people understood this was about a common, larger endeavor."[86] "That's another thing," Clinton continued. "I never, in the darkest days, I never lost sight of the fact that however many days I had left as President, every one was a privilege and a pleasure, and I should be working for the people. And I think they sensed that. I think *that*, more than anything else, answers the question you asked."[87]

To be clear, mediocre dreams and goals will not suffice. Willpower is weak without a worthwhile purpose. Invest the time in setting inspiring goals, directly aligned with a clear, vivid and compelling vision, and you will tap a tremendous source of energy and power. Driven from within, toward a purpose that resonates with you on a deep emotional, perhaps spiritual, level and the sacrifice will not seem so great, the hours of work and study and practice will not seem such a heavy price. You will easily enter a state of flow where your energy and attention are sustained well beyond your usual capacity. Immersed in the present, your sense of fulfillment from the work and people involved will increase. The work itself will seem more interesting, even exciting. As Robert Green discusses in *Mastery*, your attention will turn to increasing your skill and improving your practice.[88] You will enjoy the challenge of overcoming obstacles. You will readily see and exploit the slightest opportunities. "In fact," Greene says, "you will draw opportunities to you because people will sense how prepared you are."[89]

To succeed at the highest level, you must be like the great masters of hustle, all clearly marked by their tenacity of *purpose*. "At their best," writes Klein, "nothing deflected them from their quest. So strong was their faith in the vision driving them onward that they pushed and clawed their way through every obstacle. This quality made them fierce competitors and dangerous rivals."[90]

Such was Lincoln's vision for the preservation of the nation. When he was asked by an anxious visitor how he would respond if the rebellion, after three or four more years, was still not subdued, Lincoln said, "Oh, there is no alternative but to keep pegging away."[91] "The fight must go on," Lincoln said on another occasion. "The cause of liberty must not be surrendered at the end of one or even one hundred defeats."[92]

Howard Hughes revealed a similar tenacity of purpose when he reflected on his record-breaking transcontinental flight. At one point he began to have doubts in his equipment. "I thought somewhere over the Atlantic," he said, "long before I reached Europe, that that plane would pancake into the ocean. But I would not turn back. I would *not* turn back!"[93]

As the days stretched into weeks and months with no sign of land, the crew of Christopher Columbus grew increasingly afraid. They begged and cried and threatened him to return to Spain. But nothing could persuade him to turn back.[94]

The American aviation pioneer and bestselling author Amelia Earhart had this same mindset regarding her own dangerous aviation adventures. "Obviously," she said, "I faced the possibility of not returning when first I considered going."[95] But that wouldn't stop her. "Once faced and settled," she said, "there really wasn't any good reason to refer to it."[96]

Understand: To reach the upper echelons of power, to attain the heights of high achievement, excellence and success you too must find within yourself your own true purpose, something that motivates and inspires you, something to which you can dedicate your life. There can be no success without the drive to succeed. With a clear and compelling purpose you will begin to uncover the powers within you, the tenacity and hustle and grit you need to succeed. Remember: "Whatever else may have been lacking in the giants of the race, the men and women who have been conspicuously successful have all had one characteristic in common—doggedness and persistence of purpose."[97]

"Persistency of purpose is a power. It creates confidence in others. Everybody believes in the determined man," writes Orison Swett Marden.[98] "When he undertakes anything his battle is half won, because not only he himself, but every one who knows him, believes that he will accomplish whatever he sets out to do. People know that it is useless to oppose a man who uses his stumbling blocks as stepping-stones; who is not afraid of defeat; who never, in spite of calumny or criticism, shrinks from his task; who never shirks responsibility; who always keeps his compass pointed to the north star of his purpose, no matter what storms may rage about him."[99]

When you have a purpose firmly rooted in your mind, then you will begin to demonstrate the determination, resilience and pluck of an Abe Lincoln, Amelia Earhart, or a Howard Hughes. Then things will begin to go your way. Then you will begin to experience Foster's simple truth: All those forces that at first seem to threaten and frustrate will begin to bow to your spirit for the simple reason that your spirit will not bow to them. They will yield to your purpose. They will defer to your designs. "When a firm, decisive spirit is recognized," writes Foster, "it is curious to see how the space clears around a man and leaves him room and freedom."[100]

Expect and Plan for Problems—Preparation is Power

"By failing to prepare you are preparing to fail."
—Benjamin Franklin (1706—1790)

The stories in the newspapers in the days immediately following the assassination attempt on Theodore Roosevelt were teeming with high esteem for the former President and his fortitude under fire. More than a thousand telegrams and cablegrams from around the world poured into Roosevelt's room at the Chicago hospital, repeatedly expressing the shared sentiment that Roosevelt was one of the great world-class characters of the age.[101] "Kings and emperors, cardinals and counts, athletes and prize-fighters, financiers and social reformers were hastening to express their horror over the assault and their joy over the escape."[102] Once again, Theodore Roosevelt's courage made him into a national hero. "Mr. Roosevelt showed the indomitable courage that is ingrained in his being," wrote the *New York Times*.[103]

"Papers strongly hostile to his political ambitions were prompt to express their admiration for his courage and grit."[104] One journalist from the *Times*, for example, lauded Roosevelt, writing, "Instances of personal and physical heroism are common upon the battlefield; but probably the history of politics affords no example of it worthy to be compared with this. It was rash, it was an act of hardihood, we may say even that it was an act of folly, but it was characteristic, and the judgment of the country will be that it was magnificent."[105] The headline in another typically hostile paper, the *New York Herald*, read: "We are against his politics, but we like his grit."[106]

Establish Higher Expectations.

Given the scarcity of real courage, the strong public reaction to Roosevelt's heroics was not surprising. But there was one group who was baffled by the tremendous interest in Roosevelt's handling of the incident. As Roosevelt writes in his *Autobiography*, these men—various Rough Riders and cowboys and ranchers from the Badlands—thought Roosevelt's actions were not something to be admired. They were something to be *expected.* Carrying ahead with his commitment was "what they accepted as the right thing for a man to do under the circumstances, a thing the nonperformance of which would have been discreditable rather than the performance being creditable."[107] Hardened by the harsh realities of war, and life on the frontier "during its Viking age" these men had a very different perspective of danger and duty. "They would," writes Roosevelt, "not have expected a man to leave a battle, for instance, because of being wounded in such fashion; and they saw no reason why he should abandon a less important and less risky duty."[108]

Maintain a Realistic, Resourceful Perspective.

Roosevelt, of course, understood their perspective because it was his perspective too. He shared their experience and, not surprisingly, he shared their understanding and expectations. Roosevelt said, "I have never felt that public men who were shot whether they were killed or not, were entitled to any special sympathy; and I do most emphatically feel that when in danger it is their business to act in the manner we accept

24

as commonplace when the actor is an enlisted man of the Army or Navy, or a policeman, or a fireman, or a railroad man, or a miner, or a deep sea fisherman."[109] From this perspective of courage and duty, Roosevelt's actions followed naturally. This wasn't just TR talking a good game. Even in the midst of his Milwaukee speech, after taking an actual bullet, Roosevelt maintained this perspective. "If I was in battle now," he said, "I would be leading my men just the same. Just the same way I am going to make this speech."[110] Of course, Roosevelt was caught off guard by his assassin, but he was not caught unprepared. Nor was he unaware of how to respond. In the words of one historian, "Though the precise circumstances were a complete surprise, his course of conduct was not entirely improvised."[111] He was acting according to plan.

Think Through Possible Problems and Solutions in Advance.

Roosevelt's story reveals one of the key secrets to sticking it out: *Preparation is power*. The more trained and prepared you are, the more you understand what you're getting into, the more willing and able you are to see yourself all the way through. The most critical part of this preparation is being mentally prepared for the most probable problems and pitfalls ahead. The very act of *thinking through* the possible pitfalls—with *specific solutions* for how to handle them—significantly improves your likelihood of success.

Roosevelt, for his part, had a realistic, grounded perspective of the potential perils. In his mind, assassination was a possible hazard of the business of politics. "It is a trade risk, which every prominent public man should accept as a matter of course," he once wrote; "For eleven years I have been prepared any day to be shot…"[112] What's more, in his case, it was an assassin's bullet that allowed him to ascend to the presidency in the first place. He knew the risks, accepted them, and imagined how he might respond. "When asked how he could give a speech with a fresh bullet wound in his chest, Roosevelt later explained that after years of expecting an assassin, he hadn't been surprised. Like the frontiersmen and soldiers he admired, [and] he was determined not to wilt under attack."[113] As Roosevelt wrote to his friend, the British statesman Sir Edward Grey, "In the very unlikely event of the wound being mortal I wished to die with my boots on…"[114] This was Roosevelt's reality. It was, he said, "not a question of courage: it is a question of perspective."[115] His perspective helped him to accept the risks and prepare himself for the worst. This readiness allowed him to seize and exploit the incident in a way that few others might have imagined. And, thus, it is not entirely surprising that he was able to bear the bullet when it came.

Train Hard, Prepare for War.

When Arnold Schwarzenegger lost the Mr. Universe bodybuilding competition to Frank Zane in 1968 he was broken. In fact, later that evening, Zane's upset victory had Arnold in tears. Regardless of Zane's outstanding physique, Schwarzenegger was unprepared to be beaten by someone five inches shorter and fifty pounds lighter. "It really hurt," Arnold remembered, "I'd gone into a major competition overconfident and underprepared."[116]

Schwarzenegger was born with the ideal genetic makeup for bodybuilding, but he was not born a champion. Like everyone, he had to work at it. He had to learn to think like a champion. And, as he began to realize early, he had to learn to be better prepared. Recalling his loss years later, Schwarzenegger writes, "That afternoon at the gym, I thought more about my loss to Frank Zane. Now that I'd stopped feeling sorry for myself, I came to harsher conclusions than those I'd reached the night before. I still felt the judging had been unfair, but I discovered this wasn't the real cause of my pain."[117]

Arnold began to take ownership for his defeat. "It was," he said, "the fact that I had failed—not my body, but my vision and my drive. [...] I was not as ripped as I could have been."[118] Now with a more resourceful mindset, he could begin to explore specific factors that could be changed. "I could have dieted the week before," he said, "and not eaten so much fish and chips. I could have found a way to train more even without access to equipment: for instance, I could have done one thousand reps of abs or something that would have made me feel ready. I could have worked on my posing—nothing had stopped me from doing that. Never mind the judging; I hadn't done everything in my power to prepare."[119]

Schwarzenegger was a casualty of his own ungrounded expectations. Rather than maintaining his customarily intense routine and preparations, he admitted later, "I'd thought my momentum from winning in London would carry me. I'd told myself I'd just won Mr. Universe and I could let go. That was nonsense. Thinking this made me furious." [120]As with all great champions, Arnold was hard on himself. He expected more. At the time, Arnold remembered saying to himself, "'Even though you won the professional Mr. Universe contest in London, you are still a f...ing amateur. What happened here never should have happened. It only happens to an amateur. You're an amateur, Arnold.'"[121]

Arnold was on the path to becoming one of the greats of the sport. And this event would forever be in the back of his mind, reminding him to expect challenges, pushing him to prepare like a pro. "Staying in America," he said, "I decided, had to mean that I wouldn't be an amateur ever again. Now the real game would begin. There was a lot of work ahead. From now on if I lost, I would be able to walk away with a big smile because I had done everything I could to prepare."[122]

In sports, it is easy to see how intense, deliberate practice builds endurance and prepares athletes to persevere against a tough competitor, or maintain extreme levels of performance throughout the duration of a hard game. But these same principles are widely applicable to life.

Plan and Prepare for the Pain.

Preparation can be equally effective for enduring pain. Studies show that patients who had specific recovery goals following intense surgery (e.g. knee surgery, hip replacement, etc.) were more likely to recover faster than those who didn't. Perhaps, most interesting, in addition to the "specific, detailed plans" their preparation included how they "would handle a specific moment of anticipated pain."[123] In other words, the most successful patients had created recovery plans that included solutions to their potential obstacles ahead of time. In his book, *The Power of Habit*, Charles Duhigg writes, "Put another way, the patients' plans were built around inflection points when they knew their pain—and thus the temptation to quit—would be strongest. The patients were telling themselves how they were going to make it over the hump."[124]

In contrast, those patients who recovered more slowly or who failed to regain full movement had failed to plan and prepare for the pain. "...[T]he patients who didn't write out any plans were at a significant disadvantage, because they never thought ahead about how to deal with painful inflection points. They never deliberately designed willpower habits. Even if they intended to walk around the block, their resolve abandoned them when they confronted the agony of the first few steps."[125] What they needed, what you need when you face a challenging goal, is a plan or routine—an inflection point game plan—to follow when the inevitable adversity comes.[126]

Likewise, for soldiers in war, nothing—beyond a compelling, shared purpose—can better help to develop perseverance and grit than disciplined preparation, planning, and persistent military training and practice. The success of the Roman army, for instance, is consistently attributed to their discipline and persistence, developed through extremely rigorous physical *and* mental training. The great 4th century Roman military expert Vegetius (who wrote one of the most influential military works in the Western world) said, "We find that the Romans owed the conquest of the world to no other cause than continual military training, exact observance of discipline in their camps, and unwearied cultivation of the other arts of war."[127] In short, it is preparation and training that often enables the victors to persist, persevere, and, ultimately, prevail.

Equip Yourself to Persevere.

On December 14, 1911, the Norwegian polar explorer Roald Amundsen, already one of the dominant figures of the Heroic Age of Antarctic Exploration, became the first to reach the South Pole. His experience testifies to the fact that, in the realm of the great explorers, thorough preparation and training is equally critical to success. Indeed, in the midst of the most extreme conditions, this is often what separates those who are able to persist and endure from those who are led to an early death. Pressed to explain the success of such a remarkable expedition, Amundsen emphasized the vital significance of the work he did *before* he was flooded by grueling conditions, or challenges that demanded his depleting stamina and guts: "I may say that this is the greatest factor—the way in which the expedition is equipped—the way in which every difficulty is foreseen, and precautions taken for meeting or avoiding it. Victory awaits him who has everything in order," he said, "Defeat is certain for him who has neglected to take the necessary precautions in time..."[128]

"Our success in attaining the [South] Pole was due to the correctness of our planning," Amundsen wrote later.[129] The success of polar explorers depends on other factors, of course. "Willpower," he admits, "is the first essential of a successful explorer—only by the mastery of his own soul can he hope to master the difficulties placed in his path by opposing nature."[130] But willpower never operates as an isolated factor, nor only in the midst of battle. "Both imagination and caution," he said, "are equally essential—imagination to foresee the difficulties, and the caution which compels the minutest preparation to meet them."[131] After years of reflection, Amundsen concludes in his autobiography, *My Life as an Explorer* (1927), "Whatever I have accomplished in exploration has been the result of lifelong planning, painstaking preparation, and the hardest kind of conscientious work."[132]

The wisdom and experience of the polar explorer is echoed in the work of leading behavioral science researchers. The authors of *Extreme: Why Some People Thrive at the Limits*, sum it up well when they write, "Many experts would argue that the decisions made before an extreme mission starts are often more important than the decisions made during the mission itself. Planning and preparation make the difference between life and death."[133]

No doubt, mental preparation will be critical to your ability to stick it out. But if you can also anticipate the most critical challenges well before you are immersed in the battle, and develop specific strategies and tactics, systems or routines, for dealing with or even exploiting them before they come, this will significantly improve your ability to succeed.

Maintain a Positive Outlook.

The idea that the path to achieve a worthwhile goal will be smooth, quick and easy is foolishness. Those who maintain dreamy delusions of the road to their dreams are doomed to fail. You cannot simply coast your way to success. Challenges and setbacks are inevitable. The key is to prepare for them before they come.

"Painstaking preparation" will help you stick to your purpose and plan. It is, in fact, remarkable what people can achieve when they begin with a solid understanding of the path ahead. As Donald Trump writes from his experience in real estate, "There are a lot of ups and downs, but you can ride them out if you're prepared for them."[134]

Understand: The point is to be realistic, *not pessimistic*. "Let's be positive," Anthony Robbins reminds his listeners, "but let's also be real."[135] And the reality is, "rarely is anything that's worth doing problem free."[136] "Learning to expect problems saved me," writes another business titan, "from a lot of wasted energy, and it will save you...It's like Wall Street; it's like life. The ups and downs are inevitable, so simply try to be prepared for them."[137]

To be clear, maintaining a rationally optimistic outlook is key. It is vital, therefore, that learning to expect and prepare for challenges and setbacks does not devolve into a focus on the negative or an obsession with potential problems and pitfalls. As Anthony Robbins explains, "Eighty percent of the focus still must be on the solution."[138] Nor is the point to explore and prepare for every possible problem that might arise. This would be as foolish as not knowing anything at all. Instead, identify the most probable challenges, then turn your mind toward potential solutions to see your way through. Remember: Whatever stage of the journey you find yourself, your dominant focus must always be on achieving your vision and goals. Keep your dream at the forefront of your mind.

Prepare for the Storms.

It's not always possible to anticipate problems. Worse still, sometimes several problems will happen at once. Though temporary, this often feels crushing. This happened to Donald Trump early in his career when he was developing the Grand Hyatt Hotel in Manhattan. He faced an unprecedented number of issues and challenges that he could never have anticipated. "No sooner would I solve a problem," Trump writes, "than several more would immediately pop up."[139]

This is why, when unanticipated problems do arise, you must deal with them swiftly and directly. You never know when another problem is coming. Far better to knock one out before the next one comes. In the words of John F. Kennedy, "The time to repair the roof is when the sun is shining."[140] Don't wait for the storms.

This, of course, does not prepare you for those unfortunate times when the storms come all at once. To persevere in times like this—when problems are too big or too many to anticipate—your *mindset* is the critical factor in your success. You must become a master of the mental game. It's what you tell yourself about what's happening that matters more than anything else. Trump, for instance (long before he became the controversial presidential candidate, perpetually wrestling with his own party), admitted that, "sometimes I feel like Sisyphus, condemned to push a boulder uphill for eternity." But, he says, "I just keep pushing, shoulder to boulder, moving forward; I don't give up."[141]

In these situations, try to fix your focus on how the situation will look and feel once you make it through. In Trump's case, the lessons he learned and the mental strength he acquired in the most demanding situations he faced were the ones that proved invaluable to his later success.[142] Do not allow yourself to think of defeat. Instead, remember that the most demanding situations are those rare and special times that separate the good from the great. One way or another you will get through it. And when you do, you will find yourself at a new level of success, among a smaller, more select group of individuals.

Get in the habit of reframing your problems as the lessons you need to learn to succeed. As Steve Chandler writes in *Fearless*, "That's the fascinating thing about problems. When taken on, they are life-changing gifts. Once we can do the mind shift (from paranoid mode to creative mode) necessary to see them for what they are, all problems become advanced seminars..."[143] When Donald Trump later described his real estate fiasco with the Manhattan Hyatt, he put it this way, "Had I known from the beginning what I would have to go through, I'm not sure I would have become involved. However, in retrospect, I'm glad I did. That problem-filled project was my first big success—the development of the Grand Hyatt Hotel in New York City. I got the equivalent of several Ph.D.s from that deal."[144]

Expect Challenges and Setbacks, But Never Expect Lasting Failure.

By the time Abraham Lincoln ascended to the presidency in March of 1861 America was on the brink of civil war. The situation was grim. Lincoln knew that war was inevitable. He knew that the challenge before him was unprecedented, and that the obstacles and setbacks would be severe. And, as well as anyone could be, he was prepared for major losses and defeats. Nevertheless, President Lincoln was also confident in ultimate victory. "I expect setbacks, defeats; we have had them, and shall have them," he said. [145]"They are common to all wars. But I have not the slightest fear of any result which shall fatally impair our...strength...I do not fear it, for this is God's fight, and He will win it in His own good time." [146]

There is wisdom in Lincoln's unwillingness to expect or accept *lasting* failure. It is this hope in the *eventual* outcome that often pushes champions past their losses and defeats and into the pages of history. Indeed, many of history's greatest heroes endured considerable failures. But rather than giving up, they exploited the experience to deepen their wisdom and strengthen their resolve.

Like Lincoln, Winston Churchill knew something about failure. In fact, both of these great political figures faced considerable obstacles and setbacks throughout their lives. But they also both lived up to the truth of Talleyrand's maxim, "In war, one dies only once. In politics, one dies only to rise again."[147] Knowing this does not make it any easier, of course. As President Richard Nixon wrote in his book *Leaders*, "an adage is precious little comfort for the man who has just lost an election. Having lost a couple of them," he continues, "I know how it feels. Friends tell you, 'Won't it be great to have no responsibility and to be able to travel, go fishing, and play golf anytime you want?' My answer is," Nixon said, "'Yes—for about one week.' Then you have a totally empty feeling that only one who has been through it can understand."[148]

Churchill understood this feeling early on. After all, not only did he fail the entrance exam to the Royal Military Academy at Sandhurst *twice*, but he was only twenty-four when, in 1899 he ran for his father's old seat in Parliament and lost. The defeat left a mark. Churchill described his feelings as, "those feelings of deflation which a bottle of champagne, or even soda-water, represents when it has been half emptied and left uncorked for a night."[149] Churchill went on to lose another four elections over his career, which itself is a testament of his hope and expectations for the future.

Like Lincoln and Churchill, Nixon knew the sting of defeat. Not only did he lose the race for president to John F. Kennedy in 1960, but he lost the gubernatorial election of his home state of California less than two years later. Nixon recalled the experience of losing: "The immediate aftermath is not so bad because you are still numbed by the exhaustion of the campaign, and you also are still operating with a high level of adrenaline. Weeks or months later the realization hits you that you have lost and that there is nothing you can take back or do differently to change the outcome."[150] Recalling both Churchill's and his own experience after a failed political campaign, Nixon adds, "Unless you are wealthy, there is also the necessity of beginning another career in order to pay the bills that keep coming in every week regardless of how you feel."[151]

Nixon, of course, knew of an even deeper failure than a failure to win votes. After winning the presidency in 1968, and a landslide re-election in 1972, he made a series of stupid, unlawful, and unnecessary decisions and was forced to resign in 1974. It was an unparalleled moment of defeat for the man, and an indelible stain on the American Presidency. In his resignation speech, Nixon reveals his inner turmoil, "Throughout the long and difficult period of Watergate, I have felt it was my duty to persevere, to make every possible effort to complete the term of office to which you elected me. [...] I have never been a quitter," Nixon said.[152] "To leave office before my term is completed is abhorrent to every instinct in my body."[153] But, he was forced to acknowledge, without "a strong enough political base in the Congress," he could no longer justify staying in office.[154] "I must put the interest of America first," he said.[155]

Yet, already, even in the midst of his resignation, Nixon was working to frame his legacy, rehabilitate his reputation, and shape his future. Concluding his remarks with a catalog of his accomplishments, Nixon pledges to continue working, "as long as I have a breath of life in my body," for "the cause of peace among nations."[156] Finally, taking solace from another former President, Nixon says, "Sometimes I have succeeded and sometimes I have failed, but always I have taken heart from what Theodore Roosevelt once said about the man in the arena, 'whose face is marred by dust and sweat and blood, who strives valiantly, who errs and comes short again and again because there is not effort without error and shortcoming, but who does actually strive to do the deed, who knows the great enthusiasms, the great devotions, who spends himself in a worthy cause, who at the best knows in the end the triumph of high achievement and who at the worst, if he fails, at least fails while daring greatly.'"[157]

Some setbacks can be devastating. Losing is hard. It hurts. But to succeed you have to be prepared to lose—*without* preparing to quit. Lincoln and Churchill never lost faith in their ability to shape the future. "This was certainly the case with Churchill," Nixon writes.[158] "He resumed writing newspaper articles to bring in an income. He tried twice to get back into Parliament but failed. He showed the world a brave and resilient face, but," Nixon continues, "I am sure that each defeat was a bitterly frustrating and humiliating disappointment."[159] And, yet, Churchill never saw these setbacks as his ultimate defeat. "Defeat," Nixon explains, "is not fatal in politics unless you give up and call it quits. And Churchill did not know the meaning of the word *quit*."[160] Churchill was often down, but he was never out. Ultimately, he rose to the highest office in England twice, and today he is widely remembered as the Prime Minister who served England during, as he put it, "her finest hour."

Even Nixon, after an historic public disgrace, was able to establish himself as an elder statesman. There is much that we can learn from the examples of these historic figures. Your success will often hinge on your ability to maintain faith in the future in spite of being occasionally flooded by trials and tribulations. The key is to learn to expect challenges and setbacks. Expect temporary defeats. But never expect ultimate failure. As Winston Churchill once said, "Success is not final, failure is not fatal. It is the courage to continue that counts."[161]

Get Leverage, Change the Calculus:
The Birth of Ancient Rome

"Give me a lever long enough and a place to stand and I will move the world."
—Archimedes (287—212 B.C.)

The Ancient Greek inventor Archimedes was a renowned scientist and mathematician who, though notoriously eccentric, possessed remarkable imagination and vision. He was a genius engineer who understood the power of leverage better than anyone. During the First Punic War (264 to 241 B.C.), Archimedes inventions, particularly his great war machines, endeared him to King Hiero, the tyrant of his home city of Syracuse. Archimedes work with levers and complex pulley systems soon led him to the famous declaration, "Give me a lever long enough and a place to stand and I will move the world." When King Hiero heard Archimedes' bold assertion he challenged him to put the principle into action and help the sailors of the Syracusan fleet beach a huge navy ship. Archimedes immediately went to work. He assembled a large set of ropes and pulleys, with cogs attached to giant pillars on the shore, and with this he was able to single-handedly, with his own strength, pull the great ship out of the sea and on to the shore.[162]

Naturally, leverage is not limited to physics or mechanics or moving heavy things. Leverage can also move the minds of men.

According to the Greek historian Dionysius, when Troy was captured in the 12th century B.C. a group of Trojans secured several ships and sailed away across the Aegean Sea. After enduring a treacherous episode of violent weather and rough waves in the Mediterranean they finally landed on the banks of the Tiber River to take shelter. After a few days of rest, now fully restored by the abundance of the land, the men were ready to sail again. The women, however, who had also suffered at sea, resisted.[163] One woman of noble birth—the crafty and courageous Roma, known for her wisdom—was intent on staying in this beautiful and bountiful new land and she persuaded the women to help her with her audacious plan: The women burned their ships.[164]

Being stranded, the men were at first furious. But the women moved quickly to subdue their anger by kissing and caressing their men. Before long the men realized the women had been right.[165] They discovered the land was fertile and their neighbors were friendly. Rather than building new ships, the men agreed to stay and, in time, in honor of her daring decisiveness, they named the new hilltop settlement after Roma.[166] It was in this way that a small agricultural society situated on the Italian peninsula gave birth to the Roman civilization.

As resolved as the Trojan women were to stay, their efforts to persuade the men failed. It was not until they gained *leverage* that they were able to persevere. Of course, it was a bold plan fraught with risk, especially for Roma. And it was, naturally, beyond leverage; vision, decisiveness and courage all played a clear role in their success. But the critical factor was how the women changed the calculus of the struggle. To be sure, the men were still free to leave. They could build new ships. But now it was far easier to stay. If the men still wanted to leave, the burden to persevere was now on them.

Employ the Power of Pain and Pleasure.

Everyone struggles to some degree to achieve their goals and ambitions. When confronted with a significant obstacle, while most fall by the wayside, those people with grit will continue to struggle. They will try harder, work longer, or seek a different approach. Very few, however, will stop and think about how they might gain some leverage and thereby achieve their aim *without* all the struggle.

A powerful tool, leverage can be anything that increases your will or ability to achieve your intent. Whether that intent requires you to conquer resistance, overcome obstacles, strengthen drive, or simply improve your probability of success, leverage can give you the advantage you need to succeed.

Depending on the situation, there are undoubtedly a great many ways that you might reframe a situation or change its calculus to gain leverage. On the most basic level, however, what virtually all of these possibilities have in common is some form of pain or pleasure. Everyone is motivated to seek pleasure and avoid pain. Thus, if you can add or subtract something significant that increases or decreases the perceived pain or pleasure that you or others receive through the process of achieving your goal, or when your goal is realized, then you gain leverage and enhance your chances of success. By burning the ships, the Trojan women increased the amount of pain the men would feel—from the labor and lost time of building the ships—if they still wanted to leave. The men now *associated* leaving with considerable pain. The men also now clearly understood that staying would please the women and would likely lead to increased physical and emotional pleasure. Understand: *Associating* pleasure with achieving your desired outcome (or pain with not achieving it) is key. It is not enough to make intellectual connections. The most powerful form of leverage is when it is directly associated with powerful emotion.

As simple as this may sound there is a challenge: Understanding, identifying and resolving your competing interests. If you are having difficulty following through on a commitment, it's because there's some conflict, often in the form of a competing demand or a hidden payoff. You are somehow benefiting from not following through; there is either some perceived pleasure you are gaining or some perceived pain your are avoiding. Your success depends on your ability to reconcile this conflict, or find an acceptable tradeoff. You can either find another way of meeting your competing goals or desires or, alternatively, you can amplify the leverage around your true priorities. In other words, find additional ways of either increasing the pain of not following through or increasing the pleasure of getting it done.

Paint a Vivid Picture of the Future.

One of the simplest and most powerful ways to gain leverage is by reframing or refocusing how something is seen. Part of the magic of charismatic leaders, for example, is found in their ability to use vivid imagery and metaphors to paint a bright and compelling picture of the future, while simultaneously portraying the present with pictures of gloom and doom. With painful feelings associated with the present and pleasurable feelings associated with the future, charismatics only then need offer broad strokes for how to get there, followed by promises that they know the way—and that they are, naturally, the best qualified to lead the way.

A compelling vision can be a powerful form of leverage in your own life, particularly when backed by inspiring goals. The more clear and exciting your vision and goals, the more you can see them in your mind's eye, the greater will be your drive to see them realized. In the case of Theodore Roosevelt, for instance, he had a Progressive vision for the country, but he *also* had a clear vision for himself: Another term as President of the United States. No doubt this drove Roosevelt just as hard. After all, he loved nothing more than being president. "I do not believe that anyone else has ever enjoyed the White House as much as I have," he said upon leaving office.[167]

You can further increase your drive by simultaneously convincing yourself (i.e. with an emotionally compelling rationale) that your current situation, or whatever it is you are trying to stop or get away from, is no longer acceptable to you. Frame it in such a way that taps your own most powerful emotions. Roosevelt had a clear image of his legacy which was driving him forward, but he had also become convinced that President Taft was busy taking that legacy apart. This worked to further ensure his dedication and resolve. After all, Roosevelt recognized that at the end of his life it would be his legacy that would last. This leads to another strategy for gaining leverage.

Make a Public Stand.

Speaking to his audience immediately after he was shot outside the Gilpatrick hotel, Theodore Roosevelt broadcast his campaign as a moral cause and publicly voiced his ongoing commitment. "I am in this cause with my whole heart and soul," he said.[168] "I believe that the Progressive movement is making life a little easier for all our people…and," he continued, "I am absorbed in the success of that movement."[169] In this way, Roosevelt further linked himself and his legacy with the movement. This, in turn, further strengthened his commitment, as well as his accountability for that commitment and the possible consequences of not sticking it out. As Robert Cialdini writes in *Influence*, "the more public a stand the more reluctant we will be to change it."[170]

Roosevelt also knew that the intensity of the situation would intensify the impact of his speech and his commitment to the cause. "I want to take advantage of this incident," he said.[171] In his mind, a little more pain and risk equated with a much bigger payoff. This too strengthened his commitment to see it through. Cialdini writes, "It appears that commitments are most effective in changing a person's self-image and future behavior when they are active, public, and effortful."[172]

David Blaine, the self-described endurance artist, once fasted inside of a small Plexiglas box suspended thirty feet in the air on the bank of River Thames near the Tower Bridge in London for forty-four days. Yet when he was at home in his apartment in New York, he had trouble avoiding the food in his refrigerator. When he was asked to explain the apparent contradiction in *Willpower*, Blaine said, "I don't think I could have succeeded on a forty-four-day-straight fast if I was in this apartment. At the box in London, there was no way for me to be tempted because I was in that space. Which was part of my reason to make it public, because I knew that I would have to do it."[173]

You can use this strategy to support your own efforts to succeed. Going public with a commitment can be a powerful way to leverage the public's perception to increase your accountability, and drive you toward success. Now your reputation and credibility are on the line. You're essentially linking potential future pain with a failure to persevere and potential pleasure to seeing it through. Getting others involved can be a powerful source of leverage. Indeed, a potent form of leverage can be found in fame itself. Imagine the leverage Obama gained to quit smoking when he began his presidential campaign. Now the eyes of the world were watching.

When you share your goals with just a *few*, trusted others, you also increase the stakes (though perhaps to a lesser degree). Depending on your situation, scaling things back and limiting who you share your commitments with may be even more beneficial. If you choose your confidants carefully, you also increase the encouragement and accountability and, ideally, may get some valuable feedback, insight or support—all of which increases your likelihood of sticking to your purpose and plan. For some people, their peer group is often even more powerful than the more distant public. There may also be power in using both.

Theodore Roosevelt himself was not immune to the perceptions of his peer group. It is impossible to know what he was thinking, but it is worth noting that immediately after he was shot, TR wanted to make sure that one of his friends from the Badlands, a legendary frontier lawman, not only knew that he was shot and that he went ahead with his speech, but, historian Edmund Morris explains, "He also asked that somebody contact Seth Bullock, of Deadwood, South Dakota, and be sure to mention that he had been shot with 'a thirty-eight on a forty-four frame.'"[174] It was a curious detail. Seth Bullock was a part of TR's peer group and, for whatever reason, in the midst of this gritty moment, Bullock was at the top of TR's mind.

Leverage Your Identity.

Following the boss-controlled delegate debacle at the Republican National Convention of 1912, Theodore Roosevelt bolted from the Republican party and assumed the reins of the Progressive party. Shortly afterwards a reporter asked Roosevelt if he was feeling up to the fight. Roosevelt promptly pronounced himself as "fit as a bull moose." Cartoonists immediately recognized and quickly seized the easy parallels. Pictures of TR as a bull moose—an animal known for its size and dominance—soon spread across the land like wildfire. The 1912 campaign would be a three-ring circus: an elephant, a donkey, and a bull moose.[175] Recognizing their value to his campaign, Roosevelt was "dee-lighted" with the cartoons and began referring to himself as a bull moose—most notably when he told his audience at the auditorium in Milwaukee, "It is true. I have just been shot. But it takes more than that to kill a Bull Moose."[176] "I am going to ask you to be as quiet as possible," he added, "for I am not able to give the challenge of the bull moose quite as loudly."[177]

Beginning as a small, shy and sickly youth, TR had physically and psychologically transformed himself. He now saw himself as a man of courage and integrity, with great physical and mental strength and energy. Whether it was the heroes of history or the great game animals he hunted in Africa, TR identified with the strong and courageous. This is who he believed himself to be. This is who he was. And, to a considerable extent, this is was what drove him to do what he did.

By 1912 TR had become a living characterization of the bull moose, and the Progressive Party came to be known as the Bull Moose Party, the party that could take a bullet and keep standing. TR, the bull moose, and the progressive cause were now tightly wrapped up in the identity of one man.

TR saw himself in a certain way. He had a clear and distinct identity which he was mentally and emotionally compelled to live up to. Naturally, this went deeper than any public commitment to a particular course of action. It was now about who Roosevelt was as a man. The way you see yourself will unmistakably shape the way you think, what you say, and how you act. Imagine for example, Arnold Schwarzenegger and the way he sees himself. When Schwarzenegger broke his leg skiing he went through with his inaugural speech because—with just the *thought* of backing out—he said, "I felt like a total wimp." It was too much to bear. Schwarzenegger identified with strong men, men like Teddy Roosevelt. This was *his* identity. And it pushed him to follow through with his scheduled address.

The same can be said of Donald Trump when he found himself in catastrophic debt following the Savings and Loan Crisis of the late 1980s. His self-image was a powerful force in helping him to turn his situation around. He was eager, wrote *The New York Times* columnist Timothy O'Brien, "to avoid [personal] bankruptcy at all costs because he felt that it would permanently taint him as a failure or a quitter."[178] In his own mind, this was a temporary setback—albeit an enormous one. Trump continued to see himself as a successful developer and he was determined to prove it. And when he *did*, the accomplishment was so significant that it remains the greatest financial turnaround listed in the book of *Guinness World Records*.[179]

Understand: There is no more commanding influence over your thoughts and actions then the way you see yourself. Your beliefs about who you are, what you're capable of, and even why you're here, are all potential sources of leverage. When you effectively reframe your goal in light of your identity—including your core principles, the standards you set, or the expectations you have for yourself—you tap into a deep reservoir of energy, motivation and power. Anthony Robbins explains, "The greatest leverage you can create for yourself is the pain that comes from inside, not outside. Knowing that you have failed to live up to your own standards for your life is the ultimate pain. If we fail to act in accordance with our own view of ourselves, if our behaviors are inconsistent with our standards—with the identity we hold for ourselves—then the chasm between our actions and who we are drives us to make a change."[180] Your awareness of this gap is your source of leverage—perhaps your ultimate source.

When those standards do not exist, however, or when the way you see yourself is left unchecked or imbalanced, this powerful, driving force can lead to tragic consequences.

Counterpunch: Get Perspective. Maintain Balance.

When the Watergate scandal began to grip the nation in 1973, President Richard Nixon was doing everything in his power—as well as a number of things that were beyond his power—to hold on to the presidency. The idea that he should or even could resign was unthinkable to him. He was, however, rather than taking the fall himself, perfectly willing to eliminate members of his own staff, even knowing that some would go to prison. As the situation worsened, he became increasingly desperate to persevere. He began to lash out, blaming the press, his enemies, and even "overzealous" members of his own inner circle. He blamed everyone except himself. But as the investigation progressed the evidence began to point unmistakably to the man in the Oval Office.

When Nixon then ignored a subpoena and refused to turn over the White House tape recordings to either the Senate Watergate committee or Special Prosecutor Archibald Cox, he set the stage for a Constitutional confrontation. When he accepted the resignations of his Attorney General and Deputy Attorney General, fired Archibald Cox, and abolished the office of the special prosecutor it became a full-fledged Constitutional crisis. Political pundits dubbed it the Saturday Night Massacre, and for most Americans this was the turning point. Polls now revealed that a majority of Americans wanted Nixon out. Pressure for impeachment escalated in the U.S. Congress. And, yet, for his part, Nixon continued to maintain his innocence, declaring to the nation in a televised address, "People have got to know whether or not their President is a crook. Well I'm not a crook." [181]

Finally, on July 24, 1974 the U.S. Supreme Court ruled unanimously against Nixon, rejecting his claim of executive privilege. Within days, the House Judiciary Committee charged Nixon with obstruction of justice and recommended articles of impeachment to the full House.

Feeling defeated, Nixon was fraught with anxiety. He felt profoundly alone, and even more desperate to maintain some standing in the public's mind. On the night of July 30, 1974, Nixon was in his den in the White House unable to sleep. His presidency was embroiled in crisis. For the next few early morning hours he sat in his hideaway office contemplating his next move, carefully cataloging on a yellow legal pad the pros and cons of resigning the Presidency, acknowledging it would be best for both the country and the Republican Party. But he still could not bring himself to do it.

Nixon was a mysterious and complex individual, filled with both soaring strengths and tragic flaws. But he was also a simple man with common hopes and dreams. In the words of John Ehrlichman, President Nixon's Chief Domestic Advisor, "Richard Nixon was the strangest collection, the strangest paradoxical combination of any man I ever heard of."[182] As with Roosevelt, Churchill and De Gaulle—the leaders he admired most—Nixon identified with the great heroes of history. He wanted to be like them. He believed that he was. He was the President of the most powerful nation on Earth. He won a second term in the greatest landslide election in U.S. history. He opened the door to Red China. He brought an end to the war in Vietnam. It was unimaginable that Watergate could bring an end to the reign of Nixon. To have come so far only to be undone by a "third-rate burglary" was, in the words of Henry Kissinger, "a fate of biblical proportions." [183]

But Nixon was not like these other great leaders. Indeed, in some ways, the story of his rise to power is even more remarkable. He was not the attractive, charismatic personality, effortlessly at ease among others. He did not come from wealth and privilege. What Nixon did have—and he had it in spades—was pure, unbridled grit. Author and newspaper publisher Conrad Black writes, "lacking the quality of natural attraction was what made him vulnerable as a candidate and even as an office-holder embroiled in controversy, and was what made his ultimate attainments in his chosen career so astounding. He was vulnerable, but ultimately unstoppable."[184]

Nixon saw himself as a skilled politician, a statesman, a man of the times, a man of history. He did not see himself as a quitter or a crook. And this, in part, helps to explain Nixon's desperate, dogged desire to hold on. "One of the strongest forces in the human personality is the drive to preserve the integrity of our own identity."[185] In fact, in Nixon's case, he was willing to break the law. He was willing to let his friends take the fall. He was willing to do almost anything to protect his identity and persevere.

As dawn came up on July 31, 1974, Nixon found himself still sitting alone in his private office, contemplating his next move. He could resign, wait for impeachment, conviction and expulsion, or he could fight. And, yet, no matter how many good reasons he had to resign, he returned again and again to his gut instinct: 'Nixon has never been a quitter.' "The idea that he would be forced from his job and end his career in disgrace was "repugnant."'[186] Staying and fighting did, however, have a number of grave drawbacks. Finally, despite his concerns, Nixon made his decision. He flipped over his yellow pad of legal paper and wrote across the page: "End Career as a Fighter."[187]

Within a few short days, however, Nixon was completely finished. He was physically and emotionally beaten. There was no hope left. "The realities of common sense, politics, and daylight gave him a different message. He had no support in Congress; his own staff headed by Haig, were telling him that he could not possibly survive; and he knew he could not defend the indefensible in such a political climate."[188] Finally, on August 8, 1974, Richard M. Nixon became the first American president to resign.

Richard Nixon could have been a truly great president. But he failed because he lost his sense of perspective. And he did not have the inner compass or the accountability he needed to get himself back on track.

What is perhaps most surprising about Watergate is not that a President acted illegally and abused his power (as demoralizing as that is). What is most shocking is that the illegal actions that the Nixon administration and the President himself took in pursuit of his objectives were all completely unnecessary. There was *no need* to spy on the Democrats or break into the headquarters of the DNC—Nixon won the 1972 presidential election by a landslide.

Of course it was never really about winning the White House, or furthering his political platform. It was really about Nixon. It was personal. The reality was, Nixon struggled to handle the job, and he cracked under the pressure. He became unhinged because he didn't have anyone in his inner circle that was capable of keeping him in check.

Naturally, there are times when quitting is the best thing to do, as Nixon was eventually forced to realize. But Nixon's problem was *not* that he wasn't a quitter—we would all do well to admire that part of his personality. His problem was that that part of his personality was left fundamentally unchecked. In other words, his problem was that he didn't simultaneously identify with men of character and high honor. Throughout his remarkable career, he failed to see the power of courage and character and the role they could play in his climb to the top.

Draw On the Power of Character.

During the 1856 presidential election, the prominent American newspaper correspondent Major Benjamin Perley Poore of Newbury, Massachusetts made a bet with a friend, Colonel Robert Burbank of Boston. Poore was convinced that presidential candidate Millard Fillmore would carry Massachusetts. Burbank disagreed and the two men decided that the loser of their bet would be required to wheel a barrel full of apples from his house to the house of the winner, which was *thirty-six* miles away.[189]

On election day Fillmore failed to carry the state, the Colonel won the wager, and the Major was doomed to the long applecart hike. Fortunately, Burbank had compassion on his friend—it was just a friendly wager after all—and he wired him to tell him to forget about the bet. But Major Poore insisted on following through. It was his idea. He lost. And now he was resolved to live with the consequences. He sent a wire back to the Colonel telling him that he was on his way to Burbank's Tremont House in Boston and that he was likely to be very thirsty when he arrived. Without further delay Major Poore harnessed himself to the cart, now loaded down with a 185-pound barrel of apples, and set out for the city.[190]

It took the Major two full days to make the trek. By the time he was nearing Tremont House, Poore had lost twelve pounds. His hands were blistered from wear. And his back was badly bruised. As he got closer scores of people went out to meet him. Before long a band joined him and marchers surrounded him. As he approached the Colonel's house, he could see a sign that read, "Major Poore—may the next administration prove as faithful to their pledges as he was to his."[191] When the Major finally arrived, the Colonel leapt up on a small platform and shared a few remarks about his honorable friend before the two retired for a cool drink.[192]

Only a fool would argue against the value and importance of a strong moral character. Regardless of whether honest, reasonable people may disagree about what is right or wrong in a *particular* situation, or which competing ethical principles may apply, the reality is that most psychologically sound people want to do what they believe is right and good. What most people fail to understand is the inherent power of character in your drive to succeed. "Character *is* power," said Booker T. Washington. And the ancient Greek philosopher Heraclitus said that "character is destiny." Major Poore was a man of character and the admiring crowd that received him at the end of his long applecart slog further reinforced his identity, and further propelled him toward his destiny and the fruits of a life of integrity and honor.

Imagine how much easier it would be for Major Poore to continue keeping his commitments after he kept this one. Keeping promises and sticking to your commitments strengthens your power and resolve by developing your character. The key, writes Stephen Covey, is to start small and never over-promise and under-deliver (and the key to that is to be exceptionally careful about what you promise to do). "As we make and keep commitments, even small commitments," writes Covey, "we begin to establish an inner integrity that gives us the awareness of self-control and the courage and strength to accept more of the responsibility for our own lives. By making and keeping promises to ourselves and others, little by little, our honor becomes greater than our moods."[193] You teach yourself to keep going even when you don't *feel* like it. You learn to persevere, you stick to your commitments as a matter of course.

Character is also a commanding means of influence, and it is indispensable to true greatness. When Abraham Lincoln first entered politics in Springfield he had no experience, no credentials and few connections. All he had was his character—and that was enough. Lincoln was such a remarkably honest man of integrity that he was *trusted* by everyone who knew him—and that was key. From a young age, Lincoln had a well-developed character and the courage to do the right thing in the moment of truth. What is interesting, however, is that in his near-desperate attempt to rise out of the poverty of his youth, it was his strong moral character and his reputation for fairness and honesty that served as Lincoln's leverage, and helped him to make a name for himself and eventually win a seat in the Illinois State Legislature. "Honest Abe" they called him, both Whigs and Democrats alike.[194]

To this day, scholars habitually rank Lincoln as one of the top three greatest American presidents (usually first). So even as the presidency, the nation, and the times have all changed; historians, political scientists, scholars of leadership and law continue to place 'Old Honest Abe' on top. Theodore Roosevelt could easily have been referring to the life of Lincoln and his leadership of the nation when he said, "Character, in the long run, is the decisive factor in the life of an individual and of nations alike."[195]

This was Richard Nixon's greatest weakness. He was able to persevere through many remarkable challenges—including being defeated by Kennedy in 1960, only to turn around and lose the election for governor of California in 1962—because he did not see himself as a quitter. He was not, unfortunately, a man of great character and, therefore, there was little chance he could become a great man.

Remember: Whatever particular strategy you use, the key to leverage is finding ways to associate—through strong emotion—more pleasure and less pain with your desired outcomes. "The key is to get lots of reasons," writes Anthony Robbins, "or better yet, strong enough reasons, why the change should take place immediately, not someday in the future. If you are not driven to make the change now, then you don't really have leverage."[196]

2

FOSTER FEARLESSNESS, FORGE A SPINE OF STEEL

"You will never do anything in this world without courage.
It is the greatest quality of the mind next to honor."
—Aristotle, Ancient Greek Philosopher (384—322 B.C.)

Count the Costs, Then Forge Ahead:
General Patton's Moment of Truth

"Courage and perseverance have a magical talisman,
before which difficulties disappear and obstacles vanish into air."
—John Quincy Adams, 6th U.S. President (1825—1829)

On September 26, 1918, in the midst of World War I, George S. Patton's moment of testing had arrived. He was face-to-face with his greatest fear. Born into a long line of military heroes, this was a fear that haunted him from an early age. Patton grew up listening to stories of daring heroism and bold exploits in battle. He aspired to be a great military leader himself. Alas, he was always haunted by the fear that he would not have the guts to live up to the family name when his moment came.[197] The man who would later become the great General, "Old Blood and Guts," widely revered as an audacious hero of World War II, was deathly afraid that he would lose his courage in battle at the very moment he needed it most.

And now that moment of testing had finally come. Patton was leading a light tank brigade up a hill overlooking a German occupied town in north-eastern France. Once on the hilltop, facing directly into German machine guns, Patton and his men realized they were trapped. If they risked a retreat, they would have been picked off by German positions on the sides of the hill. To advance—though courageous—would have meant certain death. Caught in a hailstorm of machine-gun fire, Patton began to panic. "I was trembling with fear," Patton wrote later, "I felt a great desire to run."[198] His entire body began to shake. His legs softened like spaghetti. He lost his nerve. It was as if, he thought, his greatest fear had come true: He was a coward.[199]

In that moment, looking up into the clouds, Patton had a vision. It was an apparition. He could see his ancestors, his illustrious military family. There they all were standing in full military regalia, looking down on him. It seemed, Patton thought, as if they were inviting him to join them, to sacrifice his life for his men and join their company, becoming another departed hero of war.

The vision transformed Patton in an instant. "I became calm at once," he said as he looked around at his men.[200] Patton immediately called for volunteers to follow him down the hill straight into the battery of German machine guns, into what Patton said, "what I honestly believed was certain death."[201] "It is time for another Patton to die!" he said as he rallied the charge.[202]

Moments after their bold advance, Patton went down with a bullet to the leg. "The soldiers wanted to remove him from the battlefield. He said, 'No.'"[203] With the help of his orderly, Patton made it to the safety of a shell hole. "Though injured by a German bullet, Patton continued to direct his troops, showing grit and determination in the face of obvious danger."[204] Patton commanded the battle for another full hour until he was rescued.

For this incident, Patton was later awarded the Distinguished Service Medal and the Purple Heart. And the experience of charging directly into his fear changed his life forever.

The pages of the past teem with the tales of brave men and women, stories about how courage and confidence changed the outcome of a battle, the course of a game, or the result of a campaign. Throughout history humans have witnessed how a single act of courage in the midst of an impossible situation became *the* transforming incident in which a life was changed, never to regain its original arc.

Cowardice and fear have no part to play in your success. The heroes of history all became men and women of confidence and courage on their way to the top. Whatever your greatest dreams, there will always be moments where courage will be vital to your advance. Learn from the examples of the legends, adopt their strategies and tactics, employ their wisdom and insights and you will find that the person you seem to be today is a mere shadow of the potential within. Whatever fears and insecurities you may now possess, however they may have ruled you in the past, your task is to face your fears, control them, exploit them, acknowledge and dismiss them, but never allow them to define your future or dictate your next steps.

Dismiss the Counsel of Fear

"Cowardice...is almost always simply a lack of ability
to suspend the functioning of the imagination."
—Ernest Hemingway (1899—1961)

Patton was not out of the woods. He conquered his fear that day, but his fear would never be completely vanquished. Indeed, years later, speaking to a colonel in the army, Dr. T. V. Smith, Patton willingly admitted, "Colonel, I am not a brave man—the truth is, I am an utter craven coward. I never have been within the sound of gunshot or in sight of battle in my whole life that I wasn't so scared that I had sweat in the palms of my hands." [205]

Most people would look at General Patton's life and balk at the idea that he was an "utter craven coward." Indeed, the historical consensus is that George S. Patton was a man of great courage and honor, an American hero who was "indispensable" in the effort to defeat Germany in World War II.[206] In fact, Dwight Eisenhower himself later said, "It is no exaggeration to say that Patton's name struck terror at the hearts of the enemy."[207]

The fact is Patton was human. He was a man who experienced fear just like everyone else. His courage and heroism were not the result of having no fear—quite the opposite. He was courageous because he overcame his fear over and over again.

This day stands out because this was the day he got a hold of his fear and, thus, he won for himself a *lasting* advantage: He learned that giving in to his fear was a *choice*, a choice that needs to be reinforced on a regular basis. In his own words, looking back years later, Patton said, "I learned very early in my life never to take counsel of my fears."[208] To be afraid is one thing. To take counsel of or give in to your fears is something *entirely* different. Patton understood this distinction, and it made all the difference.

Whether we realize it or admit it or not, we all experience fears from time to time. Those who will be most successful, those who are consistently growing and pushing themselves beyond their comfort zones, will likely experience fear more regularly. This is a common part of high achievement. The key is awareness. To get to the next level of success, writes Anthony Robbins, "we have to be honest with ourselves; honest about our unconscious fears. Everybody has a fear of failure at some level; at times we've all been fearful that perhaps we are not enough."[209] To be unaware of your fear is to risk acting against your own best interests. It is, as Hemingway said, to risk letting your imagination get the best of you. Many people let their imaginations run rampant, until their fears start to control their lives. Patton was honest about his fears and, thus, rather than suppressing it or ignoring it, he knew he needed to watch it, manage it, and be careful not to let it take him in.

Get a Jump on Fear. Face It Down First, Fast and Often

"Do something that scares you everyday."
—Eleanor Roosevelt (1884—1962), American Politician, Diplomat, and Activist

George S. Patton was not the type to rest on his laurels. He beat back his fear, but he knew, if he was ever to achieve his ambition of becoming a great military leader, he needed to keep his fears in check. It was not enough to merely stay on guard. Patton needed to develop, and expand his capacity to lead and, thus, he knew he needed to regularly, deliberately face down his fears. He had to make courage a habit.

From this moment on, persisting throughout his rise in the ranks to four-star general, Patton repeatedly took the time to join his men on the front lines, fighting by their side in perilous places, assuming the lead in the most hazardous cases, exposing himself to danger again and again, deliberately confronting and overcoming his fears.[210] Patton's strategy worked brilliantly. "Each time it became easier to face down his fears. It seemed to his fellow generals, and to his own men, that no one had more presence of mind than Patton. They did not know," writes Robert Greene, "how much of his strength was an effort of will."[211]

Understand: General Patton was not a random outlier, or exception to the rule. He did not have some mysterious special talent or gift that allowed him to summon courage from his ancestors in the great beyond. The fact is this strategy has been helping people to free themselves from the shackles of fear since the beginning of time. Over two millennia ago, Alexander the Great took this same line of attack. Like Patton, Alexander was a bold and aggressive military commander. "He led from the front, in the vanguard of the opening cavalry charge, or as the first man up a scaling ladder."[212] This was the way of Alexander. He successfully beat back his fear by boldly driving directly through it. The portrait painted by historians is that Alexander yearned for freedom, and that only in continuing to conquer his fears anew could he satisfy his hunger to be free.

Alexander achieved greatness early in life, far surpassing the achievements of his father. But he wanted more. "Oh, he could have stayed home in Macedonia, married, raised a family. He'd have died a celebrated man," Ptolemy explains.[213] "But this was not Alexander. All his life, he fought to free himself from fear. And by this, and this alone, he was made free. The freest man I've ever known."[214]

This was an indispensable element of Alexander's success. His freedom from fear was contagious; it spread throughout his army. Arrian of Nicomedia, a Greek historian and military commander from ancient Rome, wrote that Alexander was "…very renowned for rousing the courage of his soldiers, filling them with hopes of success, and dispelling their fear in the midst of danger by his own freedom from fear."[215]

Alexander's courage went well beyond the battlefield. Beyond the strength of his army, it was this same bold courage, this same willingness to face down his fears again and again that powered his transformational vision. His vision transcended the borders and traditions of Greece. His actions pushed against the status quo mentality of his generals. By conquering his fears, Alexander pushed the human race forward. "And if his desire...to reconcile Greek and barbarian ended in failure... What failure! His failure towered over other men's successes. I've lived long life," Ptolemy said, "but the glory and the memory of man will always belong to the ones who follow their great visions. And the greatest of these is the one they now call...Megas Alexandros. The greatest of them all."[216]

Resolve to Conquer Fear Anew.

General Patton and Alexander the Great both understood an important truth: Fear is not something that can be defeated once and for all—but it *can* be managed. And they learned, more importantly, that courage can become a nearly instinctive habit. In fact, courage can become so habitual that it operates *as if* it is a natural instinct.

Some people seem to be more naturally fearless. In all likelihood, however, they have been practicing fearlessness for so long that it's all they now seem to know. Even Patton, over time, began to see himself differently. Writing to his father later, Patton said, "You know I have always feared I was a coward at heart but I am beginning to doubt it."[217]

The strategy of history's heroes is here in plain sight, waiting to serve you in your own great purpose. Every time you face down one of your fears, it loses some of its power over you. You build up a reservoir of courage that can be let loose in other areas of your life. "You gain strength, courage, and confidence," Eleanor Roosevelt said, "by every experience in which you really stop to look fear in the face."[218] Jim Morrison from The Doors put it this way, "Expose yourself to your deepest fear; after that, fear has no power, and the fear of freedom shrinks and vanishes. You are free."[219]

A little fear, held in check, can be a useful tool, a source of energy and heightened awareness. Left to run rampant, however, it will debilitate and destroy its' captive. The courage and confidence you need to follow through on your purpose requires you to deliberately put yourself in places and step into situations where you are forced to face your fear. The more you do this the more comfortable and familiar you become. Your confidence will begin to grow as your anxiety dissipates and more of your mental capacity is devoted to mastering the nuance and subtleties of your context. You will soon begin to seek out greater challenges, further feeding and fortifying your courage and confidence. Before long you too will begin to see yourself differently, you will become your own kind of battle-tested warrior, with the courage and grit you need to succeed.[220]

Act as If:
TR Facing Down His Fears

"Act as if! Act as if you're a wealthy man, rich already, and then you'll surely become rich. Act as if you have unmatched confidence and then people will surely have confidence in you. Act as if you have unmatched experience and then people will follow your advice. And act as if you are already a tremendous success, and—as sure as I stand here today—you will become successful."
—Jordan Belfort, The Wolf of Wall Street

In the summer of 1872, just before his fourteenth birthday, a serious asthma attack prompted Teddy Roosevelt's parents to send him up to Moosehead Lake in Maine. They thought some time away from New York City, camping with friends in the crisp mountain air, would do him some good.

Young Theodore had always been a small, weak, and sickly child which prodded his parents to protect and pamper him, seldom leaving him in an uncontrolled situation, never mind one where he was unprotected.[221] But this time he made the trip alone.

Traveling first by train and then stagecoach, it was here that Teddy encountered two boys close to his own age. Shy and sensitive, with weak muscles on a small frame, he was an easy target for bullies.[222] And the two boys began to taunt little TR. "They found that I was a foreordained and predestined victim," Roosevelt wrote, "and industriously proceeded to make life miserable for me."[223] He tried to ignore them at first, recognizing he was both outsized and outnumbered.[224] But as the hectoring continued, he began to lose his self-control until, finally, fear, frustration and humiliation got the better of him and he threw himself upon his harassers.[225] Unfortunately, this only served to deepen his humiliation. "The worst feature was that when I finally tried to fight them," Roosevelt explains, "I discovered that either one singly could not only handle me with easy contempt, but handle me so as not to hurt me much and yet to prevent my doing any damage whatever in return."[226]

Roosevelt would never forget the shame he felt from being helpless in the face of bullies. "During the rest of the stagecoach ride, sitting in his corner in grim silence, he determined never to be placed in such a predicament again."[227] It was turning point for TR. This was the day he made a decision that would forever change his life—not because of what *happened* to him, but because of how he chose to *respond*. The experience of being powerless roused in Roosevelt an immediate resolution to join, in his words, "the fellowship of the doers."[228] He was determined to do everything possible to develop his personal power. His efforts to build up and train both his body and his mind took on a new, heightened level of importance. "The experience taught me," he said, "what probably no amount of good advice could have taught me. I made up my mind that I must try to learn so that I would not again be put in such a helpless position; and having become quickly and bitterly conscious that I did not have the natural prowess to hold my own, I decided that I would try to supply its place by training."[229]

Naturally, Teddy continued to lift weights, but now, with his father's "hearty approval," he took up boxing.[230] Roosevelt understood, writes Morris, that "he must also learn how to give and take punishment."[231] Boxing would be ideal.

But Roosevelt was no mere brute. He knew that he had to dedicate the same long hours to developing his mind, including his mental toughness. "Transforming his body was only one step in the psychological struggle against what Teedie shamefully considered his 'timid' nature."[232] He may have become a man of action that day, but he still had to deal with his fear. In fact, in his autobiography, Roosevelt acknowledges his early struggle to overcome his fears went well beyond grade school bullies. There were indeed a great many things that struck fear in his heart.[233]

Beyond building himself up, Roosevelt found comfort in reading about the great champions and heroes of history. "I was nervous," he wrote, "and timid. Yet from reading of the people I admired,—ranging from the soldiers of Valley Forge, and Morgan's riflemen, to the heroes of my favorite stories—and from hearing of the feats performed by my Southern forefathers and kinsfolk, and from knowing my father, I felt a great admiration for men who were fearless and could hold their own in the world, and I had a great desire to be like them."[234]

Young Teddy was not reading for mere entertainment, however, or to distract himself from the realities of his own insecurities and fear. He wanted something out of these stories. He was seeking inspiration, but for a practical purpose. He was reading about history's heroic figures because he was looking for ideas, for insight, and for practical wisdom that he could use in his own life, toward his own ends.

And his search was paying off. Indeed, he reveals the tactic he found most effective in overcoming fear. It was a passage, "in one of Marryat's books which always impressed me." he wrote.[235] Over forty years later, with a lifetime of his own legendary achievements, Roosevelt still thought enough of the idea to include it in his autobiography. "In this passage the captain of some small British man-of-war is explaining to the hero how to acquire the quality of fearlessness. He says that at the outset almost every man is frightened when he goes into action, but that the course to follow is for the man to keep such a grip on himself that he can act just as if he was not frightened."[236]

This "act just as if" principle would then begin to take hold, Roosevelt explains. "After this is kept up long enough it changes from pretense to reality, and the man does in very fact become fearless by sheer dint of practicing fearlessness when he does not feel it…"[237]

This was not, moreover, simply some theoretical understanding. Roosevelt applied it to his own life. "This was the theory upon which I went," he explains.[238] "There were all kinds of things of which I was afraid at first, ranging from grizzly bears to "mean" horses and gun-fighters; but by acting as if I was not afraid I gradually ceased to be afraid."[239]

Today TR is an American icon. Nearly a century after his death, we continue to share the stories of his life. We share the stories of his bold exploits as a young progressive reformer tackling New York's corrupt, boss-controlled political machine. We share the stories of his heroic Rough Riders and his charge up San Juan Hill. We share the stories of his courage as President, fighting against the big trusts, and for the rights of workers, women and children, food safety, and a living wage.

But the confidence and courage required to accomplish his many great feats was not always his for the taking. He had to develop these qualities and, in the beginning, he had to settle for the mere outward appearance of confidence and courage.

The great Harvard psychologist William James once said, "If you want a quality, act as if you already had it."[240] That is precisely what TR did. And there can be no doubt that it worked. In fact, it wasn't long before he found himself the target of other bullies, and, in one particular case, the stakes were much higher, testing TR's mettle like never before.

Get Action:
Roosevelt and the Badlands

"Inaction breeds doubt and fear. Action breeds confidence and courage. If you want to conquer fear, do not sit home and think about it. Go out and get busy."
—Dale Carnegie (1888—1955)

One cold night in the Dakota Badlands in 1884, Roosevelt had spent the day out looking for lost horses. He was dirty, sunburned and tired when he approached the Nolan Hotel, hoping to get a hot meal and a warm bed. As he was walking up the stairs to the bar he heard a few gunshots. It was late in the evening and he had no place else to go. So, despite that he "disliked going in," he forged ahead.[241] When he entered the room he saw that there were several other men, along with the bartender, who smiled nervously at TR as he made his way across the room. Suddenly, a shabby, shady character with a revolver in each hand shouted, "Four Eyes!" in reference to Roosevelt's spectacles. "Four Eyes is going to treat!" he shouted loudly for everyone to hear. TR laughed with the others as he took his seat next to the stove, hoping to pass off the incident as a mere jest. But this was no joke. The bully was now standing over Roosevelt, with both guns cocked, cursing loudly with a tongue soaked in whiskey, repeating his command that Roosevelt "should set up the drinks."[242]

TR had had enough. He gave the man a chance to correct himself, but now it was clear that, in TR's words, this "objectionable creature, a would-be bad man, a bully who for the moment was having things all his own way," was intent on making a fool of TR, or worse.[243] Immediately taking stock of his options, Roosevelt recalled, "He was foolish to stand so near, and, moreover, his heels were close together, so that his position was unstable."[244]

Although Roosevelt was dressed in suitable Western attire, he had the unmistakable look of a fop from the big city. His buckskin tunic was elaborately decorated with beads and fringe, and had obviously been custom-made. His new calfskin boots also looked new with their shiny silver spurs. His broad-brimmed sombrero, with his rimless pince-nez glasses left the appearance of a young man with money who was wearing a costume, hoping to look the part. Moreover, standing at 5'8," speaking with a high-pitched voice, Roosevelt was not the most intimidating figure. To the hardened men of the Badlands, TR looked like a soft city-slicker, a dandy. But TR was no longer the weak and timid boy he once was. And he was certainly no coward.

Deftly playing into the mistaken perception, TR appeared to be meekly going along with the bully's demands as he got up slowly, looking past the man to avoid eye contact. "Well," he said, "if I've got to, I've got to."[245]

Once on his feet, however, Roosevelt leapt fearlessly into action. "As I rose," he writes, "I struck quick and hard with my right just to one side of the point of his jaw, hitting with my left as I straightened out, and then again with my right."[246] Both of the bully's guns went off as he fell back smacking his head on the corner of the bar. Roosevelt stood ready to crush the man's ribs with his knees, but his opponent was out cold. TR quickly snatched up both guns as the other men now loudly denounced the bully, and eagerly joined with Roosevelt. When the loud-mouth hooligan finally awoke the next morning he found himself in the shed in the back of the bar. Now disarmed and utterly humiliated, the bully immediately raced down to the train station, hightailing it out of town.

Theodore Roosevelt had just sewn another strand into his thickening cord of courage. And he continued to reinforce his habits of confidence and courage throughout his life, becoming, over time, the icon we remember today.

In the realm of human achievement, it is difficult to overstate the importance of confidence and courage. Ancient Greek and Chinese philosophers, including Aristotle and Mencius, argued that courage was one of the first and most important principles.[247] "You will never do anything in this world without courage," said Aristotle. "It is the greatest quality of the mind next to honor."[248] Winston Churchill put it this way, "Courage is rightly esteemed the first of human qualities, because it is the quality that guarantees all others."[249]

How much time has been lost because of the failure to act? How much energy has been wasted? How much treasure and life has been lost when a worthwhile endeavor was needlessly abandoned for no other reason then a lack of courage to act, to get up one more time, or endure one more defeat? Countless men and women have no doubt failed to persist with their plans because they lacked the confidence and courage to take initiative, or to continue on when they hit the inevitable wall. Do not let this be your fate. If you yearn to be successful, determine to make the development of these characteristics central to your self-development plan.

Clearly, the question is not whether we ought to value bravery and esteem acts of courage. The question is how to develop them. The following are a few of the most effective strategies we can takeaway from the legends and heroes of history, men and women like Patton, Churchill, Eleanor Roosevelt, and TR:

1. *Get Action Redux*. The challenge for many is *beginning* to become bolder and more confident. The solution, however, is far simpler than most people are prepared to admit: Just *begin* it! Take that first step! Get in the arena. "Get action," TR often said. "Seize the moment. Man was never intended to become an oyster."

A gritty hustler akin to her uncle Theodore, Eleanor Roosevelt embraced an identical outlook. When she started to get involved in the women's suffrage movement, she began to spend time with activists Esther Lape and Elizabeth Read. At times, Eleanor would grow impatient with their lack of action. "The rest of us were inclined to do a good deal of theorizing," Lape recalled. Eleanor, on the other hand, "…would look puzzled and ask why we didn't [just] *do* whatever we had in mind and get it out of the way."[250]

During the Great Depression, the leadership of Eleanor's husband Franklin Roosevelt likewise demonstrates this principle. Once FDR made a tangible commitment to take the action necessary to confront the Depression, forces began to conspire on his behalf.

Action is the key to developing all sorts of characteristics and competencies. Don't wait for courage to come. Get into action first. Indeed, courage is frequently the upshot of action. What's more, social psychologists who research this construct have found that facing up to a challenge "often brings out perseverance, ingenuity, mutual aid, cohesion, and social support in a community."[251] As Eleanor Roosevelt wrote in her book, *You Learn By Living*, "You gain strength, courage and confidence by every experience in which you really stop to look fear in the face. You are able to say to yourself, 'I have lived through this horror. I can take the next thing that comes along.'"[252]

Eleanor Roosevelt grew up terribly shy. Throughout her early life she was burdened with what she described as a, "terror of displeasing the people I lived with." Eventually, after she married Franklin, she learned that she had to face down her fears in order to overcome them. "The danger lies in refusing to face the fear," she said, "in not daring to come to grips with it."[253] "*You must do the thing you think you cannot do*," Roosevelt concluded emphatically.[254] Over time, action became the solution to her fears. "Like her uncle Theodore, like her husband Franklin, Eleanor Roosevelt would always crave action."[255]

2. *Discover and Destroy Limiting Beliefs*. The greatest obstacle to developing courage and self-confidence is often how you see yourself. Your thoughts and beliefs about who you are, what you are capable of, or what is possible for you, have a profound effect on what you achieve, regardless of whether those thoughts and beliefs have any basis in reality. Our perceptions and beliefs rarely come from the most reliable sources.

Rather than accepting ideas that don't serve your purpose and goals, your task is to discover and discard your limiting beliefs. Stop looking for excuses outside of yourself. "Here's the truth," writes Anthony Robbins, "the ultimate thing that stops most of us from making significant progress in our lives is not somebody else's limitations, but rather our own limiting perceptions or beliefs. No mater how successful we are as human beings, no matter how high we reach personally, professionally, spiritually, emotionally, there's always another level. And to get there, we have to be honest with ourselves…"[256] We have to take the time to think and reflect and identify and challenge the *beliefs behind the fears* that are holding you back. Once you identify your limiting perceptions and beliefs about your fears, you can begin to *replace* those perceptions and beliefs with more resourceful alternatives, ideas that lead to greater self-assurance and guts. Take the time to find the evidence you need to support your desired beliefs. In other words, don't just accept the beliefs you have about who you are. Instead, take the time to build, from the ground up, the beliefs you *want* to have.

3. *Act As If Redux*. In the strategy above, you are changing your beliefs first, with the understanding that new behaviors will follow these new beliefs. As Silver writes, "The mind has an amazing ability to help you create the behaviors necessary to be consistent with your thoughts."[257] With Roosevelt's "act just as if" approach, on the other hand, you are changing your behaviors first, with the understanding that new behaviors will create new experiences which will cause you to reevaluate and change old beliefs. As TR said, "I have often been afraid, but I wouldn't give in to it. I made myself act as though I was not afraid, and gradually my fear disappeared."[258]

Roosevelt's advice is echoed by Nolan Bushnell, a mentor to Steve Jobs. "I taught him," Bushnell said of Jobs, "that if you act like you can do something, then it will work. I told him, 'Pretend to be completely in control and people will assume that you are.'"[259]

This strategy may in fact be a powerful elixir to some wicked problems. In fact, Anthony Robbins maintains in *Unlimited Power* that it is possible for people suffering with depression to find relief simply by *acting as if* they are not depressed.[260] The process may not always be easy. But it is worthwhile. "It is only through labor and painful effort," Roosevelt said, "by grim energy and resolute courage, that we move on to better things."[261] Naturally, this does not mean it must happen all at once.

4. *Resolve to Keep Up the Fight*. Do not make the mistake of thinking that fear can be licked once and for all. Like Patton and Alexander, Roosevelt was constantly pushing up against the boundaries of the world, pushing through his fears and beyond his perceived limits. He learned from a young age that fear could never be completely conquered, and that the only way to live a truly fulfilling life is to continually fight back your fears, pushing forward to new unconquered terrain. "One cannot banish fear," writes Felix Dennis in *The Narrow Road*, "but one can face it down, crush it, bury it, padlock it in the deepest recesses of your heart and soul—and leave it there to rot."[262]

For TR, the way to face down one's fear was to build up one's boldness and courage over time, until a habit was formed. Quoting one of his childhood friends, Doris Kearns Goodwin explains, "'by constantly forcing himself to do the difficult or even dangerous thing,' he was able to cultivate courage as 'a matter of habit, in the sense of repeated effort and repeated exercise of will-power.'"[263]

"Most men can have the same experience if they choose," Roosevelt wrote.[264] "They will first learn to bear themselves well in trials which they anticipate and which they school themselves in advance to meet. After a while the habit will grow on them, and they will behave well in sudden and unexpected emergencies which come upon them unawares."[265] As TR understood, good habits make our lives eminently easier. Developing confidence and courage is not a one-time event. We must keep up the fight or risk slipping back toward insecurity and fear.

Stiffen Your Spine, Drive Fear to the Swine: Napoleon at Lodi Bridge

When the twenty-six-year-old Napoleon Bonaparte was given command of the French Army in April of 1796 he was not immediately respected by his soldiers. He had some presence with his palpable confidence and dapper appearance. But they quickly and foolishly judged him as an inferior commander because of his short stature and youthful appearance. The other generals and veteran officers themselves considered the young, little, insignificant General nothing more than a political appointee.

All of that, however, was about to change.

From the moment Napoleon first took command of the French Army of Italy he was in pursuit of his enemy. As a result of Napoleon's clever maneuvering, the Austrian forces, led by Johann Beaulieu, were in retreat. When the two armies finally clashed along the Adda River, just southeast of Milan, Napoleon was aggressively on the offensive, eager to find a point to cross the river and destroy Beaulieu's rear guard.

When they finally made it to Lodi Bridge, the Austrian soldiers who were holding the structure immediately began to fight desperately to defend it. Taking heavy fire from the French soldiers, the Austrians were soon resigned to abandon their position and instead began working to destroy the wooden bridge. Napoleon knew he could not let this happen. As he directed his infantry to target those seeking to destroy the structure, he ordered his cavalry to cross the river under the bridge while he sent a mass column of infantry to attack their way across.

Suddenly, the French column was being mowed down by musket fire. The effect was devastating. Within minutes the bridge was covered with scores of lifeless French soldiers. It seemed impossible to make it across alive. The French column began to fall back.

When Napoleon, who was directing the artillery to prevent the destruction of the bridge, saw his soldiers falling back he immediately swung into action. Pushing them forward, he called out to his men, much as he once said to a regiment, "My lads, you must not fear death. When soldiers brave death, they drive him into the enemies' ranks."[266] Breaking with convention and protocol, the General himself then turned to lead a second advance across the bridge. The French soldiers seeing their brave General leading the way joined him in greater numbers and with uninhibited zeal. The Austrians soldiers were dumbfounded. How could they possibly be attacking again?

As the Austrian forces began to succumb to French fire, those still standing were swept down by the French bayonets. Fear and panic ensued and the remaining Austrian soldiers retreated into the woods. In the end, the Austrians were beaten back and the French gained their position, defeating the rear guard of the Austrian army, allowing the French to take over Milan.

It was a pivotal moment for Bonaparte. "It was here, on 10 May 1796, that one of the great myths of the Napoleonic era, which helped establish the idea of Bonaparte as an irresistible, invincible force, was created."[267] In the midst of a dangerous and uncertain situation, he had distinguished himself by demonstrating intense courage under direct fire and, as a result, his life was forever changed.[268] Bonaparte later said that it was Lodi that made him certain he could become a man of great destiny.[269]

His soldiers immediately embraced him for his confidence and skill, and all the more—in spite of the fact that he was, as a general, expected to stay back—for his willingness to brave the fire of the front with his men. Bonaparte's courage endeared him to his men. Indeed, writes Asprey, "Napoleon's active role in the fighting won the acclaim of his soldiers who that night extolled him as Le Petit Caporal, "The Little Corporal" who wins battles, a nickname that would stick…"[270]

Tap the Contagious Power of Courage, Exploit It to Clear the Road.

Like Patton, Alexander, Washington and even the seventeen-year-old Joan of Arc; Napoleon was a powerful exemplar, a role model for his soldiers. It was Napoleon's courage that brought out the courage of his men. "Courage is contagious," writes Billy Graham. "When a brave man takes a stand the spines of others are often stiffened." That was the day that Napoleon stiffened the spine of the whole French army, the French people. If not for his personal valor, his men would not have persevered. They would not have taken the bridge at Lodi. And Napoleon's view of himself might never have been so dramatically transformed. In Napoleon's own words, "it was only on the evening after Lodi that I started to believe myself a superior man, and that the ambition came to me of executing the great things which so far had been occupying my thoughts only as a fantastic dream."[271]

Persevering through a tough battle or debilitating circumstances is often less about ability or endurance, and more about confidence and courage. In fact, it is remarkable the way in which a burst of confidence and courage can clear the road before you, allowing you to persist with your plan. Even before he was elevated to the rank of General, Napoleon's confidence, courage and personal power were serving his goals and ambition. His bold self-assurance and bravery gave the impression he was a force of nature. Indeed, Paul Barras, the President of the French Directory, once said to the revolutionary leader's regarding Bonaparte, "Advance this man or he will advance himself without you."[272] Another general was likewise struck by his boldness and seemingly supreme self-confidence. "I don't know why," he said, "but the little bastard scares me."[273]

Of course, Napoleon's actions on the Bridge of Lodi are not meant to suggest that courage is reckless indifference to danger. "Courage is resistance to fear, mastery of fear," Mark Twain said, "not absence of fear."[274] Napoleon and his soldiers were by no means indifferent or devoid of fear, even after they drove death away by driving fear out of themselves and into their enemy.

Fortunately for you, courage drives away far more than death. Courage drives away weakness and insecurity. Courage makes obstacles bow before you. Courage makes cooler, calmer and wiser decisions. It lowers hurdles and reduces resistance. Courage weakens the will of those who stand against you, and strengthens the spines of those who stand by your side. If you want to overcome your fears and achieve new heights, you too must forge the mindset of a warrior. Drive fear into the obstacle that stands in your way. Drive fear into the swine and send them running off the cliff. Generate the courage to take risks, put yourself on the line, attempt what may now seem beyond your reach. And when you are beaten back, make the attempt again.

COUNTERPUNCH:

Keep Hubris in Constant Check:
The Emperor's Ruinous Russian Invasion and Retreat

"True courage is being afraid, and going ahead and doing your job anyhow, that's what courage is."
—General Norman Schwarzkopf (1934—2012)

When Napoleon invaded Russia in June of 1812, in the eyes of the world he was a bold and brilliant military leader, a hero taking on a behemoth.[275] Rather than staying open to the shifting reality of the facts on the ground, however, Napoleon's invasion revealed an uncharacteristically hazardous frame of mind.[276] His confidence was becoming overconfidence. He was beginning to believe that he could will whatever outcome he desired.

Unlike Napoleon's usual openness to changing circumstances, or his careful considerations and calculations of the various alternatives; Tolstoy, in *War and Peace*, characterizes Napoleon in this battle as a man of utter and absolute determination.[277]

The Corsican was driven by a single-minded obsession with taking Russia. He was burning for a quick and decisive victory and, thus, was trapped by the idea of an immediate and direct confrontation.

The Russians, in marked contrast, were far more cautious and—to some extent, out of necessity—they remained open and flexible, continuously recalibrating their strategy as Napoleon's *Grande Armée* advanced.

Under the leadership of Mikhail Kutuzov, the Russians were also far more strategic. At sixty-seven and "older than his years," the Russian commander-in-chief would prove to be Napoleon's most dangerous opponent.

Repeatedly recalculating his maneuvers, Kutuzov continued to withdraw his troops and, thereby, lure his opponent deeper and deeper into the Russian homeland. With each passing day, Napoleon was further and further from his supply lines and hungrier and hungrier for battle. As the Russians fell further back, allowing for only minor skirmishes, they continued with their scorched earth policy, leaving nothing for Napoleon's army but the bitter cold elements of a looming Russian winter.

When Kutuzov finally offered a fight, it was far from the decisive battle for which Napoleon had hoped. There were massive losses on both sides (approximately 30,000 Frenchmen and 50,000 Russians[278]). The French were victorious, capturing the Russian positions, but the Russian army was not broken. Instead, Kutuzov led a temporary retreat that belied his intent.

Napoleon, spilling over with joy, expected the Russians to surrender. His happiness was quickly dashed, however, when he entered Moscow. The glorious holy city was ghostly calm. Where was the peace delegation? Where were all the people?

When the fires erupted Napoleon initially thought it was the looting of drunken troops. But, alas, he soon found that the city's fire pumps had been removed. It was all planned. Kutuzov left Moscow to the French. It had been evacuated, and was then burnt to the ground. Not a single person remained there for Napoleon to conquer.

In an uncharacteristically desperate act of revenge, Napoleon instructed his men to blow up the Kremlin—one of the few buildings that survived the fires. Napoleon was crushed. With trouble brewing at home, he knew he had to retreat and make his way back to France. This was the moment for which Kutuzov, the great Russian general, had been waiting. Napoleon's *Grande Armée* was weak, tired, cold and hungry. It was a humiliating retreat. By now, through it all—battle, sickness, hunger, and desertion on an "unprecedented scale"[279]—Napoleon was reduced from 450,000 to some 100,000 troops, many of whom were sick or wounded. And now they were on foot, as their horses had died from the cold or been killed for food.

Napoleon had gone into this campaign fearless, overconfident, and oblivious to the Russian winter. Kutuzov's patience had paid off. Now he attacked, inflicting terrible injuries on a retreating army. The remaining French were driven like wounded animals completely out of Russian territory.

It was here that the Russian general, Mikhail Kutuzov, emerges as the stronger leader. Harvard professor Ellen Langer writes in *Mindfulness*, "In the character of Kutuzov we can find portrayed the key qualities of a mindful state of being: (1) creation of new categories; (2) openness to new information; and (3) awareness of more than one perspective."[280]

The mindset of Napoleon, in stark contrast, was *uncharacteristically* fixed. He was closed to new information. He proved unable to consider the crisis and its context outside of his own constricted and transfixed interest in a quick and decisive victory. His confidence, left unchecked for too long, became overconfidence. He began to believe his own myth.

Be wary of letting your confidence go too far—to the point of hubris. Remember: You must master fear, not try to kill it. Make fear your servant. And keep hubris in continuous check.

Remain Grounded in Context:
The Fall of Icarus

According to the story of Icarus in Greek mythology, the Oracle at Delphi advised King Minos to command Daedalus, a prized Athenian inventor and architect, to build a labyrinth large and complex enough to contain the fearful, man-eating Minotaur. The Minotaur was a monster, half-man and half-bull, born of King Minos' wife, Pasiphae, after she was made to sleep with Poseidon's snow-white bull.

Once Daedalus and his son Icarus built the labyrinth, however, King Minos was afraid that Daedalus would share the secrets of the labyrinth and, thus, allow the Minotaur to escape. So, King Minos imprisoned both father and son within a tall tower in the labyrinth. A gifted inventor, Daedalus quickly began devising a means for him and Icarus to escape.

With so many birds flying around their lone tower on the sea, an idea quickly sprang to mind. He would build wings so he and Icarus could fly down from the tower and away to safety. They immediately set out to collect the feathers, fashioning them together with wax. Within hours, they were ready. The wings felt solid and strong. They decided to put them to the ultimate test. They would take the plunge and either escape from prison or fall to their deaths.

Suddenly, just when they were about to dive off into the wind with their wings, Daedalus turned to Icarus with a stern warning: "My son, do not fly too low. If you fly too low the mist from the ocean will weigh down your wings and you will fall from the sky and die." He paused. And they both looked down. "Icarus," he began again. "Do not fly too high. If you fly too high the sun will melt the wax and you will fall from the sky and die."

With that, they were off; first Icarus, then Daedalus. The plan seemed to be working. They were both overjoyed. Icarus began to do tricks as he laughed and soared through the air. His father cried out after him, "Icarus, stop. Your wings will not hold up to this." But Icarus dismissed his father's warnings. He was too high on their success. He began to fly higher and higher. His father again cried out, reminding him of the wax and the heat from the sun. Icarus, however, ignored his father, now out of reach, as he kept flying to greater and greater heights.

Then, suddenly, without warning, Icarus' wings began to break apart. He quickly dove toward the sea hoping to reach the surface before his wings failed. But it was too late. The melting wax, along with the speed of the dive, ripped his wings apart and Icarus fell to his death.

The lesson is clear: Keep your confidence in check. Never rely too much on, or be misled by, your past success. "Success has always been the biggest liar," wrote Nietzsche. [281]The success of his wings, and his ability to exploit them, led Icarus to believe he could fly anywhere—including where his father warned him not to go. Once his wings appeared to hold up at even greater heights, he fell under the spell of invincibility.

Like Icarus, there is a point at which our reliance on our history—on what worked and what didn't work in the past—can create a kind of naïve overconfidence that melts away under pressure and heat. It is not enough to think only of the past. We must also know and understand the context and circumstances at hand.

Acknowledge and Accept Fear, But Keep it in Its Proper Place:
Marshal Ney's Rearguard Retreat

Known as the Red Lion, the French military commander Marshal Ney was given command of the III Corps of Napoleon's *Grande Armée* during the 1812 invasion of Russia. Ney was one of Napoleon Bonaparte's eighteen original Marshals of the Empire, a rare honor granted to generals for extraordinary achievements. But it was Ney's command of the rearguard during Napoleon's infamous retreat from Moscow which turned the already heroic Ney into an immortal legend.

Expecting Napoleon to retreat, the Russians laid a trap and managed to cut Ney and some 8,000 troops off from Napoleon's main army. Napoleon, believing his rearguard to be lost, continued his retreat to Orsha. At this point, the Russian General Kutuzov extended an invitation for Marshal Ney to surrender. But Ney rejected the invitation outright, telling Kutuzov's delegation, "A marshal never surrenders; there is no parleying under an enemy's fire: you are my prisoner!"[282]

Ney plainly understood that a large contingent of Russian troops stood between him and the rest of Napoleon's army. Nevertheless, the French rearguard bravely attempted to force their way through the Russian lines, and were quickly beaten back, suffering heavy losses. Kutuzov again offered Ney the chance to surrender. But Ney would have none of it.

Ney's scouts soon discovered a parallel path back to Napoleon's main army on the other side of the Dnieper River. Ney then had his men light campfires around the camp, leaving the Russians under the impression that the French intended to stay put. But Ney's troops immediately snuck into the woods and headed for the river. The thin ice forced Ney to abandon his horses and wagons and heavy guns. Once on the other side, Ney's rearguard marched doggedly for two days and two nights without halting, encountering significant resistance, courageously withstanding heavy losses from the Cossacks at various points along the way, but ultimately succeeding in making it back to Napoleon's main army. Enduring through to the very end, Ney became known as "the last Frenchman on Russian soil."

Napoleon was so thrilled with Ney's success, which essentially allowed Napoleon's *Grande Armée* to escape complete annihilation, that it was said he leapt with joy, shouting: "I have then saved my eagles!" Napoleon said of Ney, "I have two hundred millions in my coffers, and I would give them all for Ney."[283] Indeed, Napoleon was so awed by Marshal Ney's valor in refusing to lay down his arms, though vastly outnumbered by the Russians, that he nicknamed him, "the bravest of the brave." [284]

It is normal to want to eliminate fear. Society despises cowards, and places great value on courage. But is it even possible that some people are simply devoid of fear? Not likely. The feeling of fear is an inevitable part of being human. It is a mechanism of defense designed to serve you with increased energy, attention, and strength. What is more likely is that bravery and self-confidence effectively mask fear. Real courage and genuine self-confidence are the marks not of those who have eliminated fear, but of those who have their fears completely under control.

Do not imagine, for example, that Michel Ney, Marshal of the Empire, "the bravest of the brave," was without fear. Indeed, at one point when the brave Ney was readying himself for battle he looked down to see his knees wobbling back and forth. Rather than giving in to his fear, however, he mocked it. "You may well shake," he said; "you would shake worse yet if you knew where I am going to take you."[285]

Like Ney, do not attempt to banish or suppress fear and, thereby, risk allowing it to distort your thoughts and actions, triggering you to overcompensate and, thus, under perform. Do not waste time trying to eliminate fear; this will only cause it to run and grow in unforeseen ways, and, as Benjamin Franklin said, "a person who is too fearful will end up performing defensively and thus fail to seize offensive advantages."[286] Follow instead the lead of the "bravest of the brave," and learn to acknowledge and accept fear; determine to move ahead with fear *as your servant*.

Your ultimate success, of course, is not a matter of courage or confidence alone. In fact, there is another element which, as Napoleon Bonaparte suggested, may be even more fundamental to both courage *and* grit. "Courage is like love," the Little Corporal said, "it must have hope for nourishment."[287]

3

FOCUS ON THE POSITIVE, CULTIVATE AN OPTIMISTIC OUTLOOK

"Being positive and persistent are inseparable."
—Donald J. Trump (1946—)

Maintain a Relentlessly Optimistic Outlook: Donald Trump's Epic Economic Turnaround

*"Success requires persistence, the ability to not give up in the face of failure.
I believe that optimistic explanatory style is the key to persistence."*
—Martin Seligman (1942—), Father of Positive Psychology, Author of *Learned Optimism*

When the recession of the late 1980s and early 1990s struck the real estate market in New York and Atlantic City, Donald Trump ended up in catastrophic debt. While his company was overleveraged and under water in the billions, he was personally over $900 million in debt. Trump later described it as "a horrific period."[288] Real estate broker Edward S. Gordon, recalled years later, "Donald hasn't forgotten what it's like to wake up at 2 a.m. soaked with sweat, with the bankers pounding on your door."[289]

At this point, the recession had already caused a lot of smart, capable people to throw in the towel and file for *personal* bankruptcy—people who were in far better shape than Trump. "I could easily have gone bankrupt," Trump said.[290] "This shouldn't surprise anyone because I'd always done things in a big way, and so it follows that my highs would be followed by a suitably low low."[291]

But that's not what happened. One of the lawyers, Sanford Morhouse, who represented Chase Manhattan bank during the negotiations with Trump recalled, "'I did a lot of workouts in those days on behalf of Chase, with a lot of real estate developers who had similar problems, and big ones. Almost all of them, at one point or another in that era, filed for bankruptcy protection. And Donald, to his credit, did not.'"[292]

This, of course, on one level, would make a Trump turnaround even more difficult—to the tune of 900 million dollars (his personal stake in the company). In fact, the media was trumpeting his failure as something that was *impossible* to overcome.

The situation was a "tremendous low," Trump said looking back.[293] "The banks were after me. People avoided me. There was a recession, and the real estate market was almost nonexistent. This was not a good scenario."[294]

Suddenly, when it seemed the situation couldn't get any worse, *both* the *Wall Street Journal* and the *New York Times* ran front page stories detailing Trump's financial ruin for all the world to see. "That was the lowest moment I had yet encountered in my life," Trump said years later.[295]

Rather than sending Trump into a depression, however, it made him all the more eager to prove his critics wrong. "I began to see my situation, believe it or not, as a great opportunity," he said.[296] "I had a big chance to show the press and my critics and enemies that I was a force to be reckoned with, not a flash-in-the pan success with no staying power. That's heady incentive, and that's looking at the situation positively."[297]

Even during the negotiations with the banks, "the Trumpster kept singing a happy tune."[298] A lawyer for Citibank recalled, "'He was always upbeat. One thing I'll say about Donald, he was never depressed.'"[299]

Trump refused to be beaten by his circumstances—no matter how fantastically catastrophic they were. He knew that there was no way he could come out of this without the right mindset. In fact, someone asked him about his mindset during this period when he owed billions of dollars and Trump said that "my mindset was very positive."[300] "Positive thinking really works," he adds.[301]

"I started negotiating new deals even though I was in no position to do them, because it made me feel good," Trump writes in *Think Big*.[302] "The best thing about being in deep financial trouble was that I learned that I could handle it, and by focusing on the positives, things that made me feel good, I could maintain a mindset very much like it is right now."[303] Within five years, he reversed his fortunes. "Trump has masterfully—and quickly—catapulted himself from that infamous $900 million black hole to a net worth of at least $700 million," wrote Shawn Tully in *Fortune*.[304] "The feat is a tribute to Trump's audacity. Even in the bleakest hours, he aimed not just to survive but to recapture the jackpot."[305]

Being positive, having an optimistic outlook was not, of course, the only thing that helped Trump turn his situation around—*but it was key*. As Trump says elsewhere, getting focused was a critical factor. But, he said, "I also relied on…positive thinking. Believe me, it works. It got me to where I am today—which is far richer and more successful than I was before the reversal started for me in the 1990s."[306]

Most people start to get overwhelmed when they take on too much debt. Being millions of dollars in debt would overwhelm even the most secure of business titans. Push that figure up close to a billion and you have to wonder what it is about Donald Trump that allowed him to weather such a tsunami of personal and professional debt? First and foremost, as we learn from the man himself, he stayed positive. He stayed upbeat. He maintained a persistently optimistic outlook. Regardless of whatever else he needed—hunger, vision, focus, chutzpah, action—what is most critical in times like this is watching your thoughts, and striving relentlessly to *stay positive*. Indeed, being positive itself requires persistence. "You have to be positive every single day," Trump said.[307] "You have to put a daily effort into it…"[308] This is the key point about a positive and optimistic mindset: It doesn't work if you only do it once in a while. Most everyone understands its value. Very few maintain the mindset. But why?

With roots going back as far as the French Enlightenment, the notion that there is value in taking a positive, hopeful view of things is not at all new. The work of neuroscientists and social science researchers, however, is helping us to gain a better understanding of the *power* of hope and optimism.

Research also reveals something that most people miss: Human beings have a built in "negativity bias" wherein negative events are more salient and are, thus, given more weight by our brains. What's more, if you are not steadfastly guarding your thoughts, you often risk slipping into a vicious cycle of negativity.

It is relatively easy to slip into these reinforcing cycles without even being aware of it. Something negative will happen and you will immediately become more vigilant to avoid future negative events of a similar kind. Now, through monitoring and heightened awareness, your brain will more easily and readily identify future negative information and events (even minor indicators), which often sets yourself up for a vicious cycle spiraling downward in what, *for an unfortunate few*, may end with anxiety or worse.

This all happens outside of conscious awareness—*unless* you carefully guard your thoughts. The solution is to learn to recognize the pattern and either break it or refute it with conflicting evidence or a compelling alternative explanation. Martin Seligman, known today as the "father of positive psychology," recommends what he calls the ABCDE method[309] of turning around negative thoughts:

1. *Adversity*—Write out a short description of the adversity or challenge you're facing that triggers your negative thinking.

2. *Beliefs*—Record your beliefs about the situation or circumstance. This is basically about how you are interpreting or explaining the adversity to yourself. What are you telling yourself the adversity means? Pay close attention to what comes up for you here—your *perspective* and *beliefs* about these triggering events play a major role in shaping your life.

3. *Consequences*—Record the consequences of those beliefs. In other words, answer the question: Because of your beliefs about this or your interpretation or perspective, what is happening as a result? How does it make you feel? What does it make you do?

4. *Dispute*—Generate evidence that either challenges the beliefs or interpretation you recorded above, or identifies how it is inaccurate or incomplete (look for flawed assumptions, gross generalizations, or catastrophic thinking). You can also look for evidence to support an alternative interpretation and set of beliefs.

5. *Energy*—Describe how your *new* beliefs effect your energy or attitude. Taking a few moments to acknowledge and appreciate the positive feelings and actions that follow this process can help to reinforce the practice until it becomes a habit.[310]

The key here is to focus on creating positive *emotions*, feelings that lead to positive *actions*. You do this with your thoughts. "Your thoughts are the primary cause of everything."[311] This is why Trump's advice is sound. Rather than inadvertently reinforcing the negative cycle, Trump advises, "If you ever get into deep difficulty, always focus on the things that make you feel better."[312] "It is impossible to feel good and at the same time be having negative thoughts."[313] Trump, obviously, is referring to things that are also good for you, that can improve your situation, actions aligned with your vision and goals. In his case, it was "negotiating new deals."[314] Do not underestimate the importance of your thoughts and feelings. Thoughts create emotions, and it is emotions that drive human beings. "The importance of feelings cannot be overstated. Your feelings are your greatest tool to help you create your life."[315] In the words of author and minister Michael Bernard Beckwith, "If you just intellectually believe something, but you have no corresponding feeling underneath that, you don't necessarily have enough power to manifest what you want in your life. You have to feel it."[316]

Of course, you still have to deal with your problems. To be sure, abandoning your responsibilities is the fast track to failure—which is why Trump worked so hard to avoid *personal* bankruptcy, and instead relied on Chapter 11 to restructure his companies. But the key Trump says, is not to let your problems "demoralize you or distract you from pursuing your goals."[317] Get your mindset right before you deal with your problems, and stay focused on the big picture: your vision and goals. Even in the midst of planning and preparing for potential problems—which should never devolve into a negative focus—keep your eyes on the big picture and keep your problem in perspective. "Realize that it is only a moment in time, and it will pass," Trump writes.[318] "Keep your sights on a better time in the future, which will certainly come to pass if you stay focused. Things cannot and will not continue downward forever; they will always turn around."[319] This is the secret to Trump's own world record turnaround: Stay relentlessly focused on the positive, keep your problem in perspective, and create the positive feelings you need to drive yourself forward. "That," says Trump, "is how I was able to make a comeback from the brink of utter failure."[320]

Your success depends on your frame of mind, and the way you see and interpret the world. The way you make meaning of your experience is a choice. Imagine the remarkable success of another great American showman and businessman, P.T.

Barnum, and bear in mind the perspective he chose to adopt. Reflecting on his life, Barnum said: "I was a farmhand, a merchant, a clerk, a boss, a theater director and a bank director; I lived in prisons and palaces, I knew poverty and abundance, I've traveled extensively on two continents, I've met all kinds of people and seen the human character in all its guises, and time and again I have been in the greatest danger. Amidst such a diversity of events, I had to undergo difficult times, but I'm definitely not complaining, and I believe that my life was a happy one, because I always saw the positive side of things."[321]

Regardless of what challenges you face, a subtle shift of perspective from the negative to the positive can transform virtually everything in your life. Understand: The intent is not simply to see things differently (though that is precisely where change most often begins). A shift in perspective will change what you see; it will change the way you think, what you say, and how you act in the world. Take it on as a personal challenge. Actively interpret your experiences, interactions or events—no matter how small— from an optimistic frame of mind, and you will soon see the power of your point-of-view and how exactly it can transform your life.

Build Optimism into Your Plans:
Shackleton's Miracle Trip from Elephant Island

"I tell you what I find in Browning is a consistent, a spontaneous optimism. No poet ever met the riddle of the universe with a more radiant answer. He knows what the universe expects of man— courage, endurance, faith —faith in the goodness of existence."
—Ernest Shackleton on the poetry of Robert Browning

In the late summer of 1914, the celebrated Antarctic explorer Sir Ernest Shackleton and his crew of twenty-seven set sail on an expedition in the South Atlantic Ocean. These rough and hardened men were on a quest to claim one of the few remaining prizes in the Heroic Age of exploration: First to cross the South Pole on foot. On January 18, after coming less than 100 miles from their destination, their ship, the *Endurance*, was trapped in the ice pack. That night the temperature suddenly dropped below zero. When they arose to have a look the following morning, they were crushed to find themselves surrounded as far as the eye could see by solid, snow-covered ice.

"Maddening" is how Alexander Macklin, one of the doctors on the ship, described it.[322] What seemed to leave an even deeper impression, however, was the reaction of "the Boss," as Shackleton was known by his men. "Shackleton at this time," Macklin wrote, "showed one of his sparks of real greatness. He did not rage at all, or show outwardly the slightest sign of disappointment; he told us simply and calmly that we must winter in the Pack, explained its dangers and possibilities; never lost his optimism, and prepared for Winter."[323]

Unfortunately, this was only the beginning of their troubles. The crew was, as Captain Frank Worsley describes it, "powerless to combat the inexorable laws of nature."[324] And nature wanted more with Worsley's ship than to hold her frozen in the ice. While the wind shrieked and moaned outside, and the ice floes ground against the sides of the *Endurance*, causing her to shudder as if she were alive, Shackleton met in his cabin with Frank Wild, his Second in Command, and Captain Frank Worsley.

"She's pretty near her end," Shackleton said.

Captain Worsley could hardly believe what he was hearing. "You mean that the ship will—*go*?" he asked.

"I do," Shackleton said.[325]

Worsley was beside himself. It never occurred to him that this expedition could include losing his ship. The wind continued to howl, thrashing the ship's rigging. Worsley momentarily imagined his ship was in fear of being murdered.[326]

"You seriously mean to tell me that the ship is doomed?" Worsley asked incredulously.[327]

"The ship can't live in this, Skipper," Shackleton replied.[328] "You had better make up your mind that it is only a matter of time. It may be a few months, and it may be only a question of weeks, or even days…but what the ice gets, the ice keeps."[329]

Wild, himself a relentless optimist, hastened to add cheerily, "Yes, but we are not going to let the ice get us. The poor little *Endurance* may have to go, but we won't."[330]

"It was a scenario ripe for depression, unrest and friction among the crew members."[331] When previous expeditions faced a similar challenge they tended to end in drunkenness and despair, and ultimately insanity, or even suicide. In the case of the *Karluk*, for example, the crew was transformed over the months into "a band of self-interested, disparate individuals."[332] "Lying, cheating, and stealing became common behaviors," writes Dennis Perkins, author of *Leading at the Edge*.[333] "The disintegration of the team had tragic consequences for its eleven members who died in the Arctic wasteland."[334]

In stark contrast, Shackleton kept his crew thriving. "With the strength of mind, optimism, and determination that characterized his best moments, Shackleton refused to give in to despair despite all the evidence pointing to doom."[335] "Shackleton made it his mission to keep his crew unified and positive."[336]

On June 21, 1915, a full five months after the *Endurance* had become trapped in a vast landscape of solid ice, Frank Hurley made an entry in his diary. "The Billabong [cabin] has an atmosphere poetic. Macklin in his bunk is writing poetical verses, and I am doing the same. McIlroy is arranging a décolleté dancing rig, whilst Uncle Hussey is being beset by applicants to rehearse accompaniments on his banjo."[337] It was extraordinary how Shackleton's powerful spirit of optimism and sense of hope spread through to the crew and lightened the heaviness of a dark winter and a sinister situation. "He encouraged games, skits, and music to help them through the long months of the Antarctic winter night. Remarkably, the men drew closer together and morale remained generally high."[338]

Ultimately, the menacing, tectonic masses of ice conspired to crack the hull of the ship like a brittle matchstick, and the crew was forced from the *Endurance* to the ice. Shackleton still didn't flinch. He maintained his calm demeanor and optimism, and continued to focus on the spirits and unity of his men. Setting up "Patience Camp" on the ice, the tents were kept together, and Shackleton and his crew waited patiently for nine months as they drifted on the ice floes hundreds of miles away from their destination. When the *Endurance* finally sank, Shackleton coolly turned to his men and said, "Ship and stores have gone, so now we'll go home."[339]

> *"Pessimism leads to weakness, optimism to power."*
> —William James (1842—1910), American Psychologist

Destroy the Demons, Determine that Optimism is Required.

It was not Sir Ernest Shackleton's courage or genius as an explorer that set him apart. Indeed, there were several other celebrated polar explorers of the day, of which Shackleton was only one. Moreover, Shackleton certainly did not share all of their many diverse talents. "British explorer Apsley Cherry-Garrard best expressed the feelings of his fellow 'Antarcticists,' as he called them, when he explained: 'For a joint scientific and geographical piece of organization, give me Scott; for a winter journey, give me Wilson; for a dash to the Pole and nothing else, Amundsen."[340] But, the British explorer acknowledged, "if I am in the devil of a hole and want to get out of it, give me Shackleton every time.'"[341] Shackleton's genius was in his understanding of human nature and leadership. As Captain Worsley put it, "It was his knowledge of men, quite as much as his executive ability, that made him such a wonderful leader."[342] Worsley shared an apt illustration. "It was characteristic of him," he said, "that when he ordered all superfluous weight to be cast away, he delighted the heart of Hussey, the meteorologist, by allowing him to keep his banjo. And many a weary evening was enlivened by Hussey's songs, in which we would all join, and the cheerful twang of his banjo."[343]

"Shackleton," wrote Worsley, "had a wonderful and rare understanding of the men's attitude towards one another and towards the expedition as a whole. He appreciated how deeply one man, or small group of men, could affect the psychology of the others. Therefore he almost insisted upon cheeriness and optimism; in fact his attitude was, 'You've damn well got to be optimistic.'"[344]

Optimism is essential to success, particularly in extreme situations. The more difficult the circumstances the more often hope, with a positive mindset, is key to see your way through. Pessimism and despair cloud your vision and prevent you from considering, or even *seeing*, potential solutions or avenues of escape. Understand: The more difficult the circumstances you face, the more critical it is that you maintain optimism and hope.

Tap Into Optimism as an Elixir for Failure.

Beyond any of the other great explorers of his age, Shackleton grasped the importance of a positive, upbeat spirit and optimism as a means of influence both over himself and his men, enabling him to overcome the greatest of obstacles in the most extreme of conditions. The result, not surprisingly, is that Shackleton's leadership and grit continues to influence hustlers to this day.

American media personality Jim Cramer tells the story of how his hedge fund was about to go under. Everyone was telling him to quit. But then he stumbled across an article about Shackleton. He got inspired. He read two other books about the British explorer's expedition, and soon found himself quoting Shackleton. He posted this quote on his wall: "You've damn well got to be optimistic." Over the next two years, Cramer made a dramatic turnaround, effectively catapulting himself into considerable fame and fortune.[345] Cramer openly admitted later, "'If I hadn't been schooled by Shackleton, I would have given up. It was the worst year I ever had. He got me through it because everybody,' Cramer continued, '*everybody* tells you to give up. But I came back in a style that was unbelievable, and proved the pessimists were wrong.'"[346]

Shackleton had as much cause to succumb to pessimism and despair as anyone. For years he had dreamed of crossing the South Pole, and, yet, what was likely his last chance was turning out to be a crushing disaster. But he also understood something far more important: The survival of his crew was at stake. And, thus, now the great prize was not to cross the continent, but to safely return his men home to their families. Now they needed hope and optimism more than ever.

Months after the *Endurance* sank, the ice began to break apart and the crew prepared to board the three lifeboats to sail to Elephant Island. Shackleton ensured that the three lifeboats were kept together and—ever mindful of their morale—that a cheerful spirit among the men was maintained.[347] After a full, tormenting week of rough, frigid waves and stormy weather, the wet, partially frost-bitten crew finally made it to land. The men were ecstatic.

Shackleton, however, knew they couldn't stay. He wasn't about to let his optimism become a foil for facing reality. This was a critical step toward safety and freedom, but there was no chance of being rescued here. Rather a small party, navigating a lifeboat—the 22-and-a-half-foot *James Caird*—with nothing but a sextant, would have to make the far more dangerous journey to Georgia Island, an impossible 800 miles away. As happy as they were to be on terra firma, the reality was, as one historian said, "To return from such a remote and desolate spot would demand almost superhuman effort."[348]

With all the grave decisions he had to make, Shackleton again gave careful consideration to the spirit and personalities of the two groups. He knew he needed a strong leader who could maintain the morale of those men who stayed behind on the freezing, uninhabitable island. "The twenty-two men who had been left behind on Elephant Island were under the command of Wild," Shackleton wrote, "in whom I had absolute confidence."[349] Shackleton also knew who the potential troublemakers were and, in the spirit of Sun Tzu's counsel, these few he kept even closer than his friends. In the case of the carpenter, Harry "Chippy" McNish, who had briefly been rebellious on the ice, Shackleton was sure to include him as one of the six men who set sail for Georgia Island.

After Chippy, an excellent carpenter, made some adjustments to strengthen the *James Caird*, the men loaded up some supplies—enough to last only three weeks; Shackleton knew that if they didn't make it by then, all hope would be lost—and they headed off.

The departure of the *James Caird* crew was an emotional one. Among those who stayed behind, many did not think they would ever see Shackleton and their other comrades again. In fact, Wild wrote, "I heard one of the few pessimists remark, 'That's the last of them.'"[350] This remark did not go over well at all with Wild, who also well understood the importance of optimism, and who said that he, "almost knocked him down with a rock, but satisfied myself by addressing a few remarks to him in real lower deck language."[351]

For the most part, however, Shackleton's insistence on remaining cheerful and positive had taken hold in the habits of his men. Worsley recorded his own impression of their departure: "The men ashore formed a pathetic group, waving to us and cheering Shackleton. We all cheered in reply, and as long as they thought we could see them, they kept up a wonderful appearance of optimism and heartiness."[352]

For his own part, Worsley understood the perils they were facing, but he himself also remained fiercely optimistic. "We knew it would be the hardest thing we had ever undertaken," he said, "for the Antarctic winter had set in, and we were about to cross one of the worst seas in the world."[353] But, he maintained, "I felt that whatever hardships we might be called upon to face, we were the fortunate ones...We had in fact started on the greatest adventure of our career."[354] Clearly a dangerous journey in a tiny open boat across 800 miles of the most perilous seas in the world could only be described in this way by a resolute optimist. As they fought to keep the *James Caird* afloat, they continuously endeavored to maintain hope, and a deep, down-in-the-bones spirit of optimism. "They kept cheerful. They whistled. They sang."[355]

Almost as if they willed it themselves, Shackleton and the crew of the *James Caird* miraculously made it to Georgia Island. "The six men were on the ocean for seventeen days. They endured bitter cold, scanty rations, intense seasickness, and a hurricane that they later learned sunk a five-hundred-ton steamer in the same waters."[356] In the words of historian Caroline Alexander, "They had not merely endured; they had exhibited the grace of expertise under ungodly pressure."[357] Experts would later rank their voyage "as one of the greatest boat journeys ever accomplished."[358]

The hurricane forced the *James Caird* to land far from the whaling station, but after a thirty-six hour hike over the treacherous rocky mountains of South Georgia Island, Shackleton, Worsley and Crean made it (the other three stayed behind with the lifeboat). When they finally arrived at the whaling station they were taken to see the winter manager, Thoralf Sorlle, who Shackleton knew from a dinner party just before the *Endurance* expedition began. By now the three, with full beards and long hair, were so gaunt and weathered and black from blubber smoke that they were unrecognizable.[359] Shocked to see the three "strangers" standing in his office, Thoralf said, "Who the *hell* are you?"[360] The man standing in the center quietly replied, "My name is Shackleton."[361] Shocked that they were still alive, Thoralf was overcome with emotion. He turned away and began to cry.[362]

Shackleton wasted no time in seeking to secure a ship to retrieve the men who remained on Elephant Island, men who by this time were suffering, but surviving. "In the absence of the Boss, it became clear that Shackleton's optimism had become embedded in the ethos of the team, nourished constantly by Frank Wild. He refused to entertain even the slightest possibility that they would not be rescued. As an unwavering symbol of his conviction, Wild roused the men every day with a cheery shout of 'Lash up and stow, boys, the Boss may come today.' Even the morose Orde-Lees was forced to admit that Wild's ability to maintain the spirits of those likely to be despondent was "a fine thing."'[363]

Shackleton chartered three different ships in an effort to rescue his men, but was thwarted by the ice each time. Finally, on August 30, 1916, Shackleton's fourth attempt, the *Yelcho*, a small steel-hulled steamship, made it through the ice and entered the bay of Elephant Island. Preparing a lunch of seal and limpets, one of the men looked up and spotted, "barely a mile off, a very little black ship."[364] "Wild, there's a ship," one cried out.[365] The men all scrambled to their feet to have a look. Suddenly, the men began cheering loudly out of sheer joy.[366] After 128 days "covering the worst of the Antarctic winter,"[367] Shackleton made it back, and all twenty-two of his men were rescued. Shackleton soon dashed off a note to his wife expressing his gratitude. "I have done it," he wrote.[368] "Not a life lost and we have been through hell."[369] Wild, for his part, was considerably more emotional, writing later, "I felt jolly near blubbing for a bit & could not speak for several minutes."[370]

"Optimism was at the very core of Ernest Shackleton's personality."[371] Reflecting his character, Shackleton lived true to his family's motto—*Fortitudine Vincimus* (By Endurance We Conquer).[372] Clearly, Shackleton's ability to endure such devastating setbacks, all while maintaining a sense of hope and optimism, was a critical factor in the continued sanity and survival of his crew. Indeed, writes Perkins, "the fact remains that the expedition was able to prevail against enormous obstacles largely because of Shackleton's dogged optimism—and his superb skill in spreading this positive outlook to others."[373]

But what was it about Shackleton and his optimism that was so critical to his success? There are a handful of key factors that stand out.

1. *Capitalize on Your Freedom to Choose—Fake It Until You Make It.* Maintaining optimism during a sustained trial can be difficult. You may not always *feel* like being optimistic. Do not give in to those feelings. Instead, fake the feelings of hope and optimism until you begin to feel them as real.

No matter what your situation, optimism is genuinely a matter of choice. And your feelings will follow your choices. As difficult or impossible as this may seem under certain circumstances, the reality is that it's been done before—by people who endured and emerged from some of the most harrowing tales of survival. No matter what terrible trials you face, you always have a choice about how to see it. The author of *Man's Search for Meaning*, Viktor Frankl, the famous Austrian psychiatrist who was trapped in the death camps of Nazi Germany, put it this way: "Everything can be taken from a man but one thing: The last of human freedoms—to choose one's attitude in any given set of circumstances, to choose one's own way."[374]

Given the potentially life-threatening circumstances of the expedition, Shackleton frequently framed the facts of their situation with a healthy serving of optimism. Purposefully amplifying the importance of an optimistic frame, Shackleton said, "You may know that the facts are dead against you, but you mustn't say so."[375] Shackleton insisted, "You've damn well got to be optimistic."[376] Ultimately, Shackleton refrained from withholding any of the basic facts or information about the reality of the situation from his men, but he was careful about how he framed it. And he kept his own fears and feelings of discouragement and despair locked away and out of sight.

2. Closely Monitor Your Inner Dialogue. It is not enough to decide to be optimistic. You have to train your brain to think optimistically. This means cultivating mindfulness. Learning to observe your thoughts, and manage your internal dialogue. In fact, according to Dennis Perkins, author of *Leading at the Edge*, our inner dialogue is a critical factor in shaping our outlook and, thus, our success. Perkins writes, "the first step in cultivating optimism is to pay close attention to what you say to yourself. If you are aware of this inner dialogue, especially during times of adversity or setback, you will be conscious of the messages you are sending yourself about failure or success."[377] He explains, "The right messages are energizing, and the wrong ones are deflating. The way to develop a feeling of optimism is to consistently send positive messages that override voices of discouragement and pessimism."[378]

3. Integrate Optimism into the Plan. As social beings, we are easily influenced by the emotions of others. In most cases, the individual with the most potent emotion will influence those individuals whose emotions are less potent—particularly when there are no significant power differences. If you desire success, you must be mindful of how you are being influenced by the attitudes and emotions of others. As the Apostle Paul wrote to the Corinthians, bad company corrupts. "Wicked friends lead to evil ends."[379]

Shackleton clearly grasped these social dynamics and, for his own part, remained a "fundamentally ebullient personality…a contagious force that simply infected others."[380] What's more, he was so entirely convinced of success that it was easy for others to join in his cheerful outlook.[381]

But Shackleton understood that his attitude—as critical as it was—was not enough. And, thus, he worked diligently, from the very beginning, to take these factors into account, and, thereby, ensure the psychological well-being of the entire crew. The spirit of the crew of the *Endurance* was not an accident, it was part of the way that "Shackleton had selected the men in the first place."[382] Rather than focusing on their knowledge and skills, for example, Shackleton asked whether or not the men could sing. "I suppose you can shout a bit with the boys?" he asked.[383] "The question," Alexander writes, "proved to be uncannily appropriate. What he was looking for was an 'attitude,' not paper qualifications."[384]

"Above all else, Shackleton judged a man by the degree of optimism he projected. 'Optimism,' Shackleton said, 'is true moral courage.'"[385] And for all those who failed to orient to the world in this way, said Alexander, "he regarded with transparent contempt."[386] But he didn't stop there. In fact, according to Perkins, "Shackleton also established the attitude that 'you've damn well got to be optimistic' as a core operating principle of the expedition. It was a discipline to be learned and cultivated."[387] It was not just about thinking positive. It was about being upbeat—singing, celebrating, playing games—and it was about routines to keep themselves busy. Shackleton grasped the urgent need to keep the men actively and energetically engaged in finding solutions, and ensuring their collective survival.[388]

4. *Focus on the Future.* Success is also about having hope for the future, no matter how impossible your present circumstances. When the *Endurance* was trapped in the ice, Shackleton helped to keep up the spirits of his men by planning a future expedition to Alaska—even while they were still utterly uncertain about how to free themselves from the predicament they were still in at the time. As ludicrous as the prospect of an expedition to Alaska may have seemed under the circumstances, it gave their minds an exciting alternative, something for them to do other than continuing to dwell on their current troubles.[389] "It provided a future focus," Perkins writes, "and a promise that there would be other adventures—with the obvious implication that they would triumph over their present situation. It represents just one way in which the whole culture of the expedition encouraged confidence and hope."[390]

5. *Face Reality, But Reframe it to Suit Your Intent.* "A leader who is able to reframe events in a positive light, and stick by that point of view, can turn the tide," writes Perkins.[391] Clearly, Ernest Shackleton was able to turn the tide for his crew. "'His unfailing cheeriness means a lot to a band of disappointed explorers like ourselves,' Orde-Lees wrote. 'He is one of the greatest optimists I have ever known. He is not content with saying, 'It will all come right in the end.' It is always otherwise with him. He merely says that this is but a little setback not altogether unforeseen and he immediately commences to modify his program to accord with it, even working his future plans out to given dates and to meet various possible contingencies.'"[392]

In the realm of leadership and influence, the ability to instill in others a sense of hope and optimism can help to overcome any number of significant challenges, and Shackleton's optimism no doubt made a difference—the difference between life and death. But is it possible that this power could be extended beyond a limited group?

Optimism is Infectious, Spread It Around: Roosevelt's Psychological Assault on the Great Depression

In August of 1921, at age thirty-nine, Franklin Delano Roosevelt was struck down by a debilitating disease that robbed the former Secretary of the Navy and 1920 Vice Presidential candidate of his ability to walk and stand. Eleven years later, at age 50, he was President of the United States.

Where it once appeared as if his career was doomed, it now seemed as if nothing could hold him back. With his famously jovial smile and jaunty spirit, Franklin Roosevelt strolled buoyantly into the White House to the tune of the popular 1929 ditty "Happy Days Are Here Again." Like the campaign themes of Jack Kennedy with Frank Sinatra's "High Hopes" and Ronald Reagan with his "It's Morning in America" message; the positive, upbeat campaign music reflected a reliably optimistic outlook that was a compelling component of Roosevelt's personality and leadership.

When Roosevelt's predecessor Herbert Hoover was President, it wasn't clear how, when, or even *if* America's great economic crisis would end. When FDR took office, things immediately started looking up. Once elected President, Roosevelt's unflagging cheer and optimism began to transform the nation.

From the moment he first arrived in Washington at the depth of the Depression, there was a palpable change of mood in the air. Observing the conspicuous change as

Roosevelt's train disembarked at Union Station, Arthur Krock, the 'Dean of Washington reporters,' said: "From the moment he arrived here, Washington took on almost a visible air of hope…he has become a symbol of hope, burning in the darkness that has surrounded us and which has made so many of us afraid…This single fact—this changed state of mind—is in itself of the utmost importance."[393]

Within weeks of the election, Roosevelt's message of the return of "happy days" could be found in all manner of places, including the stock ticker on Wall Street. "The new president immediately established a new, infectious atmosphere of optimism."[394] A Republican Senator from California conceded: "The admirable trait in Roosevelt is that he has the guts to try…. He does it all with the rarest good nature…. We have exchanged for a frown in the White House a smile."[395]

When Roosevelt delivered his inaugural address it came like a stirring call to arms.[396] Finally, there was energy and leadership and hope in Washington again.[397] Within days of the inauguration, historian William Leuchtenburg noted, "the spirit of the country seemed markedly changed, a feeling of hope had been reborn."[398]

A young radio broadcaster at the time, Ronald Reagan remembered listening to Roosevelt during the Depression: "His strong, gentle, confident voice resonated across the nation with an eloquence that brought comfort and resilience to a nation caught up in a storm and reassured us that we could lick any problem. I will never forget him for that."[399] Reagan, who later became a hero among conservatives, voted for Roosevelt four times. When Reagan was President, he remembered Roosevelt as "one of history's truly monumental figures," "an American giant, a leader who shaped, inspired, and led our people through perilous times."[400]

Dive Deep to Be the Catalyst in the Context.

The same spirit of bold hope and grounded optimism which allowed him to triumph over his incapacitating paralysis, and ascend to the White House, enabled Roosevelt to awaken the sleeping giant, and elicit the grit within the American people to both overcome the Great Depression, and see their way through World War II. Indeed, optimism was central to every aspect of Roosevelt's success. It played a potent role in his heroic stands against America's economic evils, the malicious attacks of the Wall Street tycoons, the dictators of the Axis powers, and his unrelenting, lifelong personal battle against the ravages of a debilitating disease.

To Roosevelt's way of thinking, America's future was very much a matter of choice. "Men are not prisoners of fate," he said, "but only prisoners of their own minds."[401] But his was no ordinary optimism. Roosevelt's sunny outlook was born out of an abiding faith in the future. Pulitzer Prize-winning American newspaper columnist and conservative political commentator George Will wrote of FDR, on the centennial of his birth, "Anyone who contemplates this century without shivering probably does not understand what is going on. But Franklin Roosevelt was, an aide said, like the fairy-tale prince who did not know how to shiver. Something was missing in FDR," Will explains.[402] But this was the key. "…What FDR lacked made him great. He lacked the capacity even to imagine that things might end up badly. He had a Christian's faith that the universe is well constituted and an American's faith that history is a rising road…Radiating an infectious zest, he did the most important thing a President can do: He gave the nation a hopeful, and hence creative, stance toward the future."[403]

Even after enduring two terms teeming with trials, *TIME* wrote, "He has one priceless attribute: A knack of locking up his and the world's worries in some secret mental compartment, and then enjoying himself to the top of his bent. This quality of survival, of physical toughness, of champagne ebullience is one key to the big man. Another key is this: No one has ever heard him admit that he cannot walk."[404]

Franklin Roosevelt's relentless optimism and heroic grit has left an indelible imprint on the American Presidency, and there is much that we can learn from his example. Pessimism is toxic to perseverance. "If you are a leader," Marcus Buckingham writes, "you better be unflinchingly, unfailingly optimistic."[405] No matter how depressing the situation or dismal the mood, leading effectively means learning to repeatedly and relentlessly return to the belief that things can, must and will get better.[406] What's more, whether you are leading a nation or pursuing your own individual goals, the environment and context you're operating in, and the people you are surrounded by, can have an effect on your success. But you are not merely at the mercy of these external forces. In fact, as we learn from Roosevelt, Shackleton, Kennedy, Reagan and others, it is possible to be the catalyst in the context, causing those in your circle of influence to adopt a more optimistic outlook, which can then ripple outwards to countless others.

When your organization or team is required to make certain, temporary sacrifices, or endure a period of hardship, hope and optimism are essential to the team's willingness to persevere. The ability to instill hope in others is often a mark of great leaders. Their secret? Lead by example. Have hope yourself. In preparing for his conquest of the Persian Empire in 334 B.C., Alexander the Great distributed all of the many estates of his crown to his followers as payment for what promised to be a long and arduous campaign. When Alexander was finished, General Perdiccas was troubled that Alexander had depleted the royal treasury. The general asked the king, "What have you reserved for yourself?" "Hope," Alexander said immediately. "Well," said General Perdiccas, as he returned his estate to the king, "we who share in your labors will also take part in your hopes."[407] Alexander's hope and optimism about their future campaign was so potent that it spread effortlessly to his men. Plutarch tells us that several others returned their estates as well.

Richard Nixon likewise understood (at least intellectually) the power of optimism and its contagious effect. Though he often had trouble pulling it off (especially when he was angry or hurt), he understood how emotional contagion could be employed to influence his listeners. Speaking to a group of young political office seekers, he instructed them: "You, as the candidate, must keep your spirit up. Any time you show the audience in front of you that you're the least bit discouraged, any time you show that you have lost your zeal, it has a contagious effect and you are doomed to lose."[408]

By the time of his illness, Franklin Roosevelt had a well-developed understanding of the power of positive thinking and how optimism could be both a factor of influence and a force for good in his own life, as well as the lives of others. When his mother, Sara, learned of his illness, however, she was completely distraught. Franklin was her only child and, with the early illness and death of her husband, she had made her son the center of her life. What would become of her dear boy now?

But when Sara Roosevelt sought out her son and saw his own optimism and determination, her own spirit was transformed. It was as if she had somehow miraculously recovered her loss. He made it seem as if everything would be perfectly okay—and, indeed, it was. The idea that Roosevelt had lost something to this disease was a matter of perception, but that perception *was not his*. Indeed, many historians have argued that Roosevelt's disability was America's great gain.

Think Positive. Be Optimistic. Project Success.

The reality is that your success rarely relies on your outlook alone. Virtually everyone operates in a social and political context of some sort, requiring a certain level of support. This invariably means that others will sometimes stand in your way. Perhaps they do not share your interests, or they do not see what you see or the way you see it. And, yet, without certain others onboard, your success is less certain.

When the famed (and controversial) Italian explorer Christopher Columbus was determined to discover a new, faster and safer route to the "East Indies," most of his potential benefactors thought he was mad. They thought his plans to sail directly across the Atlantic ocean were dangerous and foolhardy, based on gross miscalculations of the distance, and would lead to the loss of his crew and their ships. But Columbus was undeterred. His hope and enthusiasm were too great to give up. "Columbus was prepared to sell his idea to anyone and anyplace."[409] No one could extinguish his vision. In fact, according to one biographer, "The kernel, the seed, grew to such a point that it became an obsession for him."[410]

Rebuffed by John II of Portugal, and Henry VII of England, Columbus soon headed to Spain, hoping to find a patron more open to his plans. "I plow on," he said, "no matter how the winds might shake me."

Looking to the example of the scientists and sages, the heroes of history, Columbus used his powers of persuasion and skills as a communicator to work to overcome the ignorance, apprehension, and preconceptions that stood in his way.[411] He looked for *common ground* with his potential patrons, focusing on the *benefits*, he framed the voyage in terms of *their interests*, rather than his own.[412] In time, he began to win the support of influential people throughout Spain.

Unfortunately, Spain was at war with the Moors, and the dream of the Italian explorer was low on everyone's list of priorities. Nevertheless, Columbus was remarkably persistent. He too was a man of considerable grit and he persisted in his quest for seven long years.

Over time, his infectious optimism helped him to secure the resources he needed to pursue his vision of a new trade route across the Atlantic. Michael Gelb, author of *Discover Your Genius*, writes, "Columbus's compelling vision and contagious optimism gave him the power to convert those in a position of authority to sponsor his adventure, and in Spain he persuaded two archbishops, the court astrologer, two royal confessors, the royal treasurer, and finally Queen Isabella of Castile herself to support his plans."[413] When the war against the Muslims ended in early 1492 Queen Isabella and King Ferdinand, in the newly united Spain, finally agreed to sponsor Columbus and his bold voyage across the uncharted sea.[414]

In your quest for success, you will repeatedly find yourself in the position of needing the help of others. In these situations, your hope and optimism are indispensable to both winning others over and ensuring your eventual success. Everyone wants to associate with winners. Contributing to the success of someone or something makes people feel that they themselves are successful. At the very least, they tell themselves that they know how to pick the right people, projects or teams. The more you appear to be a winner, the more you focus on positive plans and hopeful goals for the future, the more others will be drawn to you. By speaking the language of a winner, you will project success. In short, the more you think about, act consistent with, and work toward success, the more others will support you and want to be a part of your plans.

Never, *never* underestimate this: Consistent, unrelenting optimism is key. Your ability to achieve your mission and goals depends on your willingness to make positive thinking a habit. In the words of Donald Trump: "It is important to think positively. Negative thinking, especially about yourself and about your prospects for success, will kill your focus and destroy any chance you have of being successful."[415]

Trump has succeeded in a number of different areas—including, most recently, presidential politics. But he has also had his fair share of failures (including some surprisingly poor decisions as a candidate). And what does he attribute to his ability to deflect failure and achieve such astonishing success? There are a number of factors to be sure. But, unlike many people, Trump does not underestimate or negate the importance of staying positive. "I'm a tough-minded optimist. I learned a long time ago that my productivity was increased by a large percentage simply by learning to let go of negativity in all forms as quickly as I could. My commitment to excellence is thorough—so thorough that it negates the wavelength of negativity immediately. I used to have to zap negativity mentally. By now, it just bounces off me within a moment of getting near me."[416] Learn to replace negative thoughts immediately. "Every time a negative thought comes at you," Trump writes, "zap it. Replace it with a positive thought. That takes energy, but the result will be stamina—positive stamina, a necessary ingredient for success."[417]

Use Positive Thinking as a Tool to Persevere.

As vital as optimism is, it's not enough. Your ability to persist is also critical. In fact, as Trump explains, "Being positive and persistent are inseparable. Persistence is essential because you can't just start out being positive and then throw in the towel at the first sign of trouble. You have to stay positive because success rarely occurs overnight."[418] Columbus waited seven years before he had what he needed to begin his great voyage across the Atlantic. Of course, he wasn't idle during this time. He remained positive and optimistic and, therefore, he continued to read and study the maps, charts and writings of other sailors, navigators, astronomers, and scientists. He continued to further develop his navigational techniques and his skills as a sailor. He never abandoned his dream because he never gave up hope. He was in it for the long haul.

Begin your new endeavors with the resolution that you are in it for the duration, write your commitment down, share it with a few, supportive friends, and you will greatly increase the likelihood that you will in fact see your way through to success. Most everyone can achieve significant success in their chosen domain, but not without optimism, persistence and hope, and not without grit. This—and this alone—will often set you apart and help to ensure your success because most people, Trump writes, "just don't have the persistence required to make positive thinking work for them. Things rarely just happen overnight. Most overnight success stories are no such thing."[419]

This, in fact, is part of what Trump believes led to his success on *The Apprentice*. Trump's success in television was not the "overnight" success that many imagined. Success can happen quickly (sometimes very quickly), but in most cases, as with Trump, reaching the stratosphere is based on years of positive thinking and working hard. Trump explains, "When my television show, *The Apprentice*, became a big hit, I had over thirty years of experience to draw upon when conducting the boardroom scenes. It wasn't just a fluke that I came across as someone who knew what they were doing."[420] Trump was new to television, but he wasn't acting. He was playing himself, a role he obviously knew well. Trump writes, "the rest wasn't particularly new to me. Business is business, whether it's being filmed or not. My business credentials and experience came into the picture as the necessary background for creating a show based on high-stake New York corporate business."[421]

Trump goes on to explain how it was positive thinking that landed him in the role in the first place. Many people tried to warn him away from the idea. Reality television was an endeavor fraught with risk. And their concerns were real. Most television shows do fail. The show might have proved to distract him from the countless concerns of his business empire. A bad performance might have undermined his credibility. But Trump was not focusing on the negatives. "I was positive about what might happen," he said.[422] "I chose a positive perspective. I asked myself the "what if" question. What if it was a success? What if I enjoyed it? What if it proved to be enlightening? What if it brought The Trump Organization the recognition it deserved? What if the jobs provided to the winners proved to be valuable stepping stones to deserving individuals? I had a long list of positives…"[423]

Many of the world's great hustlers and leaders and heroes of history were great visionaries, with bold and daring dreams for the future. But they never let their plans and goals carry them away from facing reality first. Being a positive thinker, having an optimistic outlook, maintaining hope for the future; these are all critical constituents of the grit you need to succeed. But there is a limit.

COUNTERPUNCH:

Retain a Relentless, Yet Grounded Optimism: FDR and the Great Depression

"Keep your eyes on the stars, and your feet on the ground."
—Theodore Roosevelt (1858—1919), 26th U.S. President

"Optimism is an important leadership quality, but denial is deadly."
–Dennis Perkins, *Leading at the Edge*[424]

The situation in America in the early 1930s was grim. People were desperate. Families were homeless and hungry. Banks were failing. Businesses were going bankrupt. Farms and homes were in foreclosure. Panicked depositors were withdrawing their savings at the rate of 10 percent per week. Tanks rolled in Washington against American protestors—war veterans who, while living in tents, wanted only to be paid for services and sacrifices they had already made. More than a quarter of the population was without work.[425] It was social and economic mayhem. The American dream had become a national nightmare. "Capitalism was clueless. Democracy was frozen in fear."[426]

The 1932 presidential election saw Herbert Hoover go down to Franklin Delano Roosevelt in a historic landslide. Hoover carried a mere 6 states, to Roosevelt's 42.[427] Promising Americans a New Deal, Roosevelt gave people hope. Indeed, for those Americans struggling for survival, Roosevelt was the symbol, embodiment, and last vestige of hope.

But it was not a false hope. It was more than mere rhetoric. Roosevelt believed in America's future. He believed in the American people. But he also believed in facing the hard facts. In contrast to Hoover's occasional *display* of optimism (accompanied by conspicuous inaction), FDR's optimism was grounded. Roosevelt understood that the harsh realities of the hard times were not to be ignored. And he was careful to sustain a sober optimism. According to Martin Seligman, the author of *Learned Optimism*, the actual text of his opponents' speeches was often more optimistic than those of Roosevelt himself. However, Hoover was selling false hope and people knew it. Hoover's words of hope were like seeds cast carelessly into a strong headwind, few finding the rich soil needed to take root. Moreover, Hoover's words were betrayed not simply by his weak, unconvincing delivery, but by his failure to act. He claimed the economy would turn around, but he was doing next to nothing to help make that happen. And the American people knew that too.

"Only a foolish optimist can deny the dark realities of the moment," said FDR in his 1933 inaugural address.[428] Allowing his message to be refined by the fires of the cruel economic crisis of which his audience was dreadfully familiar, Roosevelt's more judiciously reserved optimism produced a wellspring of hope upon which Americans could bank. What's more, Roosevelt's message and delivery were congruent. "Our greatest primary task is to put people to work. This is no unsolvable problem if we face it wisely and courageously," said the newly elected President.[429] When Roosevelt spoke, in contrast to Hoover, the people believed what he said. They knew he meant business; and, true to his word, once he was in the Oval Office, his vigorous whirlwind of action further strengthened their hopes.

Among the numerous factors at play, Hoover lost to FDR for largely the same reason that Carter lost to Reagan in 1980, and McCain lost to Obama in 2008. Where Roosevelt, Reagan, and Obama promised new solutions to tough problems, Hoover, Carter, and McCain represented more of the same.

When the situation is bleak, the status quo will not suffice. People naturally want to have hope for the future, but when circumstances are dire, people demand change. And this leads to the issue of credibility. People want their leaders to be positive and hopeful about the future, but they need to *believe* it can happen. As important as optimism and hope are to a your success, what we learn from Roosevelt is the importance of hope that is grounded in reality. Maintaining a relentless optimism does not mean denying reality. It is a sober optimism—backed by practical and effective action—that wins. Delusional thinking is as deadly to your goals as distorted facts. Roosevelt was unquestionably optimistic, but he never allowed his optimism to prevent him from facing the truth, as he said, "frankly and boldly."[430]

Keep It Real.

As we see in virtually every election, many candidates make promises for a better future, but they lack credibility. Rather than being equally real about the challenges ahead, they either deliberately mislead, or they come off as naïve and Pollyannish. Either way, by failing to get real with people, they fail. As Lincoln said, "You can fool all the people some of the time, and some of the people all the time, but you cannot fool all the people all the time."[431] Grounded optimism is crucial to your credibility.

People generally appreciate it when you level with them. It's not about being pessimistic—not at all. Optimism still reigns supreme, but it must be grounded. You have to be real. No one wants to feel like they're being sold.

When Ernest Shackleton took out an advertisement in the *London Times*, seeking a crew for his grand Antarctic expedition, he understood that as a renowned explorer he was likely to attract a great deal of attention. He acknowledged that a successful mission could lead to "honor and recognition." But he also understood the value of keeping his optimism in check, and being honest about the hard road ahead. As a result, his advertisement read: "Men Wanted: For hazardous journey, small wages, bitter cold, long months of complete darkness, constant danger, safe return doubtful, honor and recognition in case of success." [432]What kind of a character would volunteer for such an endeavor? Thousands of men are said to have come forward for the journey. Their ship even had a stowaway. Admittedly, the advertisement does have the lure of adventure, but there is also appeal in Shackleton's dead honesty.

Face the Hard Facts, But Reframe with Hope.

When Uruguayan Air Force Flight 571 crash landed in the Andes Mountains, there was not much room for hope. Over a quarter of the 45 passengers died on impact and several others soon gave way to their injuries and the extreme cold. When a few of them heard eight days later on the radio—their only connection to the outside world—that the search party was being called off, any flickers of hope were immediately extinguished. The three who heard the radio broadcast debated whether they should share the information with the others. "We mustn't tell them," said Marcelo.[433] "At least let them go on hoping," he said sobbing.[434] Gustavo Nicolich, who emerged as a leader during the crisis, would not have it. "No," said Nicolich, "we must tell them. They must know the worst."[435] But Marcelo refused. "I'll tell them," said Nicolich, as he made his way to the back of the plane.[436] "Hey, boys," he shouted , "there's some good news! We just heard it on the radio. They've called off the search."[437] Everyone in the crowded cabin was suddenly silent. A wave of fear and hopelessness flooded over them. Some began to weep. One of them shouted angrily at Nicolich, "Why the hell is that good news?"[438] "Because," Nicolich said in defiance, "it means that we're going to get out of here on our own."[439] It was a defining moment. This young man's courage and optimism altered the following course of events and saved the remaining survivors from total despair. They now knew what they had to do. And, as a direct result, they made it home in time for Christmas.

Keep Expectations Grounded.

On May 10, 1940, Adolf Hitler began his Western offensive with an invasion of Belgium, Holland, Luxembourg, and France. Having signed the Munich Agreement with Hitler less than two years earlier, the failure of British Prime Minister Neville Chamberlain's appeasement policies were now exposed for what they were: A naïve and near desperate optimism.

Most everyone in Britain wanted peace, but it was Chamberlain that stood face-to-face with the fanatical Fuhrer, looked into his wily eyes and walked away believing he could have it. It was not in wanting peace that Chamberlain failed. It was in wanting peace *too badly*—so badly that he deluded himself into believing that Hitler would simply give it to him, and that he could go back to Britain the brave, new benefactor of world peace.

When Hitler walked out of the private conference with Chamberlain in Munich, after signing Chamberlain's supposed *peace treaty*, he had not the slightest intention of honoring his word. That same day, to his Minister of Foreign Affairs who was disturbed about this new development, the Fuhrer said: "Oh, don't take it so seriously. That piece of paper is of no further significance whatever."[440]

Winston Churchill had been right, as he said to Chamberlain at the time in a speech to the House of Commons: "You were given the choice between war and dishonor. You chose dishonor, and you will have war."[441] The failure to more readily recognize Hitler as the wicked despot that he was cost countless lives and allowed Hitler the time he needed to become a more powerful and menacing threat. When it became increasingly clear that Hitler had not the faintest intention of maintaining peace with Great Britain, Chamberlain was forced to Buckingham Palace to offer his resignation.

Chamberlain recommend Churchill to the King and, that same day, King George VI sent for Churchill and asked him to form a government, making Churchill the Prime Minister during what Churchill would later call the British Empire's "finest hour." The King wrote of Churchill in his journal, "He was full of fire and determination to carry out the duties of Prime Minister."[442]

In Churchill's celebrated first address to the House of Commons as Prime Minister on May 13, 1940, he begins his peroration (the grand finale) with that famous line, "I have nothing to offer but blood, toil, tears and sweat." But then he quickly cuts to the brutal reality and hard facts:

"We have before us an ordeal of the most grievous kind. We have before us many, many long months of struggle and of suffering. You ask, what is our policy? I will say: It is to wage war, by sea, land and air, with all our might and with all the strength that God can give us; to wage war against a monstrous tyranny, never surpassed in the dark and lamentable catalogue of human crime. That is our policy."[443]

Clearly these were not the words of a pie-in-the-sky Pollyanna. But then, positioned on solid ground, Churchill begins to instill hope in his listeners, issuing a masterful call-to-arms:

"You ask, what is our aim? I can answer in one word: Victory, victory at all costs, victory in spite of all terror, victory, however long and hard the road may be; for without victory, there is no survival. Let that be realized; no survival for the British Empire, no survival for all that the British Empire has stood for, no survival for the urge and impulse of the ages, that mankind will move forward towards its goal. But I take up my task with buoyancy and hope. I feel sure that our cause will not be suffered to fail among men. At this time I feel entitled to claim the aid of all, and I say, "come then, let us go forward together with our united strength."[444]

And so begins Churchill's train of magnificent speeches and tireless efforts to revitalize and reinvigorate the British people for victory. With an endless well optimism and an incessant effort to sustain the valor and determination of the nation, Churchill did all that was within his power to prevail against the evil, tyrannical Nazi regime.[445] It was a long way from home for the sensitive, neglected boy with a speech impediment. And it was a far cry from what anyone would expect from a poor student who twice failed the entrance exam to military college.[446] But when Germany finally surrendered on May 7, 1945, it was this same man who would come to stand as one of the greatest prime ministers in Britain's long and tumultuous history.

There are few better examples of the value of grounded optimism and fierce resolve to your mission and goals than the example of Winston Churchill during World War II. As indispensable as Roosevelt and the American forces were in helping to win the war, Winston Churchill was the deciding factor in Europe's future. It was Churchill's hope-filled defiance and tenacious, bulldog will in the face of seemingly insurmountable odds and certain defeat, that saved England, Europe's only remaining democracy and, one might argue, the Western world's way of life. His words continue to echo across the generations. "Never give in. Never give in. Never, never, never, never--in nothing, great or small, large or petty—never give in, except to convictions of honor and good sense. Never yield to force. Never yield to the apparently overwhelming might of the enemy."[447]

Ground Hope in the Facts, Set Realistic Goals.

What was it about Churchill that enabled him to endure the intense pressure of such an epic assault? How was he able to galvanize the British people to defeat the Nazi threat? There were many things, to be sure, but beneath it all was a bedrock of hope. Churchill was a rational optimist, firmly rooted in an unshakable faith in his nation's future, and the future of freedom and democracy in the world. Churchill believed all would come out right in the end, but his expectations were grounded in a rational appraisal of the challenges ahead. Where Chamberlain frantically grasped for peace, Churchill knew there would be war first. Where most of the members of Parliament, standing alone as the last surviving democracy in Europe, put little faith in the role of their allies, Churchill knew his relationship with Roosevelt would be vital to their success. Where everyone hoped for a quick and easy victory, Churchill was prepared to invest every drop of his blood and sweat. Make no mistake, Churchill had great hope for their success, but it was a facts-based hope grounded in realistic goals, not a false hope grounded in fantasy or fear. Churchill's strategy was straightforward: survival—survival above all, survival until, as he said, "in God's good time, the New World, with all its power and might, steps forth to the rescue and the liberation of the old."[448]

This is one of the defining characteristics that sets people like Churchill and Roosevelt apart. They have hope. They are optimistic. But their expectations are grounded. They expect victory, but with significant challenges. They set highly ambitious, but, ultimately, attainable goals.

Psychology professor at the University of Scranton, John Norcross, found one dominant factor that separates those who succeed at achieving their goals and those who do not: Expectations.[449] Everyone experiences setbacks and defeats on the path to a worthy goal. What sets achievers like Churchill apart is that they *expect* setbacks, and they do *not* expect fairy-tale outcomes or instantaneous success. When the obstacles and setbacks inevitably come, the achievers view it as a "reason to recommit and a reminder to refocus on their goals with more determination."[450]

Take counsel from P.T. Barnum who wrote, "Be confident, without pulling the wool over your eyes." Barnum probably understood people better than anyone of his day and, based on his experience, he concluded, "A lot of people have remained poor, or ruined themselves, because of this destructive tendency. These people see a sure success in every undertaking," he said, "which is why they stick to nothing, abandoning one business after another. The fable about the hunter who sells the bearskin before he shoots the bear shows that this tendency goes a long way back. Unfortunately, the fable and experience have not cured people of the habit."

Maintain a Continuous Connection with Reality.

In his book *Mastery*, Robert Greene writes: "To reach mastery requires some toughness and a constant connection to reality."[451] Like the champions of hustle and grit, those who have mastered their craft have done so by enduring the harsh realities of their world. "Masters," Greene writes, "are those who by nature have suffered to get where they are. They have experienced endless criticisms of their work, doubts about their progress, setbacks along the way. They know deep in their bones what is required to get to the creative phase and beyond."[452] Yet, this is a vital path to progress: "In this day and age, you must get the sharpest dose of reality that is possible... You must go in search of it and welcome it. ...Gain as much feedback as possible, no matter how hard it might be to take. Accustom yourself to criticism."[453]

In his book, *Good to Great*, Jim Collins explains how one of the key principles of the companies that were able to make the transition from good-to-great was their willingness and ability to "confront the brutal facts of reality head-on."[454] According to Collins, "When...you start with an honest and diligent effort to determine the truth of the situation, the right decisions often become self-evident. Not always, of course, but often. And even if all decisions do not become self-evident, one thing is certain: You absolutely cannot make a series of good decisions without first confronting the brutal facts."[455]

Adopt the Stockdale Paradox.

On September 9, 1965, James B. Stockdale was on a mission flying over North Vietnam when he was struck down by enemy fire. He managed to eject from his plane and parachute safely to the ground, but he landed in a village where he was immediately captured and severely beaten. Stockdale was soon transferred to the infamous Hanoi Hilton where he was held as a prisoner of war and repeatedly, brutally tortured, within inches of his life, for the next seven and a half years.

Admiral James B. Stockdale was the highest ranking naval officer in the Prisoner of War camps of North Vietnam, and he led the prison resistance. Of the 766 Americans who are known to have been POWs in Vietnam, 114 died in captivity.[456] Stockdale eventually gained his freedom and went on to become one of the Navy's most highly decorated officers. He later became Ross Perot's running mate during the 1992 presidential campaign.

But what was it that allowed Stockdale to survive where so many other POWs perished in the camps? When Jim Collins, author of Good to Great, asked Stockdale about those who didn't make it out, Stockdale explained, "That's easy. The optimists. They were the ones who said, 'We're going to be out by Christmas.' And Christmas would come, and Christmas would go. Then they'd say, 'We're going to be out by Easter.' And Easter would come, and Easter would go. And then Thanksgiving, and then it would be Christmas again. And they died of a broken heart."[457]

Stockdale's supposed "optimists" had nothing to base their hopes upon. For all practical intents and purposes, their ideas about getting out by Christmas were nothing more than wishful thinking—at a time and in a place where that kind of thinking could be lethal. Addressing the graduating class of the U.S. Military Academy at West Point in 1983, Stockdale said, "The problem is, some people believe what professional optimists are passing out and come unglued when their predictions don't work out…babbling optimists are the bane of existence to one under stress."[458]

Stockdale, however, was not discounting the value of hope and optimism altogether—not even close. As he said himself, "I never lost faith in the end of the story. I never doubted not only that I would get out, but also that I would prevail in the end and turn the experience into the defining event of my life, which, in retrospect, I would not trade."[459] Regardless of the immediate circumstances, and his ability to accept that his fate at the moment was out of his hands, he always maintained his hope in the ultimate outcome.

He was making an important distinction. Like Churchill and Roosevelt, for Stockdale the key was to distinguish between what was under one's control and what was not.

In his book, *Thoughts of a Philosophical Fighter Pilot*, Stockdale—a student of the Stoic philosophers—draws on Epictetus's work in Enchiridion: "…a Stoic always keeps *separate* files in his mind for (A) those things that are up to him [within his power] and (B) those things that are not up to him [beyond his power]…"[460] Stephen Covey makes a similar distinction between what he calls one's broader "circle of concern" and the much smaller, inner "circle of influence."[461]

The key lesson that emerges from the story of the men who survived their captivity in Vietnam is this: Survival depends on your ability to be hopeful and optimistic, *and* face the brutal reality of the facts on the ground. And the reality is that some things are not within your power, or circle of influence.

Obviously, the idea is *not* to be negative and pessimistic about that which is beyond your power. Indeed, be hopeful about the future. Be optimistic. But be real. Focus your energy and attention on those things that are within your control.

Collins refers to this as "the Stockdale Paradox," and, according to Stockdale himself, "This is a very important lesson. You must never confuse faith that you will prevail in the end—which you can never afford to lose—with the discipline to confront the most brutal facts of your current reality, whatever they might be."[462]

Hope and optimism lead to a myriad of different thoughts and actions that inevitably influence the future in countless seen and unseen ways. It is not hard to imagine, in Stockdale's case, for example, how his perspective helped him to be proactive, working to maintain the morale of his men and, thereby, helping himself through the process.

To succeed against great odds, optimism is required. But you cannot do anything you wish. In the words of one business titan, "I'm a pragmatic positive thinker. When I hear people saying that anything you want to do is possible, that seems childish or at least uninformed to me. Some things are not going to happen."[463] Zig Ziglar put it this way, "Positive thinking won't let you do *anything*, but," he adds, "it will help you do *everything* better than negative thinking will."[464] Far better to invest time on things over which you have some influence.

Do not misunderstand: This is not about lowering your aim, or downsizing your dreams (which would be a disastrous mistake). Optimism is essential to grit. And big, *nearly* impossible dreams are key to motivation and drive. But all of this has nothing to do with living in a world of hallucinations. Delusions and denial are deadly to your dreams. "You can seize only what you can see," said John Maxwell. "Be positive, but be realistic."[465]

4

FAIL YOUR WAY TO THE TOP

"Success is the ability to go from one failure to another with no loss of enthusiasm."
—Sir Winston S. Churchill (1874—1965)

Never Fear the Failure You Need to Succeed:
Walt Disney's First Financial Fiasco

"Failure is the foundation of success, and the means by which it is achieved."
—Lao Tzu (601—531 B.C.)

It was the summer of 1923 when Walt Disney was hit with the harsh reality that he would not have the funds to complete his new silent film project, *Alice's Wonderland*. To the outside world, he maintained a positive front. He even wrote to a potential distributor of the film, Margaret J. Winkler, who knew his work, that the film "will be finished very soon."[466]

This was one of the remarkable things about Walt Disney: He believed the things that he told people, even when he had no clear idea of *how* they would happen. It wasn't that Disney's beliefs lacked grounding. The critical factor was that Disney understood that his success was still, in the words of Epictetus, "within his power."[467] Disney was operating, in the words of Stephen Covey, within his "circle of influence," not merely his "circle of concern." [468]

This time, unfortunately, his situation was desperate. Unable to pay his rent, he was living in his studio, sleeping on "rolls of canvas and cushions."[469] He had exhausted his credit at the Forest Inn Café downstairs and was eating cold beans and canned meat.[470] The only place he could shower was the railroad station where he paid a dime to rent a tub and a towel once a week.[471]

"It was probably the blackest time of my life," Walt said looking back.[472] "I really knew what hardship and hunger were like."[473] He remembered the brothers who ran the restaurant and how they grew tired of sponsoring Walt and started feeding him only leftovers. "It was a pretty lonely and miserable time of my life."[474]

The film studio, Laugh-O-Gram Films, Inc., was itself on life support. "Walt's checks kept bouncing," one of his former employees recalled.[475] "All of us eventually worked for nothing."[476] "We twice had to move during the night because we couldn't pay the rent," another remembered.[477]

A local dentist, Thomas McCrum, wanted Walt to produce a film, *Tommy Tucker's Tooth*, for the Kansas City Dental Institute. It would teach kids the importance of brushing three times a day.

When the dentist called and asked Walt to come down to his office, Walt confessed, "I can't come. I don't have any shoes."[478]

Dr. McCrum was shocked, "No shoes!"[479]

"I took my only pair to the shoemaker downstairs to have them resoled," Walt said. "They're ready, but the shoemaker won't let me have them unless I pay him a dollar fifty."[480]

The kindly Dr. McCrum temporarily rescued the studio with a $500 advance, and Walt made an excellent film that continued to play in Kansas City over a decade later.

But Walt was not out of the woods. In fact, only a short time later, Walt received an eviction notice at the studio. Utterly discouraged, even his brother Roy wrote back, "Call it quits, kid. You can't do anything more than you've already done."[481]

In July of that year Walt filed for bankruptcy, and, other than a single camera and the incomplete Alice film, all of his assets were seized to pay his debts.[482]

Remarkably, by the time of the bankruptcy proceedings, Walt was already beginning to bounce back. "Phineas Rosenberg, the attorney appointed to manage the bankruptcy proceedings, recalled, 'Most people filing for bankruptcy are disturbed or bitter. Walt wasn't.'"[483] This would give him a fresh start he thought.

By the end of the month, with a pitiful cardboard suitcase, a few spare clothing items, a print of the Alice film, and $40 cash from the sale of the movie camera, Walt dressed himself up in a colorful suit, with a bright red bow tie, whimsically bought himself a first class train ticket and headed to California to pursue his newest dream.[484]

Walt's optimism was already restored, and in full bloom. "I was just free and happy," he later recalled.[485] "I had failed," he admitted.[486] But, he added optimistically, "I think it's important to have a good hard failure when you're young."'[487]

Besides, why obsess over past mistakes? Walt was looking to the future. The hustler was headed to Hollywood. "It was a big day, the day I got on that Santa Fe, California Limited," he said.[488] Walt had a powerful sense of excitement about the possibilities ahead, which made him feel, he said, "as if he were lit up inside by incandescent lights."[489]

"Perhaps there is no more important component of character than steadfast resolution. The boy who is going to make a great man...must make up his mind not merely to overcome a thousand obstacles, but to win in spite of a thousand repulses or defeats."
—Theodore Roosevelt, "Character and Success." (1900)

Resolve to Accept Failure—Over and Over Again.

Clearly, Disney had a different view of failure than the average person. "He seemed confident beyond any logical reason for him to be so," writes Neal Gabler, author of *Walt Disney: The Triumph of the American Imagination.*[490] "It appeared that nothing could discourage him."[491] In fact, according to Craig Hodgkins, Disney writer and lecturer, "His tough experiences gave him the courage of his convictions. He was an enterprising, entrepreneurial risk-taker because he wasn't afraid to fail."[492] The fact is Disney's confidence didn't defy logic at all. It only seemed that way to others because he was operating from a different conceptual frame. In other words, in Disney's mind, failure was not something to fear because he understood a critical truth about failure: It's an inevitable part of the process of success.

"Throughout the failures...throughout the days without meals and nights with restless sleep, throughout the constant begging for funds from Cowles and Schmeltz and even Roy, throughout it all Walt Disney seemed never to lose faith."[493] "I never once heard Walt say anything that would sound like defeat," an early associate remembered.[494] "He was always optimistic...about his ability and about the value of his ideas and about the possibilities...Never once did I hear him express anything except determination to go ahead."[495]

The most successful people are, inevitably, also the people who fail the most. This is one of the secrets of success: Understanding the powerful role that failure plays in all great achievements. In the words of Michael Jordan, "I've failed over and over and over again in my life. That's *why* I succeed."[496] Arianna Huffington, editor-in-chief of the *Huffington Post,* puts it this way, "Failure is not the opposite of success, it's a stepping stone to success."[497]

This frame of mind is sewn into the psychology of all great hustlers. "Most of the great entrepreneurs did in fact suffer failures during their careers, some of them enormous, but they accepted it as part of the game."[498] If you, from this point forward, would never undertake anything without first resolving to accept failure over and over again, and be prepared to *continue failing* until you succeed, the likelihood of your eventual success will increase exponentially. It may not be precisely where or how you thought you'd succeed, but you *will* find success as long as you steel yourself for repeated failure first.

Of course, knowing that failure is a natural part of the process does not make it easier, particularly when you consider the responsibilities you have to others, but also the temporary hit you may take to your own reputation, credibility, and short-term success. Unfortunately, this is precisely where most people screw it up. Failure and rejection can be painful, humiliating, perhaps even devastating. We all want to succeed fast, early and often. The problem arises when fear stops you from trying, or the humiliation or ridicule causes you to quit too soon. But the reality is, as J.K. Rowling said in her 2008 commencement address at Harvard, "It is impossible to live without failing at something unless you live so cautiously that you might as well not have lived at all, in which case, you fail by default."[499]

Your ultimate success demands that you get a grip on your fear. Reject the false promises of playing it safe. "Security is mostly a superstition," said Helen Keller, the American author and political activist. "It does not exist in nature, nor do the children of men as a whole experience it. Avoiding danger is no safer in the long run than outright exposure. Life is either a daring adventure or nothing." [500]

Resolve to live a daring life. Take a new chance today. "Success and great wealth creation demand that you refuse to be afraid of failure or what your friends and family and neighbors might think."[501]

Understand: Failing is never the goal. The advantages are not in the failure itself. The benefits come only when you take full responsibility for your failures—rather than making the mistake of blaming others and, thereby, missing out on the chance to learn and grow from your mistakes. When you assume responsibility, you can learn and grow in a way that makes you stronger, wiser, and all the more likely to succeed in the future. But remember these words from Arnold Schwarzenegger: "Strength does not come from winning. Your struggles develop your strengths. When you go through hardships and decide not to surrender, that is strength."[502] In the words of Henry Ward Beecher, "It is defeat that turns bone to flint, and gristle to muscle, and makes men invincible, and formed those heroic natures that are now in ascendency in the world. Do not, then," Beecher added, "be afraid of defeat. You are never so near to victory as when defeated in a good cause."[503]

This was precisely the mindset of Robert M. La Follette (1855—1925), the American progressive politician. "Fighting Bob," as he was known, was both the former Governor and U.S. Senator from Wisconsin, and the 1924 Progressive candidate for President. But La Follette did not rise up to the heights of American politics without significant resistance. In fact, with the country completely controlled by the two political parties (much like we are today) this was a nearly hopeless period for all progressives. After being defeated for reelection to Congress in 1890, La Follette lost two consecutive gubernatorial elections (1896 and 1898). But "Fighting Bob" was not about to give up. In fact, he said at the time, in what later proved to be rather prophetic, "Temporary defeat often results in a more decided and lasting victory than one which is too easily achieved."[504] Running for governor a third time in 1900, La Follete finally won. He went on to transform the state into a progressive exemplar of political and economic reform, an example that stirred the nation, including sitting President Theodore Roosevelt.

"As far as failure is concerned...I just don't hold it that way, and it's not a technique or being positive, it's just being intelligent. Failure is education—if you use it. If you learn something, it's not a failure. If you don't learn anything, then it's failure."
—Anthony Robbins (1960-), American Peak Performance Coach

Double Your Failure Rate.

There is an old story told by Warren Bennis and Burt Nanus in their book, *Leaders*, about Thomas Watson Sr., the founder and long standing leader of IBM. One day a capable, young executive made a very costly mistake. He was involved in a risky venture which quickly went south and ended up costing the firm an astonishing ten million dollars. You can imagine how distraught the young man was when Watson called him into his office the following morning. Watson was eager to know exactly what happened. When he realized the young man was preparing to tender his resignation, Watson was emphatic. "Are you kidding?!" he said. "You can't quit. I just spent ten million dollars educating you."[505]

Watson understood that mistakes could be incredibly valuable and he shuddered to think of losing someone who had just learned such an expensive lesson. Keeping this executive also sent a powerful message about the relationship between risk, failure, learning and success to the rest of the staff. To this day, the story is part of the organization's lore. "If you want to increase your success rate," Watson used to say, "double your failure rate."[506]

Donny Deutsch, host of NBC's "The Big Idea," writes: "The biggest lesson I've learned over the years is that you have to make failure your friend. It is amazing how many people don't get where they want to be because they're afraid of failure. Whenever I talk to super successful people, what they always want to discuss most passionately is how their biggest growth came from the lessons their failures taught them. You cannot have greatness without some failure."[507]

Understand: You have to move forward and embrace failure as the inevitable rocks on the road to success. The secret is not to *seek* failure. In fact, you should take every sensible step you can to avoid it. The secret is to *capitalize* on it when it happens, and maximize the lessons learned. In the words of John Wanamaker, the father of modern advertising, "a man who never makes mistakes loses much that it would do him good to know."[508]

The two-term Governor of New York, Horatio Seymour (1880—1886), was known more for his speaking skills than his ability as a politician and, it was said, he was happiest when called on to give a speech not on politics, but on the philosophy of life.[509] When Governor Seymour gave a dedication speech in Holland Patent, New York he spoke on the importance of character and discipline to success. "In reviewing my life," he said, "I asked myself, 'If I were to wipe out twenty acts, what should they be? Should it be my business mistakes, my foolish acts (for I suppose all do foolish acts occasionally), my grievances? Why, no; for, after all, these are the very things by which I have profited. They are the price of wisdom. So I finally concluded it would be better to expunge, instead of my mistakes, my triumphs. I could not afford to dismiss the tonic of mortification, the refinement of sorrow; I needed them every one. The great pivotal chance by which we rise or fall turns upon the way in which we grapple," Governor Seymour concluded.[510] "If successful, the curse becomes a blessing."[511]

Fail Fast, Early and Often—Eliminate the Ways that Will Not Work:
Thomas Edison's Endless Endurance

"Our greatest weakness lies in giving up.
The most certain way to succeed is always to try just one more time."
—Thomas Edison (1847—1931), American Inventor and Business Titan

When Thomas Edison first saw a demonstration of the electric arc light in the 1870s he was instantly captivated. "This electric-light idea took possession of me," he said later.[512] He had found something that captured his creative imagination, and he was intent on further developing the arc lamp to its fullest commercial possibilities. "It was easy to see what the thing needed," he said.[513] "The light was too bright and too big. What we wished for was little lights, and a distribution of them to people's houses in a manner similar to gas."[514] And so, in 1878, he began his research into the incandescent light bulb in earnest, filing his official paperwork with the U.S. Patent Office entitled, "Improvement In Electric Lights."[515]

But Edison was nowhere near developing a light that could be used in the home. He believed it was only a matter of time, and that he had already solved the basic problems, but the reality was that he had declared "mission accomplished" far too early. Edison not only had to create a workable design for the bulb, but he had yet to discover the proper filament to keep the bulb lit—and this was proving to be one of his greatest challenges. In an interview years later, Edison reflected on the work and thought involved in his inventions, "The incandescent light was the hardest one of all;" he said, "it took many years not only of concentrated thought but also of world-wide research."[516]

After thousands of failed attempts, some of Edison's own colleagues began to think it was hopeless. They had already attempted over 3,000 different bulb designs, and tested more than 6,000 different plants searching for a viable filament to burn inside the bulb. Edison wrote later, "I recall that after we had conducted thousands of experiments on a certain project without solving the problem, one of my associates, after we had conducted the crowning experiment and it had proved a failure, expressed discouragement and disgust over our having failed to find out anything."[517] At this point, things were looking bleak. Edison did not discover electricity. He didn't invent the light bulb. And now he was proving unable to *improve* it, let alone sell it to the masses as he fully intended.

But Edison was not about to give up. "I never allow myself to become discouraged," he said, "under any circumstances."[518] Edison gently chided his dispirited associate. "I cheerily assured him that we *had* learned something. For we had learned for a certainty that the thing couldn't be done that way, and that we would have to try some other way. We sometimes learn a lot from our failures if we have put into the effort the best thought and work we are capable of."[519]

This mindset was classic Edison. "All his assistants agree," writes one biographer, "that Edison is the most patient, tireless experimenter that could be conceived of. Failures do not distress him; indeed, he regards them as always useful…"[520] When asked by a *New York Times* reporter about his extraordinary torrent of failures, Edison responded: "I am not discouraged because every wrong attempt discarded is another step forward. I have not failed 10,000 times. I have successfully found 10,000 ways that will not work."[521] And, he added, "When I have eliminated the ways that will not work, I will find the way that will work."[522]

"All of us fail. Successful people fail often, and...learn more from that failure than everyone else."
—Seth Godin (1960—), American Author, Entrepreneur and Marketing Maven

See Setbacks as Prized Lessons Learned.

Imagine—after *thousands* of failed experiments, Edison still had a positive, forward-thinking mindset. The secret of Edison's perseverance was his perspective of defeat. Edison did not believe in defeat as such. Failure for him was simply another step on the road to success. Not only were mistakes and setbacks inevitable, but they were a valuable part of the learning process that helped him to discover the proper path to his ultimate goal. "From the moment he took the problem in hand he had no faintest doubt of being able to solve it, and to this, probably, is due the fact that however many disappointments he met with, he was never really down-hearted or despairing."[523]

Finally, Edison came upon the idea of using the black carbon soot found on the inside of the dirty glass lanterns. Testing various materials for the thread, Edison immediately found the carbonized materials were staying lit much longer. It was October 21, 1879, Edison remembered. "We sat and looked, and the lamp continued to burn, and the longer it burned the more fascinated we were. None of us could go to bed, and there was no sleep for any of us for forty hours. We sat and just watched it with anxiety growing into elation."[524]

Ultimately, they discovered that a filament from carbonized bamboo could burn for more than 1,200 hours. Finally, on December 21, 1879, Edison announced to the press that he had attained his aim. He invited the public to come down to his Menlo Park laboratory on New Year's Eve to ring in the New Year, and see his spectacular display of incandescent lamps, set up around and throughout the buildings. Edison had successfully transformed the arc lamp from what was largely perceived as a cool trick, or even a gimmick, into a revolutionary new invention that changed the world in a way that even he could not have imagined. The price of gas securities on the stock market plummeted, while stock in the Edison Electric Light Company soared to $3500 per share.[525]

All this from a man whose teachers said was, "too stupid to learn."[526] For Edison, intelligence had nothing to do with it. "Genius," he said, "is ninety-nine percent perspiration and one percent inspiration."[527] This is what allowed Edison to endure such a prolonged and persistent onslaught of defeat: He never saw it as defeat. He was simply taking necessary actions, doing the work that needed to be done. According to the American political consultant Frank Luntz, "When it comes to a trait like persistence, it's all about action. No amount of IQ, cunning or skill makes work finish itself, or inspires others to fight with you. You must be willing to put in the effort required to get the results that stand apart from—and miles above—everyone else's. I'm not," Luntz said, "talking about the drive to get things done. I'm talking about doing them over and over again until you win."[528] No matter how much failure Edison encountered, he knew that hard work and perseverance would always be critical to his success. "Our greatest weakness," he said, "lies in giving up. The most certain way to succeed is always to try one more time."[529]

Increase Your Capacity to Fail Fast, Early and Often.

Edison's quest to invent the first practical, commercially viable electric lamp is a pitch perfect illustration of the old adage: *The road to success is paved with failure*. There is no doubt that Edison's invention was a scientific success. It was a clear breakthrough beyond the arc lamp and other competing ideas for harnessing electricity. The incandescent electric light bulb was not, however, enough to ensure Edison's *financial* success. That fight was only just beginning.

People wanted this product. But Edison had yet to develop the electrical system for getting power to the lamps and lighting systems of his customers, or the power stations for generating the electricity. He sold the public on the idea of lighting their homes and businesses, now he was in a race to meet demand, his competitors were on his heels, and time was of the essence.

Meanwhile, the gas and oil interests were desperate to stop him and, in fact, were effectively scaring off potential investors, grossly exaggerating the dangers of electricity and the risks of catastrophic fire. Edison, of course, was not about to back down now. "If there are no factories, to make my inventions," he said, "I will build the factories myself. Since capital is timid, I will raise and supply it. The issue is factories or death."[530]

Edison's mindset and attitude about failure was an indispensable component of the grit that led to his greatness as an inventor and entrepreneur. This characteristic has countless applications. "Indeed, most of the great things of the world have been accomplished by grit and pluck," writes Orison Swett Marden.[531] "You can not keep a man down who has these qualities. He will make stepping-stones out of his stumbling blocks, and lift himself to success."[532]

What is your mental framework about failure and success? What price are you willing to pay to achieve your most cherished goals? How can you reframe your failures so that, rather than fearing them, you look forward to the lessons they have to teach? Your influence, power and ultimate success requires that you stop thinking of your mistakes and failures as something to be ignored or hidden or, worse still, evidence that you should throw in the towel. Instead, recognize that your failures are revealing important lessons you must learn on your path to ultimate victory. Find ways to use failure to your advantage—the value is in the learning. "Repeated failure will toughen your spirit and show you with absolute clarity how things must be done. In fact," writes Robert Greene in *Mastery*, "it is a curse to have everything go right on your first attempt. You will fail to question the element of luck, making you think that you have the golden touch. When you do inevitably fail, it will confuse and demoralize you past the point of learning."[533]

Remember: Failure is not final. Recognize that, as Edison himself said, "Many of life's failures are people who did not realize how close they were to success when they gave up."[534] Interestingly, most of the retellings of this story report that Edison failed 1,000 times. Apparently, 10,000 failed experiments is just too hard to believe. Who could possibly be *that* persistent? How many times would you be willing to fail in pursuit of your dreams? Is 10,000 failures really all that unthinkable? How many thousands of times did you fall before you learned to walk? Do you think there was some point at which your parents should have insisted that you stop trying?

The reality is Edison did conduct close to 10,000 different experiments before he found the proper filament and bulb design he needed for commercial application. But there's an important lesson here beyond the obvious significance of mindset, pluck and grit. Edison set himself up so that it was possible for him to fail thousands of times. In fact, he didn't just create a culture where bold experimentation was encouraged. He created a system and an environment in which he could speed the process of experimentation and, thereby, fail fast and frequently until he found success. At his famous Menlo Park Laboratory, Edison had an entire team of people working for him, including mechanical assistants, glass blowers, mathematicians, carpenters, draftsmen, machinists, lab assistants, bookkeepers, secretaries, a photographer, a chemist, and a lawyer.[535] And these people came from all over the world. If not for this remarkable team—of few of which went on to some acclaim themselves—Edison could never have secured an astonishing 1,093 U.S. patents.

This is one of the secrets of success. Instead of making great efforts to avoid failure, hustlers look for ways to pick up the speed and fail faster. Knowing that failure is inevitable, even beneficial, they embrace it when it comes. They learn from it. And, if necessary, they fail again and again, faster and faster, until they succeed. As Tom Peters put it, "Test fast, fail fast, adjust fast."[536] "Fail often," writes Carol Dweck, pointing to Silicon Valley's unique record of success, "and you'll succeed sooner."[537]

In the documentary film *I Am Chris Farley*, based on Chris Farley's life as an actor and comedian, Dan Aykroyd and Mike Meyers point to the influence of Del Close on their own careers, as well as the life and career of Chris Farley. Meyers says, "Del Close was a fantastic improviser, great teacher, the creative Svengali of Bill Murray, Aykroyd, Belushi."[538] Del Close, in fact, taught a number of notable students, including Tina Fey, John Candy, and Stephen Colbert. Chris Farley was reportedly thrilled just to get into the classes at The Second City, where Del Close performed and directed. Dan Aykroyd highlighted one of the critical factors that allowed so many in their group to succeed: "Del was the chief anarchist artist there. What he taught all of us was to be free. And to be unafraid. And to go out and fail as often as possible. To try things. To die on stage. Who threw off convention and kinda blew the lid off the form so that we could really do the freest work that we were capable of."[539] This is it. This is one of the great keys to success: You must give yourself the freedom to fail. In the words of Anthony Robbins, "Most successful people are successful because they failed more than anybody else." Your task is to find ways to support or speed up your failure rate and, as a result, significantly increase your likelihood of success.

Embrace Public Failures, Teach Your Tribe to Take Risks.

In the summer of 1932, New York Governor Franklin D. Roosevelt was running for president. The United States was in the midst of the Great Depression and Roosevelt, in his address at Oglethorpe University in Atlanta, was subtly criticizing the gross inaction and passivity of President Hoover. FDR hoped to inspire the nation to overcome the dark days of depression, as he made the case for a much more industrious, action-oriented leadership. "The country" he said, "needs and, unless I mistake its temper, the country demands bold, persistent experimentation. It is common sense to take a method and try it: If it fails, admit it frankly and try another. But above all, try something." [540]

Political partisans are quick to criticize FDR for his policies in dealing with the Depression, but it was this very spirit and willingness to take initiative that was most helpful in generating the inspiration, motivation and momentum needed to turn the country around. It's true that a number of his policies and programs failed. But the fault lies not with those who strike out with new ideas, quickly moving forward until a solution is found. The fault lies with those who fail to act. It was Hoover's inability and unwillingness to risk intervening in the market that let the situation spin so horribly out of control.

The fact is that failure is an inevitable reality of the complex and uncertain world we live in today, particularly in positions of leadership and influence. James Fallows, former speechwriter to President Jimmy Carter, writes in the *Atlantic Monthly*, "The sobering realities of the modern White House are: All presidents are unsuited to office, and therefore all presidents fail in certain crucial aspects of the job."[541] The solution is not to freeze up and back off. "The only way to succeed is to have the courage to fail, and fail publicly."[542]

"Given this truth," writes *Slate* journalist John Dickerson, "presidents would be wise to follow that maxim from Silicon Valley: fail fast. Otherwise, they'll be stuck late in their administration with inevitably low approval ratings, the punishing requirements of getting re-elected, and the regret that they no longer have the room to maneuver that they once did."[543] The solution is to recognize failure as an inevitable part of leadership. "If they accept failures," Dickerson concludes, "they can learn from them and chart a new course while their administration is still young enough to act."[544]

Most people are willing to experience some degree of failure, provided that failure is only known to a few close friends. But failing in a small circle is inconsistent with large circle success. Of course, your goal is never to *intentionally* fail, particularly when, as president for example, the stakes are so high. "We obviously don't want a chronic fumbler in office," writes Dickerson, "but no one can be successful without having made some mistakes. If they've never made a mistake, it means they weren't taking risks. And every president must take risks."[545]

What's more, the very willingness to try new things can itself serve as a powerful source of momentum to push you and your team forward. As Harvard Kennedy School professor David Gergen, advisor to four U.S. Presidents, writes of FDR, "As long as he kept trying, he knew the public would invest hope in the future. Sometimes a leader doesn't solve a crisis; he helps followers get through a crisis."[546]

This was one of FDR's great strengths: He wasn't afraid to experiment. He wasn't afraid of defeat. "He was willing to try lots of things. Some failed and when they did, he learned and moved on. 'I experimented with gold and that was a flop,' he once told a group of senators. 'Why shouldn't I experiment a little with silver?' Roosevelt wasn't afraid of failure."[547] If you want to succeed, adopt Roosevelt's way of thinking about failure. "I have," he plainly confessed, "no expectation of making a hit every time I come to bat. What I seek is the highest possible batting average, not only for myself but for the team. Theodore Roosevelt once said to me: 'If I can be right 75 percent of the time I shall come up to the fullest measure of my hopes.'"[548]

Dare to Fail Big:
Andrew Carnegie and James Eads' Bridge

"My fear was of mediocrity, of being just another cog in the relentless system that would eventually grind our spirits down to dust. I refused to be a prisoner in a gilded cage from which there was no escape...I was determined to overcome my limitations, to stare my mediocrity in the face, to step up and dare to fail big, to go for the gold, live on the edge of uncertainty.
At least I'd be alive to feel my own pain, as John Lennon had commanded.
Dive rather thank sink, and dare the current to take you!"[549]
—Billy Idol, Dancing with Myself (1955—)

"Only those who dare to fail greatly can ever achieve greatly."
—Robert F. Kennedy (1925—1968)

Andrew Carnegie was still in his twenties in 1865 when he incorporated the Keystone Bridge Company. It was the end of the Civil War, and Carnegie was an ambitious young man ready to make his mark on the world. Carnegie was itching to conquer new terrain and help advance the new nation, and he was thrilled with the idea of "building glorious structures spanning America's mighty rivers and canyons."[550]

With the great bulk of the railroad system confined to the Eastern United States, a railway bridge across the mighty Mississippi River represented an unprecedented opening to the American West. Equally important, Carnegie understood the significance of railways and bridges to America's future. And he was eager to take advantage of the opportunity to be in the vanguard of what was still an emerging industry. "After all, winning the contracts to build such bridges would not only be lucrative, but would represent monuments to man's ingenuity, to the progress of America, and to the river itself, eulogized by Mark Twain in *Life on the Mississippi*."[551]

Be Ready to Risk It All.

When he learned of the renowned civil engineer and inventor James Buchanan Eads' interest in building a bridge across the Mississippi River at St. Louis, Carnegie immediately began to court Eads. He was determined to win from him the metal work contract for the Keystone Bridge Company.[552] Carnegie did not have the experience he thought he needed for such a massive, monumental structure, and he was not entirely sure he could pull the project off. But he knew that securing the contract to help build such a magnificent bridge would be a tremendous boon to his business, helping him to beat out competitors for future contracts.[553]

In 1870, Carnegie succeeded; operating as the Chief Engineer under the Illinois and St. Louis Bridge Company, Eads awarded Carnegie with the contract to build the bridge's superstructure.

Gearing up for such a colossal undertaking would require significant capital investments. "But Carnegie knows there is no reward without risk. He invests everything he has into the bridge."[554] In the words of historian H.W. Brands, "Andy Carnegie stepped up. He decided he could do it. One striking thing about Carnegie—and this is true of the great entrepreneurs—they are willing to take risks. They are willing to roll the dice and bet—in later days, the whole corporation—or, in this case, bet his career."[555]

With his experience in the stock market, Carnegie even went so far as to help Eads sell bonds to his connections in Europe. Building a major railway bridge across the Mississippi was a mammoth ambition and Carnegie was jumping in with both feet. He even convinced many of his friends and associates to do the same. Carnegie was risking almost everything, including the goodwill of his business partners and the livelihood of his workers. But he was taken by the enormity of the task, and he believed a bridge across the Mississippi would be a game changer for everyone involved.

Most people prefer to work their way up slowly. They imagine that they are not ready to move several steps ahead at once. They assume that those operating at a higher level deserve to be there, that they are somehow better, that they have greater knowledge, talent or skill. Some people tell themselves that they want to pay their dues first, but the fact is that experience can only take you so far—it's confidence not ability that they lack. With a significantly greater appetite for risk, the great heroes and hustlers of history never miss an opportunity to step up their game. In fact, they deliberately look for ways to break free from the shackles of convention. They regularly act contrary to the status quo mindset of the masses. They ignore archaic rules, customs, and norms. And when they see that fear is guiding thought and action, they look for chances to change the game.

When Christopher Columbus was planning his journey across the Atlantic, to what would become known as the "New World," he was setting a course into uncharted waters. Rather than staying close to the shore—as sailors had always done, in order to ensure a safe return—Columbus was heading directly into the vast and mighty and utterly unexplored Atlantic Ocean. Abandoning convention and conquering his fears, he was ready to risk it all. Columbus, in the words of Oxford University historian Felipe Fernandez-Armesto, "was the first to succeed precisely because he had the courage to sail with the wind at his back."[556] What previous explorers refused to attempt, Columbus dared to do. "Columbus sailed perpendicular to the shoreline, straight away from civilization as he knew it, even though he did not know what, if anything, lay ahead."[557]

Expect Problems, But Think Solutions.

Problems are a natural part of any worthwhile endeavor, and they should be expected. Eads and Carnegie's bridge across the Mississippi was no exception. Unfortunately for Eads and Carnegie, their first problem was a potential deal-breaker.

At the time, nearly a quarter of all bridges failed, many collapsing under the weight of loaded trains. Yet, these bridges were nowhere near the length required to cross the Mississippi. The unprecedented length and, thus, the increased danger of collapse, moreover, turned out to be just one of their obstacles. Local companies that operated the steamboats that used the river for shipping saw this potential new development as a threat to their business interests and, thus, sought to fight the building of the bridge every step of the way. Hoping to kill the bridge, they began by pressuring Congress to require the bridge to be significantly *higher* than any existing bridge. They insisted that the bridge had to be high enough—*an unprecedented 500 feet*—to accommodate their steamboats, which, they argued, would be significantly taller in the future. Congress acquiesced to the powerful steamboat interests, and Eads was forced to rethink his design—and the feasibility of the project.[558]

Eads determined that the height requirement could be solved by building a cantilever bridge, which had never been made before. The fear, however, was that a cantilever bridge made of iron would not be strong enough to withstand the rail traffic and the currents of the mighty Mississippi.

Eads suggests to Carnegie that if the superstructure was made out of steel—which, at the time, was the strongest material known to man—the bridge could still be built. But steel was still far too expensive to manufacture in mass quantities. Fortunately, Carnegie had also been following the development of steel and he immediately began to consider the possible ways to manufacture steel at a cost cheap enough to prevent the financial collapse of their endeavor.

Carnegie soon visits iron and steel mills around the world, he meets with engineers and chemists. And, before long, he learns that Henry Bessemer, a celebrated English inventor and ironmaster, accidentally discovered a process of making steel that reduced the time to manufacture a steel rod from two weeks down to fifteen minutes. Carnegie immediately sails to England to meet with Bessemer.

Through the progression of his problem solving adventure, Carnegie comes to believe that steel is the future. Biographer Peter Krass writes, "As Carnegie stood before the dazzling Bessemer converter, the white ingots glowed in his eyes and the heat of the blow inflated his five-foot-three inch frame until he was as big as President Ulysses S. Grant. He felt a surge of power, of enthusiasm, of confidence that steel would indeed replace iron, and he became determined to build a majestic steel mill."[559]

Carnegie had made up his mind. He agreed with Eads. They would build the railway bridge over the Mississippi with steel. It would be the world's first attempt to build a large steel structure.

Most everyone hopes to avoid problems. We all relish the thought of effortlessly achieving our most cherished dreams. This is the mentality that drives raffles and lotteries. This is why messages of the quick-fix swindlers are so seductive. People want (sometimes desperately) the fraudster's exaggerations and falsehoods to be true. The reality, however, is that with any significant endeavor problems are virtually inevitable.

85

Those who do not expect troubles to surface from time-to-time often find themselves deflated and discouraged when the inevitable problems arise.

The heroes of hustle and grit, however, understand that problems are a natural part of the process of pursuing any significant objective and, therefore, that they should be expected. They know problems will come up and they are, therefore, prepared to respond when they do. Rather then getting dispirited or lamenting their luck, they immediately move into the mode of either finding solutions, or, better yet, transforming their problems into opportunities. Congress and the steamboat operators nearly derailed Eads and Carnegie's plans. Instead, however, focused on finding a solution, Carnegie discovered Bessemer's steel-making process, which quickly and completely transformed his business, eventually helping him to become the wealthiest man in the world.

Think Big: Beyond Problems and Solutions.

On August 29, 1945, two weeks after Japan's official surrender at the end of World War II, and less than three weeks after the atomic bombings of Hiroshima and Nagasaki, President Truman sent General Douglas MacArthur to be the Supreme Commander for the Allied Powers in Japan (SCAP).

Leading the Japanese people out of a feudal system which had been in place for nearly 2,000 years was an impossible challenge. Of course MacArthur knew there would be problems. The entire endeavor was a mass of complex, multifaceted problems. A strong military element had dominated the leadership of the Japanese government—including Emperor Hirohito himself—for decades. Rich landowners ruled the markets. And women were completely subservient to men. Worse still, MacArthur was essentially coming in as the enemy occupier.

But MacArthur had high hopes. His mindset went beyond merely turning problems into opportunities. MacArthur wanted Japan to become one of the great reformation stories of modern history. Besides, MacArthur was not one to back down from a challenge, no matter how big. In fact, MacArthur was notoriously cocky and took pleasure in chewing on what most men wouldn't dare to bite off.

MacArthur's most brilliant move was the way in which he worked to reframe his role in Japan. He was not going in as a conqueror, but as a collaborator. He did not merely want to help put Japan back together. He wanted to help Japan rebuild for the future. MacArthur had a heart for the Japanese people, and he respected their culture. He wanted Japan to succeed, and he immediately went to work to help make it happen.

Land reforms dramatically reduced the cost of land and effectively redistributed a remarkable 90 percent of the land, which greatly increased productivity. Japanese women, who had previously been seen as the property of their families, were essentially emancipated and given the right to vote. A constitution was written which shared considerable power with the parliament, empowered labor unions, and greatly increased freedom of speech throughout the nation. The Emperor, who was revered by the Japanese as a god, formally renounced his claim to divine status, becoming instead, like the monarch in England, a figurehead ruler. Japan soon emerged as a model of postwar recovery and, in the end, the Japanese people surpassed even MacArthur's high expectations. In an address to Congress on 19 April 1951, MacArthur declared: "The Japanese people since the war have undergone the greatest reformation recorded in modern history."[560] Today, Japan is one of the greatest powers in the world, and America and Japan remain among the closest of allies.

General Douglas MacArthur did not go into Japan with any illusions about the task before him. He understood the difficulties ahead. And, of course, the Japanese people deserve the lion's share of the credit for their transformation and ascendency following the defeat of the Axis powers at the end of World War II. Nevertheless, MacArthur succeeded in his role because he dared to think big. It wasn't simply that he expected problems, or that he remained focused on solutions—both of which are often critical to success. MacArthur succeeded because he had a clear and compelling vision for the future of Japan, a big and bold vision rooted in the interests of the Japanese people.

Thinking big is risky. Things will not always work out. Big ambitions are often accompanied by big problems. But there is power in thinking big. A shared vision, with big, bold and inspiring goals can go a long way toward overcoming difficult challenges. As Goethe once said, "Dream no small dreams for they have no power to move the hearts of men."[561] Lofty dreams inspire hard work. Hard work builds confidence. Confidence dreams lofty dreams. It's a virtuous cycle. Big dreams force new ways of thinking from our minds, new actions and habits from our lives.[562] And for this reason, visions must be idealistic. "A vision has no power to inspire or energize people and no ability to set a new standard or attract commitment unless it offers a view of the future that is clearly and demonstrably better for the organization, for the people in the organization…or for the society within which the organization operates…The vision, in short, must be manifestly desirable, a bold and worthy challenge for those who accept it."[563]

Moreover, highly capable, competent people are not drawn to mediocre leaders with mediocre dreams. Highly effective people want to continue to learn and grow and achieve great things. "The greater your dream is," writes John Maxwell, "the greater the people who will be attracted to you."[564]

From the earliest histories of leadership we can discover examples of the great significance of a bold and bright vision—from Alexander the Great's vision of an ethnically integrated society to John F. Kennedy's vision of putting a man on the moon. As President Richard Nixon wrote in his book Leaders, "Great leadership requires a great vision, one that inspires the leader and enables him to inspire the nation."[565]

Prepare Your Plan of Escape.

Carnegie's discovery of Bessemer's steel-making process was not the end of his problems. In fact, not surprisingly, the problems were only just beginning. Carnegie had no idea what he was getting into with Eads. "Eads presented Keystone with minutely detailed plans and specifications that called for a quality of steel never before produced."[566] Author and historian John Barry reports, "At the time, steel making was really an art, and Eads demanded the precision of a science. He essentially required steel makers to become scientific and to impose rational methods that would produce a standard reliable product."[567]

To Carnegie's way of thinking, however, Eads was an idealistic perfectionist. Whereas, for his own part, Carnegie was far more of a pragmatist. Carnegie's thinking was aligned with that of the French philosopher and historian Voltaire, who said, "perfection is the enemy of excellence."[568]

Over the next couple of years, Carnegie began to lose his patience with Eads. The operation was way behind schedule, and well over budget. The time delays and Eads' endless demands regarding the specifications of Carnegie's steel went well beyond the "custom of the trade," and was driving Carnegie's costs far beyond what was calculated in the original contract. "Of all men, your man of real, decided genius is the most difficult to deal with practically," Carnegie writes to a mutual friend. "This Bridge is one of a hundred to the Keystone Company—to Eads it is the grand work of a distinguished life. With all the pride of a mother for her first-born, he would bedeck the darling without much regard to his own or others' cost. Nothing that would please and that does please other engineers is good enough for this work."[569]

Carnegie began to have his doubts about whether the bridge would ever be finished and, importantly, about his and his associates' investments in it. He was so discouraged, in fact, that he began to fear that his stock portfolio would end up hemorrhaging the way this project was now.

Carnegie's assessment began to shift. He had taken a big chance and now it looked as if failure would be his. Maintaining a positive front, Carnegie began to sell his holdings in the St. Louis Bridge Company at a substantial loss. Writing to one associate, he said, "I am disgusted with the affair, throughout, & may have sold at panic prices..."[570]

Strictly as an investor, Carnegie took a big hit. But he was not about to abandon the bridge. And, in fact, he was prepared to "buy an unfinished Bridge," force Eads out, and finish it himself if the situation required.[571]

In time, Carnegie, Eads, and the many loose pieces eventually started to come together, patience and understanding started to win out, and the spectacular shape of the bridge began to take form. "Despite the difficulties between the two sides, and the many delays and cost overruns, Carnegie marveled at the bridge when it was finally completed. In December 1873, he wrote to a financier in Europe that 'the entire work—bridge, tunnel & approaches, are magnificent.'"[572]

Eads Bridge opened on July 4, 1874. With a parade and fireworks, a marching band and a 100-gun salute, nearly 150,000 spectators witnessed the dedication, with celebrated Civil War hero General William Tecumseh Sherman driving in the last spike, completing the "world's first steel arch bridge and the biggest bridge built up to that time."[573]

As the world's first major steel structure, Eads bridge would prove to be the beginning of a revolution in construction.[574] It established James B. Eads as one of the greatest technical and artistic engineers of the era.[575] Eads was celebrated around the nation (some even considered him as a potential candidate for president). The American architect Louis Sullivan, known as "the father of skyscrapers," said of Eads, "Here again was Man, the great adventurer, daring to think, daring to have faith, daring to do."[576] Eads was indeed a bold man of action. As he said in his own words, "Fortune favors the brave. 'Drive on' is my motto."[577]

Together, Carnegie and Eads ushered in the age of steel. Steel would constitute the core of Carnegie's career. Less than a year after the bridge was completed, Carnegie opened the J. Edgar Thomson Steel Works in Braddock, Pennsylvania. For railroads and bridges and skyscrapers, the orders began to pour in, swamping his steel mills for the next quarter of a century. Using Bessemer's steel-making process, focusing on efficiency and cost-cutting, Carnegie, as a direct result of this venture, became the greatest steel producer in the world and, by 1901—when he sold his empire to J.P. Morgan—the richest man of his era.[578]

Jump in the River with Both Feet.

Eads and Carnegie's success was by no means certain. Clearly, Carnegie himself had major doubts; to the point of hedging his bets and absorbing significant stock sale losses half way through the ordeal. But taking calculated risks is precisely what hustlers do. Indeed, Carnegie had demonstrated a willingness to take huge risks from an early age. When he was only 21 he risked the loss of his mother's house in order to purchase stock in a package delivery business.[579]

Not every self-made success story has been an economic daredevil, of course. But they all rejected the safe (but deceptive) road of certainty.[580] Do not assume, however, that this is just the way they were made—sometimes it is, oftentimes it's not. The reason they take chances is because they understand they must in order to achieve significant success. There are plenty of *relatively* safe roads to mediocrity, but there is virtually no risk-free road to success. In fact, many of the most successful people have taken some of the greatest risks. But these people also understand something else: Success rarely comes overnight. More often than not, success comes *after* all the setbacks, failure, and costly mistakes. And this explains why the most successful people are almost always the ones who have failed the most.

In 1908, Andrew Carnegie challenged Napoleon Hill to research the principles of success and achievement by studying the leading business and political figures of the day. Carnegie introduced Hill to a remarkable collection of high achievers, including Henry Ford, Alexander Graham Bell, Thomas Edison, John D. Rockefeller, Theodore Roosevelt, Woodrow Wilson, FDR and numerous others. From this twenty year project—detailed in his multi-volume *The Law of Success*—Hill gained a wealth of valuable insights. He also discovered an interesting finding: "Most great people," Hill writes, "have attained their greatest success just one step beyond their greatest failure."[581]

Consider Hill's finding for a moment. What if your absolute greatest success in life could not happen *until* you endured the greatest failure of your life? Might that change your view of failure? Of course it would be a fool's mistake to run ahead with foolish plans. Risks should be calculated not reckless. But would you not, as you examine the possibility of failure, be reassured knowing that there is a remarkable record of people who, after suffering some great failure, responded in such a way that led to their life's greatest success? What kind of life do you want to live anyway? "What kind of man would live where there is no daring?" asks Charles Lindbergh.[582] "I don't believe in taking foolish chances," said the aviation pioneer, "but nothing can be accomplished [if we don't take] any chance at all."[583]

Dare to Go Big, It's Easier in the End.

To succeed at a high level, you must dare to fail big. Naturally, the idea is not to aim for big failure. The idea is to have the guts to go big, regardless of whether you fail or not. "I guarantee if these guys [Vanderbilt, Carnegie, Ford, Rockefeller] were alive today," says Donny Deutsch in The Men Who Built America, "they wouldn't be telling you about their successes. They would be telling you about their early failures or the places they almost failed. That's the great motivator," Deutsch adds, "and you have to be able to embrace that. If you can't embrace both failure or the possibility of failure or the tremendous fear of failure you can't be wildly successful. It's an axiomatic truth."[584]

Most people are beaten not by failure, but by fear. It is the risk of failure that occupies their minds. Fear replaces reasonable thought. It degrades their decision-making. It wastes time with worry. The solution is to set your sights on your target and, come what may, charge ahead. Stop living your life fearing things that virtually never come true. Heed the wise words of Herodotus (c. 484—425 B.C.), the ancient Greek historian, who said, "It is better by a noble boldness to run the risk of being subject to half the evils we anticipate than to remain in cowardly listlessness for fear of what might happen."[585] Your ultimate success depends not on the particular outcome of some chance endeavor, but on your ability to forge ahead through whatever failures you face. In the words of the Roman statesman Seneca, "It's not because things are difficult that we dare not venture. It's because we dare not venture that they are difficult."[586]

Prepare to Risk It All.

Donald Trump loves to take chances, and he loves to make a deal. High stakes deals are in his DNA. In fact, he writes in the opening of *The Art of the Deal*, "I don't do it for the money. I've got enough, much more than I'll ever need. I do it to do it. Deals are my art form."[587] Besides, Trump adds, "I like making deals, preferably big deals. That's how I get my kicks."[588]

The only thing Trump loves more than making deals is himself. The idea of furthering his personal brand and putting his name on another luxury building, product or service is usually too good to pass up. That's why when Trump had the opportunity to put his name in the sky, in a big airline deal, he jumped in with both feet. He imagined a luxury service, focusing on flights between Boston, New York and Washington. It was going to be, he said, "a diamond in the sky."[589]

Almost from its inception, however, Trump's airline was hammered by problems. He invested close to $400 million in the airline before it was up to a level that met his high expectations.[590] But he soon found himself overleveraged. Moreover, given that many of his potential passengers were not interested in paying extra for luxury, the business was not booming. When the economy started to nosedive, Trump defaulted on his loans.[591] "When the markets crash, you negotiate with banks," Trump said later.[592]

In less than three years, Trump was out. Aviation consultant George Hamlin said, "Trump said the shuttle was going to be a diamond in the sky, but it turned into a lump of coal."[593] Trump, of course, the consummate hustler, was quick to bounce back, and he soon began to frame the fiasco to his advantage. "It worked out well for me," he said later.[594] "I ran an airline for a couple of years and made a couple of bucks. The airline business is a tough business, [but] I did great with it."[595]

This, of course, was not Trump's only business (or personal) failure. Trump has tried—and failed—to sell vodka, chocolate, and even steaks. But it is this willingness to endure failure—over and over again, if necessary—that sets the great heroes of history apart. Yes, Trump is often admired because he has succeeded beyond the wildest expectations of most people. But among his most admirable qualities includes his willingness to go big, and—if and when he fails—to pick himself up and go big again, and again, and again.

Obviously, we don't all start off life playing on the same field. But we can all learn to play the game. We can watch and learn from the all-stars, including what they do to win and how they handle failure when they lose. "I've seen some people get completely swallowed up by failures," Trump said.[596] "The worst thing you can do to yourself is to believe that bad luck is your due. It isn't! It's not just intelligence or luck that gets us places, it's tenacity in the face of adversity."[597]

The fact is sometimes you will take a big chance and you will fail. Alexander the Great wanted to unite the cultures of the world, and he worked hard—but failed—to do it. "Oh, but what failure!" wrote Ptolemy, the Greco-Egyptian writer. Imagine what he *was* able to achieve even while his broader ambition remained unmet.

The reality is that failure is a most natural part of life. It happens to us all—*especially* those who achieve extraordinary success. Why? Because taking big chances is what it takes to succeed big. Rarely does anyone ever achieve anything great by constantly playing it safe. In fact, not only is it often easier to succeed by taking big risks, there are times when taking a big chance is the *only way* to move ahead. "Did you know that Walt Disney mortgaged everything he owned, including is own personal insurance, to fund the $17 million construction of Disneyland?"[598] It's true. There was no other way. None of his potential funders believed in his vision the way he did. So, he risked it all. "Walt

Disney founded an empire on fantasy and risk taking."[599] Fortunately, his gamble paid off, and it paid off big. In fact, Disney continues to reign as a premier global brand,[600] while 2015 revenues for the Walt Disney Company exceeded fifty *billion* dollars.[601]

Failure is inevitable. Learn to accept it and never let it rob you of the courage to get back up and go after your dreams. Imagine, the great Dutch painter Vincent van Gogh said, "what would life be if we had no courage to attempt anything?"[602] Isn't life always worth taking another big chance? Mark Cuban thinks it is. "You don't have to break the Mendoza Line (hitting .200). In fact, it doesn't matter how many times you strike out," writes Cuban.[603] "The beauty of success," he said, "whether it's finding the girl of your dreams, the right job or financial success, is that it doesn't matter how many times you have failed, you only have to be right once."[604] But here's the key: Don't just attempt anything. Attempt something big!

Find the Seed of Advantage in Adversity, Use It for Your Success: P.T. Barnum and the Greatest Elephant on Earth

"Every great man, every successful man, no matter what the field of endeavor, has known the magic that lies in these words: every adversity has the seed of an equivalent or greater benefit."
–W. Clement Stone (1902–2002), American Businessman, Philanthropist, Author

Around Christmas in 1860, the year that Abraham Lincoln was elected President, a curiously large elephant was born near the Takkaze River in East Africa. The infant elephant was discovered by Arabian hunters who had been hired to capture animals to sell to European zoos. The elephant soon found himself at the London Zoological Gardens where he became known as "Jumbo" and was put under the care of animal keeper Matthew "Scotty" Scott.

Jumbo and Scotty quickly connected, and soon developed a close bond that lasted a lifetime. Jumbo appeared to adjust exceptionally well to his new environment and he soon became the zoo's leading attraction. He was remarkably gentle, even with small children. Jumbo allowed tens of thousands of children to ride on his back—something not all elephants are keen to do—including the children of Queen Victoria (who also became quite fond of Jumbo),as well as young Winston Churchill, and Teddy Roosevelt. According to the magazine *Harper's Weekly*, Jumbo was, "as gentle with children as the best-trained poodle dog."[605] He would even eat biscuits and small cubes of sugar out of children's tiny hands. With his reputation for being so gentle and well-behaved, Jumbo quickly earned the love of people everywhere, becoming the first international animal superstar.

As Jumbo continued to grow to his full, massive size, he soon became known as the biggest elephant living in captivity. This caught the interest of P.T. Barnum, the famous entertainment impresario, widely believed to be the greatest showman on earth. Barnum was a master entertainer and promoter with a genius for knowing what would appeal to people and how to further stir their excitement. Known as the "Shakespeare of Advertising," Barnum understood an audience's fascination with anything odd or extraordinary, including people and animals unusually large or curiously small.[606] Barnum and his partner Bailey soon wrote to the London Zoological Gardens with an offer to purchase Jumbo for $10,000. And though they were reluctant to sell, in the end—recognizing that Jumbo, following his years of sexual maturity, was entering a period of increased testosterone and aggression—they finally agreed.

Use Storytelling, Reframe Adversity to Your Advantage.

Suddenly, the people of London began to protest the sale of their beloved beast. Even Queen Victoria expressed her disapproval. But Barnum was undeterred. When Jumbo himself appeared to resist the trip to America, by refusing to walk into the large crate made for him for the trip, the protests and public outrage quickly swelled. People wrote letters to the newspapers. Petitions were sent to Parliament. Barnum even began to receive threats on his life. Still, he was undeterred. In fact, as difficult and dangerous as this may have been, Barnum recognized the intense criticism and resistance as a spectacular opportunity, and he deftly used the free worldwide publicity as a means of telling the story of Jumbo and intensifying the anticipation for his arrival in the United States. Barnum was more than happy to wait until Jumbo was ready leave. "Let him lie there a week if he wants to," Barnum wired to the London zoo.[607] "It is the best advertisement in the world."[608]

Barnum readily agreed to welcome Jumbo's trainer and friend Scotty to the team and within a week—with the help of a few bottles of whiskey—the two were on a ship headed for America. Stories soon circulated in America that Jumbo was drinking and dancing the hornpipe with the sailors as they crossed the Atlantic Ocean. It was Barnum, of course, who was working his magic as he began to build anticipation for the launch of a new American star. Jumbo was to become the symbol and face for what Barnum called, "The Greatest Show on Earth."

Storytelling was a crucial part of Barnum's brilliance. He understood people's hunger to escape the mundane details of their own lives and the power of storytelling to take them away to another world. He also understood how stories could be used to reframe events both for the public and for ourselves. As Barnum's own example illustrates, storytelling is a powerful tool you can use in dealing with your own adversity. It is not what happens to you that matters most. It is the story you tell yourself about what and why it happened. In Barnum's case, he always seemed to find or fashion a story that would lead to his continued success. He was resolved to look for reasons why his presently difficult situation was actually to his advantage and, as a consequence, he readily seemed to find it. As Harvard psychologist Ellen Langer writes, "What we have learned to look for in a situation determines mostly what we see."[609]

By the time of Jumbo's arrival in America, Barnum drummed up the hoopla and set the stage for an entrance unlike any the world had ever seen. Thousands upon thousands of people populated Jumbo's path from the docks in Battery Park to the home of the circus in Madison Square Gardens. Jumbo's arrival went on record as New York City's largest crowd in history. With Jumbo joining the show that year, the circus broke all previous records of attendance.[610]

Clearly, P.T. Barnum was a master storyteller, a marketing and promotion genius. After spending nearly triple the price he paid for the elephant to transport him to the U.S., Barnum later acknowledged that he recouped his costs in the first two weeks of Jumbo's debut. Even before he arrived, there was an explosion of "Jumbomania," a fascination and craving for all things Jumbo—from hats, canes, ties and cigars to jewelry, polkas, soaps and souvenirs. The very word *jumbo* (from Swahili, *jumbe*, meaning chief), which did not yet exist in the English language, became the byword for anything very large.

Take Time to Pause and Regroup.

Alas, the fascination with the enormous elephant, and the fanfare and fun surrounding his circus life was on a collision course with destruction and death. Just over 3 years later, on September 15, 1885, Jumbo was tragically killed in a train accident in Ontario, Canada . At only 24, Jumbo lived less than half of the average lifespan for his breed. Scotty, who had shared a beer with Jumbo virtually every night of his life, was distraught. In his final moments, according to eyewitness account, Jumbo reached out his trunk and wrapped it around his friend Scotty, while Scotty dropped to his knees and cried like a baby.[611]

When Barnum got the news, he too was crushed. Barnum had experienced numerous devastating setbacks throughout his life—including many fires, a few of which burned his museums to the ground—but he always seemed to emerge unfazed. When Jumbo died, however, Barnum was momentarily beat. Within days, believing that the circus was lost without Jumbo, Barnum began the first steps of bankruptcy proceedings.

Not long thereafter, however, Barnum was bouncing back. He was determined that Jumbo would live on in an "afterlife with the circus."[612] He produced a story about how Jumbo went down as a hero, how Jumbo had saved baby elephant Tom Thumb, who was on the tracks with him at the time of the accident, and how he had tried to stop the train by charging directly at it.[613] Describing Jumbo as a "mountain of bone and brawn," Barnum's account has Jumbo taking on "the leviathan of the rail" and meeting his end "with a becoming dignity and fortitude."[614]

Recognizing the power of storytelling and people's ongoing fascination with Jumbo's life story, Barnum then had Jumbo's hide stuffed by taxidermist, Henry Ward. Barnum also had Jumbo's bones erected, separately, to exhibit Jumbo as a standing skeleton. Jumbo would now be displayed in two places simultaneously. It was, Double Jumbo—"two Jumbos for the price of one."[615]

To deepen interest, Barnum began to portray Jumbo in a new light, making him into a kind of animal divinity. The new circus advertisements read: "The Tremendous Skeleton of Jumbo, Lord of Beasts." Including a more scientific angle, he added "Prepared by the distinguished scientist and naturalist, Professor Henry A. Ward of Rochester, New York." Understanding the principle of scarcity in motivating people to act, Barnum further added: "for a brief season only."[616]

To the surprise of some, "Jumbo proved as popular dead as he was alive."[617] The demand for Jumbo and Jumbo paraphernalia continued for years afterwards. His skeleton was later donated to the Smithsonian, finally resting at the Natural History Museum in New York. His hide was donated to Tufts University, where Jumbo became the University's mascot. And Jumbo's big heart was sold to Cornell.[618]

Never Simply Accept Adversity, Find a Way to Use It.

To Barnum's competitors and critics, his continued success with Jumbo after the elephant's death was too much to bear. Not only did he effectively have "two Jumbos," but he had them without the risk of an accident with the children, without the awful, insidious smell and cleanup of his waste, and without the expense of feeding him (which included a daily intake of 200 pounds of hay, 15 loaves of bread, 2 bushels of oats, a barrel of potatoes, and a bag of onions[619]). That Barnum was able to effectively transform a tragic loss into an even greater success, led a few unscrupulous characters to spread rumors that Jumbo was sick and dying and that Barnum *intentionally* had the animal killed (leading to conspiracies that still exist today). But herein lies yet another example of the genius of Barnum, and his ability to turn adversity to his advantage. Rather than getting upset by such outrageous and hurtful lies, Barnum would use the claims of his critics to create controversy which would inevitably lead to greater publicity, public interest and increased traffic to his shows. Barnum hardly cared at all what lies his critics charged. In fact, he said, "I don't care what people say about me as long as they say something."[620]

The most successful people are *not* those who effectively skirt setbacks, avoid adversity, deflect defeat and, in so doing, rise to the top. In fact, have you ever considered that setbacks, failures and adversity may be critical components of your success; that if not for challenges and hardships you would never develop the competence and self-confidence so essential to your success? This is certainly the perspective of hustlers like Sir Richard Branson. "In fact," Branson said, "failure is one of the secrets to success, since some of the best ideas arise from the ashes of a shuttered business."[621] In the words of the ancient Roman Emperor Marcus Aurelius, "The impediment to action advances action. What stands in the way becomes the way."[622] Writing in his journal (known later as Meditations), Aurelius continues, "Our actions may be impeded...but there can be no impeding our intentions or dispositions. Because we can accommodate and adapt. The mind adapts and converts to its own purposes the obstacle to our acting."[623]

It is not enough to endure adversity. Success requires that you find a way to use it. High achievement demands that you foster a skill for transforming setbacks into success. It demands that you develop a talent for turning adversity to advantage, a knack for finding profit in failure. Your dreams and goals are not served when you see only obstacles and setbacks. Learn to rethink, reframe and transform those things that appear to be working against you. Learn to see instead new discoveries and opportunities, the growth of wisdom, the cultivation of competence, the development of strength and power, or a chance to pivot, or regroup and start anew. "A man of genius makes no mistakes," wrote James Joyce in *Ulysses*.[624] "His errors are volitional and are the portals to discovery."[625]

"Many of our failures sweep us to greater heights of success, than we ever hoped for in our wildest dreams. Life," wrote William George Jordan, former editor of *The Saturday Evening Post*, "is a successive unfolding of success from failure."[626] This is the mindset of men and women of grit, and it is a recurrent source of potential power. In the words of Nietzsche, "I assess the power of a will by how much resistance, pain, torture it endures and knows how to turn to its advantage."[627]

Abraham Lincoln knew something about mastering adversity. Lincoln's entire life was a succession of overcoming challenges and pushing through painful setbacks. And, yet, through all of the personal losses and numerous electoral defeats, he grew stronger and rose higher until at last he was elected President of the United States, and then re-elected. Lincoln, evidently, found ways to profit from these setbacks. Indeed, he was clearly learning from his experiences, gaining valuable insight and wisdom. In notes he prepared for a law school lecture circa 1850, Lincoln writes, "I find quite as much material for a lecture in those points wherein I have failed, as in those wherein I have been moderately successful."[628] And, of course, at the very least, by willing himself to push ahead, he built up a resistance to adversity and became, in time, as he put it, "too familiar with disappointments to be very much chagrined."[629]

As we learn from the example of Lincoln, sometimes the key advantage in adversity is the sheer power of the lesson learned. When Richard Branson was busted in 1971 for evading Customs and Excise taxes on a shipment of music records, he was arrested and spent the night in jail. The experience of losing his freedom and being "utterly dependent on somebody else to open the door" shook Branson to his core.[630] "That night was one of the best things that has ever happened to me," he wrote later.[631] "I vowed to myself that I would never again do anything that would cause me to be imprisoned, or indeed do any kind of business deal by which I would ever have cause to be embarrassed."[632]

Branson learned to steer clear of such ethical lapses of judgment, but this was far from his final failure. From selling Christmas trees and Virgin clothing, to Virgin Cola, Vodka and Brides, Richard Branson has continued to see his fair share of failures. But this is a key part of what enables Branson to achieve such extraordinary success. He does not succeed in spite of his failures. He succeeds because of his failures and, importantly, the lessons he is able to take away as result. "Failure and rejection are an inevitable part of business," Branson says, "and how you deal with them will ultimately affect your success."[633] Success is not about avoiding failure. It's about learning from it. "We have had many great successes at Virgin," Branson said, "but we've also experienced a number of failures. Every time something hasn't worked out as we hoped it would, we have picked ourselves up, looked at what went wrong, and learned from our mistakes."[634] *Learning* is the key, Branson says. "Learn from failure. If you are an entrepreneur and your first venture wasn't a success, welcome to the club!" In his book, *Like a Virgin*, Branson writes, "Most entrepreneurs' first ventures fail—I know, because mine did—but the lessons you learn from failure are invaluable and will help you with your next attempts."[635]

Assume Responsibility for Moving Ahead.

Nelson Mandela's participation in 1994 in his nation's first multiracial elections was an historic event in itself. His election victory as South Africa's first black president represented an epic transformation, celebrated around the world, marking "an official welcome for the world's newest democracy into the community of nations."[636] "The sun shall never set on so glorious a human achievement!" Mandela said in his inaugural address as he called for healing and reconciliation.[637] That Mandela could achieve such a remarkable feat after spending over a quarter of a century in prison is a testament to the strength of human will and the power of the human spirit to overcome adversity. Nelson Mandela was a master at using setbacks to his advantage. In fact, in many ways, Mandela became even more powerful from behind prison bars. He never let his time go to waste, he explains in an interview on Larry King.[638] Rather, he used the time to think and reflect, and write his life story. "Especially for those of us who lived in single cells," Mandela said, "you had the time to sit down and think, and we discovered that sitting down just to think is one of the best ways of keeping yourself fresh and able, to be able to address the problems facing you, and you had the opportunity, also, of examining your past. You could," he continued, "stand away from yourself in the past and examine whether your behavior was befitting to a person who tried to serve society..."[639]

"Every condition, be it what it may, has hardships, hazards, pains," wrote W. E. Channing, America's leading 19th century Unitarian preacher.[640] "We try to escape them; we pine for a sheltered lot, for a smooth path, for cheering friends, and unbroken success. But Providence ordains storms, disasters, hostilities, sufferings; and the great question whether we shall live to any purpose or not, whether we shall grow strong in mind and heart, or be weak and pitiable, depends on nothing so much as on our use of the adverse circumstances."[641]

Make this mindset your own. Never simply endure adversity. Look for the opportunity in the problem. Find the benefits in setbacks, the advantages in defeat. Whatever difficulty life throws your way, it is your mindset that matters most. Remember, Channing writes, "Outward evils are designed to school our passions, and to rouse our faculties and virtues into more intense action."[642] Indeed, he adds, "sometimes they seem to create new powers."[643]

Do not complain about the hardships you face. "Difficulty is the element, and resistance the true work of man."[644] The growth of your strength and power, Channing writes, "…never goes on so fast as when embarrassed circumstances, the opposition of men or the elements, unexpected changes of the times, or other forms of suffering, instead of disheartening, throw us on our inward resources, turn us for strength to God, clear up to us the great purpose of life, and inspire calm resolution. No greatness or goodness is worth much, unless tried in these fires."[645]

5

STEEL YOURSELF FOR CRITICISM, OPPOSITION AND RESISTANCE

"It is not the critic who counts; not the man who points out how the strong man stumbles, or where the doer of deeds could have done them better. The credit belongs to the man who is actually in the arena, whose face is marred by dust and sweat and blood, who strives valiantly; who errs and comes short again and again; because there is not effort without error and shortcomings; but who does actually strive to do the deed; who knows the great enthusiasm, the great devotion, who spends himself in a worthy cause, who at the best knows in the end the triumph of high achievement and who at the worst, if he fails, at least he fails while daring greatly. So that his place shall never be with those cold and timid souls who know neither victory nor defeat."
—Theodore Roosevelt (1858—1919), "Citizenship in a Republic," Paris, April 23, 1910

Brace for the Brickbats, Critics, Haters and Trolls: Harry Truman Following in the Footsteps of FDR

"Genius has been well defined as the infinite capacity for taking pains."
—Orison Swett Marden (1848—1924), Pushing to the Front

By the time of his death on April 12, 1945, Franklin D. Roosevelt was the longest serving President in U.S. history, and was widely judged to be one of the greatest. Under his leadership, America had emerged from the Great Depression and turned the tide in World War II.

When Vice President Truman got the news from Eleanor Roosevelt that FDR had died, he suddenly found himself fighting back tears. "Is there anything I can do for you?" he asked.[646] "Is there anything *we* can do for *you*?" Eleanor shot back. "For you are the one in trouble now."[647]

That's when it hit him. The humble, plain speaking man from Missouri was now the leader of the most powerful nation on Earth. "Boys," he said to the press corps later, "if you ever pray, pray for me now. I don't know whether you fellows ever had a load of hay fall on you, but when they told me yesterday what had happened, I felt like the moon, the stars, and all the planets had fallen in on me."[648] Everyone immediately understood. After all, many of Roosevelt's supporters thought, 'how could *anyone* fill the shoes of such a great man,' let alone a pedestrian politician like Harry Truman?

Truman had no college degree and no fixed profession. As a failed haberdasher and sometime dirt farmer, Truman got into politics at age 50 because he was failing at everything else. When he ascended to the Presidency, Truman had been serving as Vice President for less than 90 days, without any mentoring from FDR. He knew very little of the intimate details of the war or U.S. foreign policy, and he knew *nothing* of the ongoing development of the atomic bomb. "But now," he wrote later, "the lightning had struck, and events beyond anyone's control had taken command."[649] The awesome responsibilities of the world's mightiest nation had fallen on him.[650]

Virtually no one thought Truman could handle the job. In the words of journalist Hugh Sidey, who covered the Presidency for *Time*, "The forecasts of his stewardship ran the gamut from hopeless to hopeless."[651] Even Truman didn't think he was up to the task. "It was," he said later, "a terrible thing to have to take over after a three-term President who had been so nearly unanimously elected every time."[652] But Harry Truman was determined to try. In fact, no matter what happened, he was resolved to give it his very best.

The criticism of Truman began immediately. Even Cabinet members were critical of the new President. In fact, Roosevelt's funeral had barely finished when Truman overheard Harold Ickes, Secretary of the Interior, "carrying on about how the country would go to hell now that Roosevelt was gone."[653] In what was an obvious slight, Truman recalled how Ickes spoke loud enough so that Truman could overhear him, "He said there wasn't any leadership anymore."[654]

The press attacked Truman even more viciously. "Most of the newspapers didn't hesitate to lie," Truman said.[655] Some of the Hearst papers even made the outrageous (and utterly false) claim that Truman was a member of the Klu Klux Klan.[656] The attacks were more intense than Truman had expected, or ever before experienced. He was often hurt by the criticisms and he was not immune to an occasional emotional outburst.

In just over a year, Truman's approval rating plummeted precipitously, eventually falling from 87 to 33 percent. At this point, a Senator from his own party, William Fulbright, suggested that Truman resign. In his typical blunt, plain-spoken style, Truman said that he didn't care what "Senator Half-bright" said.

Taking little heed of his critics, he continued to forge ahead. You just have to do the best you can, Truman figured. "That's the main thing," he said. "A man can't do anything more than that."[657]

It was the same outlook that Abraham Lincoln adopted during the Civil War. When he was up for re-election in 1864, the attacks greatly intensified. When he was asked if he had read some of the more prominent, vitriolic speeches made against him, Lincoln replied, "I have not seen them, nor do I care to see them."[658] Lincoln understood the gist of their attacks, and he knew that any further consideration was a waste of his time. "Time," Lincoln said, "will show whether I am right or they are right, and I am content to abide its decision."[659]

"Lincoln had pure grit," wrote Orison Swett Marden.[660] "When the illustrated papers everywhere were caricaturing him, when no epithet seemed too harsh to heap upon him, when his methods were criticized by his own party, and the generals in the war were denouncing his 'foolish' confidence in Grant, and delegations were waiting upon him to ask for that general's removal, the great President sat with crossed legs, and was reminded of a story."[661]

Naturally, to the man who wanted to share these vitriolic speeches with the President, Lincoln explained that the way he felt about his critics was like the way an old Illinois farmer felt one day when he was eating cheese. When the farmer's son suddenly rushed in to stop him, he exclaimed, "Hold on, dad! There's skippers in that cheese you're eating!" "Never mind, son," the farmer said as he kept munching on his cheese. "If they can stand it, I can."[662]

"Despite a steady barrage of criticism, Truman became increasingly self-confident, and even cocky, as he familiarized himself with the duties and responsibilities of his office."[663] With a deep knowledge of history and leadership, Truman continued to do what he thought was right, regardless of whether or not it was good politics, or popular with the people. Slowly, the American people's confidence in Truman began to grow.

Still, the consensus in the mainstream media was that Truman's loss in the 1948 election to New York Governor Thomas Dewey was a forgone conclusion. Truman disagreed. He campaigned relentlessly, delivering fiery speeches from the platform of the *Magellan* railcar on his famous whirlwind whistle-stop tour, effectively building his case with the American people. "When almost no knowledgeable observers gave him a chance," Truman defeated Dewey by a decisive 2 million popular and 114 electoral votes.[664] It was one of the greatest upsets in the history of presidential elections.

Accept It and Let it Go.

When Truman ascended to the presidency he was unprepared for the harsh criticisms and public attacks. The grossly unfair and frequently untrue criticisms hurt. And his blunt, often heated, responses frequently left the impression that he was sensitive and immature, unable to handle the demands of the presidency. And, no doubt, as a result, he lost some of the public's esteem. But Harry Truman had an inner core of steel. And, regardless of how he dealt with his critics and opponents outwardly, it was this inner core of character and conviction that continued to guide his decisions as President no matter what the opinions of his opponents, or critics in the press.

Richard Nixon also struggled with what he believed was unfair and uninformed personal and political attacks. In stark contrast to Truman, however, Nixon lacked the inner core of character and confidence. Robert Dallek writes, "His fear that political enemies would see through his veneer of self-assurance was a breeding ground for anger at critics."[665] Like Truman, Nixon also frequently responded to his critics in public, but for Nixon that was never enough. Even after he voiced his displeasure he was unable to let it go. "He could not bear to read negative comments about himself and his administration. Scanning daily media stories for anything unflattering, Nixon responded by ordering aides to deny White House access to offending journalists."[666] He continuously compared himself with other successful political figures, including Jack Kennedy. But when he would look at their relationships with the people and the press, for example, instead of working to model those relationships, he would instead feel resentful about the way he was treated.

He allowed his critics to get under his skin, to the point that it began to infect his Presidency. Nixon's inability to handle the criticism and opposition he faced as President led to increasingly poor decision-making, and unresourceful, paranoid thinking; which eventually precipitated an unnecessarily prolonged involvement in Vietnam, the Watergate scandal, and, ultimately, worldwide disgrace when he became the only president in U.S. history to resign from office. Nixon was indeed so incapable of handling criticism or managing his emotions that, if not for his other extraordinary political talents, it is unlikely he ever would have won any election at all, let alone the American presidency.

When most people find themselves in a position of increased visibility or responsibility, they often find themselves unprepared for the increased resistance, criticism and attacks. Lacking a strategy and plan, the increased pressure quickly begins to expose and magnify their weaknesses, thereby, escalating the resistance and attacks. The way to succeed here, is to see this resistance for what it is. This is not personal. This is about power. When you are no longer guided by your own inner purpose and principles, you lose power. When you control your emotions and accept the criticism and resistance as a natural part of the path to the top, you increase your power.

President Bill Clinton, for instance, has always considered himself to be a Christian of strong faith. Throughout his life he attended church regularly and frequently fellowshipped with other Christians. After he became President, however, he said that he was completely unprepared for the hate he experienced from some of the leaders in the Christian community. Naturally, attacks from those we consider to be a part of our own community can leave a mark. Nevertheless, Clinton consistently kept his emotions in check and, as a result, he was able to endure the unexpected attacks.

The heights to which you can climb will depend on your ability to acknowledge and accept criticism and then quickly let it go. Whatever attacks may come, learn as much as you can, but never let yourself take criticism personally. That is the path to failure. Understand: It's never really about you. The things your critics say will always reveal far more about themselves. Increased pressure and opposition often takes some time to get used to. And that's fine. Permit yourself to make some mistakes. But remember this: Criticism is a small price to pay for increased influence and power. Find ways of dealing with it and you will find it well worth it in the end. "It's all up to you," writes Chris Matthews in *The Hardball Handbook*. "If you want to push your ideas, ambitions, or dreams, you have to get out there and champion them. You need to be able to face rejection, hostility, and, more often, indifference. The higher your ambitions take you, the more stamina you'll need, the more willingness to get a "No!" slammed in your face. The more failure you can accept, the greater your chance of success."[667]

Truman succeeded because he was able to let go. He was often temporarily hijacked by his emotions, but he quickly returned to his own inner compass. You may never control your emotions completely. But you can learn resourceful strategies for dealing with criticism and managing your emotions more effectively. Even Abraham Lincoln had to find ways to deal with his anger. He would, for example, often write out "hot letters" when he was angry, later burning them in the fireplace after he had cooled down.[668] Like Lincoln, Harry Truman, in time, learned to more effectively manage his emotions, though never completely. But then something suddenly happened that left an indelible imprint, an experience that altered his outlook, and pressed him to adopt a much more resourceful perspective.

Get Perspective.

On December 5, 1950, President Truman's daughter Margaret Truman sang at Constitution Hall in Washington D.C. Her singing career had just begun a few years earlier, and her critics were not always so kind. But *Washington Post* music critic Paul Hume's review the following day was especially harsh. In fact, he wrote, "she cannot sing very well," and "she is flat a good deal of the time." Heaping on the insults, he concluded, "Miss Truman has not improved in the years we have heard her…she still cannot sing with anything approaching professional finish."[669]

When President Truman read the review the following morning, he was livid. He immediately and foolishly fired off a letter of rebuke to Hume on White House letterhead. He denounced the critic, saying that he was an "eight ulcer man on four ulcer pay."[670] "When you write such poppy-cock," Truman wrote, "as was in the back section of the paper you work for it shows conclusively that you're off the beam and at least four of your ulcers are at work."[671] Truman wrote that if he ever met the man, "you'll need a new nose, a lot of beefsteak for black eyes, and perhaps a supporter below!"[672]

The private letter was immediately leaked and carried on the front page of the nation's papers. Some Americans wrote in to support the President's emotional defense of his daughter. Far more criticized his lack of self-control. "Truly we have chosen a 'common' man President. Yes—very common," wrote one.[673] *The Chicago Tribune* warned the American people that Truman's "mental competence and emotional stability" were insufficient to remain in the Oval Office.[674] The general consensus was that Truman was taking himself far too seriously. And, in the context of the ongoing war in Korea, the timing of his outburst could not have been more misguided.

There was one letter, however, that seemed to have an enduring effect on Truman and his attitude toward his critics. It was a letter from a couple who had lost their son in Korea and the envelope included their sons' Purple Heart. "Mr. Truman," the letter began,

"As you have been directly responsible for the loss of our son's life in Korea, you might just as well keep this emblem on display in your trophy room, as a memory of one of your historic deeds. One major regret at this time is that your daughter was not there to receive the same treatment as our son received in Korea."[675]

For years, Truman kept that letter in his desk.[676] It was as if the entire incident provided Truman with some much needed perspective. In the context of war, in the face of thousands of American lives lost, Truman's concern over a critic's review of one of his daughter's talents was shockingly petty. It dramatized his extraordinary position of privilege and the awesome responsibilities he had to the American people. From this day forward, Truman would always have that Purple Heart to remind him of how truly fleeting and meaningless were the words of his critics.

Of course, the criticism, resistance and attacks never stopped. But now he would accept it as part of the territory. "If you can't stand the heat," he would say, "get out of the kitchen."[677]

With the ongoing war in Korea, racial tensions at home, charges of corruption against his administration, and the rise of McCarthyism, Truman's approval rating continued to sink throughout the remainder of his presidency.[678] Nevertheless, sticking to his principles and purpose, Truman forged ahead. Despite his unpopularity, he continued to ignore his critics and do what he thought was best for the country as a whole. "If you want a friend in Washington," he would joke, "get a dog." [679]

Alas, when his Presidency finally concluded, Truman was among the least popular political figures in the nation.[680] Fortunately, for him, however, he would live to see the redemption of his reputation. From the moment Truman left politics and returned to his private life in Missouri, his standing began to soar. With increasing time and distance, it became increasingly clear that Truman—throughout his tumultuous years in office—was making great decisions for the country, despite the harsh, unrelenting attacks of his critics. Assessments of his presidency began to change and, over time, it would be one of the greatest turnarounds in presidential politics. Particularly throughout the 1970s, continuing on after his death, esteem for Truman and his presidency continued to rise. Today, historians, political scientists, scholars of leadership and law consistently rank Truman within the top ten of America's greatest presidents, usually seventh.

Devalue the Critic.

Criticism is inevitable. The higher you climb, the more you can expect. The more others feel threatened by your power and success, the more enemies you will accumulate. Most people tend to back down in the face of fierce critics or powerful opponents. True hustlers, however, recognize this resistance as indications of their success and, thus, they forge ahead. History's heroes take the mindset of Alexander the Great who said, "There is something noble in hearing myself ill spoken of when I am doing well."[681]

Indeed, critics and adversaries are part and parcel of doing great things. "You have enemies?" asks Victor Hugo, "Why, it is the story of every man who has done a great deed or created a new idea. It is the cloud which thunders around everything that shines. Fame must have enemies, as light must have gnats. Do no bother yourself about it; disdain. Keep your mind serene as you keep your life clear."[682]

"It is not the critic who counts," said TR. It is your ability to deal with it that determines whether your succeed or fail. And it is your mindset that makes the difference. Forget whether or not the criticism and attacks you receive are accurate or fair. That's a distraction. Whatever criticism may come, respond with grace and poise. "Do not give your enemies the satisfaction of thinking that they cause you grief or pain. Be happy, be cheerful," writes Hugo, "be disdainful, be firm."[683] Focus your energy and attention on ways to turn them to your advantage instead.

Understand: There are times when you must answer the charges of your critics, and there are times when you must counter-attack. Controlling your emotions is the critical factor, never letting anyone get under your skin. "The best fighter is never angry," said the ancient Chinese philosopher Lao Tzu.[684] When you are unmoved by your opponents and critics, when you receive their attacks with self-assurance and grace, then you begin to elevate yourself. Then you will begin to win others over. Even many of your detractors will be seduced by your easy confidence, your seemingly effortless equanimity and power.

When the thirty-four year old gubernatorial candidate Huey Long burst on to the political scene in Louisiana, he faced opposition and resistance from nearly every corner, including the newspapers. It was unthinkable that some young upstart might steal the Governor's Mansion from the entrenched political elites. "One day you pick up the papers and see where I killed four priests," Long told a crowd of spectators at a country fair in Ascension Parish in 1927.[685] "Another day I murdered twelve nuns, and the next day I poisoned four hundred babies. I have not got time to answer all of them."[686]

Huey Long was never upset by the harsh, deceptive attacks he received. Instead, he turned them to his advantage, using them for both publicity, and to position himself in his listeners minds. He mocked and belittled his critics with his obvious exaggerations. In one swoop, he made them seem ridiculous and untrustworthy and, therefore, irrelevant. Equally important, he portrayed strength and power. Even though he often engaged in similarly sordid assaults, he projected an image of being above the guttersnipes, invincible to their attacks. And he did it all in a way that was endlessly entertaining. "Everywhere Huey campaigned, the newspapers followed. He made good copy and the papers gave him wide coverage," even as, according to Long biographer Richard White, "most of the reporting soundly denounced him."[687]

It's not that you're unaware of the criticism or that you don't learn what can be learned. It's that you are not injured by it, or diverted away from what matters most. In fact, sometimes the greatest damage is done when you fail to receive the criticism and feedback you need to succeed. "The trouble with most of us," said Norman Vincent Peale, "is that we would rather be ruined by praise than saved by criticism."[688]

Never Let Your Critics Determine Where Your Talents Lie.

After his first few attempts before the House of Commons failed, the Irish playwright and Member of Parliament Richard B. Sheridan was told that he would never be a good speaker. Sheridan, however, refused to believe it. "It is in me and shall come out," he said.[689] Years later, Sheridan gained a reputation for being one of the greatest orators of his day.[690] When Walt Disney first started out as a cartoonist, he struggled to survive. The newspapers kept turning him away. Some even suggested that he lacked talent and should try another field. But Walt didn't listen. Cartoons, animation, movies—this was all part of Disney's dream. And he didn't waver. Eventually he caught a break, invented Mickey Mouse, and the rest is history. Looking back over his life years later, Disney said, "All the adversity I've had in my life, all my troubles and obstacles, have strengthened me... You may not realize it when it happens, but a kick in the teeth may be the best thing in the world for you."[691]

Never let others decide what talents you do or do not have. Decide for yourself. The point is not to ignore legitimate, constructive feedback. The point is to be very careful about accepting what is both legitimate and constructive. It means you give yourself a bona fide chance to uncover talents that may, for the moment, be entirely undeveloped and, thus, hidden from view. It means you invest time in exploring your possibilities. And it means recognizing that "talent" may in fact be fundamentally overrated, and that it's really about putting in the thousands of hours of *deliberate* practice.[692] It means success has very little to do with your critics. It's really about grit.

Demand Debate—
Solicit Conflicting Perspectives and Constructive Criticism, Then Use it to Recalibrate.

When John F. Kennedy became President in 1961 the CIA's plan to assist Cuban exiles in overthrowing Fidel Castro's communist regime in Cuba was already well underway. Approved by President Eisenhower, it was not until after Kennedy's election that he was made aware of the clandestine operation. Within three months, however, all of his top advisors—a group of esteemed, educated men from Harvard—supported the CIA's invasion plan.

Nevertheless, the Bay of Pigs plan turned out to be a complete militaristic, political and diplomatic catastrophe. Irving Janis, author of *Groupthink*, writes: "The Kennedy administration's Bay of Pigs decision ranks among the worst fiascoes ever perpetrated by a responsible government."[693] Kennedy himself asked: "How could I have been so stupid to let them go ahead?"[694] He was livid. Privately, he told friends he wanted to "splinter the CIA in a thousand pieces and scatter it to the winds."[695] Publicly, however, Kennedy took full responsibility for the Bay of Pigs fiasco and did everything he could to make sure such a tragic blunder would never again happen on his watch.

Kennedy's handling of the CIA's invasion plan still stands today as a potent example of poor decision-making. What is perhaps most remarkable is the extent to which Kennedy and his advisors maintained a blind commitment to what, in hindsight, was a disastrous strategy for dealing with an unruly neighbor. James MacGregor Burns writes that the CIA, taking advantage of the young, new president, played right into "JFK's bias for action and eagerness to project strength."[696]

Arthur Schlesinger, a top aide to the President, describes sitting silently in group meetings deliberating the plan, surrounded by "a curious atmosphere of assumed consensus."[697] Pushing forward with an ill-conceived plan riddled with faulty assumptions, the level of groupthink operating around the President was so thick that openness to alternative interpretations and legitimate criticism was scarcely seen as an option.[698]

It was Kennedy's first major mishap as President. He failed to manage the personalities in his cabinet and, therefore, he failed to ensure he was getting the information and alternative perspectives that he needed in order to question and challenge their faulty assumptions, misguided perceptions and mistaken beliefs. Kennedy's apparent lack of openness to criticism and dissent—whether real or perceived—and his failure to effectively solicit thoughtful feedback and alternative interpretations resulted in the Executive Committee's failure to critically examine the CIA's strategy and goals, or to even consider other, potentially far more viable and legitimate, alternative actions. The defective plan was ultimately doomed from its inception.

Kennedy, in essence, failed the inner game of leadership. His confidence in himself and his team was overinflated. The fact that not a single member of his Executive Committee was opposed to the plan should have been a warning sign, triggering Kennedy to reassess his leadership of the team, their communications and collective decision-making. But instead, tragically, he read it as a genuine consensus to move ahead.

Robert Kennedy said later that he was surprised to learn how the men that made up his brother's cabinet shied away from expressing an opinion differing from that of the President. In his memoir of the Cuban Missile Crisis, *Thirteen Days*, he writes: "We had virtual unanimity at the time of the Bay of Pigs. At least, if any officials in the highest ranks of government were opposed, they did not speak out. Thereafter, I suggested there be a devil's advocate to give an opposite opinion if none was pressed."[699]

Kennedy's handling of the Cuban Missile Crisis a year and a half later stands as a story with stark contrasts.

Win the Inner Game—Stay Cool Under Fire:
Missiles, Soviets, Cuba and JFK

"Whoever is slow to anger is better than the mighty,
and he who rules his spirit than he who takes a city."
—Proverbs 16:32

On October 15, 1962, the U.S. intelligence apparatus discovered the installation and buildup of offensive nuclear weapons a mere 90 miles off the coast of Florida on the island of Cuba. Deployed under the leadership of Russian Premier Nikita Khrushchev, with the aid of Fidel Castro and his Marxist regime, these weapons were believed by many leaders in the Western hemisphere to be a threat to world peace, and a violation of the policies of the hemisphere.[700]

One week later, President Kennedy announced to the world that Soviet nuclear weapons had been discovered in Cuba and that he, as a result, ordered a naval "quarantine"—a blockade—of the island nation.[701] While he addressed his television audience, a presidential directive was underway which put all U.S. Armed Forces on DEFCON 3—high alert and increased readiness. Kennedy made it clear that the United States would not permit offensive nuclear weapons in Cuba, and he demanded that the ballistic missiles be dismantled and returned to the USSR.

Kennedy then voiced the crux of what historian Michael Beschloss later described as "probably the most alarming address ever delivered by an American president":[702] "This secret, swift, and extraordinary build-up of Communist missiles," Kennedy said, "...in violation of Soviet assurances, and in defiance of American and hemispheric policy...is a deliberately provocative and unjustified change in the status quo which cannot be accepted by this country if our courage and our commitments are ever to be trusted again by either friend or foe..."[703]

He then issued an unmistakable warning to Khrushchev and the Russians, "Should these offensive military preparations continue...further action will be justified...It shall be the policy of this nation to regard any nuclear missile launched from Cuba against any nation in the Western Hemisphere as an attack by the Soviet Union on the United States, requiring a full retaliatory response upon the Soviet Union."[704]

It was a shocking announcement. As the gravity of the crisis suddenly sucked the air out of the lungs of anyone who heard, a still silence swept across the nation. The world was at the brink of nuclear war. Witnesses described how people in homes, offices, pubs, and dorms—normally full of loud and rambunctious energy—were now suddenly speechless, motionless as Kennedy spoke. "My fellow citizens, let no one doubt that this is a difficult and dangerous effort on which we have set out. No one can foresee precisely what course it will take or what costs and casualties will be incurred."[705] Finally, Kennedy concluded with a call for "sacrifice and self-discipline" to face the unknown dangers ahead.[706]

Suddenly, the world was on edge. Nuclear war seemed imminent. People hung on every news bulletin. Protests broke out in friendly nations where many people opposed the belligerence of the world's two superpowers. People everywhere began stockpiling canned food, water, and supplies. Families drew closer and made emergency plans, while they completed any lingering work on their backyard bomb shelters. Many others felt helpless as they scurried through crowds with no clue where to turn. "I'm here because I feel completely hysterical about the world situation," said one young woman. "I don't know what else to do.[707]"

The weeks that followed the discovery of the surreptitious deployment of missiles in Cuba is widely considered "...the closest the world has come to World War III," and, quite possibly, the closest we have come to the extinction of humankind.[708] Arthur M. Schlesinger Jr., Special Assistant to the President, called it "the most dangerous moment in human history."[709]

Thirteen days and many sleepless nights later, the intense internal deliberations of Kennedy's Executive Committee of the National Security Council (ExComm), and the delicate, precarious negotiations between Kennedy and Khrushchev appeared to reach a resolution. But as the Soviet ships continued to sail directly toward the U.S. Naval blockade, everyone held their breath. Had Khrushchev been bluffing? Was he backing out? Was an insubordinate General acting on his own? "The great danger and risk in all of this," the President said to his brother, Attorney General Robert Kennedy, "is a miscalculation—a mistake in judgment."[710]

Keep Mistakes in Context,
Create a Buffer to Absorb the Inevitable Mishaps and Miscalculations.

President Kennedy's seemingly insignificant remark to his brother reveals what was in actuality an invaluable understanding of both the precariousness of the situation and the critical need to remain cool. Missteps, miscommunication, and misjudgments are endemic to any significant undertaking. Alas, in the midst of a crisis between two hostile actors, a single miscalculation could prove catastrophic. Kennedy's understanding of the need to remain calm and collected and, more importantly, his ability to do so was critical.

In stark contrast to Kennedy's coolness under fire, a few of the members of ExComm—particularly General Curtis LeMay—were operating with little apparent restraint. Willing and ready to escalate tensions so as not to appear weak, these men appeared to have little concern or understanding for how quickly and easily the situation could spiral completely out of control, resulting in a nuclear exchange, and the loss of potentially millions of lives on both continents.

When President Kennedy asked General LeMay how he thought Khrushchev would respond to force from the United States, "General LeMay assured him there would be no reaction."[711] It was an absurd assumption. LeMay was clueless. Too often men like LeMay have an irrational fear of *appearing* weak. Their idea of courage gets warped into bold recklessness. In their minds, anything that might be misinterpreted as weakness, wreaks of cowardice. But even Theodore Roosevelt—celebrated for his courage, and well-known for his readiness to fight provided there was *just cause*—said that, when people are facing dangerous situations, "What such a man needs is not courage but nerve control, coolheadedness."[712] Fortunately, in the case of LeMay, the President remained unconvinced.

Building on his failed experience with the Bay of Pigs Invasion, Kennedy was further influenced by his recent reading of the origins of World War I. His brother Robert writes of the President, "A short time before, he had read Barbara Tuchman's book *The Guns of August*, and he talked about the miscalculations of the Germans, the Russians, the Austrians, the French and the British. They somehow seemed to tumble into war, he said, through stupidity, individual idiosyncrasies, misunderstandings, and personal complexes of inferiority and grandeur."[713] Kennedy was determined not to let that happen to them. "We were not going to misjudge, or miscalculate, or challenge the other side needlessly, or precipitously push our adversaries into a course of action that was not intended or anticipated."[714] In fact, Kennedy was even prepared to absorb a few less consequential offenses in order to avoid a much greater loss.

The President's will was tested on October 27, when U.S. Air Force Major Rudolf Anderson Jr. was shot out of the sky while piloting a U-2 reconnaissance plane over Cuba. A couple of Kennedy's military leaders immediately urged him to launch airstrikes in response.[715] However, believing—correctly, as it turned out—that the strike was not approved by Khrushchev, Kennedy again kept his cool. Fearing that a retaliatory strike would end in all-out war, Kennedy said, "It isn't the first step that concerns me, but both sides escalating to the fourth or fifth step and we don't go to the sixth because there is no one around…"[716]

Khrushchev was likewise grasping the slippery, perilous path they were on, and the need to maintain a cool restraint. Khrushchev's son Sergei would later write, "It was at that very moment—not before or after—that father felt the situation was slipping out of his control."[717] The surface-to-air missile that killed Major Anderson could easily have become the trigger of World War III. Instead, it was the incident that began the de-escalation of the crisis.[718]

Master Coolness: Maintain Grace Under Pressure.

History teems with tales of those who remained cool under pressure, and achieved important triumphs as a result. Lincoln, JFK, Eleanor Roosevelt, Gandhi, Mandela and King were all famously cool under intense pressure—as was Jackie Robinson in the heat of segregated sports. Indeed, Robinson's ability to perform at the plate while being loudly ridiculed by racist spectators was a testament to his nerves of steel. Too often we give in to our emotions. We may start out determined not to let our emotions rule our responses, but in the heat of an argument, a battle, or a public performance we lose our footing and begin to respond to whatever impulse arises. Human beings are emotional creatures. It is normal to be moved by our feelings and moods. But giving ourselves over to our emotions is never the path to personal power and success. In the words of Stephen Covey, author of *The Seven Habits of Highly Effective People*, "The ability to subordinate an impulse to a value is the essence of the proactive person."[719] Your success depends on your ability to manage your emotions. To begin to unleash your true potential and achieve your greater purpose, you must learn to subordinate your moods and emotions to your objectives and goals.

Jackie Robinson was a fighter who was not afraid to stand up against racial injustice. When Branch Rickey—club president and general manager of the Brooklyn Dodgers—began looking to bring Robinson onto the team as the first black player (both for his superb athletic ability and his high moral character), he had one overriding concern: Could Robinson keep his emotions in check when it mattered most?

Rickey knew that Robinson was arrested while in the Army for refusing to move to the back of a segregated bus. He also knew that the racism in the Major Leagues would likely be brutal, and that an angry response from Robinson could spoil their shared ambition to integrate the sport. When Rickey asked Robinson if he thought he could face the racism without reacting in anger, Robinson was taken aback, "Are you looking for a Negro who is afraid to fight back?" Robinson asked.[720] Rickey responded, "I'm looking for a ballplayer with enough guts not to fight back."[721]

Robinson soon resolved to "turn the other cheek" and, with a few initial bumps along the way, the rest was history. Scott Simon, author of *Jackie Robinson and the Integration of Baseball*, writes, "The valor with which Jackie Robinson responded to the jeers and the hatred and the bigoted remarks and the catcalls is one of the great silent portraits in American history. Under that hail of threats and epithets he would walk into the batter's box…and get a hit. That's what he did. He certainly didn't cower. He certainly didn't flinch."[722] In 1947, the same year he joined the Major Leagues, Jackie Robinson was named Rookie of the Year. In 1949, he was voted Most Valuable Player. And in 1962, he was inducted into the Baseball Hall of Fame. Jackie Robinson mastered more than the game of baseball. He mastered the inner game, and his example of remaining cool under pressure continues to inspire to this day.

Maintain Restraint.

Jack Kennedy also had to learn to manage his emotions, and keep his ego in check. Yet, he too learned to master the inner game, remaining rational and cool under one of the most stressful and potentially catastrophic confrontations in human history.

When the Russian ships continued to advance toward the U.S. Naval blockade, despite recent assurances from Khrushchev that they had an agreement, time seemed to stand still. Why were the Soviet ships still advancing? What should they do? With his generals following his lead, Kennedy kept his cool—and it paid off.

Suddenly, Khrushchev ordered the Soviet ships to stop. Then, within minutes, the ships began to turn around and head home.

"We are eyeball to eyeball, and I think the other fellow just blinked," said Dean Rusk, Kennedy's Secretary of State.[723] The Soviets backed down. Khrushchev agreed to remove the missiles. The bold and bombastic Cold War combatant's reckless maneuver collapsed, and ended in retreat.[724] CBS News broadcaster Charles Collingwood called it a "humiliating defeat for Soviet policy."[725]

Looking back decades later, MIT's Noam Chomsky wrote, "The events of October 1962 are widely hailed as Kennedy's finest hour. Graham Allison joins many others in presenting them as 'a guide for how to defuse conflicts, manage great-power relationships, and make sound decisions about foreign policy in general.' In a very narrow sense, that judgment seems reasonable," writes Chomsky.[726] "The ExComm tapes reveal that the president stood apart from others, sometimes almost all others, in rejecting premature violence."[727]

Kennedy, together with Khrushchev's reluctant (yet heroic) compliance, successfully averted a nuclear holocaust as well as the potentially crippling political and diplomatic position of the United States with the rest of the world—but not without a price. In exchange for removing the missiles, Kennedy agreed to make a public declaration that the United States would not invade Cuba, unless there was a direct provocation. Privately, Kennedy also agreed to secretly remove the nuclear missile installations that existed—unknown to the public—in Turkey and Italy. Though the missiles in Turkey were technically obsolete, removal represented a weakened commitment to an ally.[728]

The crisis proved to be a sobering learning experience for both nations. A key takeaway for Kennedy was the extent to which it reinforced his understanding of how events themselves can take over; how mishaps, misunderstandings, mistakes and miscalculations can lead to an unpredictable and often uncontrollable chain of events that ends in consequences that neither party either anticipated or desired. The wisdom gained from the crisis echoed the sentiments of Abraham Lincoln following the end of slavery and the triumphant conclusion of the Civil War. "I attempt no compliment to my own sagacity," Lincoln said, "I claim not to have controlled events, but confess plainly that events have controlled me."[729]

An understanding of the powerful, unruly forces at play did not foster in Lincoln or Kennedy a sense of helplessness—quite the opposite. It heightened the urgent need to be at the top of their game. The more volatile, uncertain, complex and ambiguous the situation, the greater the necessity of effective leadership, critical thinking and rational decision-making. In the case of Kennedy and Khrushchev, the crisis reinforced the need for perspective and humility and the value of putting oneself in the other's shoes. And, thus, it reinforced and dramatized the need to remain calm, collected and cool. In essence, it highlighted the immeasurable value of being unshakable. And, as the record reveals, Kennedy succeeded brilliantly. "Kennedy was the coolest man in the room," Lyndon Johnson said later.[730] And, Arthur M. Schlesinger praised the 'mathematical precision' with which Kennedy calibrated his threats of force against Cuba and the Soviet Union and the 'composure, clarity and control' the president displayed."[731] "It was this combination," he wrote in *A Thousand Days: John F. Kennedy in the White House*, "of toughness and restraint, of will, nerve and wisdom, so brilliantly controlled, so matchlessly calibrated, that dazzled the world."[732]

Of course, it wasn't just Kennedy. "The real good fortune," writes Michael Dobbs in *One Minute to Midnight*, "is that men as sane and level headed as John Fitzgerald Kennedy and Nikita Sergeyevich Khrushchev occupied the White House and the Kremlin in October 1962."[733]

"He who controls others may be powerful, but he who has mastered himself is mightier still."
—Lao Tzu (Circa 5th Century B.C.), Ancient Chinese Philosopher

Be Unshakable, Manage Emotion to Facilitate Grit.

The pressures you face in pursuit of your own ambitions, and the potential consequences of your actions will of course never be as severe as they were for Kennedy and Khrushchev during the Cuban Missile Crisis. Nevertheless, mastering your emotions, and maintaining an outer confidence and inner cool can be equally transformational in your own individual life, no matter what challenge you face. Whatever your ambition or goal—whether it's succeeding in business, winning public office, defeating a competitor in sports, or an enemy in war, or even pursuing a potential mate—the inner game is indispensable to your success.

Inner game is essentially what's happening in your head. It's the inner dialogue or self-talk that emerges from your beliefs and assumptions, principles and values, perceptions and perspectives, your personal theories, hidden rules and rules of thumb. Inner game is what lets you overcome outer limitations (whether they be physical characteristics, health or financial difficulties, or a lack of education or experience). And this is key because, "You have power over your mind," wrote the Roman Emperor

Marcus Aurelius, "not outside events."[734]   "Realize this," he wrote, "and you will find strength."[735]

Winning the inner game is about effectively mastering your mind and emotions. It's about maintaining your confidence, composure, and cool. This is the frame of mind and emotional state that allows you to receive the input, feedback, and criticism you need to succeed. This is what allows you to invite dissenting opinions, consider alternative perspectives, and review conflicting information without defaulting to a predetermined response.

Virtually everyone has certain emotional triggers which, when pulled, can derail them from their plans. The more easily and often you are derailed, the more your goals and dreams are at risk. Strong emotions can be a powerful ally, but only when they are harnessed and directed toward worthwhile ends. Misdirected, imbalanced or unchecked emotions, whether positive or negative, can be a barrier to perseverance and grit. Impulsiveness and overconfidence can be just as detrimental to your plans and goals as unbridled anger, desperation or fear. It is a clear, stable mind and a cool, steady hand that enables you to persist with your plans. It is emotional stability that facilitates grit. "What makes your mind stronger, and more able to control your emotions, is internal discipline and toughness."[736] You can not expect to maintain your resolve when you lose control of your emotions. Nor can you expect to master your emotions overnight. You can, however, make significant progress by adopting some of the strategies and tactics of the legends of cool.

Let No One Rattle Your Cage.

Our emotions are easily influenced by others, particularly when the emotions of others are strong, and perceived as authentic. Thus, part of managing your emotions and moods includes managing or resisting the emotional contagion of others.

This was a critical component of the challenge that Kennedy and Khrushchev faced during the Cuban Missile Crisis. A number of the military leaders on both sides were characteristically eager to get into action. Nikita Khrushchev had a particularly difficult time keeping his internal aggressors at bay. But Kennedy also had a handful of the military's top brass who were eager to carry out an all-inclusive attack, including an invasion of Cuba. One particularly belligerent General, Curtis LeMay, nicknamed "The Demon"[737] and "Bombs Away,"[738] supported a full-scale attack on Cuba throughout the crisis. According to LeMay's logic, "If you kill enough of them, they stop fighting."[739]

The bombshell, however, was that LeMay still insisted on the use of force even after the crisis had been resolved. "'After Khrushchev had agreed to remove the missiles, President Kennedy invited the Chiefs to the White House so that he could thank them for their support during the crisis, and there was one hell of a scene. LeMay came out saying, 'We lost! We ought to just go in there today and knock 'em off!'"[740]

Another one of the Joint Chiefs, Admiral George Anderson, was similarly upset. "We have been had," he said angrily.[741] Kennedy, fortunately, writes Noam Chomsky, "repeatedly rejected the militant advice of his advisers and associates who called for military force and dismissal of peaceful options."[742] He remained unrattled by the hawks, and cooler heads prevailed. Had one of these men been President, their apparent inability to manage their emotions might have cost the world dearly.

Kennedy was able to maintain his composure, in part, because he didn't allow himself to be the exclusive audience or target of the alternative views. In fact, in contrast to the Bay of Pigs fiasco, Kennedy intentionally sought out conflicting perspectives. He played members of ExComm off of one another rather than responding to each position or argument himself. In essence, he acted as facilitator, leading the members through a rational dialogue and reasoned debate. What's more, he used questions to respond to disagreements, which allowed him to probe deeper, or even subtly challenge positions or arguments that he saw as weak, rather than getting caught up in an emotional debate. In essence, Erwin Hargrove writes in *The Effective Presidency*, "He did not so much manage the process as guide it. He asked hard questions and gradually felt his way to a decision."[743] All this allowed him to make the wisest decisions possible—given the knowledge, experience, intelligence, wisdom, and insight of ExComm—rather than making decisions that were primarily driven by emotions.

Reframe Resistance, Reassess Threats: Doc Holliday and the O.K. Corral

"If there is no contradictory impression, there is nothing to awaken reflection."
—Plato (427—347 B.C.), Philosopher in Classical Greece

In the events leading up to the infamous Gunfight at the O.K. Corral in Tombstone, Arizona in 1881, outlaw Ike Clanton had been stirring up trouble in town. The loud-mouth, quick-tempered outlaw was notorious for his heavy drinking and public boasting. He and his brothers were members of "The Cowboys"—a loose gang of cattle thieves and stagecoach robbers—and they were constantly pushing up against the law.

Ike Clanton had been spreading rumors that Doc Holliday, and his friends and lawmen Virgil, Morgan, and Wyatt Earp had been involved in the Benson stagecoach robbery, which left two people dead. Encountering the outlaw at a saloon one night, Doc Holliday publicly called Ike Clanton out as a liar. A disorderly dispute ensued as Clanton, who was already drunk and running his mouth, was angered and publicly humiliated by the incident.

Following the intervention of his friend, Tombstone City Marshal Virgil Earp, Holliday headed to bed at Fly's boarding house. Meanwhile, Ike Clanton stayed up. And he continued to drink. By the time dawn neared, Clanton had been drinking all night and was now threatening to kill Doc Holliday and the Earps. According to witnesses, Clanton was outside Holliday's hotel room howling like a coyote. Clanton, according to Ned Boyle, a bartender at the Oriental, "said that as soon as the Earps and Doc Holliday showed themselves on the street, the ball would open, and that they would have to fight."[744]

As word of Clanton's threats spread, the townspeople grew increasingly anxious, and began to fear that a showdown between the legendary lawmen and the infamous Cowboys was imminent. Suddenly, once day broke, the boarding house proprietor rushed in to wake Doc Holliday, telling him that Clanton had been howling like a coyote all night, threatening to kill him and the Earps as soon as he saw them.

Doc Holliday, famously cool-headed and quick on the draw, was unfazed. As he struggled to open his eyes after a night of drinking, he turned toward the woman and coolly remarked, "I read about a coyote's howling in a book once. It's supposed to be a warning;" Holliday said, as he looked at her with one eye squinting, "the truth is, they only howl when they're scared."[745]

Virgil Earp deputized Doc Holliday later that morning as they, along with Wyatt and Morgan Earp, prepared for a confrontation with Clanton and the outlaw Cowboys.

When the two sides finally met that afternoon near the O.K. Corral, their guns were drawn. Yet, Ike Clanton, after spending the better part of the day threatening to kill Holliday and the Earps, saying, "that they would have to fight on sight," now ran forward crying to Wyatt that he did not want to fight and that he was unarmed.[746] Wyatt pushed Ike back saying, "Go to fighting or get away."[747] With that, Clanton immediately ran off through Fly's boarding house and escaped. In the famous 30-second gunfight that immediately followed, three Cowboys were dead. Virgil, Morgan, and Doc Holliday were grazed by bullets, but all quickly recovered. Wyatt Earp walked away without a scratch.

Reframing is a powerful tool for dealing with criticism, threats, opposition and resistance, and there are countless ways it can be done. In the case of Doc Holliday and the Earps, rather than letting Ike Clanton and the Cowboys get under their skin, or absorbing the fear that the other townspeople felt, they reframed the loud public threats as the cries of frightened cowards.

Shifting paradigms and changing frames is useful not only in dealing with opposition and resistance, but can also be a game changer in terms of overcoming entrenched obstacles, making leaps of progress, or simply attaining strategic goals. In fact, one of key lessons from the Cuban Missile Crisis (i.e. the incredible ease with which a miscalculation could slip into a nuclear confrontation) lead both sides to rethink nuclear weapons and the strategy of "mutually assured destruction" (MAD) as a viable deterrent. Rather than leading to increased hostilities between the two superpowers, the prospect of nuclear war and the recognition that they were much closer to mutually assured destruction than they previously imagined, led them to see each other in a new light. The crisis caused a paradigm shift. It provided a rationale and became an *opportunity* for a reduction in tensions. They began to see, perhaps for the first time, how their own survival depended on better communication and cooperation with their purported *enemy*. This, in turn, led to the installation of a direct telephone line from the Oval Office to the Kremlin, and talks on nuclear test bans and non-proliferation treaties followed soon after.

Crises, accidents and disasters have a way of breaking even the most stubborn people out of old, ineffective patterns of thinking. But why wait? It's not difficult to identify useless or harmful perspectives or unresourceful points of view (e.g. just look for where the pain is, then start examining the relevant underlying assumptions and beliefs). Whatever criticism, resistance, or opposition you face, it is how you see it—your perspective, paradigm, or frame—that matters most. Is your perspective limiting your options or reducing your power, or are you adopting the most resourceful point of view? "If you are distressed by anything external," wrote the Roman emperor Marcus Aurelius, "the pain is not due to the thing itself, but to your estimate of it; and this you have the power to revoke at any moment."[748] Get in the practice of reframing opposition and resistance so that your options are increased and your position or power is strengthened. You may find that the criticism you face is not the howling of a fierce hunter, but the cries of a coward—and your increased insight and awareness on the matter will lead to a far more resourceful response.

Build Capacity to Detach:
Roosevelt the Cyclone Assemblyman

Not long after Theodore Roosevelt first entered the New York State Assembly in 1882 he was emerging as a fearless, young reformer with a bright future. He was unafraid to confront the corrupt controlling forces that ruled New York, including the powerful New York Supreme Court judge Theodore Westbrook and the notoriously crooked financier Jay Gould. TR railed against the bribery, corruption, and fraud with rousing speeches in the Assembly, warning his fellow legislators, "You cannot cleanse the leper. Beware lest you taint yourselves with this leprosy."[749]

The press was taking notice. "It is with the greatest satisfaction," wrote *Harper's Weekly*, "that those who are interested in good government see a young man in the Legislature who...does not know the meaning of fear, and to whom the bluster and bravado of party and political bullies are as absolutely indifferent as the blowing of the wind."[750]

In his second term, at only twenty-four, he was already the head of his party as Minority Leader. And he was as eager as ever to disrupt the status quo, reform the government, and bring change to New York. The young legislator was proving to be a hurricane of energy and emotion, bolting into rooms "as if ejected from a catapult."[751] Itching to gain the floor, Roosevelt thought nothing of shouting at the speaker for over a half an hour.[752] "Mis-tah-Spee-kar! Mis-tah-Spee-kar!" he would carry on until he was recognized. TR soon became known as "the Cyclone Assemblyman."[753]

Alas, rising so quickly, he began to get carried away by his success. He began to think of himself as right about everything. He was unable to step outside of himself to consider another point of view. His own friends griped, "He won't listen to anybody. He thinks he knows it all."[754] "He showed a dangerous tendency to see even the most complicated issues simply in terms of good and evil. As a result," writes Edmund Morris in *The Rise of Theodore Roosevelt*, "his speeches often sounded insufferably pious."[755] Before long, his rapid rise began to reverse.

He continued to stand for reform and against corruption, but his ego was clouding his judgment. He wanted what he believed was right and good, but his fight for reform was increasingly about *him*, about whether or not *he* could beat the crooks and their machine. "It was not that he did not love politics," one legislator remembered, "and know the game well enough from the start—but he loved himself more."[756]

Intent on tackling the widespread corruption, he charged ahead even more vigorously, unaware that he was increasingly standing alone. He moved with reckless haste. He failed to build a coalition or establish a solid case. More and more Theodore was seen as "a destructive force in the House. Indeed, Roosevelt seemed better at scattering the legislation of other men than whipping up any of his own."[757]

When he proved unable to produce legislative victories, he began to imagine that the whole legislature was corrupt. It seemed as if simply disagreeing with him meant that you were crooked.[758]

"What's got into Roosevelt?" his friends complained.[759] Rather than stepping back to see the big picture, Roosevelt hunkered down. "Before he knew what was happening, his influence had evaporated. He was a leader without a following—the laughing-stock of his enemies, the despair of his friends."[760]

The newspapers began calling him, "His Lordship."[761] No longer was it just Jay Gould's *World*, but several newspapers were now coming down on the "Dude" from New York.

Control Your Impulses. Pause, Step Back, and Detach.

In March of 1883, Roosevelt delivered a speech that hastened his decline, and nearly wrecked his career. After Governor Cleveland vetoed a bill that would have reduced Jay Gould's Manhattan Elevated Railroad fare from ten to five cents, on the grounds that it was unconstitutional—a bill that Roosevelt eagerly and publicly supported—TR immediately reversed his position. He hastily, heedlessly decided that Cleveland was right, and he had been wrong. To everyone else, however, TR looked like a fool.

It wasn't that he should or should not have voted for the bill. At issue was the sense that he was being driven not by a consistent set of principles or political beliefs, but by unmitigated emotion. Wholly unnecessary and inappropriate, his speech smacked of egotism. "I have to say with shame that when I voted for this bill I did not act as I think I ought to have acted," he said frankly, "...I have to confess that I weakly yielded, partly to a vindictive spirit toward the infernal thieves who have the Elevated Railroad in charge, and partly in answer to the popular voice of New York."[762]

Furthermore, as he came out supporting the veto which greatly benefited Jay Gould he simultaneously attacked "Gould and all of his associates," arguing that, "they have done all possible harm to this community, with their hired newspapers, with their corruption of the judiciary and of this House. ...It is not a question of doing right to them. They are common thieves...they belong to that most dangerous of all classes, the wealthy criminal class."[763]

TR's speech caused an uproar in the press. When he was ridiculed by the newspapers—both hostile and friendly papers alike—rather than recognizing his error or stepping back to reevaluate, "Roosevelt doubled down."[764] He was bitter and resentful and unable to step back.

Theodore Roosevelt was flailing. He was so caught up with himself and carried away by his initial success, that he was unable to pause, step back and detach. Driven by impulse, he had lost his way. He had been assaulted by his opponents before, but now they were all on the attack. "For the first time in his career, both friends and enemies seemed genuinely outraged."[765]

"If Roosevelt had been a hero to the press before," writes Edmund Morris, "he now found himself its favorite clown. Democratic newspapers joyfully quoted his 'silly and scandalous gabble' and intimated that he, too, was a member of 'the wealthy criminal class.' He was dubbed 'The Chief of the Dudes,' and satirized as a tight-trousered snob, given to sucking the knob of an ivory cane."[766] New York's newspapers began to print that young Roosevelt's career was over.

Despite widespread criticism, Roosevelt was proving slow to learn. "A day or so after the Five-Cent debacle, Theodore again let his emotions get the best of him."[767] Having lost all perspective, he was at the mercy of his own emotions. David McCullough writes in *Mornings on Horseback*, "He was acting as though he were under some kind of emotional strain, seemed not to know how to handle himself."[768] Unable to distance himself from his feelings of frustration over recent events, he again lashed out with another "grandstand play on the floor, suddenly tendering his resignation from a committee" before launching into a speech McCullough describes as "a wild, childish diatribe against the whole Democratic Party. It was as if, like the tiny shrew in the cage, he would fling himself at the great Democratic snake and tear it to pieces before anyone knew what happened."[769] His speech was a rash and disastrous show of emotion, incoherence and egotism. "He was proving himself a pompous know-it-all that nobody wanted to follow."[770] "Worse, the more pushback he received, the more independently radical he acted. The more radically he acted, the less people wanted to follow him. Theodore's impulsiveness derailed any chance he had to lead."[771]

Explore Alternative Frames

Roosevelt had clearly been wrapped up in his own success. He had been carried away by his swollen pride and unhindered emotional reactions to events. "Years later, in a letter to his son, he would admit that he lost perspective."[772] "Success had come to him too fast."[773] He had risen "like a rocket," he said, "and the result was I came an awful cropper, and had to pick myself up after learning by bitter experience the lesson that I was not all-important and that I had to take account of many different elements in life."[774]

Rather than taking a step back to get some distance, to try to look at things more objectively, or from alternative perspectives; when the inevitable opposition, resistance and criticism arrived, he abruptly reacted from an emotional state. Roosevelt's ego was at the helm, and it was undermining everything he was trying to do. "I suppose that my head was swelled," Roosevelt later admitted to his friend Jacob Riis.[775] "It would not be strange if it was. I stood out for my own opinion, alone. ...My own conscience, my own judgment, were to decide in all things. I would listen to no argument, no advice. I took the isolated peak on every issue, and my people left me."[776] "When I looked around...I found myself alone. I was absolutely deserted."[777]

By allowing himself to be impulsively driven by his own thoughts and feelings alone, Roosevelt said, "My isolated peak had become a valley; every bit of influence I had was gone. The things I wanted to do I was powerless to accomplish."[778] "The result was that I speedily and deservedly lost all power of accomplishing anything at all; and I thereby learned the invaluable lesson that in the practical activities of life no man can render the highest service unless he can act in combination with his fellows, which means a certain amount of give-and-take between him and them."[779]

The critical issue for young Theodore was that he was too eager to succeed. His goals were laudable, but his deep emotional attachment to those goals was undermining his efforts. He was like an exposed nerve. There was no space between stimulus and response. One young, fellow reformer, Isaac Hunt, was asked about Roosevelt's temperament years later. "No," Hunt said when asked if Roosevelt was cool.[780] "He was just like a Jack coming out of the box; there wasn't anything cool about him. He yelled and pounded his desk, and when they attacked him, he would fire back with all the venom imaginary. In those days he had no discretion at all. He was the most indiscreet guy I ever met..."[781]

This is the problem with those who are driven by their moods and emotions rather than their purpose and goals: They are ineffective. They lose influence with others. They are often powerless to accomplish anything at all.

Learning to detach gives you the advantage of your greatest and most powerful asset: Your mind. Clear, rational thinking is far simpler when you are able to distance yourself from your emotions. When your mind is calm and your emotions are cool, it is much easier to explore alternative frames, to see things from another's point of view.

Get Outside of Yourself, See Things from Another Point of View.

Throughout the Cuban Missile Crisis, Kennedy kept putting himself in Khrushchev's shoes. When the crisis was finally ending, Kennedy could easily imagine the distress and humiliation that Khrushchev was experiencing in the midst of the Russian retreat. Given the gravity of the circumstances they had just navigated, and the pitfalls that still lay ahead, Kennedy understood that their fragile resolution could be easily weakened or even reversed. He knew that humility was the proper response from the Americans and, therefore, he quickly warned his jubilant aides not to gloat.[782]

But it was not just with Khrushchev. Kennedy worked to see things from the perspective of others throughout the crisis. Of course, he valued his own background and experience, but he was not so foolish as to imagine that he could see all that he needed to see in any given situation.

The failed Bay of Pigs Invasion was a humiliating, yet powerful, learning experience for Kennedy. By the time of the Cuban Missile Crisis a year and a half later, several key leadership lessons had been learned. By mastering the inner game of politics and power, and learning to more effectively manage his and others' emotions, Kennedy was able to expand his capacity for high stakes leadership, which, in part, translated to a number of strategic insights and more practical tactics. In fact, in stark contrast to the decision making that took place prior to the Bay of Pigs Invasion, from the very beginning of the missile crisis, Kennedy adapted the conditions of decision making within his group of advisors and, consequently, he emerged with a far more effective set of solutions. More specifically, President Kennedy adopted several tactics in an attempt to ensure a more effective outcome, some of which included: (1) Establishing new role definitions, (2) Assigning a rotating devil's advocate, (3) Having periodic leaderless meetings, (4) Mixing up the group participants at different times, (5) Seeking out reports that offered conflicting or alternative views, (6) Holding meetings of subgroups, (7) Encouraging debate, and (8) Scheduling changes in the group atmosphere.[783]

Identify a Friendly Critic, Receive Feedback from Those You Respect.

Detachment is a powerful tactic for dealing with difficult problems and people. Criticism, opposition and resistance are handled best with the calm, coolness of mind that comes from being able to mentally separate yourself from your situation. Whether an outward *show* of emotion is appropriate or not (sometimes it is); a calm, collected, inner coolness always beats out the overwrought.

Getting distance can be difficult. The more something means to you, the more difficult it is to separate yourself from it. Learning to loosen your grip and detach yourself from circumstances requires self-control and strength of mind. This is where a trusted team, advisor, or friend can be especially valuable. Strength and synergy can be reaped from the simple fact that they are different people with different experiences, backgrounds, beliefs, frames of reference, and points of view. The more you are able to get outside of yourself and your own narrow view, the more wisdom will be accessible to you.

Effectively dealing with criticism and opposition is often about the people with whom you surround yourself. Find people who can provide a reality check on your assumptions, share constructive feedback, help you see yourself the way others see you, offer alternative interpretations, challenge misguided beliefs, or help you see things from a broader, more complete and resourceful perspective. Whatever helps you to increase your capacity to detach, to get outside of yourself, and see things in a fresh, innovative, and resourceful way can be tremendously valuable, and will expand your capacity for high achievement.

Getting the distance and perspective you need to succeed can be particularly challenging for those in positions of great power (not many people are confident, or skilled enough, to tell their king he isn't wearing any clothes), especially for those who fall into young Theodore's trap of thinking they know better than everyone else. This is precisely what has made Donald Trump's 2016 campaign for president both scandalously entertaining and predictably precarious: Trump appears to lack the capacity (or at least the inclination) to pause, step back, reflect and assess. What's more, there appears to be very few who can help him to see himself, his words, and actions from a distance, in a broader context, or from other conflicting, yet equally legitimate, points of view.

Alas, when an occasional bit of feedback does penetrate Trump's defenses, he largely neglects to receive it in a way that could prove considerably helpful. Trump, for instance, has admitted that his wife Melania and daughter Ivanka told him that he needed to "act presidential."[784] Yet, he has, thus far, remained unfazed. He said that he enjoys being "unpresidential" too much. While the Republican establishment believes this is his biggest weakness with voters, Trump is determined to do things his own way. "I don't care," he says. "It's so much fun for me. I love doing it. Please don't take that away from me!"[785]

There is no doubt that Trump's campaign has been, in part, a great gamble by a savvy showman, who has proven to be a masterful manipulator of the media. It has been equally clear, however, that Trump has been at times tightly, emotionally wound up in his presidential campaign. Trump appears impulsive by nature. He lacks a filter. He shoots from the hip. And this makes him both highly entertaining, and highly susceptible to error. In the words of *The New York Times*, "Trump is a high-risk candidate who is in constant danger of self-immolation."[786]

No doubt, it is refreshing to hear *any* political candidate speaking their mind. And Trump's (apparent) candor and occasional outrageousness has greatly contributed to his near constant, "earned" (i.e. free) media coverage—which has been tremendously beneficial to his campaign (to the tune of an astonishing two billion dollars).[787] It is a mistake, however, to imagine that Trump's surprising success as a candidate does not leave room for significant improvement.

Trump is a smart guy, he is often witty, and a fair amount of what he says makes sense. Too often, however, when things start to heat up, he lacks the cool detachment he needs to offer a more effective and resourceful response. Whether he is reacting to a slump in the polls, criticism in the media, attacks from his opponents, or simply challenging questions; Trump consistently reveals a lack of restraint. Worse still, when he does screw up, and is immediately attacked by his opponents or criticized by the press, he gets further wound up and proceeds to double or triple down on his original remarks, refusing to learn and correct course (never mind making amends for any damage done). It's as if he is unable to let go and get the distance he needs to hear even the most legitimate criticism. "Trump does not back down, retract, or apologize, ever, not even for the most trivial thing."[788]

As a result, he may come off as strong with his supporters, but he misses an opportunity to expand his base. Rather than listening to the feedback, and adjusting course as needed, he comes off as being rash, brash, and—as his own wife and daughter have cautioned—unpresidential.

Trump's apolitical approach to campaigning affords him considerable latitude in terms of gaffes and a lack of polish. Tapping into the anger and fear of his followers also fosters a degree of loyalty to him that is far more accepting and forgiving of his blunders than the media or the political establishment appears capable of recognizing. Nevertheless, lacking the capacity or tendency to pause, step back and take stock, Trump is far less likely to recognize his errors, learn from his experience, and gain the wisdom and understanding he needs to win the presidency, even if he was able to bulldoze his way through to the Republican nomination. Like Icarus, Trump keeps flying higher and higher, unaware that the sun is melting the wax that binds his wings, and he will soon come crashing down. The only question seems to be whether he can make his opponents fall first.

Be the Witness: Observe Your Emotions, Never Be Captive to Them.

John F. Kennedy's ability to remain collected and cool stands in stark contrast to Donald Trump. Whereas Trump's emotions are often triggered by minor infractions, rarely would anyone get a rise out of JFK. In fact, Kennedy said, "I don't think I ever react emotionally to a problem."[789] And, according to one biographer, "Kennedy usually maintained objectivity even under pressure."[790] In the words of author Evan Thomas,

"He had a very great ability to step back, to be cool, to be detached, to not get sucked in by the passions of the moment, to not just ride the wave."[791]

When his mother Rose Kennedy was asked if he was emotional, she said, "I suppose the reason for the question is that he always seemed so self-possessed, unruffled, equable, with a certain air of 'detachment'"[792] She went on to explain how her son seemed to operate "as though he were in the scene and living it fully yet observing the scene with himself in it."[793] "I think by and large," she added, "this was true. He did have an even temperament."[794]

Kennedy's Secretary of Agriculture Orville Freeman once described it thus: "You always had the feeling that to some extent he was standing in the corner kind of looking at all of this with something of an air of detachment."[795] Clark Clifford, advisor to the President, once explained,

I felt at times that, as he dealt with personal or professional crises, he was able to step away from himself and look at a problem as though it involved someone else. Sometimes, watching him during a discussion on some contentious issue, I felt as if his mind had left his body and was observing the proceedings with a detached, almost amused air. Something within him seemed to be saying, 'This may seem supremely, even transcendently important right now, but will it matter in fifty years? In one year? I must not permit myself to become involved to the point where my judgment is suspect."[796]

Biographer Michael O'Brien adds, "He seemed to have an 'extra eye,' outside of himself, which surveyed a scene."[797] This practice is part of the training in the ancient Japanese art of swordsmanship.[798] Practitioners are taught to look at their adversary as if he was a mountain far away. One of the greatest samurais, Musashi, referred to this as taking a "distanced view of close things."[799] The purpose is to get emotional distance, to create some space between you and your natural impulses.[800]

Understand: John Kennedy was, for the most part, just like everyone else—including Trump. The difference was that he understood the significance of effectively managing his state. "He had an exceptional capacity for detachment."[801] "That doesn't mean I'm not emotional," Kennedy said. "I probably have as many emotions as the next person...it simply means I reason problems out and apply logic to them."[802]

With his lifelong love of reading and learning about the titans of history, Kennedy tended to take an historian's view of world affairs. He had an eye for the bigger picture—the broad, sweeping view of how things would appear on the pages of history. His early experience as a journalist also, no doubt, played a part in his tendency to witness events as a detached observer, imagining how he would write the story later.

Whatever else may have driven him to it, his ability to emotionally detach served him well, particularly in difficult situations when rational and objective thinking were at a premium. As Harvard historian David E. Kaiser wrote in *American Tragedy*, "Kennedy's detachment, curiosity, and quick intelligence allowed him to deal rapidly with a variety of issues as President, even while maintaining a relatively relaxed routine. ...His detachment and flexibility...combined with his personal grace, also enabled him to maintain his emotional equilibrium during three very turbulent years of American history—and, far more important, helped the vast majority of his fellow citizens to maintain theirs as well."[803] Kennedy thought people were often held captive by their own emotions. "He believed that hysterical or overly excited people usually did not have good judgment."[804] And, therefore, this was something he assiduously sought to avoid. As it turns out, detachment is a powerful way to do it. In fact, psychological research has now repeatedly revealed that those who are able to detach from their emotions (e.g. by imagining that they are watching themselves from a distance) are able to eliminate unwanted feelings, emotions that stand in the way.[805]

Naturally, developing the habit of detaching allowed Kennedy to deal with criticism and resistance with greater thoughtfulness and objectivity, and without all the useless, emotional excess. As Arthur Schlesinger noted, "He has a capacity to view a problem with detachment free from petty prejudices."[806] But more importantly, this made Kennedy a stronger and more steady leader, a Commander in Chief that inspired confidence in the American people, and respect around the world. Equally important, in addition to finding serenity in his faith, Kennedy's facility for detaching himself from his situation and surroundings to look at matters with clear eyes was, in the words of historian Robert Dallek, "a singularly useful attribute in dealing with awesome burdens."[807] "Kennedy had enough detachment about himself and the magnitude of the problems he confronted not to let criticism or negative perceptions control his public actions toward the USSR."[808] Throughout the Cuban Missile Crisis, Kennedy kept his nerves steady as he continued to play it cool. He had so effectively mastered his ability to detach that, writes another historian, "he could coldly go to the brink of nuclear war without being unnerved by a normal man's sensitivities."[809]

Stand Tall and Strong and Firm.

The ability to maintain a certain level of composure, and detachment from the drama that surrounds you is essential to being at the top of your game. It is the mark of many of history's great heroes. Indeed, some see this as the characteristic that stands out above all others (perhaps especially those who consistently *failed* to keep their emotions in check). In early 1974, at the height of Watergate, when he was deeply mired in the scandal, Richard Nixon visited the Lincoln Memorial to place a wreath on the monument in celebration of Lincoln's birthday. In his brief remarks, Nixon reminded his audience of the circumstances that Lincoln was forced to endure, and what he was able to accomplish in the face of such formidable resistance, opposition and war. "He freed the slaves. He saved the Union," Nixon said.[810] "He died of an assassin's bullet just at the height of his career, at the end of the War Between the States."[811] And through it all, President Lincoln was one of the most hated men in the country. In fact, Nixon said, "When we examine the American Presidents, it is quite clear that no President in history…was more vilified during the time he was President than Lincoln."[812]

Many Presidents have confessed that the personal attacks deeply hurt them. Lincoln was no exception. "He was very deeply hurt by what was said about him," Nixon said.[813] And, yet, according to Nixon, it was the way that he handled it that made Lincoln great. "Lincoln," he said, "had that great strength of character never to display it, always to stand tall and strong and firm no matter how harsh or unfair the criticism might be."[814] There were, of course, many characteristics that made Lincoln great— vision, compassion, integrity, humility, humor. But this was one, Nixon thought, that stood out above all the rest, and helped to explain why Lincoln was "of all the American Presidents, more revered, not only in America but in the world."[815] Lincoln's greatness, Nixon believed, " perhaps more than anything else" was his "strength, the poise under pressure."[816]

Never Try Too Hard.

To detach is to let go of *outcomes* on an *emotional* level. When you are too attached you are weakened by your emotions. Your judgment is clouded. Your perspective is narrow. Your thinking is short-term. In essence, your ego is wrapped up in the result. To succeed under pressure you must develop the habit of managing your emotions. To effectively handle your critics, to triumph over your opponents requires you to keep calm and cool. Detaching helps you to quiet your mind. "In short, 'getting it together,'" writes W. Timothy Gallwey in *The Inner Game of Tennis*, "requires slowing the mind. Quieting the mind means less thinking, calculating, judging, worrying, fearing, hoping, trying, regretting, controlling, jittering or distracting."[817]

Detachment is not about being disengaged, or indifferent to your goals. In fact, "the real trick," Deepak Chopra writes in *The Soul of Leadership*, is "to practice detachment while still being fully engaged."[818] Your desire for a particular outcome does not change, only your emotional attachment to it. And this, paradoxically, helps you to work more effectively toward your desired outcome. As Gallwey taught, learning to detach can help you to stop trying so hard. And, he said, "the secret to winning any game lies in not trying too hard."[819] As the English author Tom Butler-Bowdon writes, "The wise always have an outcome or result in mind, yet their detachment from it makes them all the more effective."[820]

"In order to acquire anything in the physical universe," writes Chopra, "you have to relinquish your attachment to it."[821] In other words, he explains, "This doesn't mean you give up the intention to create your desire. You don't give up the intention, and you don't give up the desire. You give up your attachment to the result."[822]

The more you are attached to the outcome, the more vulnerable you are to the emotions that will get in your way. "The angry general loses," writes Sun Tzu in *The Art of War*.[823] Tame your desires, do not abandon them. Master self-control and, as Solomon writes in Proverbs, you will surpass even the mighty who captures a city.[824]

Understand: The point is not to *remain* detached. The point is not to become an aloof, reserved, indifferent, or dispassionate person. The point is to develop the capacity to detach. Think of it as a cognitive tool available to you whenever you need it, a tool that becomes more powerful with practice.

Get 'On the Balcony' to Avoid Being Swept Up By Events.

Your ability to endure criticism, to overcome opposition and resistance, to persevere through trying times will often depend on your mental discipline. Wisdom is readily available to those who take the time to stop, step back and reflect. People are often surprised by the wisdom, insight and discernment they gain when they take the time to get outside of the arena, to explore alternative viewpoints, to place circumstances and events in their broader context, to review relevant background and history, to consider unconventional ideas, or simply to pray, meditate, journal and reflect. Taking a few minutes each day to detach and reflect can be an eminently useful practice. Do not underestimate the power of a simple tool. As Harvard's Ronald Heifetz puts it, to be effective you have to make time to "get on the balcony."[825] Getting distance, "observing the patterns of action from afar," says David Gergen, helps to foster more effective action.[826] Your success depends on your ability to both act and reflect. To be highly effective is to both participate and observe. It is, in the words of Walt Whitman, to be "both in and out of the game."[827]

"Although the principle may be easy to grasp," writes Heifetz, "the practice is not. Rather than maintain perspective on the events that surround and involve us, we often get swept up by them."[828] This, in fact, was part of Soviet Premier Nikita Khrushchev's problem during the Cuban Missile Crisis. He was too emotionally attached to the outcome and thus he was temporarily swept up in subsequent events. Whereas Kennedy remained cool and detached, and emerged as a heroic leader; Khrushchev had a much more difficult time—both during and afterwards (and lived to regret placing nuclear missiles so close to U.S. shores). Rather than striving to maintain some emotional distance from the crisis, Khrushchev appeared to be deeply and emotionally attached. Indeed, the long awaited message from Khrushchev was indicative of the emotional duress that he was experiencing. "A great deal has been written about this message," wrote RFK in *Thirteen Days*, "including the allegation that at the time Khrushchev wrote it he must have been so unstable or emotional that he had become incoherent. There was no question that the letter had been written by him personally. It was very long and emotional."[829] Khrushchev was, in part, able to see things from Kennedy's perspective. He did have some appreciation for the President's position—that it was the Soviets who had instigated this most recent crisis. Fortunately, for humanity, the limitations and weaknesses of the belligerents were overcome. Had either Kennedy or Khrushchev ultimately proven unable to handle the profound emotional duress we might not be around to talk about how they did.

Get Perspective, Project Beyond Resistance: Robert Kennedy Learning to Take the High Road

"You will never reach your destination if you stop and throw stones at every dog that barks."
—Winston Churchill (1874—1965), British Prime Minister

By the time Robert Kennedy was running for president in 1968, he was widely seen by his opponents as a ruthless, cold-blooded political operator. It was a reputation he had acquired, in part, through the calculated, no-nonsense, hard-driving way in which he ran his brother's political campaigns. As far as Bobby was concerned, however, he was only doing what he had to do to make sure his brother won. "I'm not running a popularity contest," he once told Hugh Sidey of *Time*.[830] "It doesn't matter if they like me or not. Jack can be nice to them…Somebody has to be able to say no."[831] At the time, Bobby didn't see any other way. "If people are not getting off their behinds and working enough," he said, "how do you say that nicely? Every time you make a decision in this business you make somebody mad."[832]

Later, after Jack won, Bobby would be the guy behind the scenes, doing all the hard jobs, making sure things went according to Jack's plans. This included, as Attorney General, Bobby's relentless "get Hoffa" pursuit of the notorious organized crime boss Jimmy Hoffa.

Perhaps it all started as far back as high school sports. Robert Kennedy, his football coach once said, "He loved to hit his man. And when he hit, he seemed to come alive."[833] Wherever it began, "ruthless" was an expression that stuck, that "seemed to explain something about him," and that he would shoulder throughout his life.[834]

When the celebrated journalist Sir David Frost was interviewed by *Cigar Aficionado* he was asked if he had a favorite or most memorable interview. Frost, of course, had many names to choose from, including Nelson Mandela, John Wayne, and the famous interview with Richard Nixon which later became the movie Frost/Nixon. There was one, however, that stuck out above the rest. "It was," he said, "when I interviewed Robert Kennedy in 1968 at the Benson Hotel in Portland, Oregon, in what, alas, turned out to be the last long personal interview he ever gave."[835]

"I wanted to talk to him about his boating down the rapids," Frost recalled, "and the quote of Edith Hamilton's he often used about how 'men are not born for safe havens,' and I said, 'Some people have described you as reckless.' And he looked at me and smiled and said, 'No, no. Ruthless.' Which was so sweet. He was helping me out with the insult. It was a very attractive quality," Frost said.[836] "All the people who criticized him at that time said he was ruthless. I said, 'Some people have said that your reputation for ruthlessness dates back to when you had to do the difficult dirty things behind the scenes in the 1960 election as campaign manager for your brother.' And he said, 'No, no, that's just my friends making excuses for me.'"[837]

For Frost, a man who had interviewed scores of famous and infamous people, Kennedy's response—his entire demeanor—surprised him. It was such an atypical response. Frost walked away from the interview thinking that Kennedy, he said, "had an incredible charisma."[838] Frost continued, "I've always said that I don't know how you define charisma except as Robert Kennedy on that particular day."[839]

Focus On Adding Value.

When most people are criticized they immediately get defensive. Their hearts start to race and they launch into a litany of excuses, attempt to change the subject, or perhaps even counter-attack. In essence, they *react* to the criticism without realizing they are surrendering their power. They're being driven by the agenda of their critics. Yet, in an attempt to defend themselves, they often look weak and reactive. They may even cause themselves unnecessary humiliation. With their emotions getting the best of them, some people may even come off as irrational, incompetent, or even guilty of something that was entirely made up. Moreover, an emotional reaction often brings greater attention to an issue or criticism that they would prefer to see disappear. Finally, many people, driven by unbridled emotion, will react in a way that further escalates the matter, to the point that it begins to take away time, energy and other resources from their own mission and goals.

Rarely, however, is any of this necessary. More often than not, one of the best and most graceful ways to handle criticism is simply to rise above it. Whether the criticisms of your opponents do any real damage is largely dependent not on the attacks themselves, but on how you choose to respond.

Robert Kennedy gave the impression that he was beyond the criticism. In fact, he was happy to share it with you if you didn't know. It was no skin off his back. He just wanted to help you with your interview. He was perfectly comfortable in his own skin, with who and what he was, even in the face of an insult. It didn't matter what anyone else thought or said about him. In that moment, his sole focus was on you, and how he could help you. And that, in fact, is the heart of a charismatic bond.

A lot of people experience anxiety for the simple reason that they're too wrapped up in their own reality. They're too focused on themselves. People who learn to balance their time by also thinking about how they can help others, tend to be much more calm, confident, and secure. This is a law of nature: Doing good for others is good for you too. In contrast, continuously thinking only of yourself is a recipe for anxiety, insecurity, depression, or worse. By focusing on adding value to others, you can overcome many of your own limitations, insecurities, and feelings of emptiness.

Understand: It is not always possible to ignore or even wise to try to rise above the criticism and attacks of others. Largely depending on the *perceived severity* and *legitimacy* of the criticism and the critic; some things must be dealt with head on and straightaway.

Preserve a Presidential Cool, But Keep Critics in Check.

During the 2016 presidential election, much was made in the media of Donald Trump's persistent personal attacks on his adversaries. "Lyin' Ted," "Crooked Hillary Clinton," "Little Marco," and "Low-Energy Bush" are just a few of the insults Trump repeatedly hurled at his opponents.[840] But it was never simply Trump's insults that did the damage. It was the failure of the response. Rubio, for example, sunk to a new low for a presidential candidate during the GOP primary when he attempted to counter Trump's insults by referring to Trump's anatomy in relation to the size of his hands.[841]

Rather than elevating himself above the tactics of a schoolyard bully, Rubio only made himself look desperate and immature.[842]

In stark contrast, Carly Fiorina responded to Trump's personal attacks very differently. At one point, Trump, who had been attacking Fiorina's appearance, said, "Look at that face. Would anyone vote for that? Can you imagine that, the face of our next president?"[843] CNN's Jake Tapper, playing into the lowest common denominator, attempted to get Fiorina to respond in kind to Trump's attacks on her appearance. Rather than taking the bait, however, Fiorina, doubling back to Trump's previous comment (i.e. that women all over the country heard what Bush said about cutting funding for women's health issues), said simply, "Mr. Trump said that he heard Mr. Bush very clearly—and what Mr. Bush said—I think women all over this country heard very clearly what Mr. Trump said."[844]

Trump was also an outspoken voice within the "Birther Movement," a conspiracy theory which questioned the legitimacy of Barack Obama's citizenship and, thus, the legitimacy of his presidency.[845] Given the absurdity of the charge, Obama was reluctant to respond. As the movement gained ground, however, Obama finally saw fit to put the issue to rest by releasing first his birth certificate and, eventually, his long form birth certificate. Alas, as conspiracy theories tend to go, this did very little to appease his enemies. Then, finally, with Trump as a captive audience member at the White House Correspondents Dinner, Obama played what he said was a video of his birth. The video, however, designed to ridicule Trump and the Birther Movement, was a clip from Disney's *The Lion King* movie wherein the cub Simba is born in Africa. Joking that this would finally put the issue to rest, Obama effectively cast Trump as a conspiracy nut when he concluded, "No one is prouder to put this birth certificate to rest than The Donald. He can finally get back to focusing on the issues that matter: Did we fake the moon landing? What really happened in Roswell? And where are Biggie and Tupac?"[846]

Hunker Down on Your Purpose: Lincoln's Enduring Cool

"We are not trying to entertain the critics. I'll take my chances with the public."
—Walt Disney (1901—1966), American Entrepreneur

Suffer Fools When It Serves Your Purpose.

In April of 1954, President Dwight "Ike" Eisenhower visited the birthplace of Abraham Lincoln. He had always wanted to visit "this Shrine," he said, "which is so truly American."[847] He spoke of his admiration for Old Honest Abe saying that, "Abraham Lincoln has always seemed to me to represent all that is best in America."[848] He went on to share a few of the characteristics he admired most and which he thought made him a "great leader."[849] And what do you think were the characteristics that Ike admired most? Forbearance and self-control. "You can find no instance," Ike said of Lincoln, "when he stood up in public and excoriated another American. You can find no instance where he is reported to have slapped or pounded the table, and struck the pose of a pseudo-dictator, or of an arbitrary individual."[850] Even when Lincoln himself was insulted or provoked, he maintained his composure and poise. Lincoln had learned long ago the utter futility of letting his feelings dictate his actions.[851] In the words of Eisenhower, "Never did he fall into the false habit of striking a Napoleonic attitude at any time and under any provocation."[852]

President Eisenhower had served as a five-star general during World War II, and he well knew the trouble that some "glory-hopping," "prima donna" generals could cause for their commander-in-chief. During his remarks at Lincoln's birthplace, Eisenhower shared the story of how President Lincoln, one day during the Civil War, needed to see General McClellan and, so, the President went over to the General's house. General McClellan, however, decided that he did not care to see the President and, so, he went to bed. Well, you can imagine, Eisenhower said, "Lincoln's friends criticized him severely for allowing a mere General to treat him that way."[853] But Lincoln, with all of his cool and collected self-control said, "All I want out of General McClellan is a victory, and if to hold his horse will bring it, I will gladly hold his horse."[854]

President Lincoln, kept his pride in check, and he maintained his cool by keeping his mind on his mission and goals. As Eisenhower said, "Lincoln's leadership was accomplished through dedication to a single purpose, the preservation of the Union."[855]

Keep Your Mission at the Top of Your Mind.

It's not that Lincoln never felt angry, insulted, or hurt—he certainly did. But he never lost site of his greater purpose, and he did his best to subordinate his emotions to his mission. Lincoln believed wholeheartedly in the work he was doing and, thus, in the end, the attacks of his opponents and critics meant very little. In is own words, Lincoln once said when he was attacked by his opponents in the Committee on the Conduct of the War, "If I were to try to read, much less answer, all the attacks made on me, this shop might as well be closed for any other business."[856] Lincoln said on another occasion, "I do the very best I know how—the very best I can; and I mean to keep doing so until the end. If the end brings me out all right," he continued, "what is said against me won't amount to anything. If the end brings me out wrong, ten thousand angels swearing I was right would make no difference."[857]

It is natural to be hurt by the criticisms of our fellows, but when your purpose is so powerful, so significant, it can go a long way toward strengthening your resolve. In essence, with your mind on your mission, it is perspective that helps you to endure the attacks.

Lincoln, not surprisingly, also found other tactics for releasing his destructive emotions. Carl Sandburg, for example, writes that Lincoln would often write emotional letters when he was angry—"hot letters," Lincoln called them—but then he would throw them in the fireplace.[858] Or he would put them in his desk drawer, and read it the following morning. If he still felt like sending it the next day, then he would. But he almost never did, because he was always cooled off by then and, with greater emotional distance, it was easy to see how his letter was unlikely to further his broader aims.[859]

Lincoln endured fierce criticism throughout his time as Commander-in-Chief. "He knew that there were divisive influences at work," Ike said, "but he knew also they were transitory in character—they were flaming with heat, but they were made of stuff that would soon bum itself out."[860] But he also believed in the enduring values of America and he believed America was destined to endure. "And so he was patient. He was forbearing. He was understanding. And he lives today in our hearts," Eisenhower said, "as one of the greatest that the English-speaking race has produced, and as a great leader."[861]

Have Faith in the Ultimate Future.

In June 1961, President Kennedy was flying home after meeting with Nikita Khrushchev. Kennedy left the discussions with the disheartening realization that nuclear war was even more possible than he had imagined. The possibility of a nuclear holocaust lured Kennedy into a state of deep reflection. Later, when Kennedy's secretary, Evelyn Lincoln, was clearing his desk on Air Force One she found a note Kennedy had written out to himself.[862] He was quoting Abraham Lincoln, a message of hope and faith that Lincoln had written to himself before the Civil War: "I know that there is a God and I see a storm coming. If he has a place for me I am ready."[863]

Whatever your existential beliefs, there is much to be said for trusting—no matter what challenges, criticism, or attacks you may be facing in the moment—in your greater purpose, and that all things will work out for the best in the end. Whatever skepticism or doubts you may have, the lesson from Lincoln, Eisenhower, Kennedy, and countless other leadership legends and heroes of history is that when faced with awesome burdens there is nothing so reassuring and empowering as faith in an ultimate, moral purpose.

Exploit the Advantage of an Adversary: Roosevelt Riding a Parade of Criticism

"A wise man gets more use from his enemies than a fool from his friends. Their ill-will often levels mountains of difficulties which one would otherwise face. Many have had their greatness made for them by their enemies."
—Baltasar Gracián, 17th century Spanish Jesuit, *The Art of Worldly Wisdom*

When Theodore Roosevelt became president of the board of the New York City Police Commissioners in 1895, the New York Police Department was reputed to be the single most corrupt force in the country. And, yet, with his keen interest in reform, this was just the kind of job Roosevelt relished. Working with a couple of leading, reform-minded journalists—Jacob Riis and Lincoln Steffens—Roosevelt had come to believe that "the tap-root" of the corruption was the money that the nearly 10,000 saloons across the city were funneling to the police and political bosses in exchange for being permitted to sell alcohol on Sundays, in violation of New York law.[864] Passed to satisfy constituents nearly four decades earlier, New York's Sunday law had been, writes Doris Kearns Goodwin, author of *The Bully Pulpit*, "warped into a massive vehicle of police and political blackmail."[865] If the saloon keepers refused to make the monthly payments or otherwise fell out of favor with the Tammany Hall political machine, they would quickly find their businesses shut down and themselves in jail.[866]

As police commissioner, unable to *change* the law, Roosevelt knew exactly what he had to do: He had to *enforce* the law. Roosevelt was no Puritan, nor did he believe in Prohibition, but he understood that a law on the books that is not uniformly enforced is a law that breeds conflict and corruption.[867]

Unfortunately, for the working people, most of whom worked everyday *except* Sunday, the Sunday closing law was wildly unpopular. The workers had no part in the corruption or the saloonkeepers profits, they simply wanted to enjoy a drink with friends while they played cards, threw darts, and shot pool on their one day off.[868]

Nothing could stop Roosevelt, however, from doing what he believed to be right—not the workingmen, and certainly not the corrupt politicians or police. Of course, Roosevelt understood the political fallout that enforcement would provoke. "The corrupt would never forgive him," wrote Lincoln Steffens, "and the great mass of the people would not understand."[869] Roosevelt forged ahead and, within two months, Roosevelt's strict Sunday enforcement policy had closed the doors on over 95 percent of the city's saloons.[870]

Star in Your Opponents' Show.

As expected, it provoked a tidal wave of brutal backlash. The attacks on TR were fierce and unrelenting. "I have never been engaged in a more savage fight," Roosevelt confessed to an old Harvard friend.[871] Roosevelt's office was flooded with telegrams. "You are the biggest fool that ever lived," read one.[872] "What an ass you have made of yourself," read another.[873] There were even a couple of "dynamite bombs" placed in TR's desk which, fortunately, never exploded, and which he basically ignored.[874]

Roosevelt, of course, being Roosevelt, was undeterred. In the words of his friend, newspaper editor Joseph Bishop, "This was a fight after Roosevelt's own heart."[875]

The outrage grew to such a fever pitch that the people began to organize a parade in protest of the Police Commissioner and his unpopular policy. When they sent a mocking invitation to Roosevelt, hoping to strike fear and humiliation in his heart, they were dumbfounded when Roosevelt happily accepted. "They think he won't show up because he won't be able to bear the criticism."[876] But Roosevelt was not the man they imagined. His confidence and courage went well beyond enduring a literal parade of criticism. What's more, TR understood that this was a priceless opportunity for national publicity. Whatever side stories might be told, he knew that his actions on that day would be the main story and, therefore, this was a chance for him to exploit his opponent, and further his national ambitions.

More than 150,000 people lined the route of the parade. It proved to be an impressive event with, according to New York's *World*, "gilded floats, decorated and peopled in a manner most pleasing to the eye...and long lines of men in shining uniforms and all the glitter and splendor of mounted paraders."[877] In fact, more than 30,000 paraders and performers passed by, many with scathing banners and placards denouncing him as the "worst police commissioner in U.S. history."[878] "Send the Police Czar to Russia," read one banner; "Rooseveltism is a farce and a humbug," read another.[879]

And, yet, there too, positioned center stage for hours, was the target of all the derision, disrespect and disdain—standing and smiling and laughing and waving. The man who was meant to be publicly roasted and cut down to size was enjoying himself to the hilt, laughing harder than anyone, complimenting his critics on their clever attacks.[880] "'That is the best yet,' Roosevelt chuckled, pointing to a wagon entitled 'The Millionaire's Club.' The float," Goodwin explains in *The Bully Pulpit*, "sported three gentlemen in frock coats and tall hats, with one bearing 'a striking resemblance to Theodore Roosevelt.' The trio sipped champagne at a 'private club,' while at the rear of the wagon a mock arrest of a beer-drinking laborer was staged. 'That is really a good stroke,' Roosevelt burst forth with admiration."[881] A few of the contemptuous creations were so witty, in fact, that the good-natured and uninhibited Roosevelt asked if he could keep them as souvenirs.[882]

One German workingmen did not see Roosevelt and figured he was too much of a coward to show up. "Now, where is Roosevelt?" he shouted in German.[883] Suddenly, to the man's astonishment, Roosevelt, standing on a stage nearby, shouted back (also in German), "Here I am! What do you wish, friend?"[884] The man was astounded. He immediately snatched off his hat and waved, "Hurrah for Roosevelt!" as the crowd erupted in laughter and cheers.[885] Suddenly, the entire column of the parade took up the cheer, "Hurrah for Roosevelt."[886] As each section of the parade made its way to the place where Roosevelt was standing, the man they marked for removal was met by a spontaneous roar of approval. "What had been intended as a rebuke was turned into an endorsement."[887]

Even Roosevelt's critics in the press, including Jay Gould's *World* which had been attacking Roosevelt with a "shrieking" fury, had to admit that Roosevelt had stolen the day by delighting the crowds with his good-natured showing, and cool handling of the affair.[888] "It looked almost as if the whole affair were in his honor," wrote the *World*, "and the long lines to whom he bowed, took off their hats in salute."[889] "Bully for Teddy!" the marchers shouted.[890] "Teddy, you're a man!"[891] A parade meant for humiliation became "a procession in his honor."[892] "His ability to turn the tables," Goodwin concludes, "to relish his protracted self-mockery in public, was compressed into the headline of a Chicago newspaper: 'Cheered by Those Who Came to Jeer.'"[893]

Master Your Emotions, Win the Psychological Game.

In the realm of influence and power, people are often derailed by their own overreactions to the criticism and attacks of their opponents.[894] Theodore Roosevelt himself, early in his political career, was often carried away by his emotional reaction to the actions of his adversaries in the New York legislature, and the words of his opponents in the press. But he learned his lesson. And by the time of his appointment as police commissioner, TR was becoming a master of the art. Indeed, it is hard to imagine anyone who could better handle a literal parade of opponents who marched with scathing banners, floats and other spectacles intended to ridicule, demean, and destroy, as they passed through one of the most populous cities in the world. A weaker man might easily have been ruined by such an affair.

With a spine now infused with steel, TR was free to master the psychological game of political warfare. He was no longer compelled to operate on the level of emotion alone. He had the mental space to think strategically about his broader purpose and long-term goals. He was, essentially, in a psychological state where he could turn the attacks of his opponents to his own advantage.

Human beings seem to have lost something of the art of profiting from our enemies. And, yet, if our early ancestors had not practically mastered this art, we would not be here to talk about it today. Throughout the history of humankind, it has never been enough to defend ourselves from our enemies. The most successful have always found ways to use their enemies to their advantage. "Primitive men were quite content if they could escape being injured by strange and fierce animals, and this was the aim and end of their struggles against the wild beasts;" writes the ancient Greek historian and biographer Plutarch in the 2nd century, "but their successors, by learning, as they did, how to make use of them, now profit by them through using their flesh for food, their hair for clothing, their gall and colostrums as medicine, and their skins as armor, so that there is good reason to fear that, if the supply of wild beasts should fail man, his life would become bestial, helpless, and uncivilized."[895]

There will, no doubt, be times when your success will depend on how you respond to the attacks of an adversary or the criticism of a competitor. The key is to get your mindset right. The object is not to run and hide and hope to avoid the attacks. But this is precisely what most people do. As Plutarch said, "it is enough for most people if they can avoid suffering ill-treatment at the hands of their enemies."[896] But this approach, often born of fear, will do very little to protect you or strengthen your power. Nor can you hope to achieve anything of significance if you're preoccupied with avoiding criticism and attacks.

The solution is simple: Recognize that there are always numerous options for how to respond, many of which will actually enhance your position or strengthen your power. Rather than cowering in fear, think of how you can exploit the advantage of an adversary. As Plutarch suggests, "look at your enemy, and see whether, in spite of his being in most respects harmful and difficult to manage, he does not in some way or other afford you means of getting hold of him and of using him as you can use no one else, and so can be of profit to you."[897]

Show Yourself as Above the Attack.

Most people get so emotionally carried away by the words and actions of their adversaries that they fail to stop and think strategically about how they might best exploit the attacks, and turn the criticism or negative attention to their own advantage. Indeed, in many cases, in their hasty overreaction, they fail to appreciate the extent to which their wisest possible move is not to react at all. Exploiting your adversary is not always about fighting or countering your opponents attack. In fact, as the ancient Chinese military strategist Sun Tzu wrote, "The supreme art of war is to subdue the enemy without fighting."[898]

Power is often a matter of perception. When you lose perspective, and reduce yourself to the level of an insignificant critic or an immaterial attack, you lose power— often while inadvertently elevating the critic. When President Harry Truman sent a private letter to music critic Paul Hume, who had published a harsh review of Margaret Truman (the President's daughter) and her recent performance singing at Constitution Hall, Truman's mind was focused entirely on the critic. He lost his perspective. Apprehended by his own emotions, his focus was insular and his thinking was short-term. As a result, not only did he fail to ignore the insignificant criticism—or, better yet, find a way to use it for his own purposes—but, when his private letter was made public, Truman suffered even greater criticism from a broad swath of the American people. Rather than revealing himself as a gracious and magnanimous leader, Truman came off to many Americans as a petty and embarrassing bumpkin who lacked self-control.

Understand: To ignore naysayers, doubters, and critics is *not* to ignore legitimate input or feedback. Legitimate criticism can be powerful friend—*if* you let it. Most everyone likes to be praised and lifted up. Very few people appreciate, fewer still actively seek, the feedback and constructive criticism they need to succeed. "Unfortunately," writes USC's Morgan McCall in *High Flyers*, "people often *like* the things that work against their growth…People like to use their strengths…to achieve quick, dramatic results, even if…they aren't developing the new skills they will need later on."[899] Do not fall into this trap. Remember: Diamonds are born out of extreme pressure and heat. Pearls do not form without grains of sand. Be wary of what is too easy and smooth. "Flattery is more dangerous than hatred," writes the 17th century Spanish Jesuit Baltasar Gracián, "because it covers the stains which the other causes to be wiped out. The wise will turn ill-will into a mirror more faithful than that of kindness, and remove or improve the faults referred to."[900] "Fools spoil even their friendships," writes Plutarch, "while wise men are able to make a fitting use even of their enmities."[901]

Confront Your Critics:
Turn Attacks into Opportunities for Greater Exposure and Increased Support.

When Senator Richard Nixon was a Vice Presidential candidate on the ticket with Dwight Eisenhower in 1952, he faced harsh criticism from his opponents, including many from his own party who wanted him off the ticket. When rumors began to spread that Nixon had a political "slush" fund, and that he was using the money for personal expenses and, in exchange, providing special favors to the contributors, it became a major crisis for the Republicans. Nixon became a liability in the race, and Eisenhower began to consider dropping Nixon from the ticket.

Rather than caving to the criticisms of his opponents, however, or succumbing to his feelings of frustration and anger over the pressure he was getting from Republican leaders to drop out, Nixon began looking for ways to exploit the attacks. And, in one brilliant blow, establishing himself as a political force to be reckoned with, Nixon went on television, taking his case directly to the American people. In his address, Nixon defended himself, his family, and his finances as he appealed to the hearts of Americans. Revealing himself as a man of modest means, Nixon challenged those who questioned the legitimacy of the donations he received, and how the money was being spent. In a masterful stroke, Nixon finished his address with a mention of the gift that he would not give back: It was, he said, "a little cocker spaniel dog…sent all the way from Texas. And our little girl—Tricia, the 6-year-old—named it Checkers….And you know," Nixon concluded, "the kids, like all kids, love the dog and I just want to say this right now, that regardless of what they say about it, we're gonna keep it."[902]

The sappy, emotionally charged "Checkers speech," as it was later known, was a masterpiece of political theater. It aroused a massive outpouring of support for Nixon, solidifying his position as Eisenhower's running mate, and, according to *The New York Times*, giving the ticket "a shot in the arm," and, thus, ensuring their victory in the 1952 presidential election less than six weeks later.[903] In Eisenhower's own words, delivered before a stadium audience, Nixon had been subjected to "a very unfair and vicious attack," but he had "vindicated himself" and now "stood higher than ever before."[904]

Politicians, celebrities, and other public figures frequently face harsh, fallacious and unfair criticism and attacks that are intended to destroy. It is natural to get angry and frustrated by these destructive or deceptive attacks. It is not until they succumb to their emotions, however, that they risk surrendering their power. The solution is to get distance and detach. Then use that space to think clearly about whether or how to respond. Nixon succeeded, in this instance, because he got the distance and took the time he needed to think strategically about how he might exploit the damaging, political attacks. When Harry Truman's daughter received an unfavorable review by the music critic, Truman succumbed to his emotions. Rather than taking time to stop and step back, Truman rushed to respond—even to the point of immediately sending a White House messenger out to drop his letter in a post office box across the street, intentionally acting out before an aide could stop him.[905] Truman effectively gave his power over the situation away and, as a result, made a fool of himself before the entire country.

To successfully achieve your ambition and goals, you must steel yourself for the inevitable opposition. To *exploit* the efforts of your adversaries, however, to turn their attacks to your advantage, necessitates moving beyond mere confidence and self-control. Managing your emotions is a critical first step, but it is not enough. To use your opponents to advance your cause requires greater perspective and a higher degree of calculation. Rather than thinking of your opponents and their attacks, think of the spectators, your wider audience, and those you may reach as a result. Rather than thinking of the immediate situation, consider the many alternative ways that things might play out. Most people think only of their next move. Their psychology is tit-for-tat. You must imagine life as a game of chess, considering a more complete range of options, while working to think through several moves ahead.

Use Conflict to Connect.

Most people make the mistake of assuming that being attacked is an automatic negative. In the game of influence, however, there are significant advantages to having an adversary, and criticism is often exceptionally useful. In fact, conflict can be a powerful tool for engaging interest and building an audience. Indeed, Benjamin Franklin, America's original hustler, deliberately concocted controversy, and critics for his newspaper, the *Pennsylvania Gazette*, who would write letters to the editor as a way of entertaining his readers.

In one instance, Franklin had a certain, fictitious "J.T." stirring up trouble with another local paper as a strategy for creating a rivalry designed to engage readers on both sides. The crafty Franklin had J.T. write in to correct one of Franklin's own typographical errors (Franklin had mistakenly written that a patron had "died" at a restaurant, when he meant to say "dined").[906] J.T. went on about other errors including a misprint in a Bible that reported King David was "wonderfully mad" (rather than "wonderfully made"), leading one loopy preacher to carry on about the benefits of "spiritual madness."[907] Soon J.T. slyly made his way over to the real purpose of his letter to the editor: To incite editor Andrew Bradford, of Franklin's rival paper, the *American Weekly Mercury*, and to engage Bradford's readers. Walter Isaacson writes, "Franklin then went on (under the guise of J.T.) to…criticize Bradford for being generally sloppier, and (with delicious irony) praise Franklin for not criticizing Bradford: 'Your paper is most commonly very correct, and yet you were never known to triumph upon it by publicly ridiculing and exposing the continual blunders of your contemporary.'"[908]

The wily Franklin had a reputation for engaging in these sort of clever tactics, pen names, and innocuous ploys. He understood the benefits of criticism and the power of conflict to attract attention and connect with an audience. (He also understood that reasonable people don't mind being fooled in superficial matters, but what they will not tolerate is boredom.) Benjamin Franklin knew how to leverage this power and, as a result, he was not only open to the opportunity to engage his adversaries in public, he relished it. Ultimately, conflict was another way for him to increase his influence. As the celebrated Italian author Pietro Aretino once said, "Even when I'm railed at, I get my quota of renown."[909]

Use Controversy to Engage.

Another great American hustler, P.T. Barnum, was most concerned when there was *not enough* criticism. Barnum understood that people saying pleasant, positive things about his museums, concerts and three-ring circus was good for business. But he also understood that adding a fair amount of controversy to the mix of public opinion would bring far more traffic and support to his endeavors than positive reviews alone. In fact, if Barnum ever found that things were proceeding too peaceably he would intentionally work to stir things up. In several instances, like Ben Franklin, Barnum wrote anonymous letters to the editors of newspapers attacking himself, his show, or some particular curiosity. This would then pique people's interest in the affair and, before long, Barnum would find new streams of revenue from people stirred to investigate matters for themselves.

When Barnum first heard about Joice Heth, who claimed to be 161-years old, and the former childhood nurse of the illustrious George Washington, he was eager to get in on the act. This, after all, was George Washington, the "Father of Our Country," and though Heth's claims seemed too fantastic to believe, she appeared to Barnum to be shockingly old, her knowledge of the minute details of the Washington family was unparalleled, and Joice Heth herself insisted, "I raised him."[910] Rather than hesitating because of his own doubts, however, Barnum recognized that while many others would be equally skeptical, and while still others might consider Heth's story a fraud, skepticism left room for curiosity, and curiosity could draw a crowd. "In fact, whenever there was a whiff of doubt about the authenticity of what the public crowded to see, so much the better. Sometimes that very doubt was a necessary ingredient and had to be manufactured."[911] What's more, Barnum didn't fear the likely criticisms and attacks that would ensue. Rather, he delighted in them. After all, according to Barnum's calculations, controversy was a key component of their formula for success.

Throughout her run, in which Heth herself took "great delight" (and considerable profit), as she told audiences stories about "little George," the controversy over her age continued in the press.[912] To Barnum's surprise, other critics protested not because they thought her story was a sham, but they objected to anyone reaping commercial profits from such a sacred link to the late, great General George Washington.[913]

When the popularity of Joice Heth's act finally began to taper off, Barnum sought to further stir the pot. He wrote an anonymous letter to a Boston newspaper claiming that Joice Heth was a fake. But he didn't simply challenge her age or the authenticity of her story, as others had already done. Instead, hoping to stir enough controversy to reinvigorate the show, Barnum added a new twist: Barnum (anonymously) claimed that Joice Heth was actually a *machine*, a "curiously constructed automaton, made up of whalebone, India-rubber, and numberless springs," and, he wrote, that the exhibitor was "a ventriloquist."[914] And with that, once again, Joice Heth was a sensation. "The media swallowed it and printed it," writes Joe Vitale in *There's a Customer Born Every Minute*.[915] "The public again lined up to see Heth, to try to detect if she was indeed a machine."[916] It was around this time that Barnum had, writes one biographer, a "breakthrough" discovery. Barnum came to understand that, "the public actually enjoyed being deceived, as long as they were, at the same time, being amused."[917]

Barnum and Franklin both understood that conflict and controversy could be good for business. However they may have dealt with the attacks personally, they knew that criticism was unavoidable. The bigger their audience, the more criticism they expected. It was simply the price that had to be paid. They both also understood that the criticism and attacks of their opponents was something that they could use. The real danger, they came to believe, was when the criticism and attacks began to fade away.

Let Your Enemies Lift You Up.

When Huey Long first ran for governor in Louisiana in 1924, the deck was heavily stacked against him. The corporate corruption and gross economic inequality that Long was determined to fight against was widespread and well-established. In fact, the political machine and corporate powers he opposed had their roots in the Antebellum era, characterized by wealthy plantation owners and slavery, leading to the Civil War. Increasing the political and economic power of the poor in Louisiana was, thus, in many ways, to go against the tide of history. And, not surprisingly, Huey Long endured all manner of contemptuous ridicule as a result. Representing the status quo, New Orleans' *Times Picayune* said that Long was "unfit for the post of governor."[918] An executive of one of Long's greatest opponents, John D. Rockefeller's Standard Oil, said that Long's speeches were "as much moment as the braying of an ass or the yelping of a locoed coyote."[919] Even former Louisiana Governor Ruffin Pleasant took part in the attacks, calling Long a "vainglorious, egotistical and selfish...pompous, inflated, chesty, loose-mouthed rattletrap."[920]

All of this did nothing to stop voters from turning out in droves to support the brash, bold political novice from the poor hill country in Northern Louisiana. In fact, the attacks had the opposite effect. Rather than damaging his campaign and destroying his fledgling career as his opponents intended, the brutal attacks helped to bring his campaign the extensive, ongoing attention he needed to educate the voters about what he stood for, and what exactly he intended to do. The press, of course, was largely critical of Long. It was, after all, owned or controlled by the ruling elites. But the malicious attacks helped Long by clearly and publicly identifying who his enemies were—Louisiana's super rich ruling elites—and, therefore, who stood to gain from a Long victory—Louisiana's poor, powerless, and dispossessed. In the end, what was most notable about the 1924 election was not that this radical, young, rule-breaking upstart lost. What shocked the political establishment more than anything was Long's unexpectedly strong third place showing. "Observers were astounded by the large vote for Long."[921] In a three-way race, the young, relatively unknown country lawyer took over thirty percent of the vote. Perhaps most important, the 1924 election convinced Long that the Pelican State's political elites could be beaten. He had chosen his enemies well and they had inadvertently helped to lift him up. Long would go on to *win* the next election, becoming the youngest Governor in Louisiana's history. And politics in Louisiana would never again be the same.

Whatever the specifics of your most significant ambitions, there is little doubt that influence can be a critical factor in your success. What most people mistakenly believe, however, is that harsh criticism or attacks from their opponents will lessen their influence, if not sink their chances before they even begin. The media in fact tends to perpetuate this myth by overestimating its own level of influence and power to damage and destroy. Donald Trump's 2016 campaign for president is a case-in-point. Regardless of the overwhelmingly negative attention Trump receives in the press, he dominated in the primaries. In fact, the mainstream media deserves the lion's share of the credit (or *responsibility*, depending on your perspective) for enabling Trump's rise.

Fear of criticism too often has people playing it safe, so safe in fact that they hesitate to offend anyone. They find themselves working so hard to be perfect that they never increase their visibility or influence at all. As Benjamin Franklin said, "If all printers were determined not to print anything till they were sure it would offend nobody, there would be very little printed."[922] What these fearful people fail to realize, however, is that criticism may be exactly what they need to help get their message out. In your own efforts to expand your circle of influence, a well chosen enemy may be the ideal leverage you need to succeed. As the ancient Greek historian Plutarch said, "Wise men are able to make a fitting use even of their enemies."[923] In fact, the Spanish Jesuit Baltasar Gracián took it a step further arguing, "Many have had their greatness made for them by their enemies."[924]

Use Your Adversaries to Define Where You Stand.

Franklin Roosevelt faced intense opposition to his New Deal legislation, policies designed to dig American out of the Great Depression. There were powerful interests profiting greatly from the status quo that were aligned against him. In fact, Roosevelt said in his 1936 speech at Madison Square Gardens, "Never before in all our history have these forces been so united against one candidate as they stand today. They are unanimous in their hate for me," he said.[925] Nevertheless, Roosevelt concluded, "I welcome their hatred."[926] It may seem odd to some to "welcome" hatred, but Roosevelt was a masterful political leader, and he knew how to use enemies for his own purposes. He understood how enemies can define you and help to lift you up. Indeed, FDR said on another occasion, "Judge me by the enemies I have made."[927]

Most people will never face the powerful and entrenched opposition, or the cruel and malicious attacks faced by Huey Long, Donald Trump, Hillary Clinton, Barack Obama, Bernie Sanders, or FDR. Most everyone, however, will have their fair share of critics and adversaries. There may be times when you can win your opponents over, destroying an enemy, as Lincoln said, by making him a friend. And, in the long run, this is often the wiser move. But there may also be times when you must accept the reality of fierce critics and treacherous opponents, find ways to exploit their attacks, and use them to lift yourself up. Remember: The sheer attention and support you can gain may alone outweigh the damage of the attack.

Whether in business, politics, entertainment, or sports, to deliberately provoke a powerful enemy is not a strategy without risks. The attacks can be relentless, deceptive, and brutally unfair. Nevertheless, there is always another side to the story that people will be eager to hear. And as long as there is a free press, there will always be people who are happy to profit from publishing your response to the attacks. And if you are ready, willing and able to counter the attacks, you can turn the aggression of a powerful enemy into a priceless opportunity to gain exposure, get your message out, and increase your influence with your own base, the people you need to succeed.

Earn a Following By Enduring Punishment—with a Grin.

It was Theodore Roosevelt's response to his first defeat in the Republican Association at Morton Hall that began to win over the support he needed launch his career in New York politics. Roosevelt came out in favor of a non-partisan street cleaning bill, but was soundly defeated by the party machine. Nevertheless, he "took his defeat with a grin," writes a Roosevelt biographer.[928] And it was this simple thing— Roosevelt's demeanor and endurance, even in the face of defeat—that made the difference. "His fellow Republicans of the Twenty-first District liked that grin and began soon to have the kind of respect for the man behind the grin that they had for prize-fighters, political "bosses," and all others who could give and take vigorous punishment."[929] Indeed, if not for the critics and opponents Roosevelt faced throughout his life, he never would have had the opportunity to showcase his ability to handle his critics, or to "give and take vigorous punishment." Remember: It is often the case that what your opponents say or do has little lasting significance. Far more often, it is your response that determines your fate. Remember these words from Amelia Boone, American obstacle course racer, and three-time winner of the World's Toughest Mudder, "I'm not the strongest. I'm not the fastest. But I'm really good at suffering."[930]

Elevate Yourself Above Shallow Concerns.

During the 1984 presidential campaign, President Reagan, at 73, was being criticized for his age. His opponents were attacking him, saying he was too old to be president, that he couldn't handle the pressure if things started to heat up. His campaign was working hard to counter that image, releasing pictures, for instance, of him playing football with his shirt off on the beach. Finally, in his debate with his younger opponent, Walter Mondale, moderator Henry Trewhitt confronted Reagan directly. "You already are the oldest President in history," Trewhitt began, "and some of your staff say you were tired after your most recent encounter with Mr. Mondale. I recall yet that President Kennedy had to go for days on end with very little sleep during the Cuban missile crisis. Is there any doubt in your mind that you would be able to function in such circumstances?"[931] Reagan was ready to put the issue to rest. "Not at all," he began, "and I want you to know that also I will not make age an issue of this campaign. I am not going to exploit for political purposes my opponent's youth and inexperience."[932] The audience erupted with laughter and thunderous applause. Trewhitt, taking a few seconds to regain his composure, immediately recognized Reagan's response as a home run. Even Mondale couldn't wipe the smile off his face, even while he knew he was beat. The exchange, in retrospect, was seen as the turning point, finally giving Reagan some rest. Two weeks later, Reagan defeated Mondale in a landslide, carrying 49 of the 50 states.

Whatever criticism or attacks you are faced with, or defeats you are forced to endure, never assume that the damage is done and there is nothing worthwhile left to do. It is not the attacks of your opponents, but the way you handle them that will determine your future.

Never Take Yourself Too Seriously.

When Dwight Eisenhower was Supreme Commander of the Allied Forces in Europe during World War II he made a trip to visit the troops stationed near Aachen, the westernmost city in Germany. The troops were enduring some intense hardships and Eisenhower wanted to check in on the soldiers, and see if he could boost their morale. After he delivered a short speech, the GIs responded with warm applause. But then, suddenly, when Eisenhower stepped off the platform and slipped backwards into the mud, the troops all burst into uproarious laughter. Then Eisenhower looked up at the soldiers all standing their laughing at him and he burst into laughter himself. "Something tells me," Ike said, "that my visit with you fellows has been a howling success."[933]

Your success depends on your ability to roll with the punches, laugh at yourself, and readily embrace the great bulk of your gaffes, mishaps, limitations, and mistakes. When a particular criticism of you sticks, rather than working overtime to defend yourself or shutter the attack, see if you can't turn it around, or embrace it and make it your own. Then you can begin to subtly redefine it to serve your own ends. When Huey Long first picked up the nickname "Kingfish," his critics immediately jumped at the opportunity to use it to deride and discredit him. *Vanity Fair*, for example, thought the nickname was an apt fit for Long, writing that the Louisiana kingfish has a "big mouth, feeds off suckers, thrives best in the mud and slime, and is very hard to catch."[934] Rather than protesting or discouraging its use, however, Long took the nickname on as his own. He embraced it. He began answering the phone, "This is the Kingfish."[935] He even used the nickname when referring to himself to lighten the mood. "It has served to substitute gaiety for some of the tragedy of politics," he wrote in his autobiography.[936] "I have made no effort to discourage it."[937]

> *"Of all the virtues we can learn, no trait is more useful, more essential for survival, and more likely to improve the quality of life than the ability to transform adversity into an enjoyable challenge."*
> —Mihaly Csikszentmihalyi (1934—), Hungarian Psychologist

Learn to Laugh at Yourself, Master Self-Deprecating Humor.

Prior to the 1960 presidential campaign, John F. Kennedy was ridiculed by his opponents for his perceived dependence on his father, the wealthy magnate Joseph P. Kennedy. Many accused his father of attempting to buy the presidency for his son. This was becoming a significant problem for the candidate, so much so that Kennedy began looking for ways to deal with some of the criticisms. Finally, just before delivering a speech one evening, Kennedy reached into the breast pocket of his suit and withdrew a slip of paper, informing his audience, "I have just received the following wire from my generous daddy."[938] At last, the press probably figured, this telegram was evidence that young Kennedy was on a tight leash with his father. Kennedy continued, "Dear Jack, Don't buy a single vote more than is necessary. I'll be damned if I'm going to pay for a landslide."[939] Kennedy's audience erupted in laughter, and the issue of his father's influence soon began to fade.

People frequently ridiculed Abraham Lincoln for his appearance. Rather than letting it get to him, however, he would use it as a way to connect with his audience. During a debate, for instance, one of Lincoln's opponents, Stephen Douglas, accused Lincoln of being deceitful, saying that he was "two-faced." Always quick with the wit, Lincoln responded: "I leave it to my audience. If I had another face, do you think I would wear *this* one?"[940] The laughter of the audience immediately deflated his opponent's attack.

People who take themselves too seriously are at a significant disadvantage. They have a hard time dealing with criticism, opposition, and attacks. They are, therefore, weaker and more vulnerable to the agenda of their adversaries. As a result, they are more dangerous and unpredictable, often finding themselves reacting to events, rather than following through with their own strategy and plans. Learn not to take yourself too seriously. Learn to laugh at yourself, roll with the punches, and make fun of your mishaps and gaffes. Understand: There is power in being able to laugh at yourself. Self-deprecating humor puts others at ease. It makes you seem more likeable, relatable, accessible and charismatic. It disarms your critics. When you are able to laugh at yourself, you also give people the impression that you understand the world and your place in it. You see the world as it is. It projects an image of confidence, strength, reliability, and power. As the character Tyrion Lannister (played by Peter Dinklage) said to Jon Snow (Kit Harrington) in Game of Thrones, "Let me give you some advice bastard. Never forget what you are. The rest of the world will not. Wear it like armor, and it can never be used to hurt you."[941]

6

BE OBLIVIOUS TO REJECTION AND DEFEAT

Find a Way or Make One:
Walt Disney's Impossible Dream

"I will either find a way or make one."

—Hannibal Barca (247—c. 183 B.C.), Ancient Carthaginian Military Commander

It was not until the early 1950s that Walt Disney turned his attention to a dream which he had been harboring for years: The creation of an amusement park and resort that would captivate and entertain the masses, "a place," he said, "for people to find happiness and knowledge."[942] By this time, Disney had already achieved remarkable success, winning awards as an animator with Mickey Mouse and, in 1939, an Academy Award for *Snow White and the Seven Dwarfs*, which at the time was the highest grossing film in Hollywood.

When Walt Disney set out to create Disneyland, however, he met with a steady stream of harsh resistance. His own brother, Roy, called the Disneyland idea a "carny" concept, which left the impression of circus geeks and sideshow freaks, smelly animals, dirty grounds, and amusement rides, all run by vagabond hucksters eager to make a quick buck off their unsuspecting guests.[943] Walt, however, had something entirely different in mind, something much more safe, family-friendly, and "clean."[944] But when he tried to describe to Roy exactly how Disneyland would be different, Roy said, "It's a fantasy and won't work."[945] Even the alleged experts thought the Disneyland concept would fail. In fact, the Stanford Research Institute rejected the idea outright and "advised the board of directors of Disney to not invest one cent in the concept."[946] Others balked because they were "afraid it was too ambitious."[947]

The lack of willing investors nearly bankrupt Disney and the entire endeavor. A whopping 302 banks reportedly rejected his request for a loan.[948] Disney's vision was so big and bold that the bankers thought he'd lost his mind.[949]

Look for Opportunity in the Impossible.

The Punic Wars between Rome and Carthage were some of the greatest and most costly confrontations in history. Largely a result of the ever expanding and rapacious reach of the Roman Republic, along with the Carthaginian's unwillingness to surrender Corsica, Sardinia and parts of Sicily—all of which they considered part of the Carthaginian Empire—Rome and Carthage were locked in conflict for over a century. It was not until the rise of Hannibal Barca, widely considered one of the greatest military leaders in history, during the Second Punic War (218—201 B.C.), that the future of the Roman Republic was in doubt.

The First Punic War (264—241 B.C.) saw the Carthaginians with unquestionable Naval superiority, handily defeating the greenhorn Roman navy at the Battle of the Lipari Islands. Rome responded to the defeat by rapidly and dramatically expanding their fleet to over one hundred warships.

The Roman legions had long been considered a superior land fighting force. Now, Rome was determined to focus on her navy, protecting the Italian peninsula from any future sea-based attacks. It was a turn of attention that Hannibal would soon exploit, as he began preparations for one of the most audacious military assaults in history.

Rather than attacking Rome by sea, as the Romans expected, Hannibal resolved to launch an invasion through Northern Italy. With winter fast approaching, Hannibal would attempt the impossible. Stretching the endurance of man and beast to the utter limit, Hannibal set out to bring an army—including some 90,000 men, 12,000 horses and 37 elephants—across the Alps.

Entering the foothills of the Alps at the onset of winter, Hannibal's army would have to cross 120 miles of snow, ice and rock, reaching elevations over 8,000 feet, with no shelter, little food, and little rest; with miles of jagged, narrow pathways carved into the mountainsides, with sheer drops of hundreds of yards, everything covered by the slippery, perilous elements of winter, all while facing down barbarian tribesmen who lurked and hovered waiting for the opportune moment to attack. "Never," Hannibal explained to his generals, "in his wildest dreams, would the Roman think us capable of such audacity."[950]

Indeed, the Romans were not prepared for an assault by land. Stretching across eight countries, with peaks exceeding 15,000 feet, the Roman people had always assumed they were protected from a land invasion by the perilous, snow-capped mountains. They never suspected Hannibal's bold breach across such treacherous terrain.

But when Hannibal told his generals of his plan they were dumbfounded. Of course the Romans would never expect such an assault. It was impossible. To his generals, the idea of taking an army with horses and elephants across the Alps was unthinkable. It was madness. It could not be done.

Hannibal, however, remained impervious. "I will," he said, "either find a way or make one."[951]

To both the awe and alarm of the Romans, Hannibal and his army made it across the Alps. And, in three decisive battles, Hannibal unleashed a tactical and strategic genius the likes of which the Romans had never before seen, a force so powerful it rattled the very foundations of Rome.

Stockpile Victories as an Antidote for Subsequent Rebuffs.

As with many of the heroes of history, Hannibal's words reveal the mindset of success. No doubt, this was an outlook Walt Disney maintained throughout his life. After all, Walt Disney's struggle to build Disneyland was not the first time he had experienced a heavy dose of rejection and defeat, and found his way through nonetheless. In fact, rejection, setbacks and defeat had been a regular part of his life, beginning with his own father who "told him he could never make a living by drawing cartoons."[952] It wasn't, however, just the banks, the experts, or his own family that rejected his ideas—as if all that was not enough. And it wasn't just the ambitious and majestic ideas like Disneyland that spawned such rejection either. According to Disney's friend, author Ray Bradbury, "Everything Walt achieved in his life was something he was told he couldn't do."[953] Over time, however, by stockpiling his successes, Walt Disney became increasingly immune to rejection. And, moreover, as Bradbury puts it, "He spent his entire career proving the doubters wrong. And he had a wonderful time doing it.'"[954]

Disney was determined to make his dream a reality. He would build Disneyland or go bankrupt trying. "Once again Walt listened to his own internal messenger and ignored all the experts..."[955] He refused to be defeated by the banks. "He wasn't crazy," writes Anthony Robbins, "he was a visionary and, more important, he was committed to making that vision a reality."[956]

Walt Disney was one of America's great visionaries. But it was not vision alone that led to his success. Wendell Warner, who worked for years as an engineer and draftsman for Disney, put it this way, "'Walt was successful because of one rock-solid Midwestern value. It's called perseverance.'"[957] In the words of a Disney biographer, "Walt succeeded because he was persistent and determined. He didn't let rejection and criticism stop him. He didn't listen to the naysayers who told him he couldn't do this or that. Walt was a finisher."[958] And he would follow through on Disneyland despite the bankers and experts, regardless of the many skeptics, naysayers, and critics.

Vision and grit—that was the secret of Walt Disney's success. He believed in his vision, and had the grit to follow through, regardless of the resistance and rejection that seemed to stalk nearly every move. Like Hannibal, Walt believed he was left with little choice. Finally, he determined to sell his home in Palm Springs and put his insurance policy up as collateral to get the money he needed to buy the Anaheim property, reaching what he said was, the "limit of my personal borrowing ability."[959] And, as a result, hundreds of millions of people around the world have experienced the delights of Disney's dream.

History's heroes of hustle and grit all learned to become increasingly immune to rejection and defeat. At first, you may have to rely on small victories, or successes in other areas of your life to neutralize or counteract rejection and defeat. Even without any real significant triumphs, you can use your creative imagination to construct experiences that serve the same end. Over time, as you begin to stockpile your victories and successes—and periodically recall them in vivid detail, or, better yet, by keeping a success journal—you will build a shield of resistance and develop a kind of hardiness that makes you, essentially, more and more oblivious to future rejection and defeat.

Cultivate Mindfulness, Let Your Purpose Dictate Your Response.

To feel the sting of failure and rejection is a natural part of our survival as social animals. The pain is intended to help us learn from our misjudgments, miscalculations, and mistakes and, thereby, better adapt to our environment, community and tribe. Even in the modern world, our instinctive responses often maintain much of their value. Problems begin to arise, however, when people mindlessly let their default responses run like master programs.

It is virtually inevitable that you will face rejection and defeat in the pursuit of your most ambitious dreams and goals. Whether or not you succeed depends in no small part on your capacity to carry on, to be essentially oblivious to such resistance. Paradoxically, the easiest way to be oblivious to the social and emotional sting, to forge ahead in spite of such rejection and resistance, is to adopt a more mindful, intentional response. Rather than instinctively falling back on your automatic programming, deliberately decide how you will respond to rejection and defeat. Resolve to make choices aligned with your purpose and goals, rather than your emotions and moods or, worse still, the moods and emotions of others. It is easy to disregard rejection, to ignore naysayers, to say "no" to those who deny you, when you have a deeper "yes" burning inside.[960] Understand: To succeed at a high level demands withstanding relentless rejection. It requires functioning at a higher level of awareness and intention, driven by a clear sense of purpose and inspiring goals.

This unwillingness to accept rejection is a recurring theme in the biographies of the great champions and legends of grit. It's as if rejection as such does not register in their minds. They are utterly oblivious to defeat. "If you look at any of the most successful people in history," writes Anthony Robbins, "you will find this common thread: They would not be denied. They would not accept no. They would not allow anything to stop them from making their vision, their goal, a reality."[961]

The first time General Douglas MacArthur applied to West Point, his application was rejected. Determined to gain entrance to the prestigious military academy, MacArthur was resolved to apply again. Unfortunately, his application was rejected a second time. Most men would have given up after the first attempt. Almost everyone would have given up after the second. But Douglas MacArthur was not most men. He would not be denied. And, thus, he applied a third time. Finally, he was admitted. West Point's admissions committee, ultimately, made the right decision, and General MacArthur made history. Today, West Point is home to the MacArthur Monument, a statue of the great General just outside the North entrance of the MacArthur Barracks.

General Douglass MacArthur's distant cousin Winston Churchill had this same mindset of obliviousness in the face of rejection and defeat. "When he was after something that he was determined to get, he did not know the meaning of the word no, no matter how often he heard it," writes President Richard Nixon in his book *Leaders*.[962] "Once he was engaged in a military battle or a political campaign, he purged the word defeat from his vocabulary."[963] The British Bulldog understood that it is not defeat unless you yourself recognize it as such.

When the British troops were forced to retreat during the Battle of France, after facing a devastating defeat in Dunkirk, Churchill went before Parliament to rally the nation. The Nazis were winning the war, but it was not over yet. Churchill marched ahead unfazed by the grave setbacks, and he was determined to instill in the British people that same unshakable resolve. "Even though large tracts of Europe and many old and famous States have fallen or may fall into the grip of the Gestapo and all the odious apparatus of Nazi rule," Churchill said, "we shall not flag or fail."[964] Churchill ended his address with a call to arms that brought several Members of Parliament to tears:[965] "We shall go on to the end, we shall fight in France, we shall fight on the seas and oceans, we shall fight with growing confidence and growing strength in the air, we shall defend our Island, whatever the cost may be, we shall fight on the beaches, we shall fight on the landing grounds, we shall fight in the fields and in the streets, we shall fight in the hills; we shall never surrender."[966]

Be the Punching Bag that Strikes Back.

The crushing rebuke President Bill Clinton suffered when he lost the House and Senate, *and* the governors mansions to the GOP in the 1994 mid-term elections was billed as "one of Clinton's great electoral spankings."[967] Clinton was starting to look like a one-term president who would be unlikely to achieve anything of lasting significance. Yet, to the disappointment of his opponents, and the surprise of most everyone in Washington, Clinton emerged in the subsequent years stronger and with greater political capital than he had in the beginning of his presidency.[968] In fact, from the '94 mid-term elections, Clinton's approval rating continued its upward trend until 1999, never again falling to its '94 lows.

In a charged interaction with his nemesis, Speaker of the House Newt Gingrich, Clinton revealed an illuminating metaphor for one of the key characteristics of his success. "Do you know who I am?" Clinton rhetorically asked Gingrich. "I'm the big rubber doll you had as a kid, and every time you hit it, it bounces back. That's me—the harder you hit me, the faster I come back up."[969]

When Clinton was asked to explain how he, in one interviewer's words, "survived travails that would have sent other politicians either running for cover or killed them," Clinton replied, "I have a high pain threshold. That's pretty important."[970] Crediting his "indomitable mother," Clinton added, "I was raised to believe that every person should live on Churchill's edict, 'Never quit.'"[971] This was not just Clinton's perception of himself either; as indicated by Rahm Emanuel's remark to Barack Obama about both Bill and Hillary Clinton in 2008: "'Quitting,' he said, 'simply wasn't in the Clintons' bloodstream.' Certainly there had never been any evidence of that particular form of plasma in the former president's veins. And his recent behavior gave no indication that he'd received a transfusion."[972]

It is not defeat, denial, or rejection that ruins most people—it's their reaction to these events. It's always the response which determines the succeeding outcome. But your objective is to go even further. Focused on your greater purpose and goals, rejection fails to register as such in your mind. You are entirely unfazed by defeat. You see only feedback and lessons learned. Consequently, like Clinton, you gain experience, insight, and wisdom from every experience, regardless of the results.

Do not misunderstand: Only a fool would imagine there are no reasonable limits to this approach. Being oblivious to rejection and defeat is a matter of attitude and emotion, not strategy and logic—or ethics. In other words, you remain emotionally unfazed. Your motivation to attain your overall purpose remains unchanged. And, yet, as with all legitimate feedback, your strategy is flexible, and open to change. Being oblivious to rejection and failure did not mean that Clinton was not listening and learning. Clinton is indeed famously open to feedback. In fact, part of Clinton's comeback following the '94 mid-terms was grounded in his increasing willingness to govern as a centrist, a moderate, even borrowing ideas from and adopting some of the policies of the moderate right.

Play the Long Game, and Do Not Give Up.

When Donald Trump faced the prospect of personal bankruptcy in the early 1990s it was, he said, "a tremendous low." Problems seemed to surround him on all sides. "The banks were after me," he said.[973] "People avoided me. There was a recession, and the real estate market was almost nonexistent."[974] When everyone else thought he was finished, when they were trumpeting his fall on the front pages of *The Wall Street Journal* and *The New York Times*, Trump was hard at work figuring out how to come back.

"Giving up," he said, "is something that never entered my mind. Not for one second, and that's one reason I think I confounded my critics. They were trying to skewer me, but it had the opposite effect—it just made me want to make a comeback and in a big way. I knew I could prove them wrong by being stubborn, being tenacious, and not giving in or giving up."[975] Looking back years later, Trump said, "I became a stronger person very quickly during this time."[976]

More recently, throughout the 2016 campaign for president, Trump continues to endure endless negative attention from the media (often for good reason, but more often simply because Trump's name sells). And, yet, Trump has proven remarkably resistant to the criticism. In fact, it often seems as if his campaign is further propelled by the attacks; his poll numbers have continued to rise even while he's widely reviled in the press.

Whatever their political positions or personal flaws, there are clear lessons to be learned from both the successes and failures of people like Clinton and Trump. Both Bill and Hillary Clinton have endured withering political attacks throughout their careers. But they never gave up and, in the end, they came out stronger as a result. The lesson is clear: "Quitters do not get anywhere," says Trump.[977] "You will not be successful if you listen to nos."[978] "When most people say no, they are doing it to further their own ends. Do not let somebody's arbitrary 'no' stop you. Find a way to turn the 'no' into a 'yes,' or find a creative way to sidestep the 'no.'"[979] Again, he adds, "Do not let anybody stop you!"[980]

Focus instead on being self-reliant. "It's all up to you," writes Chris Matthews in *The Hardball Handbook*.[981] "If you want to push your ideas, ambitions, or dreams, you have to get out there and champion them. You need to be able to face rejection, hostility, and, more often, indifference. The higher your ambitions take you, the more stamina you'll need, the more willingness to get a "No!" slammed in your face. The more failure you can accept, the greater your chance of success."[982]

Remember: It's not a matter of how fierce the rejection you face, it's how you face it. Keep your focus always on the outcome at the end. In Churchill's words, "If you're going through hell, keep going."[983] Be oblivious to rejection. Smile in the face of those who deny you or refuse your requests. Steal a play from the champions and focus your mind on the bigger game, several moves ahead.

When you play the long game you understand how roles and positions of power can be easily reversed. Imagine a future where those who reject you now become your most outspoken advocates, your greatest champions. Adopt this mindset, practice these tactics and you will find yourself becoming increasingly able to absorb temporary setbacks and defeat, becoming, over time, increasingly indomitable, emotionally and psychologically invincible.

Even as others reject or defeat you, they are noticeably affected by this certainty, self-confidence, and poise. They are perplexed by your grace in the face of even the harshest rejection or bitter defeat. There seems to be something special about you. They may experience you as charismatic, or perhaps they are simply unable to understand why their rejection appears to have the opposite effect. They sense that you know something. Many will begin to question whether they misjudged you. They think they defeated you, but there you are: Standing, impenetrable, unable to be conquered.

"If you want to succeed in life, remember this: Massive rejection is the key to success."
—Anthony Robbins (1960-), American Speaker, Author, Coach

Erase Failure and Rejection, Shut the Door and Move On.

Arnold Schwarzenegger has faced a number of challenges and setbacks throughout his life and various careers. A number of his films became box office fiascos, and he's endured the harsh rebukes of Hollywood and the entertainment media on numerous occasions. But Arnold faced some of his greatest challenges and most intense criticism, along with outright rejection, in the realm of California politics, most notably when all four of his pet ballot initiatives were defeated in the 2005 special election.

And, yet, none of this ever stopped Schwarzenegger from finding success, in part, because he had a proven strategy for dealing with it: He simply kept moving forward with his plans. "…Unconcerned with the foibles and failures of the past, Arnold took what he needed from his earlier life and moved on."[984] In his book, *Fantastic: The Life of Arnold Schwarzenegger*, Laurence Leamer explains, "Arnold obsessed over nothing but endlessly moved on, discarding whatever was unpleasant and negative and carrying forward only what inspired and moved him."[985] Arnold always knew exactly what he wanted; he refused to let anyone stop him. In an interview with Lesley Stahl on *60 Minutes*, Schwarzenegger reveals this same mental approach:

Stahl: "Someone said about you that one key to your success was your resolute, non-introspection. And you also say in the book, I think, that if you have had a failure in life, you just erase it. You don't think about it, and just keep going."

Schwarzenegger: "I don't dwell on it. Dwelling on it, like some people do, you know, years later, say, 'Oh, yeah, I lost this, and I will never forget that. I'm still suffering.' No, that's not me. I don't suffer for anything that I've lost."

Stahl: "You're able to just keep going?"

Schwarzenegger: "Oh, yeah."[986]

Arnold's ability to always keep moving forward has been central to his success. "Schwarzenegger never lets perceived setbacks or obstacles interfere with his vision for the future."[987] None of this is to suggest Schwarzenegger didn't learn from rejection and defeat—he certainly did. To be oblivious to rejection and defeat does not mean you neglect taking responsibility for your mistakes. After all, in order to succeed, you *must learn* from your blunders and gaffes. In fact, being oblivious to rejection and defeat is the opposite of being irresponsible. It's about taking *full* responsibility. It's about refusing to let anyone have responsibility for your ultimate success. As Schwarzenegger said in a televised news conference at the capitol following his failed ballot initiatives, "The buck stops with me. I take full responsibility for this election. I take full responsibility for its failure."[988] But he was also learning from his failure. Arnold elaborated on the event in his autobiography, "I'd taken too confrontational an approach, I'd been in too much of a hurry, and I hadn't really listened to the people. We overreached. And it had backfired."[989]

This, of course, was all that would be said. "Arnold was not a man to obsess over momentary setbacks. He was already moving on…"[990] "I promised the fighting was over," he said. "Next year would begin with a different tone."[991]

The industrial titan Andrew Carnegie possessed this same quality. He too weathered his fair share of setbacks, including failed business investments, patent struggles, failed technologies and processes in his plants, severe service disruptions with the railroads, and major conflicts with labor.[992] Carnegie also had to work, on more than one occasion, to rebuild his reputation.[993] But he never let any of this hold him back. Like Schwarzenegger, Carnegie possessed the remarkable ability to, as one biographer put it, "shut the door on the past with so resolute a slam and with hardly a backward glance."[994]

Never dwell on the mistakes of the past. Never obsess over rejection or defeat. But take full responsibility for learning what you can, and quickly moving ahead.

7

Bounce Back, Rebuild, Begin Anew

"I don't measure a man's success by how high he climbs,
but how high he bounces when he hits bottom."
—George S. Patton (1885—1945), U.S. Commanding General

Make Up Your Mind to Comeback:
The Resurrection of FDR

In 1920, when the Democratic National Convention nominated Franklin Delano Roosevelt, at just 38-years-old, as the vice-presidential candidate—with James Cox on the top of the ticket—Roosevelt was living his dream. An aristocrat with a famous last name and a cousin who had been one of the most popular Presidents in recent memory, FDR seemed destined to succeed. He was a tall, white male who was attractive, fit, personable, young and rich, and he was married to the niece of the former President. It was as if the world was being handed to him on a gold-plated platter. Previously appointed as the Assistant Secretary of the Navy, it looked as though he himself was destined to follow in his cousin Theodore Roosevelt's footsteps to become President of the United States.

FDR relished every minute of the campaign for Vice President, and though he and Cox lost that election, the campaign was, for FDR, a considerable triumph. He gained national name recognition, and experience with a national campaign. He joined hands with and earned the goodwill of thousands of party leaders across the nation, and now the presidency itself was clearly within reach.

Alas, a dark cloud was approaching.

Suddenly, in August of 1921, Roosevelt fell gravely ill while vacationing at Campobello Island in New Brunswick, Canada. Within days, Roosevelt was unable to move his legs.

Two weeks later, he was diagnosed with polio. The illness left him permanently paralyzed from the waist down. It was a devastating turn of events.

A few short weeks earlier, FDR was riding on top of the world, then suddenly everything seemed to come crashing down. His life, as he knew it, was over. "He was thirty-nine years old. No one knew what sort of life might now be possible for him," David McCullough said, "but one thing seemed certain: His political career was finished."[995]

Roosevelt spent the next several years largely out of the public eye. Even if Roosevelt had wanted to, the idea that he might somehow bounce back from this and reenter the harsh, competitive world of politics was unthinkable at the time. The ignorance, unfounded fear, and primitive social attitudes toward people with disabilities was widespread. Biographer Hugh Gallagher explains, "In the 1920s, why, polio was a terrifying thing. Something like 25 percent of people who caught polio died of it within the first two weeks. If you survived and you had paralysis, they didn't know what to do, and "nice" families kept their disabled members at home in the back bedroom with the blinds drawn. There was a certain shame attached to it somehow."[996]

But Franklin Delano Roosevelt refused to be beaten. In fact, he refused to accept his paralysis at all. He was determined to walk, no matter how awkward, painful, and humiliating it might be. He was determined not to allow this setback to diminish his dreams. It might be a long road back, but he was going to make his way. "He would devote the next seven years to one single goal: To get back on his feet."[997]

> *"Using the power of decision gives you the capacity to get past any excuse to change any and every part of your life in an instant."*
> —Anthony Robbins (1960—), American Author, Speaker, Coach

Decide to Bounce Back.

High achievement and success requires becoming the kind of person who bounces back, regardless of the blows or series of setbacks that life sends. This is not just words. The story of human history is the story of men and women rising to meet and master the challenges before them, overcoming obstacles and bouncing back from setbacks they did not yet know they could. Indeed, the reputations of many of the heroes of history came not from easy success, but were forged in their efforts to absorb setbacks and bounce back from defeat. General Ulysses S. Grant faced a number of grave setbacks throughout the Civil War, and yet he recovered time after time, to the point that Grant's success as a General was primarily attributed not to his courage or renowned capacity as a strategist, but to his ability to recover from defeat. Indeed, Lincoln said, "It is the dogged pertinacity of Grant that wins."[998]

The American showman and entrepreneur P.T. Barnum faced a number of devastating fires, business fiascos, costly lawsuits, and a failed run for Congress. And, yet, somehow he always seemed to find his way back. "At fifty, Barnum was a ruined man, owing thousands more than he possessed, yet," writes one of America's early self-improvement authors, "he resolutely resumed business once more, fairly wringing success from adverse fortune, and paying his notes at the same time."[999] Nothing seemed able to keep the showman down. "Again and again he was ruined; but phoenix-like, he rose repeatedly from the ashes of his misfortune each time more determined than before."[1000]

Resilience is an indispensable factor of success. In the words of Richard Branson, "This ability to bounce back after a setback is probably the single most important trait an entrepreneurial venture can possess. If innovation is at the heart of your business, obstacles come with the territory. How you react to and navigate those hurdles will make the difference between failure and success."[1001] The simplest and most important thing to do when adversity strikes is to *decide* to bounce back. The very act of determining in your mind that you will not be beaten is an indispensable key to your comeback, and ultimate triumph.

Far too many people get so caught up with the pain of the past that they begin to destroy their future. They dwell. They obsess. They fixate on what happened; they fail to learn and move on. "Every one ought to make it a life-rule to wipe out from his memory everything that has been unpleasant, unfortunate. We ought to forget everything that has kept us back, has made us suffer, has been disagreeable, and never allow the hideous pictures of distressing conditions to enter our minds again. There is only one thing to do with a disagreeable, harmful experience,' and that is—forget it!"[1002]

The celebrated New York City preacher and author Norman Vincent Peale repeatedly encountered people who were suffering not from what happened, but from their inability to let it go. "The person," he explained, "who has the philosophy of the new beginning is the person who will never continue to associate with his failures." Peale advised his audience: "Never hang around with your failures. Never talk about them. Never think about them. Walk away from them—no matter what they are. Never settle for a failure."[1003]

Have you made costly mistakes in the past? Fine. You're not alone. Now accept it and move on. "Don't be mortgaged to the past...There is no use in castigating yourself for not having done better. Form a habit of expelling from your mind thoughts or suggestions which call up...bitter memories, and which have a bad influence upon you."[1004]

In his book, *Like a Virgin*, Richard Branson shares how he learned this same "enduring" lesson from his mother, Eve, "who always taught me," Branson wrote, "never to look back in regret but to move on to the next thing. The amount of time people waste dwelling on failures," wrote Branson, "rather than putting that energy into another project always amazes me."[1005]

One of the tricks of resilience—rather than letting go of the past—is simply to reframe it. You can work your *perception* of failure to your advantage. Columbia University psychologist George Bonanno, who has been studying resilience for nearly twenty-five years, explains, "Events are not traumatic until we experience them as traumatic."[1006] In essence, it's not an exaggeration to say that it's not what happens to you, but how you construct that experience in you mind that determines how it effects you. Similar findings have emerged in the research around stress. Stress is only harmful to your health when you interpret it as being harmful.[1007] In essence, Bonanno concludes, "We can make ourselves more or less vulnerable by how we think about things."[1008]

It is your freedom in the moment to choose what each new adversity means that will determine your future. "Your life changes the moment you make a new, congruent, and committed decision," writes Anthony Robbins.[1009] "It's in your moments of decision that your destiny is shaped."[1010]

Rejuvenate and Regroup to Rise and Fight Again

"The greatest glory in living lies not in never falling, but in rising every time we fall."
–Nelson Mandela (1918—2013), President of South Africa

Within weeks of his paralysis Roosevelt began the excruciatingly painful and tedious exercises that his doctors recommended for his condition. The exercises "took up endless time," and, biographer Geoffrey Ward added, "I think it's a measure of his ambition and his grit that he kept at them as long and as hard as he did."[1011]

Unfortunately, Roosevelt's paralysis was not getting better. Whether he would admit it or not, he had lost forever the use of his legs. He was not able to walk, or even stand on his own. And that, Roosevelt understood, was a political problem. He knew that if people saw him struggling to walk that it would elicit pity—and, thus, it was "political poison."[1012] But neither was this enough to beat FDR. "And since he wasn't getting better, he developed better techniques for appearing to look better."[1013]

Utterly dependent on the metal braces around his legs, he learned to use only his cane, and the strength of his sons or an aide who acted as a brace. "You must not let people see that this is difficult or takes effort or it hurts," Roosevelt instructed his sons.[1014] It was highly risky. He could've easily fallen over. "It was not a practical way" of walking, one biographer said, "but it was a political way."[1015]

And, so, as Roosevelt made his way from his car to the platform of one event after another, using the sheer strength of his upper body to hold himself up on his son, they would ever so slowly joke and laugh and carry on as if nothing unusual was happening, indeed making it look as if they were going slow simply so they could smile and say hello to as many people as possible. "It was show biz," said Hugh Gallagher, and "it worked."[1016]

Three years after he had been diagnosed with a debilitating disease, FDR was invited to deliver the nominating speech for Governor Al Smith at the Democratic National Convention in New York City and, on June 26, 1924, testing the waters, Roosevelt reentered the public arena. Backstage, out of sight from the people and the press, Roosevelt wheeled himself as close to the podium as he could get without being seen.[1017] With his legs wrapped in metal braces, Roosevelt had to be lifted to his feet. With a cane supporting him on one side and his son, Elliott, holding up him from the other, Roosevelt stepped out onto the stage, and was immediately met with the wild cheers of a mass of delegates some 15,000 strong. Balancing precariously on his supports, Roosevelt set out to walk across the stage to the podium. "An accidental fall would leave him sprawled helplessly on the convention floor, his political hopes destroyed."[1018]

"He appeared to be walking."[1019] "And he was smiling, a great, happy smile that took eyes away from his withered legs. It was as courageous a performance as any in American political history. Roosevelt's brow was soaked in sweat once he reached the podium and gripped it with both hands to steady himself. And still he smiled. The warring delegates hushed in shared admiration."[1020] A commentator at the time depicted the drama unfolding: "'Here on the stage is Franklin Roosevelt, a figure tall and proud even in suffering, pale with years of struggle against paralysis, a man softened and cleansed and illumined with pain. For the moment we are lifted up.'"[1021]

Roosevelt may have lost the use of his legs, but he did not lose his spirit or guts. And that, in the end, proved to be enough. "Thousands of men" wrote the Founder of Success magazine over a century ago, "have put grit in place of health, eyes, ears, hands, legs and yet have achieved marvelous success. Indeed, most of the great things of the world have been accomplished by grit and pluck."[1022]

Roosevelt's speech was a rousing success.

The nomination went to Al Smith, but the triumph was all FDR.[1023] Party leaders immediately began to discuss the possibility of FDR running for governor of New York, another post his cousin Theodore once held. "When Smith urged him to run for governor of New York, Roosevelt said he was ready."[1024]

When someone asked Governor Smith why he risked raising up a potential rival by helping FDR win New York, Smith showed no concern. "He'll be dead within a year," he said.[1025] Several months later, however, Smith failed in his bid for the presidency. FDR, on the other hand, was now the Governor of New York.[1026] By 1932, just eleven years from the time he was struck down with paralysis, Franklin Delano Roosevelt was President of the United States.

> *"In the fell clutch of circumstance, I have not winced nor cried aloud.*
> *Under the bludgeonings of chance, my head is bloody, but unbowed."*
> —William Ernest Henley, "Invictus" (1875)

Take Time to Bleed.

One of the key steps in bouncing back from a serious setback is taking the necessary time to recover and regroup. It is often wise to take time to mourn, heal, or more fully process and assimilate a life-altering experience. As Ecclesiastes tells us, there is a time and a season for everything. It is, after all, impossible to run on a broken leg. What's more, getting up before you grasp what happened is a good way to risk breaking the other leg. In FDR's case, he still had to get a handle on what he was dealing with before he could move ahead.

President Richard Nixon faced a number of setbacks throughout his political career. One of his biggest upsets followed his loss of the presidential race to John F. Kennedy in 1960. When Nixon lost the race for governor of California just two years later, it was widely agreed that Nixon's political career was finished. It was one thing to lose the presidency to JFK, but now he was viewed as the man who couldn't even win over voters from his own home state. Even Nixon himself—rarely an exemplar of emotional self-control—admitted (foolishly) that he was finished, telling the press that he would no longer be their political punching bag, "…because, gentlemen," he said, "this is my last press conference."[1027]

Knowing that others had defied their political obituaries, however, Nixon always got back up and carried on. Nixon was fond of St. Barton's Ode: "I am hurt but I am not slain! I will lie me down and bleed awhile—then I'll rise and fight again!"[1028] And, indeed, after several years in the wilderness, Richard Nixon did rise to fight again, winning the White House in 1968, and again in 1972.

Stay Down But Never Out.

Spending years in the wilderness or benched from the big game may be painful, frustrating, or even humiliating, but it can also be eminently useful. The key is to turn you attention toward being strategic with the use of the time. Roosevelt did not remain idle during this period—quite the opposite, he was working harder than ever before. He worked aggressively to rehabilitate himself, including a rigorous, daily exercise routine and regular swimming. He developed methods for moving around; including a wheelchair which he designed himself, and modifications to his 1936 Ford Phaeton which allowed him to drive with only hand controls. He came up with creative ways to camouflage his condition from the public and the press. He also used this time to create a rehabilitation center for other polio patients. Meanwhile, his wife Eleanor, and his friend and political advisor Louis Howe worked assiduously together with FDR to maintain his political prospects.

In Nixon's case, he traveled throughout Europe meeting with world leaders, giving press conferences, and increasing his knowledge of global affairs. He also moved to New York and joined a prestigious law firm, paid off his debts and made more money than he had at any other time in his life. He stayed out of the 1964 election, which helped to rebuild his reputation as a team player and party elder. He also worked to support a number of congressional candidates in 1966, giving back to his party, keeping his name before the press and fresh in voters minds, and effectively laying the groundwork for his successful presidential bid in 1968.

Never Linger Too Long, Prepare to Run New Risks.

The other key here is to take the time you *need*, but no more than you need. As with a physical injury, if you wait too long you risk limiting your future range of motion. When Eleanor Roosevelt and Louis Howe arranged to have FDR give Alfred E. Smith's nominating speech at the DNC in 1924 Roosevelt thought it was too risky. He knew that if he fell on his way to the podium, his political career would be finished in an instant. He also knew, however, that time was running out, and that if he ever hoped to get back into politics now was the time. The opportunity for national exposure might not come again until 1928, and even then he would have to work much harder to reacquaint himself with voters and rebuild his base of support. Roosevelt made the attempt, delivered his famous "Happy Warrior" speech and effectively lit the fire for his political resurrection.

Frame a New Beginning:
Never See Failure as Final, or Defeat as a Dead End

"Failure is often the turning-point, the pivot of circumstance that swings us to higher levels."
—William George Jordan, *The Majesty of Calmness* (1900)

At the peak of his public esteem and political power, President Richard Nixon was driven by personal demons to destroy his presidency.[1029] After many months of struggling to survive the sins of Watergate, he was finally forced on August 8, 1974 to become the first American president to resign from office. One of the darkest and most mesmerizing moments in the American presidency, a saga of midnight capers and malicious criminality, of unbridled corruption and the abuse of power was at last at an end. "Our long national nightmare is over," President Ford would later say to the American people.[1030]

Watergate was Nixon's most disgraceful defeat and, in the final analysis, it remains a lasting part of his political legacy. But it was not his final chapter. All of the dogged determination, resilience, and grit that Nixon had demonstrated throughout his life and political career, including his relentless struggle to hold on to the presidency which elevated the Watergate scandal into a constitutional crisis, would now be directed toward a new beginning. Before he even left the White House that new beginning was already underway.

In his final remarks to his staff at the White House, Nixon recalled the story of young Theodore Roosevelt and his beautiful young wife Alice Lee who died when she was only twenty-two. Roosevelt was distraught, Nixon said. He wrote in his diary only a large 'X' with the words, "The light has gone out of my life."[1031] Six months later, preparing a printed memorial for private publication, Roosevelt remained inconsolable.[1032] "She was beautiful in face and form and lovelier still in spirit," Roosevelt wrote,

"...None ever knew her who did not love and revere her for her bright and sunny temper and her saintly unselfishness...When she had just become a mother, when her life seemed to be just begun and when the years seemed so bright before her, then by a strange and terrible fate death came to her. And when my heart's dearest died, the light went from my life forever."[1033]

Nixon was fond of Theodore Roosevelt and frequently quoted him in his speeches. But what is perhaps most telling is that Nixon recalled—of the many dark episodes and defeats TR faced—*this* episode in Roosevelt's life to share with his staff in his final address. Perhaps losing the Presidency, which he had coveted for so long, under such shameful and scandalous circumstances, *was* like having the light go out of his life.

Rendering Roosevelt as a kind of role model, Nixon continued his remarks. "He thought the light had gone from his life forever," Nixon said. "But he went on. And he not only became President, but as an ex-President, he served his country, always in the arena, tempestuous, strong, sometimes wrong, sometimes right, but he was a man. And as I leave," Nixon continued, "let me say, that is an example I think all of us should remember."[1034]

"We think sometimes when things happen that don't go the right way...We think that when someone dear to us dies, we think that when we lose an election, we think that when we suffer a defeat that all is ended. We think, as TR said, that the light had left his life forever. Not true," Nixon said.[1035] Roosevelt, of course, still had most of his life before him. Nixon, on the other hand, was now sixty-one. But Nixon understood that this is a way of thinking. It is part of the mental framework of success. "It is only a beginning, always," he said.[1036] "The young must know it; the old must know it. It must always sustain us, because the greatness comes not when things go always good for you,

147

but the greatness comes and you are really tested, when you take some knocks, some disappointments, when sadness comes, because only if you have been in the deepest valley can you ever know how magnificent it is to be on the highest mountain."[1037]

These were not merely the words of some presidential speechwriter. This was part of Nixon's operational code. He would find a way to absorb this knock too. He would turn the page and begin a new chapter. Indeed, even before his fall from power was fully realized, he was already hard at work rebuilding his reputation. In his final speech, delivered from the Oval Office, rather than acknowledging wrongdoing (which he might also have done), Nixon was actively framing events to suit his own future purposes. Referring to the speech as "a masterpiece," biographer Conrad Black wrote, "What was intended to be an unprecedented humiliation for any American president, Nixon converted into a virtual parliamentary acknowledgment of almost blameless insufficiency of legislative support to continue."[1038] He then devoted the other half of his address to a catalog of his accomplishments as President.[1039]

The great military strategist Carl von Clausewitz taught that, "even the ultimate outcome of a war is not always to be regarded as final."[1040] After coming back many times before, Nixon would now be hard at work to make this his latest great comeback. But it wasn't just the way Nixon mentally reframed events. He actively worked to make it—and, in time, it truly became—a new beginning. His first step was to write his memoirs. This would give him the chance to reframe his legacy. As another one of his heroes, Winston Churchill, once said, "History will be kind to me for I intend to write it."[1041] With the publication of *RN: The Memoirs of Richard Nixon* he suddenly became a bestselling author. He began to travel internationally, visiting heads of state (many of whom thought the Watergate fiasco was overblown), and slowly building a reputation as a wise, elder statesman. Beginning with Jimmy Carter, presidents began consulting with Nixon particularly in matters of foreign affairs. "He remained an acknowledged expert on foreign policy, gave countless speeches around the world, and authored several well-regarded books, including *Real Peace* (1983), *No More Vietnams* (1985), *1999: Victory without War* (1988), *In the Arena* (1990), *Seize the Moment* (1992), and *Beyond Peace* (1994)."[1042]

In time, Richard Nixon effectively reclaimed his place on the national stage.[1043] In what historians have called "the high-water mark" of his comeback campaign, Newsweek carried Nixon on the cover in a 1986 story with the title, "He's Back: The Rehabilitation of Richard Nixon."[1044]

When he finally passed away in 1994, scores of foreign dignitaries, international luminaries, and all four of the living American Presidents were present to pay tribute. Focused on Nixon's many notable achievements, President Bill Clinton said in his eulogy, "May the day of judging President Nixon on anything less than his entire life and career come to a close."[1045]

Let Go, Look to Your Next Goal.

President Richard Nixon was in the practice of doing what all of the great hustlers of history have done when faced with defeat: Rather than dwelling on the setbacks and failures of the past, they look forward to the future, and toward their next great dream. Nixon, no doubt, was a flawed leader. But he was a man of action, and he needed a new mountain to climb. What was done was done. Whatever transgressions he committed were now in the past. As Paul wrote to the Corinthians, "The old has passed away; behold, the new has come."[1046] Regardless of all that was coming to an end, for Nixon it was but the beginning of something new—always a beginning. In his eulogy, Clinton put it this way, "The enduring lesson of Richard Nixon is that he never gave up being part of the action and passion of his times. He said many times that unless a person has a goal, a new mountain to climb, his spirit will die."[1047]

Imagining a new beginning is essential to bouncing back and moving on. Publicly disgraced, driven from office, widely condemned across the country, if Richard Nixon can imagine his most ignominious moment as a new beginning, anyone can. This is one of the secrets of the resilient. Part of their power is in their way of thinking, their mental framework, their way of looking out at the world. They never see failure as final, or defeat as a dead end. There is always something new on the road ahead.

Whatever setback, failure or defeat you face, resolve to frame it as a new beginning. Acknowledge that there is something somewhere in this that you needed for the journey ahead—and begin it. "Failure is not fatal," Churchill said. "It is the courage to continue that counts."[1048]

Learn to See Adversity as Preparation for Future Success.

This practice of reframing failure and defeat as the chance for a fresh start or a new beginning, or "an opportunity," as Henry Ford put it, "to begin again more intelligently,"[1049] stems from a hustler's capacity and inclination to see the future through the lens of hope and positive expectation. Naturally, their positivity bias about the future tends to become a self-fulfilling prophecy—they see good things happening in the future and, therefore, they think, speak and act in ways consistent with bringing those good things about. This positivity bias also enables them to interpret their past struggles as having some unknown value for whatever lies ahead. In Franklin Roosevelt's case, he saw his struggle with paralysis not as something that might have held him back from achieving his dreams, but rather that his struggle to triumph over his paralysis was preparing him for the political struggles ahead. "If you have spent two years in bed trying to wiggle your big toe," FDR said, "everything else seems easy."[1050] And Americans apparently agreed. When the Great Depression brought the nation to its knees, the American people put their faith in the man who, against all odds, found a way to raise himself up. By triumphing over his own personal paralysis, Roosevelt was especially equipped to help America overcome hers.

However difficult or impossible your situation may seem, it may be precisely what you need to achieve your greatest dream. When British novelist J.K. Rowling, author of the Harry Potter fantasy series, was hit with her greatest defeat, she said, "I was set free because my greatest fear had been realized...and I had an old typewriter and a big idea. And so rock bottom became a solid foundation on which I rebuilt my life."[1051] Rowling's is not an uncommon case. As leadership authority Warren Bennis once said, "The leaders I met, whatever walk of life they were from, whatever institutions they were presiding over, always referred back to the same failure—something that happened to them that was personally difficult, even traumatic, something that made them feel that desperate sense of hitting bottom—as something they thought was almost a necessity. It's as if at that moment the iron entered their soul; that moment created the resilience that leaders need."[1052]

People often make the tragic mistake of thinking that some great failure they faced is evidence of their inadequacy or unworthiness, confirmation of their feelings of inferiority. They never stop to imagine how this may have been exactly the lesson, hardship, pain, split, or, in the words of Jack Mezirow, "disorienting dilemma,"[1053] that they needed to most effectively make it to or through the next stage of their lives.

And, yet, there is much to learn from our defeats and failures, often far more than from our victories and successes. Knowing that resilience is such a critical component of high achievement, perhaps just the opportunity to build resilience is worth the passing pain. Examining the lives of history's heroes—people like Theodore Roosevelt who lost his father early, and then his mother and beloved wife on the same day, all by the time he was twenty-five—leaves little doubt that resilience was an indispensable element of their ultimate success. The very fact that they find the strength to come back is what transformed their future. It is as if resilience, as much as anything, is what enables success to take place.

When historian Doris Kearns Goodwin was asked about the qualities of Lincoln, TR, LBJ, and JFK, and what allowed them to be successful in the presidency, she said, "I think one of the most important qualities is the ability to withstand adversity and come through trials of fire. They all seem to do that. I mean, think of Lincoln," she said.[1054] "How many times did he have to get through failure before he finally succeeded? And once you get to be president, if you've done that, and seen yourself come out the other side, it just gives you perspective."[1055]

It is not always easy to determine what precise takeaway, insight, or lesson you needed to learn. Perhaps it is about forging a character. Think for example of how FDR was changed by his paralysis and, it was said, "he was able to identify with people with whom fate had also dealt an unkind hand."[1056] Perhaps, as Goodwin suggests, the greatest value is in the perspective you gain, the wisdom that comes, as the ancient Greek dramatist eschylus put it, "through the awful grace of God."[1057] When he was still just twenty-five, contemplating a future in politics, TR wrote, "Although not a very old man, I have yet lived a great deal in my life, and I have known sorrow too bitter and joy too keen to allow me to become either cast down or elated for more than a very brief period over success or defeat."[1058] Indeed, part of perspective is seeing the fleeting nature of setbacks, failure, and defeat, and seeing just how persistently true it is that the end "is only a beginning, always."[1059]

Seize Responsibility for Your Advance:
Napoleon Escapes from His Island Prison and Retakes France

"Take time to deliberate, but when the time for action has arrived, stop thinking and go in."
—Napoleon Bonaparte (1769—1821), French Military and Political Leader

By the time of Napoleon's disastrous Russian Campaign of 1812—a landmark loss in military history—his Grande Armée was in tatters, the French Empire was crumbling under financial burdens, and the French people had become painfully weary of war. After a quarter a century of fighting, France was emotionally, militarily, and financially exhausted.

With his army reduced by nearly a half a million men, Napoleon's enemies recognized this as an opportune time to attack the once unbeatable military commander. When the forces allied against Napoleon entered Paris—while he was preoccupied in the South—rather than staging a popular uprising, as was expected, the French people capitulated. By the time Napoleon learned he had lost Paris, it was too late. His own men now refused to fight, and urged him to surrender. Napoleon's secretary wrote of his Generals, "the turn of the wheel of fortune had ravaged these souls of iron."[1060] At long last, Europe's great "Man of Destiny" was defeated.

For Napoleon, being forced to abdicate the throne was an utterly devastating turn of events. In his mind, this was a great, historic humiliation. He was severely discredited. His star had faded. His life was at an end. After being one of the most powerful leaders in the history of the world, he was now suffering the lowest and most degrading experience of his life. He was so distraught, in fact, that within days of his defeat, he attempted to kill himself by drinking poison. "Life had become intolerable," Napoleon said to Caulaincourt, his close personal aid.[1061]

But, as fate would have it, he failed at this as well. The poison, which he had kept from the time of his invasion of Russia, had lost its potency and, instead of killing him, made him only temporarily, violently ill.

Within days, Napoleon was exiled by the allied nations of Europe to the tiny island of Elba. In a kind of geopolitical mockery, Napoleon was designated as the official sovereign of Elba and permitted to preserve his title as Emperor. Widely considered one of the greatest military minds of the modern era, the man who controlled the entire continent of Europe, and dominated European affairs for over a decade; the humiliation of being the "Emperor" of an island less than twenty miles long, with a population of less than 12,000, was unbearable for Napoleon. "Life," writes Robert Greene, "was a mockery of his previous glory."[1062] "As Elba's "king" he had been allowed to form a court—there was a cook, a wardrobe mistress, an official pianist, and a handful of courtiers. All this was designed to humiliate Napoleon, and it seemed to work."[1063] Whereas most people might have been perfectly content to live out their days on the beautiful, charming and temperate island, for Napoleon, Elba was akin to solitary confinement. And, yet, in his mind, it hardly mattered. "I shall not need anything," he said upon ratifying the terms of his surrender, "a soldier does not need much space to die in."[1064]

Hold On, Stay Open to the Unfolding of the Future.

Virtually anyone who has ever achieved anything of great significance has at some point, prior to their rise, experienced the negative thoughts and feelings spawned from setbacks and defeat. At the time, it may even seem as if there is no point in going on. When Nixon lost the race for the White House against Kennedy, and then the Governorship in California—all within two years—he believed, for a time, that he was finished. "You won't have Nixon to kick around anymore," he famously said at his "last" press conference.[1065]

Abraham Lincoln—who was known by his law partner to be "keenly sensitive to his failures" and was often "miserable" when faced with defeat—considered "himself a failure as a lawyer and a politician" when he returned to Illinois at age forty after serving only one term in the U.S. House of Representatives.[1066] In fact, for the following "five desolate years," Lincoln "was losing interest in politics."[1067] Looking back as President, Lincoln remembered being "so disgusted" with politics during this period that, he said, "I made up my mind to retire to private life and practice my profession."[1068] Some of his friends went even further, saying that Lincoln during this period was afflicted with, "a sadness so profound that the depths of it cannot be sounded or estimated by normal minds."[1069]

Fortunately, for the vast majority of people, these feelings and doubts inevitably fade in time. Circumstances may change ever so slightly, altering your point of view. New people may enter your life which shifts your focus. Time and distance may expand your perspective about past events. Or, perhaps, as was the case with Napoleon, old acquaintances with new information may redirect your thinking, or refocus attention on your broader purpose.

Contrary to how Napoleon may have felt at first, Elba was no island prison at all. To be sure, it *was* patrolled by Britain's Royal Navy. And the British commissioner of the island, Sir Neil Campbell, who was appointed to watch over Napoleon, *did* send regular updates to Britain's Foreign Secretary. What's more, King Louis XVIII sent "a swarm of spies to watch Napoleon."[1070] "Almost every ship brought secret agents disguised as friars, sailors or commercial travelers; they crept in among Napoleon's grooms and lackeys, so many they sometimes shadowed each other by mistake."[1071]

Nevertheless, Napoleon was given considerable latitude, and complete autonomy over the Island. In fact, as part of the Treaty of Fontainebleau (1814), Napoleon was allowed to keep (unwisely, as it inevitably turned out) a small garrison of 1,000 men, mostly members of his Old Guard—his fearless and fanatically loyal veterans—in order to defend the island from any would-be heroes who wanted to see the Emperor's head on a spike. Remarkably, he was also allowed a sixteen-gun brig, *The Inconstant* to serve as the flagship of Elba's navy.[1072]

As time went by, Napoleon began to entertain visitors at his residence, the Palazzina dei Mulini (House of Mills) in Portoferraio, including a number of foreign dignitaries, English tourists, and old friends. Reports began to trickle in about the French people's dissatisfaction with the Bourbon monarchy. The monstrously fat King Louis XVIII was proving to be widely unpopular. After experiencing the progressive reforms of the French Revolution and the Napoleonic era, many of the French believed that Louis' leadership was a step backwards, a return to the tyranny they had sacrificed so much to escape.

Napoleon was troubled by the idea that France's future might be in jeopardy. "There is no sacrifice," he once said, "which is above my courage when it is proved to be for the best interests of France."[1073] News of the deteriorating situation under Louis' leadership began to eat away at Napoleon. The idea that he would end his days on Elba became increasingly intolerable. "At last," he said, "I could stand it no longer."[1074] He was finally determined to escape from his idyllic island prison. It was a defining moment. It was here that he once again seized the initiative and assumed responsibility for his advance, and the future of France.

Napoleon soon determined he must find a way to regain the reins of power. "The idea of returning to France attracted both his gambler's instinct and his sense of mission."[1075] If the reports were true that the majority of the French people would welcome him back with open arms, then perhaps all he had to do was escape from Elba.

Despite the risks, he began to plan his escape. He sent a letter to General Douot, his Military Governor of Elba, giving the order to stock *The Inconstant* with provisions for the journey, and to have the aptly named ship disguised with paint and flags as an English Brig.

When British Commissioner Campbell left for a medical appointment in Italy, Napoleon seized the moment and, on February 26, 1815, just 10 months after being exiled to Elba, Napoleon and his small garrison of soldiers stealthily slipped past his enemies and sailed for France. Within days they landed on French soil without incident.

Seize Responsibility, Assume Ownership Of Your Fate

When most people are confronted with a severe setback or debilitating defeat they are flooded with feelings of helplessness. Their confidence gets sacked. They begin to doubt themselves and question their ability to handle what happened, and bounce back. Alas, they lose their initiative.

When Bill Clinton lost the Governorship of Arkansas in the 1980 election he took it as severe blow, and slipped into depression.[1076] According to long-time political advisor Dick Morris it was, as *Time* put it, "impossible for him to climb out of his hole."[1077] Clinton began to question whether he would continue in politics at all.

After spending some time licking his wounds, Clinton began to meet with political leaders and regular folks he connected with in his previous campaigns around the state.

He wanted to visit with them, apologize for his mistakes, and listen to what they had to say. Before long, Clinton was beginning to regroup, and rethink his experience. With this small, but consequential decision to get out and meet with people, Clinton was retaking the initiative. Whether consciously or not, Clinton was beginning to once again seize responsibility for his advance—a series of steps that would prove to be the road back to the Governorship, and then on to become the 42nd President of the United States.

No one is completely immune to the sting of failure and defeat. Most everyone struggles with insecurity and self-doubt in the face of a great fall. What marks the high achievers and heroes of history, however, is that, in one way or another, they find a way to bounce back. It may not happen right away. And it may begin with some small, seemingly insignificant step. But eventually they retake the initiative and seize responsibility for figuring out what's next. They begin searching for opportunities to comeback. They assume ownership over their future. And they act.

The record of human history is clear: We are all capable of far more than most anyone imagines. We have far more power over our individual lives than most people are willing to admit. And we have complete responsibility for how we choose to respond to our lives' individual events. The winners of the world know this and, as a result, they *own* their decisions and the *results* of their mistakes and failures—not in a prideful or sacrificial way, but in a way that maximizes their ability to learn and grow from these experiences and move on. M.J. DeMarco, author of *The Millionaire Fastlane*, writes, "when you own your decisions, something miraculous happens. Failure doesn't become the badge of victimhood—it becomes wisdom."[1078] Understand: It's not about accepting blame or finding fault at all. In fact, don't emphasize the problem so much. Focus instead on the solution.[1079] The key is taking ownership of the *consequences*, and responsibility for pressing on. "It's a mindset that works," writes one billionaire businessman, "and it's one way to accentuate the positive without being blind to the negative."[1080]

Before becoming the first black President of South Africa, elected in a full democratic election, Nelson Mandela spent over 27 years in prison. During that time, Mandela kept a scrap of paper with him in his cell. On that paper was a poem, written by William Ernest Henley, called "Invictus." The poem ends with words that match Mandela's own mindset throughout this great human trial for his soul, and which buttressed his indomitable belief that somehow he would once again manifest freedom: "I am the master of my fate," Henley wrote, "I am the captain of my soul."[1081]

Never Assume Someone Will Save You, Prepare to Fight Your Way Back.

No one ever became the master of their fate or the captain of their soul by remaining idle, or waiting to be saved by someone else. No doubt, a critical part of resilience is taking time to rejuvenate, regroup, and break through your own mental blocks. Your mindset is critical to surviving a setback.[1082]

But this alone is never enough. Action is equally indispensable. In fact, as the historical record reveals, you will often have to fight your way back into the arena. Do not labor under the illusion that coming back from failure or defeat will be easy, or that justice will prevail and you will eventually be saved. "If you want to aim high, you have to have the guts to handle the inevitable bumps in the road."[1083] And be prepared to handle them yourself. "If you strike out, nobody is going to help you—not your friends, not the government. You have to look out for yourself…"[1084] But remember this: It *will* be worth it. And the greater and harder fought your comeback is, the greater its worth.

When Napoleon Bonaparte safely landed on the French coast following his escape, the King did not roll out the red carpet to welcome the would-be usurper. Rather, he sent a regiment of his army—led by none other than Marshal Ney, the former General who had served Napoleon with great honor and distinction, even earning the designation, "bravest of the brave."[1085]   Regarding his former Emperor, the impetuous Marshal Ney promised the King that he would bring the usurper back to Paris like a wild beast in an iron cage."[1086] Napoleon never would have expected Ney to rescue him from his island prison, but he likely never expected to be facing him as an enemy either.

The idea that Napoleon could retake France with such a small detachment of troops was ludicrous. Not even the cowardly, incompetent King was concerned when he heard the news that Napoleon was in France. But Bonaparte was a man of faith and action and he had already made up his mind that he would do everything he could. As he once said himself, "Impossible is a word to be found only in the dictionary of fools."[1087]

When Napoleon encountered the infantry regiment barring his path, he boldly ordered his fanatically devoted men to lower their muskets, as he causally advanced toward the regiment alone.

Before long, the hasty Ney gave the order to fire. But his men were frozen. They stood mesmerized. Their mouths hung half open as Napoleon continued to slowly saunter toward them. Sporting his familiar gray overcoat and his signature two-cornered hat—the "bicorne," which he had always intentionally wore sideways in order to stand out and be easily identified[1088]—Napoleon shouted to the King's army: "Here I am."[1089] Utterly oblivious to the probability of a miscalculation, Napoleon threw open his iconic gray overcoat, inviting a shot. "Soldiers, I am your Emperor. Recognize me!" he said.[1090] "If there is one among you who wishes to kill his general, his Emperor, he may: here I stand."[1091]

"A single shot would have finished the adventure."[1092] But it was all too much for the soldiers to bear. Ignoring the commands to fire, they broke ranks, abandoned their weapons, ran toward and surrounded Napoleon, reaching out to touch him, overwhelming him with acclamations of "Long live the Emperor!"[1093] Ney attempted to offer his sword to Napoleon as an act of surrender, but Napoleon swept him into a merciful embrace as the men cheered and wept. In a matter of mere minutes, Napoleon's courage, charisma, and connection to his men had transformed his preposterous, pitiable invasion into a victory parade to Paris.

As they marched their way to the capital, they were met with great fanfare. People celebrated in the streets. Portraits of Louis were torn down and immediately replaced with portraits of Napoleon that had been hidden away. "People of all classes threw themselves at his feet…Volunteers swelled the ranks of his new army. Delirium swept the country. In Paris, crowds went wild."[1094]

When King Louis learned of Ney's defection, he panicked and fled the Tuileries (the imperial palace in Paris) and sought safety in England.[1095] By the time Napoleon arrived at the Tuileries the crowd was so exuberant that they carried him up the steps, nearly crushing him in their excitement.[1096] Balzac wrote later, "Before him did ever a man gain an empire simply by showing his hat?"[1097] Napoleon later recalled the march from Cannes to Paris, now known as "Route Napoleon," as "the happiest period in my life."[1098] Within a month, Napoleon Bonaparte was once again Emperor of France.

"I beg you take courage; the brave soul can mend even disaster."
—Catherine the Great (1729—1796), Empress of Russia

Be Reborn in the Ashes.

Disaster is the ultimate test. When everything around us collapses overnight, life itself can seem to be at an end. Our hopes for the future fade away, or perhaps our dreams now seem meaningless in the face of all that's been lost. Even Napoleon, prior to his abdication, thought poison was his only real choice.

But perhaps disaster itself also carries the very seeds needed to comeback. Like the Phoenix in Greek mythology, it is the *ashes* from the flames which consume the bird that then allow the bird to be reborn. If all is truly lost than this may be the ideal time to reinvent yourself, reimagine your life, or repurpose your career. Disaster also has a way of melting away the mental shackles that have been keeping you from taking worthwhile risks. Courage and boldness tend to grow exponentially when you imagine you have little left to lose.

In Napoleon's case, he had always been a bold man of courage and guts, willing to assume significant, *calculated* risks. And, yet, following his abdication and exile to Elba, it is easy to imagine how he was now—with virtually nothing left to lose—prepared to take whatever risks were necessary, and thus displayed a depth of courage that could only be expected from a Man of Destiny, an individual who seems to *know* he is acting in accord with Providence itself and, therefore, is willing to face down anything that might stand in his way. This was how Napoleon, with unflinching bravery in the face of a probable barrage of bullets, seized responsibility for his comeback. And it left the King's troops in awe. Napoleon's message was unmistakable: 'I will either go forward, or you will have to kill me.' That was the moment Napoleon reasserted authority and power over his destiny. That was the moment he retook France from the Bourbon monarch. In that moment, the stature of *The Little Corporal* was over ten feet tall. As the mythology goes, each time the Phoenix is resurrected from the ashes, she is even more beautiful than before.

Understand: Disaster offers a kind of freedom of action. There is a sense of liberty in knowing that you must rely on yourself. The power that you unleash when you stop waiting for something or someone else to save you is often all you need to succeed. When the survivors of the Uruguayan Air Force Flight 571, which crashed in the Andes Mountains, learned that the search party was being called off, they were all devastated. One of the survivors, however, saw it differently. It was "good news," he said defiantly, "because it means that we're going to get out of here on our own."[1099] Now desperately motivated to move, they made the long, perilous journey through the snow-capped mountains and were, miraculously, home by Christmas.

Most people will never have to put their lives at risk in order to make a great comeback. And, yet, every road to excellence, high achievement and success is riddled with setbacks, failure and defeat. In fact, as one billionaire business titan writes, "The biggest doers often suffer the biggest setbacks in life."[1100] What separates those who succeed from everyone else is how they respond when the inevitable failures and setbacks strike.

Avoid Alibis, Excuses are Toxic to Success.

When the U.S. economy was struggling and his efforts to invent a viable commercial product from gum elastic (natural rubber) repeatedly failed, Charles Goodyear eventually ended up in debtor's prison. Fortunately, Goodyear did not focus on finding fault with himself, or waste time wallowing in his misfortune. He didn't obsess over past mistakes, or fixate on the unfairness (and absurdity) of the prison system. Goodyear understood that failing to take responsibility for his circumstances was to give away his power—something he was unwilling to do. Instead, Goodyear assumed ownership for his situation, and asked his wife to bring a batch of this gum elastic and some tools and other materials from his lab down to the prison where he continued to experiment, hour after hour, late into the night. Nevertheless, success continued to elude the self-taught chemist. Unable to keep the substance from turning into a sticky, formless mess in summer or becoming bone hard in winter, Goodyear's brother-in-law told him emphatically, "rubber is dead."[1101] Refusing to admit defeat, however, Goodyear replied, "And I am the man to bring it back."[1102] And indeed he did. Goodyear eventually discovered a process for developing vulcanized rubber, received a U.S. patent, and went on to international acclaim.

People often fail to recognize the damage they do to themselves with their excuses. The more they make excuses, the less likely they are to achieve their goals. The better they get at making excuses, the further away they push their dreams. In the words of the immortal Benjamin Franklin, "He that is good for making excuses is seldom good for anything else."[1103] Whether excuses make you look weak, unlucky, or out of control, they do not inspire confidence or trust. Excuses may elicit pity, but they kill attraction and success.

Everyone experiences setbacks and failures which could easily serve as an excuse for not achieving your goals. But the superstars of success do not make excuses. Rather, they find ways to forge ahead regardless of the failures they face and, as a result, emerge stronger and more alluring than before. "Roosevelt could have hidden behind his lifeless legs; Truman could have used 'no college education;' Kennedy could have said, 'I'm too young to be president;' Johnson and Eisenhower could have ducked behind heart attacks."[1104] All of these leaders could have made excuses. Instead they boldly seized the moment, took action, and rose to become some of the most storied stars in American history.

Focus Not on the Fiasco Itself, But on Responsibility for Moving Ahead.

Most people fail to effectively deal with their failures because they fail to control their focus. They allow themselves to be mentally and emotionally consumed by the affair. They focus on the fiasco itself, rather than moving ahead. This was one of the secrets of President Bill Clinton's ability to consistently comeback: Time and again he turned his attention to his primary purpose and focused on the responsibilities of the job at hand.

In stark contrast to Clinton, President Richard Nixon seemed to fixate on the failures he faced. When the Watergate scandal erupted, Nixon was quickly consumed by it. The more the story led the headlines, the more it dominated his distrustful mind and dictated his every move. Before long, he began to reveal cracks in his armor. As the weeks and months went by, Nixon became increasingly consumed with a long, mounting list of perceived enemies. He was losing control of himself and his presidency. Tragically, he was his own worst enemy. Days before the U.S. House of Representatives was to consider articles of impeachment, Nixon resigned.

Unlike Nixon, Clinton's approach to the threat of losing the presidency during the Lewinsky scandal was not to turn away from his responsibilities, but to lean even further in. Where Nixon obsessed over the Watergate break-in and worked tirelessly to cover it up, Clinton focused all of his time and energy on moving ahead with his job. "Clinton amazed his staff, many of whom seemed poised for nervous breakdowns themselves, with his iron resolve to fight back, and by using the best weapon at his disposal: being presidential."[1105]

By the time of Clinton's State of the Union address in 1998 the Lewinsky scandal had reached a fever pitch. It was only a week earlier that several major news organizations broke the story of the alleged sexual relationship. The President was under intense fire, and now as Jim Lehrer said on PBS the night before, "This ongoing crisis has drawn great attention to the President's State of the Union address tomorrow night."[1106] It was, said journalist Haynes Johnson, "a drama that we've not seen before in the history of the presidency."[1107] Harvard's David Gergen added, "I think he'll have a huge audience tomorrow night, Jim, just people who want to tune in and see what he looks like, how he's doing, and see if anything happens, you know, if there's going to be any crack in the facade, or anything like that."[1108]

Many were expecting Clinton to crash and burn that night. Some were hoping he would. Others speculated that Clinton might resign at the end of his speech. But Clinton had good news for the American people, and he had no intention of abandoning ship now. Clinton began his address citing a litany of remarkable facts: Unemployment was at a twenty-four year low. Inflation was the lowest in thirty years. "Incomes are rising," Clinton said, "and we have the highest homeownership in history. Crime has dropped for a record five years in a row. And the welfare rolls are at their lowest levels in twenty-seven years. Our leadership in the world is unrivaled," Clinton added.[1109] "Ladies and Gentlemen," he said as he lowered his voice and raised the volume for effect, "the state of our Union is *strong*."[1110]

Whoever had tuned in to see Clinton flail under the pressure of his enemies' intense assaults was sorely disappointed. The man they so desperately wanted to bring down had just unleashed a spectacular set of statistics on the state of the nation—the nation which he had been leading for the last five years. When Clinton then announced that he was submitting "the first balanced budget in thirty years" there was nothing his enemies could do except stand and applaud.[1111] "By now, the Democrats were cheering the semicolons. The Republicans were slack-jawed. On a purely personal level," wrote biographer Michael Waldman, "measured solely by grace under pressure, it was a remarkable performance. The simple fact that he's standing there. The added fact that he was poignant, confident. The room was united in one thought. How does he do it?"[1112]

How *did* Clinton do it? And what was so different about Nixon's approach? Even in the midst of the impeachment crisis following the Lewinsky scandal, rather than getting caught up with the media maelstrom or his partisan opponents—as Nixon was prone to do—President Clinton focused the great bulk of his time and energy on doing the job the voters elected him to do. "While it would have been understandable if Clinton had become distracted by the crisis, Clinton's focus on the presidency, paradoxically, seemed to increase, prompting much speculation about what in Clinton's psychological makeup allowed him to do this."[1113] Clinton biographer David Maraniss describes how, "From an early age, he developed a capacity to block out unpleasant aspects of his life."[1114] And, the Pulitzer Prize-winning journalist adds of Clinton, "His capacity to block out and compartmentalize his life…helps explain his optimism in the face of difficulties and his remarkable ability to recover from setbacks."[1115]

Whereas the attacks inflicted by Nixon's enemies seemed to penetrate his defenses (often causing him to dig further in, exacerbating his situation), Clinton was often able to effectively fend off the attacks. And, yet, as critical as this was, Clinton's strategy was more than just successfully shielding himself from the arrows of his opponents. Clinton also recognized another, even greater potential source of power: The American people. Rather than getting pulled down into a fight with his enemies—something Nixon was consistently unable to resist—Clinton understood that the real power was with the people. And, thus, he believed that focusing on fulfilling his responsibility to the voters would be a far more effective strategy for winning in the end. And it worked. In the wake of the impeachment proceedings, Clinton's approval rating reached 73 percent, which was an all-time high for Clinton.[1116] What's more, rather than losing seats in Congress in the 1998 midterm elections which, in light of the Lewinsky scandal, most political pundits expected—and which would have been consistent with the "six-year itch" effect—President Clinton became the only two-term President since Reconstruction to actually gain seats in the House.

Know that You Have What It Takes.

There is probably nothing more important to regaining your initiative, and seizing responsibility for your comeback than believing that you have what it takes. Everyone, of course, has their doubts at times. But your ultimate success depends on your ability to push these doubts aside—and act. The unlikely story of Napoleon Bonaparte retaking the throne of France could never have happened if he had not believed that he was capable of doing it. Of course, he too had grave doubts about his future—to the point of attempting suicide. But when it came time to act, Napoleon was acting with as much belief in himself as he had ever had. And this was key. As John F. Kennedy once wrote to a girlfriend, he had, he said, "...the feeling that no matter what happened I'd get through."[1117] And, he added, "It's a funny thing that as long as you have that feeling you seem to get through."[1118]

Your ability to bounce back demands that you believe that you can. "You have to know that you have what it takes to come back from anything," writes Trump.[1119] And you can handle it, you can come back from anything—if you make up your mind to believe that you can. "Whether you think you can or you think you can't," said Henry Ford, "you're right."[1120] No matter what failure or setback you face, someone has faced it before and found a way to come back. Never doubt that you will overcome your setbacks and failures. Instead, resolve to find a way.

Learn from Failure, Strengthen Through Defeat: Washington's War of Posts

"Failure is instructive. The person who really thinks learns
quite as much from his failures as from his successes."
—John Dewey (1859—1952), American Psychologist, Educational Reformer

Following their victory against the British in Boston in March of 1776, General George Washington and his troops were riding high. Exulting over their fortuitous triumph, the Continental Army marched confidently onward to New York to defend the strategically important city from slipping into British hands.

By August, however, British General William Howe had built up his forces with a bay full of battleships, supply ships, cannons, and a disciplined, veteran army of 32,000 men. It was the greatest seaborne attack the British Empire had ever staged. Unlike Boston, Washington now faced a military force far larger than his undisciplined, ragtag band of civilian recruits, and the ensuing Battle of Long Island, the biggest in his career, proved to be a withering defeat. 300 soldiers in the Continental Army were killed, 700 were wounded, and another 1,000 were captured and imprisoned, or enslaved.[1121] Howe, who only lost 64 men, was so certain of his victory in the war that he set up camp to wait for Washington's inevitable surrender.[1122]

Washington had no intentions of surrendering to the British, but he also recognized the futility of continuing this fight. And, so, on a dark night of heavy rain and thick fog, Washington secretly evacuated his army across the river to Manhattan.

The Battle of Long Island was the lowest moment in Washington's long, illustrious career. Though it was only the beginning of a series of setbacks and defeats, historian Joseph Ellis argues, "This is the one he doesn't want to remember...This is where he nearly loses everything—including his life, on a couple of occasions."[1123] Washington was so dejected, in fact, that his correspondence during this time seems to have said, in effect, 'I want to die.'[1124] The pain and humiliation of such defeat was unbearable for Washington.[1125] Indeed, in one particularly harrowing incident, according to General Nathanael Greene, Washington appeared to be offering himself to a small, rapidly approaching band of British troops as if he wants to be killed. In fact, if General Greene had not grabbed the reins of Washington's horse to pull him out of his suicidal stupor, Washington would likely have died that day.[1126]

Washington's army was soon forced into New Jersey, and finally into Pennsylvania, as the British captured New York. Washington was devastated by the series of bitter defeats. It now looked to almost everyone as if America's stand against the British was at its end.

"But," Joseph Ellis, author of *Revolutionary Summer*, has argued, "Washington's greatest asset—apart from his resilience—is that he *learns*."[1127] Indeed, Washington was not finished. He was as resolved as ever to do everything in his power to reverse the direction of the war.

Washington was also beginning to grasp an important lesson from his mistakes in New York. Humiliating defeats on Long Island and Manhattan pressed him to question his strategy, and helped him to understand the flaws of fighting pitched battles (frontal assaults or encounters on prearranged battlegrounds) against an army of superior size and experience. He was starting to appreciate the importance of a strategy better suited to the limits of his army and the strengths of his men. "It's an expensive way to learn, but out of this experience he begins to fashion a strategy that will win the war for independence."[1128] As he grapples with the limits of his resources, he begins to abandon his preconceived ideas about what it will take to win. He begins to recognize the value of a more defensive strategy, a war of attrition, or, as he called it, a war of posts. "And it is this experience," said Ellis, "in the summer of 1776 that initiates that learning process for Washington."[1129]

> *"Be independent of the good opinion of other people."*
> —Abraham Maslow (1908—1970), American Psychologist, Columbia University

Avoid Surrendering to Popular Opinion, Focus on Doing What Works.

By the time Fabius Maximus was appointed dictator of the Roman Republic in 217 B.C., the great Carthaginian military commander Hannibal Barca had already reduced the Roman Republic to a state of panic. Hannibal's epic surprise advance through the Alps, and his stunning victories in the battles of Trebia and Lake Trasimene, were making it increasingly clear that the Romans were up against a military genius. With its very existence in jeopardy, the Roman Republic was now facing the worst crisis in its history. With Hannibal at the gates of Rome, destruction of the city seemed imminent.

Given his advanced age and notable experience, the Roman Senate turned to Fabius, desperately hoping that he could lead the Republic to victory. Fabius was a wise, thoughtful politician and general who had been carefully watching and learning from the army's failures against Hannibal. He soon determined that defeating the militarily superior Carthaginians would require a new, more patient approach.

Alas, Fabian's strategy of harassing Hannibal's troops, attacking their supply lines, and withdrawing his troops whenever their fate was in jeopardy, did not inspire confidence in Rome. His scorched-earth tactics—which were often a severe blow to the local villages—and his willingness to protract the conflict with a war of attrition was, before long, ridiculed and rejected by the Romans. While some senators and generals began to see the wisdom of his approach, many thought his unwillingness to confront Hannibal head on was a strategy born out of cowardice.

When Fabius' term as Dictator ended, the Romans immediately returned to a strategy of direct engagement—with abrupt, catastrophic consequences. In fact, the subsequent Battle of Cannae is remembered today as one of Hannibal's greatest tactical feats and, for Rome, one of its greatest, most historic defeats. With as many as 50,000 Romans killed, including several dozen senators and officers, it was near total annihilation for Rome. Not a single family in Rome was not either related to or connected with someone who had been killed in Cannae.

Suddenly, reduced yet again to a state of panic, Rome's leaders rush back to Fabius for advice, now believing that his wisdom was given from the gods themselves. Following his counsel, the Romans reengage the Carthaginians with Fabian's strategy and, to the relief of the Roman people, steadily begin to reduce Hannibal's army. Before long, with a shortage of men and supplies, Hannibal is forced to retreat to Croton. From here, he is called back to Africa to defend his homeland where the Roman army, led by Scipio Africanus, has now taken the fight—and where Hannibal will at last face defeat.

Where the other Roman generals encountered epic failures, Fabius' willingness and ability to learn from their mistakes enabled him to identify an alternative strategy, a strategy that ultimately rid Rome of the Carthaginians. But his genius was also in his ability to abandon limited or incomplete mental models about what sort of victory was possible. His wisdom was in his ability to stand apart from the longstanding beliefs and assumptions grounded in popular opinion.

The pressure of popular opinion is often too much for most people to resist. In the face of fierce opposition, they lose confidence in themselves and their ideas. If they are publicly ridiculed or rebuked, most people will abruptly reverse course. And, yet, how often has popular opinion turned out to be wrong? The Roman people's initial assessment of the Fabian strategy was not about military effectiveness. It was about pride, impatience, and fear. Rather than focusing on what worked, they gave into their emotions. And they lost tens of thousands of men as a result.

Widely known today as the "Father of Guerrilla Warfare," Fabius Maximus was also an effective *political* leader who understood the power and importance of public opinion. And, yet, he possessed the courage and wisdom to avoid surrendering to it— even at great cost to his reputation—when he believed popular opinion was wrong. Understand: The aim is not to simply ignore popular opinion—after all, very often it is the leaders who are wrong and the people who are right. The lesson is to beware of being held captive by the opinion of others, or surrendering so completely that you fail to think critically, and do what you know will work.

"Experience is simply the name we give our mistakes."
—Oscar Wilde (1854—1900), Irish Author and Playwright

Learn and Adapt, Learn and Adapt.

People often fail to bounce back from failure because of the story they tell themselves about what happened. By absolving themselves of any responsibility, they fail to see what they might change in order to move ahead. When General Washington lost the Battle of Long Island and was subsequently beaten back by the British into

Pennsylvania, it was clear that his civilian soldiers lacked the discipline and fighting experience necessary to defeat the British. This fact alone exasperated Washington—to the point that, in the midst of battle, he actually "struck several officers in their flight" from the enemy.[1130] "Good God! Have I got such troops as these?" he shouted on another occasion.[1131] "Are these the men with which I am to defend America?" he said, as he flung his hat to the ground.[1132]

It was not just the troops, however, who lacked experience. Washington was making more than his fair share of costly mistakes. "We lost every time we confronted the British," writes historian David McCullough, "and very often it was Washington's fault."[1133]

But Washington was not looking to cast blame, and as he got over the shock and horror of his army's lack of discipline, and the humiliation of his own defeats, he began to think about how he could learn and adapt to the reality of their situation, and the limits of his men. "He had a lot to learn," McCullough said, "but he always learned from his mistakes."[1134] And, as Washington himself once said, "Errors once discovered are more than half amended."[1135]

As Washington began to examine the problem, he began to see the flaws in both his strategy and his mindset. He began to think in terms of a defensive strategy and the need to, as he said, "avoid a general action, or put anything at risk."[1136] Writing to the Continental Congress, Washington said that he was, "persuaded that it would be presumptuous to draw out our young troops into open ground against their superior numbers and discipline."[1137]

Washington was also astutely aware of his own mindset about this approach. "It was a shift in thinking that did not come naturally to Washington. A Fabian strategy, like guerrilla and terrorist strategies of the twentieth century, was the preferred approach of the weak."[1138] "Washington did not believe that he was weak, and he thought of the Continental Army as a projection of himself. He regarded battle as a summons to display one's strength and courage; avoiding battle was akin to dishonorable behavior, like refusing to move forward in the face of musket and cannon fire."[1139] Nevertheless, Washington knew that this was not about pride or courage. It was about employing the method that was necessary, as he put it, to "derive the greatest benefit."[1140] "I am sensible," Washington admitted, keeping his mind focused on the larger purpose, "that a retreating army is encircled with difficulties, that declining an engagement subjects a general to reproach; but when the fate of America may be at stake on the issue, we should protract the war, if possible."[1141]

"Retreating was against the grain for an aggressive leader like Washington, but over time he learned to control his feelings and think strategically."[1142] Given the Continental Army's limited resources, as well as the men's greater familiarity with the terrain, the Fabian strategy was an attractive alternative and proved to be a superior choice. "In the nature of things, he had to fight a defensive war. But by fighting an aggressive defensive, which was also fluid, he raised the cost of victory for the British to an unacceptable level."[1143]

As Washington's strategy began to prove itself, his success encouraged the French to join the war against the British. The greatest watershed, captured in Leutze's famous oil painting, *Washington Crossing the Delaware*, was the Christmas 1776 surprise attack on the Hessian forces in Trenton and their success, a week later, at the Battle of Princeton. In the words of one historian: "Washington's daring actions since Christmas had been electrifying. Not only were some heads of state in Europe impressed by his boldness and resolve, but Trenton and Princeton, as a British traveler in Virginia noted, had "given [the Americans] fresh spirits" to prolong the war. This was precisely what

Washington sought."[1144] These two victories, in the words of one British historian, Sir George Otto Trevelyan, left an enduring imprint: "It may be doubted whether so small a number of men ever employed so short a space of time with greater and more lasting effects upon the history of the world."[1145]

"It is not a little pleasing nor less wonderful to contemplate," Washington wrote from White Plains, "that after two years maneuvering…both armies are brought back to the very point they set out from and that which was the offending party in the beginning is now reduced to the use of the spade and pickaxe for defense."[1146] Washington's own excitement in the success of his strategy is evident: "The hand of Providence has been so conspicuous in all this," he said, "that he must be worse than an infidel that lacks faith, and more than wicked, that has not gratitude enough to acknowledge his obligations…"[1147]

Washington and his men ultimately proved more than equal to the task. But it was not so much due to their success on the battlefield. Beside the fact that, as McCullough puts it, "Washington would not give up; he would not quit," their success was due to Washington's ability to keep learning from his mistakes.[1148] "Washington was self-aware enough to admit to himself and to others that he made mistakes."[1149] And this was key. "He would then correct the situation if possible and move on without delay or excuses."[1150] "Despite his inexperience and hesitancy, Washington had courageously abandoned a flawed strategy, replacing it with a plan consistent with the realities of his strengths and weaknesses," and those of his men.[1151] And for this he continues, from the perspective of historians today, to earn an "honorable mention" for the military strategist that he became through the protracted war; but also for the dexterity, determination and grit that allowed him to bounce back from his bitter defeats in New York, survive long enough to learn, adapt, and execute a strategy that could win.

Let Learning Become the Catalyst to Your Comeback.

Months after Bill Clinton fell from power in 1980, after serving a single term as Governor of Arkansas, he slowly began to open to the idea of another run. "I began to drive around the state and talk to people," he said later.[1152] Through this process of spending time with people, and considering their different perspectives about his surprise defeat, he began to identify and learn from his mistakes. By the time he collected the courage to throw his hat back in the ring, he knew he would have to change some things. Speaking at a Yale alumni dinner years later, Clinton recalled the lessons he learned from the experience. "When I decided I didn't want to give up and I wanted to go on in politics," he said, "I realized I had to be in better communication with the voters."[1153] As Clinton began to take the lessons learned and make them the center of his campaign things started happening again, and the 1982 comeback started to look like a distinct possibility.

Widely recognized today as "The Comeback Kid," this was not the last time that Bill Clinton would bounce back from a significant setback or defeat. And, yet, what people consistently fail to recognize is Clinton's ability to learn from his mistakes, and the role that his "capacity to take correction" plays in his ability to comeback.[1154] In essence, Clinton bounces back because he learns from his failures; he profits from his mistakes. And this, not surprisingly, has been central to his success in politics. In fact, Clinton's resilience, grounded in his ability to learn and grow from his failures, is one of his *greatest* strengths. Indeed, in his assessment of Clinton's leadership, the distinguished political scientist Fred Greenstein writes of what he calls "Clinton's most redeeming traits—ones that bode favorably for his leadership in the long, if not the short, run: His remarkable capacity to rebound in the face of adversity, his fundamental pragmatism

162

and his capacity (in spite of his thin-skinned tendencies) to admit his own failings."[1155] In spite of Clinton's many well-known flaws, Clinton was consistently able to meet and exceed expectations because, as Greenstein concludes, "This cluster of traits helps account for the commonly made observation that he is incapable of sustained error."[1156]

There is a simple reason why most people neglect to learn from their failures: They get so caught up blaming someone or something else, that they neglect to take responsibility for bouncing back. Learning is always easier when your mind is focused in on moving ahead. Understand: It is often impossible to stage a great comeback without learning. There can be no comeback if you only rise to repeat the same costly mistakes. In fact, it may be that learning is the best kept secret of resilience.

Virgin's Richard Branson, who has faced far more than his fair share of failures, has repeatedly found learning to be a key part of turning his failures and setbacks around. Whether it was one his daredevil adventures gone awry—like his first attempt to take the jet stream across the Atlantic in a hot air balloon—or whether it was a disastrous business failure—like the time he lost his shirt by taking Virgin public only to buy it back less than two years later—Branson's ability to examine himself and learn from his mistakes has been critical to his success. In his own words, "…The secret to bouncing back is not only to be unafraid of failures but to use them as motivational and learning tools."[1157] It's not the failure that counts, it's the learning that's key. Thomas Edison, one of the world's greatest inventors, put it this way: "Just because something doesn't do what you planned it to do doesn't mean it's useless."[1158] Your task is to find the usefulness in failure, to learn from it. "Conduct a thorough postmortem," writes Branson, "and use the findings to your advantage to make sure you get it right the next time around."[1159] "There's nothing wrong with making mistakes," he adds, "as long as you don't make the same ones over and over again."[1160]

No doubt, Branson admits, "Setbacks are discouraging, but you should always try to channel that feeling into positive action. The key to Virgin's continuing success has been this simple idea: when we get something wrong, we try to understand why and quickly make a change. Then we focus on what works and take it to the next country or industry or sector."[1161]

There is always something to be learned from failure. It is success that tends to mask mistakes from our own minds. Failure often makes our mistakes painfully clear to us, often allowing more than a few lessons to be learned. What most people fail to acknowledge is how failure speeds up the process of learning and growth. This is the strategy of the superstars of success. And Thomas Edison is a case-in-point. In fact, he got so good at learning from his mistakes that it not only became a key part of his ability to bounce back, but failing—over and over again, faster and faster—became a fundamental part of his strategy for success.

Harvest the Power of Overcoming.

When Arnold Schwarzenegger got his first real taste of weightlifting in 1961, he went well beyond what his body could handle. Rather than the standard 3 sets of 10 reps, some older boys at the gym pushed him into doing 10 *sets* of every exercise. When he was riding his bike home later on, he couldn't understand why his arms and legs felt "rubbery and sluggish," like spaghetti.[1162] Before long he ended up falling off of his bike. "This was strange," he said, "I noticed how my arms and legs didn't feel connected to me."[1163] He immediately got back on the bike, but he said, "I couldn't control the handlebars, and my thighs were shaking like they were made of porridge."[1164] Suddenly, he fell off his bike again, only this time he landed in a ditch. Finally, sitting there in the dirt, a grin spread across his face. He figured it out. And he was thrilled. The rubbery pain he was feeling was from the workout. He knew that this pain meant his muscles were going to grow. The fact that he had to walk his bike, as he put it, "an epic four-mile hike" home—all because he had worked out so hard—this was *fantastic* to Arnold; there was only one thing on his mind, he said, "I couldn't wait to get back to the gym."[1165]

Do not underestimate the power that comes and the wisdom that's gained simply from overcoming your failures. Most people would prefer to avoid failure and have an easy ride. But that is not the way of excellence and success. Strength is built through resistance. Power is gained through overcoming. It is often the case that just moving through the pain of failure will cause you to learn and grow, enabling you to forge and strengthen your will. "To overcome one barrier gives us greater ability to overcome the next. History is full of examples of men and women who have redeemed themselves from disgrace, poverty, and misfortune, by the firm resolution of an iron will."[1166]

Abraham Lincoln's entire life was a succession of bouncing back from one rejection or failure after another. But this part of his story is key: *He was never just failing.* With each failure he was continuously strengthening his ability to overcome. He was learning from his experience. He was getting to know himself, his strengths and weaknesses, his opportunities and threats. He was deepening his wisdom and understanding of the world, and the place he intended to have in it. All of this was critical in further enabling him to continue rising up.

Men and women of grit rejoice in the lessons learned, and the potential progress they can gain, regardless of the pain. In the words of Walt Disney, "All the adversity I've had in my life, all my troubles and obstacles, have strengthened me... You may not realize it when it happens, but a kick in the teeth may be the best thing in the world for you."[1167] Napoleon Bonaparte put it this way: "Adversity is the midwife of genius."[1168]

Let Disappointment Drive You to Find Success.

For six months, driven from office, a disappointed Clinton drove around the state meeting people and apologizing for not being a better listener, for not paying closer attention to their problems and concerns.[1169] Then one day he had a conversation that inspired him to get back in the game. Sharing the story with an audience years later, Clinton related the pivotal incident:

"One day I was going to see my mother, who lives about fifty miles from Little Rock, the state capital. I stopped midway at an old service station, which is kind of a political watering hole. I walked in and smiled."[1170]

"'You're Bill Clinton, aren't you?'"

"I said, 'Yes, sir.'"

"'Well, I cost you eleven votes, son. And I loved every minute of it!'"

"'You did?'"

"'I did. It was me and my two boys and their wives and six of my buddies. We just leveled you.'"

"'Why did you do it?'"

"'I had to—you raised my car license tax.'"

"'Let me ask you something. Look out there across this road. Remember when that road right there was in the front page of the biggest newspaper in this state, because cars were buried in it and I had to send tractors down here to get cars out?'"

"'I don't care, Bill. I still don't want to pay it.'"

"'Let me ask you something else. Would you ever consider voting for me again?'"

164

"He looked down at his shoes, and he looked back at me, and he said, 'You know, I would. We're even now.'"

"So I went out, put a dime in the pay phone, and said to Hillary, 'We're gonna run.'"[1171]

That February, 1982, Clinton headed back out to the airwaves. He admitted he had made some mistakes, promised he learned his lesson, and announced his candidacy for Governor with a new slogan: "You can't lead without listening."[1172]

No question—Clinton's loss of the governor's office in Arkansas was a major disappointment. He loved being governor, and he screwed it up. But that wasn't the end of the story. "Those things that hurt, instruct," wrote Benjamin Franklin.[1173] In Clinton's case, the sting of losing taught him one of his greatest lessons about leading: The central importance of listening. And this may have been the very setback he needed to learn how to succeed long-term. Bill Clinton won back the governorship that year. "And, thereafter, his political comportment," writes Greenstein, "was by all accounts far more measured and responsive to political realities, enabling him to remain as governor for a further decade."[1174] "Disappointment is inevitable when you are attempting to do anything of great scale," writes Anthony Robbins.[1175] But rather than letting it permanently keep you down, he continues, "let your disappointments drive you to find new answers; discipline your disappointments. Learn from every failure, act on those learnings, and success becomes inevitable."[1176]

Recalibrate and Begin Anew

By the time Huey Long was elected Governor of Louisiana in 1928, at age 35, he had already acquired a number of powerful enemies, and a reputation for boldly attacking the corrupt, bloodthirsty corporations in his State; including powerful monopolistic trusts like John D. Rockefeller's Standard Oil. Growing up in a political family during America's Progressive Era and the age of muckrakers, Long was well aware of the crooked relationship between Louisiana's business and political elites, and how they effectively squeezed the life out of the lower classes. As a young lawyer who prided himself on never taking a case against the poor, he fought and frequently won significant settlements against many of these powerful business and banking interests, making a name for himself as a champion of the common man.

Unfortunately, for the new Governor, these powerful interests had already co-opted the machinery of government, and had a virtual lockdown on Louisiana's legislature. Every attempt Long made to curb their interests, or check their power was met with fierce resistance in both the House and Senate, but also in the newspapers, and the high society of Baton Rouge, the political hub of Louisiana. When Long came out with an "occupational license tax" on Standard Oil and the other petroleum interests, after less than a year as Governor—which he wanted to use to fund new schools and colleges for the poor, and new roads, bridges and hospitals to modernize the State—his actions effectively amounted to a declaration of war.

When Standard Oil's pawns in the House began organizing to impeach the new Governor, he was caught off guard. Huey Long was by no means an exemplar of moral rectitude, but he'd done nothing to justify impeachment. "Huey, realizing he was on dangerous ground, prepared to retreat."[1177] But it was too late.[1178] The movement to impeach Long had already begun to build steam. A mass meeting was organized in Baton Rouge, complete with food and music by the Standard Oil Company band.

Faced with 19 allegations—ranging from the serious to the comical—Huey Long was broken, and he thought he was beat. Despair began to set in. Huey's brother said later that he found Huey sobbing on the bed in his room at the Roosevelt Hotel. Other associates testify that he spoke "darkly" about giving up.[1179] Huey never imagined his efforts on behalf of the poor would end with his impeachment. It looked as if his crusade to return power to the people was at an abrupt end.

Before Huey was convicted in the Senate, however, he had an epiphany. He realized that his thinking was all wrong. Impeachment was not about him, or his personal behavior, as the allegations suggested. It was about his purpose and position. It was about his policies and plans regarding Louisiana's gross economic inequality—*and all of that was about the people*. If he lost, they lost. In fact, the reality was that the people would be losing the only true champion they'd ever had in the Governor's office.

With this shift in thinking, Long was immediately aware of the source of power he needed to bring an end to impeachment: The very people who elected him to office. He quickly recalibrated his approach to impeachment, and came up with an ingenious plan. Rather than attempting to fight with the legislature, Long took his case back to the people of Louisiana. He ran because he wanted to fight economic inequality and put big money in check. Now he could write this impeachment incident into that same narrative. "He held a mass meeting of his own, on the same site his opposition had used; an enormous crowd flocked to Baton Rouge from all over the state, and he told it that the impeachment was simply a plot by Standard Oil and its allies to thwart his program for the people."[1180]

Next, Huey hit the road, covering the state with his famous circulars, speaking to audiences large and small. Calling out the corrupt legislators, Long said at one stop, "I fought the Standard Oil Company and put them pie-eating members of the gang out of office. I used a crowbar to pry some of 'em out, and I'm using a corkscrew now to take the rest out, piece by piece."[1181]

Word traveled fast. People began contacting their state senators, imploring them to save their champion and vote against his impeachment. Meanwhile, Huey was finding support in the Senate. In time, he was able to persuade fifteen Senators to sign a round-robin (one more than he needed to avoid conviction), which stated they would—based on the fact that the vote in the House was illegal—not vote to convict no matter what the evidence. Huey Long was back from the dead. The movement to remove him from office dissolved, and, less than two years later, the people of Louisiana elected Long to the United States Senate.

Stop, Heighten Awareness, Prepare to Adjust Course.

Far too many people react emotionally to threats to their interests. The mere suggestion that they might lose something of value to them—love, power, money, public esteem, etc.—often provokes a subtle but instinctual, fight-or-flight response. Their thinking is clouded and distorted by emotional reactions to events.

Rarely does this lead to the wisest, most strategic response. In fact, responding out of anger or fear often makes things worse. If you yearn to make a successful comeback, never plan maneuvers or devise strategy in an emotional state. Never simply respond. What you must do instead is take time to step back and expand your perspective, heighten your awareness, and think. Look for what may be missing or distorted in your map of the terrain. "The key to mastery is a shift in awareness."[1182] It wasn't until Long shifted his attention back to the people of Louisiana that his awareness centered on a strategy for overcoming impeachment.

By the time all four of Arnold Schwarzenegger's pet ballot initiatives were defeated at the polls in the 2005 special election, the Governor's approval rating had fallen to the low thirties.[1183] His reelection the following year was now in jeopardy. Taking such a public beating at the polls, however, suddenly made Schwarzenegger aware of his mistakes. "I've thought a lot about the last year and the mistakes I made and the lessons I've learned," he said at his State of the State address on January 5, 2006.[1184] "I have absorbed my defeat, and I have learned my lesson. And the people," he continued, "who always have the last word, sent a clear message: cut the warfare, cool the rhetoric, find common ground, and fix the problems together. So to my fellow Californians, I say: message received."[1185] Within months, his approval rating started to rebound. By the time of the election in November, Schwarzenegger was reelected with a comfortable 56% of the vote, compared to the Democratic candidate, Phil Angelides, 39%.

Long and Schwarzenegger succeeded because they stopped to adjust course. They recalibrated before they began anew. To effectively come back from defeat, take time to think about *how* you will respond. When most people make up their minds to bounce back from a failure or setback, they get back in the ring and proceed to do exactly what they were doing before. Their strategy is purely one of persistence. Sometimes this is enough. Other times it's not. Do not respond without *thinking*. Return to your primary purpose. Make an intentional, resourceful choice that's aligned with your long term dreams and goals. The setback you suffered may have changed your situation or position and, therefore, to realign with your purpose, you must adjust course. Achieving your vision and goals requires recalibrating based on where you are now. Get back to the big picture, and look for an alternative route to the top. Maintain your vision, but be more flexible in your approach. This could include adjusting your timing, or fine-tuning your team, or it might even include adopting a new strategy.

Never Assume a Higher Stage is Harder to Win.

Sometimes recalibrating is about a different starting point. Sometimes you can lose on a small stage and immediately turn around and succeed on a large stage. You may fail with a small business endeavor only to succeed with a major enterprise. Too often people are defeated in a relatively easy situation or when the stakes are low. They then automatically assume they would lose even worse in a more difficult situation or when the stakes are high. But this is not always true. Abraham Lincoln lost several lower offices, including the U.S. Congress (1843) and two consecutive U.S. Senate races (1854 and 1858), but then he went on to become the 16th President of the United States. Nixon lost the California governorship in 1962 and went on to win the U.S. Presidency in 1968. Theodore Roosevelt lost his bid to become mayor of New York City in 1886 and promptly left elective politics, only to return to win the Governorship of New York in 1898. Bill Clinton lost his run for the 3rd congressional district in Arkansas in 1974 only to win a statewide office in 1976, and the Governorship of Arkansas in 1978. George W. Bush lost his race for the 19th congressional district of Texas in 1978, but won the gubernatorial election in 1994. Barack Obama lost a race for the U.S. House in 2000, but won his race for State Senate in 2002, and the U.S. Senate in 2004. Napoleon Bonaparte failed on the much smaller island of Corsica, but won in France. "Having been beaten on a tiny stage, he would triumph on a huge one. It was only by coming to France as a refugee that Napoleon was able to have a career that could match his dreams. It was only as a Frenchmen that his gifts for political maneuvering could make him famous and it was only as a French soldier that he could show the world that he was a military genius."[1186]

Remember: The size of the stage or the status of the arena may have little if anything to do with your defeat. Perhaps the context on the small stage is all wrong, or you may simply be better suited to a game with higher stakes. No matter what the particular circumstances of your defeat, learn what you can from the experience, use the lessons learned, then recalibrate and begin anew.

8

COUNTERPUNCH:

Be Prepared to Pivot, Know When to Quit

"We are not retreating—we are advancing in another direction."
—Douglas MacArthur (1880—1964), Five-Star General

Know When to Pivot

"A foolish consistency is the hobgoblin of little minds."
—Ralph Waldo Emerson (1803—1882)

Avoid Blind Adherence, Adapt to Implacable Facts.

When Jimmy Carter campaigned for president in 1976 he ran as a political outsider. Following Watergate and the fall of Nixon, Carter believed that his lack of Washington experience was a decisive strength of his candidacy. Contrasting himself with Nixon and the Washington establishment, Carter promised in one campaign ad, "I will never tell a lie. I will never make a misleading statement. I will never betray the confidence any of you has in me…"[1187] Despite various gaffes and slip-ups during the campaign, Carter's outsider approach ultimately proved to be an effective strategy for winning the White House.

It was not, however, an effective strategy for winning relationships with or leading the individual members of the U.S. Congress.

And, yet, even after becoming the very center of Washington, Carter continued to portray himself as an outsider. He dressed informally, adopted a folksy speaking style, and, eschewing many of the trappings of power, he maintained his down-to-earth image as a modest peanut farmer from the Georgia plains.

Carter was not merely maintaining an image, however. Rather than acclimating to Washington and getting to know the people and power relationships of the town, Carter worked hard to maintain his status and identity as an outsider. It was a mentality that extended to his team of advisors. In the words of one Washington correspondent, "His top people had no experience in Washington and they were sort of contemptuous of Washington."[1188]

It was as if Carter believed that his railing against Washington's professional politicians during the campaign meant that he would be hypocritical or duplicitous if he later, as president, began to develop effective working relationships with these same people. But this was shortsighted. As journalist Elizabeth Drew said, "It's one thing to sort of run against Washington, but you have to live there, and you have to govern there, and you have to work with the people who are there. And it really doesn't get you anywhere to have this attitude if you want to get anything done."[1189]

Alas, Carter continued to break with the Washington "insiders" in his effort to govern; becoming, as his National Security Advisor Zbigniew Brzezinski described it, "like a sculptor who did not know when to throw away his chisel."[1190] He even went as far as alienating Speaker of the House Tip O'Neill, a Democrat from Massachusetts. "He never understood how the system worked," O'Neill would later complain; "and although this was out of character for Jimmy Carter, he didn't want to learn about it either."[1191] According to Congressman Dan Rostenkowski, "Carter's attitude was members of the House and Senate are bad guys."[1192]

At times, Carter's behavior bordered on disrespect. "Often he wouldn't return phone calls of leading senators. There was," reports historian Douglas Brinkley, "a kind of an abrasive attitude he had towards them. He never showed them the respect. So they all eventually got bitter and turned on him."[1193]

Somehow it failed to occur to Carter that his hopes for the American people required the help of key lawmakers on the Hill. In fact, Carter even went as far as threatening Congress, asserting in essence that if they refused to support his legislative agenda, he would go over their heads and appeal directly to the American people, asking them to pressure their representatives to support his proposals.[1194] But, in Carter's case, the strategy failed. He was asking for too much, and the American people never responded the way Carter had hoped.

What is perhaps most remarkable about Carter's failed approach to Congress and, thus, the failure of his legislative agenda, was that his party held significant majorities in both the House and Senate for both the 95th and 96th Congress (i.e. Carter's entire term). Carter's failed relationship with another Massachusetts Democrat, Senator Ted Kennedy, was so bad that Kennedy took the risk and controversial step of running against Carter in the 1980 primary. Later that year, Ronald Reagan defeated Carter in an electoral landslide.

> *"A pivot is a change in strategy without a change in vision."*
> —Eric Reis (1978—), American Entrepreneur

Know When to Pivot.

There is a long history of American presidents who ran as Washington "outsiders" (i.e. those who never served in either the House or Senate), including eighteen presidents to date.[1195] Unlike those who successfully made the transition, and were later reelected to a second term, President Carter, apparently in an effort to be consistent, proved unable to effectively pivot to the presidency. "Anything but a master strategist,"[1196] Carter failed to appreciate the seismic shift from running as the Democratic nominee, to leading the nation as America's Chief Legislator. He was apparently oblivious to the fact that this strategy ultimately failed to serve the American people. "Jimmy Carter," as one prominent politician put it, "reminds me of a south Georgia turtle who's been blocked by a log—he just keeps pushing, pushing, pushing straight ahead, he doesn't go around…until he finally gets a soft spot in the log and right on through he goes."[1197] Unfortunately, Carter's problem with Congress was that there were a lot of logs, but not a lot of soft spots.

Carter's inability to pivot and adapt serves as a cautionary tale. A reluctance to bend—particularly on principle—is often seen as an admirable trait. We respect those who stand on principle, and succeed purely through a kind of dogged determination. There is also considerable power in consistency. Without consistency there is no track record or accountability. There is no reputation or results to measure and assess.[1198] Consistency allows us to build trusting relationships, businesses and brands. And it is, no doubt, a powerful component of success.

Too often, however, consistency is overvalued. Too often people are consistent because they fear inconsistency. They worry it will appear hypocritical, unintelligent, confused, or weak. They would rather fail than be inconsistent. But this is a mistake.

> *"The only way a man can remain consistent amid changing circumstances is to change with them while preserving the same dominating purpose."*[1199]
> —Winston Churchill (1874—1965), British Prime Minister

Adjust Course, But Maintain Your Ultimate Destination.

President Lyndon Johnson often told the story about the unemployed high school teacher who was desperately looking for a job during the dark days of the Great Depression. One of the school boards in the Texas hill country was impressed with the young man's application, and thought he would be a strong addition to the school. They had, however, one hesitation. There was an ongoing controversy in the community about geography, and they wanted to know where the young man stood.

"We think we'd like to hire you," began one of the board members.

"But..." the chairman interrupted his colleague as he stood up.

Now standing bent over, looking down at the teacher, the steely-eyed redneck continued. "But tell us this," he said, pausing for effect. "There is some difference of opinion regarding whether the world is round or flat." The chairman paused again as he watched a drop of sweat run down the job applicant's face. Finally, he said in a slow southern drawl, "How...do...YOU...teach it?"

Without hesitating a moment, the applicant wiped the sweat from his brow, smiled up at the redneck chairman and said, "I can teach it either way."[1200]

The chairman stood up as a smile slowly spread across his face. He extended his hand to the young man, and said, "Son, you just talked your way into a job."

Johnson often used this story to illustrate the importance of flexibility in the pursuit of a purpose. Known as the "Master of the Senate," LBJ understood as well as anyone the importance of adjusting course as needed throughout the journey in order to reach his ultimate destination.

Live to Fight Another Battle, Another Day.

A frequent theme of Ronald Reagan's 1980 presidential campaign was devoted to a message of lowering taxes. Yet, less than two years later, Reagan signed the Tax Equity and Fiscal Responsibility Act of 1982, which amounted to a substantial tax *increase*.[1201] As dedicated as Reagan was to lowering taxes, he was flexible enough to take what he believed were the necessary steps to respond to a deepening recession. Few would accuse Ronald Reagan of lacking commitment to his vision and goals. And, yet, he was flexible enough to adapt as needed to the reality on the ground.

The welfare reform bill that President Clinton signed in 1996 did not appear to be his party's philosophical ideal[1202] (three members of his administration resigned in protest when he signed welfare reform into law), but, recognizing the pressure and understanding the power of Newt Gingrich's "Republican Revolution," Clinton forged ahead hoping to foster a new approach to the problem of poverty, particularly its dreadful intergenerational cycle.[1203]

The heroes of history recognize the power of fortitude, consistency and grit. And, yet, they also have the courage and confidence to change, pivot, or adjust when they must. The great military strategists all understood that a general's strategic intent in any particular battle is not always to win. Sometimes simply surviving a confrontation, distracting the enemy, or averting a conflict altogether serves the grand strategy and purpose better in the end. George Washington faced more than his fair share of defeats on the battlefield. He also dodged, ducked and evaded others. And, yet, with flexibility on strategy and a firm focus on holding his army together in order to win the war, Washington and his men ultimately survived long enough to triumph against the British. Napoleon Bonaparte's invasion of Russia in 1812 was a cataclysmic failure, in large part because the Russians (under the leadership of the aging Russian commander, Mikhail Kutuzov) were open and flexible enough to repeatedly back away from a fight they could not win, while luring Napoleon and his *Grande Armée* into a cold winter trap the French could not survive.

It was the application of these same principles—firmness of purpose, flexibility of approach—that allowed Ronald Reagan and Bill Clinton to win second terms, emerge as masters of the presidency and rank, in retrospect, as two reasonably effective executives.

Their critics will argue that they were willing to abandon their purpose and principles, but that is hardly the case (though they were willing to abandon their pride, and make a whole new set of friends and enemies along the way). Certainly, they surrendered some ground. But this is precisely what set them apart. It was their ability to recognize what they were up against, and their willingness and flexibility to adapt that ensured the success of their greater purpose.

Writing in *The New York Times* on the anniversary of the Personal Responsibility and Work Opportunity Reconciliation Act, Clinton put it this way, "Ten years ago, neither side got exactly what it had hoped for. While we compromised to reach an agreement, we never betrayed our principles and we passed a bill that worked and stood the test of time. This style of cooperative governing," Clinton said, "is anything but a sign of weakness. It is a measure of strength, deeply rooted in our Constitution and history, and essential to the better future that all Americans deserve, Republicans and Democrats alike."[1204]

Clinton and Reagan both understood that the triumph of a long-term vision often means adapting to a hard, and perhaps a temporarily painful and frustrating, short-term reality in order to live to fight another day. Indeed, with at least one notable exception, nearly every two-term president since FDR has been (or learned to be) a master of adaptability.[1205]

"Stay committed to your decisions, but stay flexible in your approach."
—Anthony Robbins (1960—)

Stay Flexible on Strategy, Remain Resolute on Principles and Purpose.

Charles Darwin argued that it is not the strongest of the species that survive, nor even the most intelligent. The ones that survive are those most responsive to change. Sadly, the truth is that most people are not at all responsive to change. In fact, people often fail outright by failing to recognize the point at which their consistency and determination has devolved into rigidity or blind adherence. Holding fast to a failed strategy or plan despite the immediate reality, or even long after the facts on the ground have changed, has led to many strategic blunders, including Carter's failed approach to pushing policy through the U.S. Congress.

A willingness to adapt to a given set of circumstances is often a critical factor of success. Whether it is a significant shift in power, an emerging opportunity or threat, or a change in the business or political landscape; rather than remaining intractable, hustlers adjust to the reality at hand. "The lesson here," in the words of political consultants James Carville and Paul Begala, "is that the battle does not always go to the biggest or the strongest. Especially in a fast-paced, ever-changing environment, the winner is going to be the person with the greatest ability to adapt."[1206]

Understand: The objective is not to be flexible about everything, adapting the moment there's a shift in the wind. True champions remain committed to their purpose and principles, their vision and values, but remain flexible on strategy, tactics, and objectives, adapting as *needed* to the environment, the landscape, or emerging opportunities and threats. As Jim Collins writes in the *Harvard Business Review*,

171

"Companies that enjoy enduring success have a core purpose and core values that remain fixed while their strategies and practices endlessly adapt to a changing world."[1207] The ancient Chinese philosopher Confucius put it this way: "When it is obvious that the goals cannot be reached, don't adjust the goals, adjust the action steps."[1208]

Keep Flexibility as a Core Principle of Success.

One of the nineteenth century's most brilliant strategists, Carl Von Clausewitz taught that, as important as planning was to victory, the battle plan was always based on a myriad of certain assumptions—assumptions about everything from the terrain and weather to the utility of weapons, from the strength and capacity of the forces to the unity of command. Clausewitz referred to this collection of assumptions and unknowns and the inevitable differences between real war and this "war on paper" as *friction*. Once the battle plan was enacted and, as Clausewitz wrote, the "fog of war" drifts in, the strategy rarely ever looks as clear. "In war more than anywhere else things do not turn out as we expect. Nearby they do not appear as they did from a distance," Clausewitz wrote in his book *On War*. "Every fault and exaggeration of [a] theory is instantly exposed in war."[1209] This reality led another of the great nineteenth century strategists, Helmuth von Moltke, to conclude that, "no campaign plan survives first contact with the enemy."[1210]

The answer to this dilemma, according to Clausewitz, was flexibility—flexibility in the formation, implementation, and execution of strategy. "War is the realm of uncertainty," he argued.[1211] And in this realm, the need for flexibility is paramount. In matters of modern warfare and military intelligence, this is a widely accepted principle. In fact, the armed forces of many nations, including the United States Armed Forces, the Royal Air Force and the Canadian Armed Forces, consider flexibility to be one of the top principles of war.

Given the volatile and uncertain environment we live in today, flexibility is a critical component of success in virtually every field of endeavor. From business and politics to sports and entertainment, the ability to quickly and readily respond to face new circumstances requires a high degree of flexibility, including a certain level of awareness, responsiveness, resilience, agility and adaptability.[1212] "Recognizing this reality," says Carville and Begala, "is one of the keys to success. The ability to adapt to a changing environment, to adjust to new realities, is essential."[1213]

Maintain the Course, Adjust the Sails.

Napoleon Bonaparte once said, "I am sometimes a fox and sometimes a lion. The whole secret of government lies in knowing when to be the one or the other." Machiavelli regarded a leader's ability to accurately assess the circumstances and act accordingly as a critical factor in his or her effectiveness, noting that leaders who are foxes are unable to defend against wolves, and that those who are lions are vulnerable to snares.[1214] "Those who rely simply on the lion do not know what they are about," Machiavelli wrote, "...he who has known best how to employ the fox has succeeded best."[1215]

This is one of the challenges of high achievement: Knowing when to stand strong, like the lion, in the face of obstacles and threats to your vision and goals, or whether the critical issue is to find, like the fox, a clever, alternative approach. The key is to find the balance between sticking with a workable strategy and adjusting the tactics as opportunities arise, and as the context and conditions demand. Being open to the possibility of changing your strategy does not mean that your strategy should change on a whim. Until a careful reassessment reveals the need for a change in the strategy, it should also remain relatively fixed. The effective pursuit of your purpose means adapting the strategy because the strategy is failing, not because of a failure of your resolve.

World War II general George S. Patton considered it a matter of *strategy versus tactics* that determined the degree of flexibility. Patton advocated a greater steadfastness with respect to *strategy* and greater flexibility with respect to *tactics*. In a letter from North Africa dated November 2, 1942, Patton wrote: "Have been giving everyone a simplified directive of war. Use steamroller strategy; that is, make up your mind on course and direction of action, and stick to it. But in tactics, do not steamroller."[1216] Celebrated political consultant James Carville likewise sees a need to remain more resolute on strategy—along with the overall purpose—but more flexible on tactics and tasks: "You have to keep your ultimate objective in mind at all times, design a multistep strategy for getting there and then—within that strategy and in pursuit of that objective—have the flexibility to tack one way or another as circumstances dictate moment by moment."[1217] In the words of Sun Tzu: "Do not repeat the tactics which have gained you one victory, but let your methods be regulated by the infinite variety of circumstances."[1218]

Know When to Quit

"God, grant me the serenity to accept the things I cannot change,
the courage to change the things I can, and the wisdom to know the difference."
—Reinhold Niebuhr (1892—1971), American Theologian, Serenity Prayer

Sarah Palin made history in 2006, at age forty-two, when she became both the youngest and the first woman to be elected Governor of Alaska. As she followed through on her campaign promises to reform the government and cut expenses—which included selling the governor's jet on eBay—Palin saw her approval rating shoot up to 93%, the highest in the nation, leading the media to dub her "the most popular governor in America." When John McCain selected Palin to run as his Vice President, she made history again as the Republican party's first female vice-presidential nominee. Palin then became a national celebrity overnight.

From the size and adoration of the crowds, to the headlines and pictures in the press, it was immediately apparent that Sarah Palin's star power was eclipsing John McCain's. The people, the press, and the Republican party operatives were all captivated by the sassy, patriotic, gun-toting 'mama grizzly.' McCain's staff began to struggle to manage Palin and her messaging problems as she began going her own way. As it became increasingly clear that McCain and Palin were going to lose the election to Obama and Biden, Palin became increasingly cocky, listening to McCain's top advisors less and less. Sarah Palin was going rogue. After all, in her mind, it was John McCain that was losing the 2008 election. *She* was the future.

Resist the Temptation to Quit Without a Rock-Solid Rationale.

But then just eight months after the election, Sarah Palin made a major political miscalculation when she suddenly, inexplicably resigned as Governor of Alaska. Political pundits collectively gasped as everyone held their breath waiting to discover the real reason for the dramatic turn. Certainly, they figured, some looming scandal must have forced her out. But no real compelling rationale ever followed. Palin apparently did not care to be governor any longer. Whether she succumbed to boredom, impatience, or the fear of having to fight off further ethics violations; Palin mistakenly assumed she could simply walk away without doing irreparable damage to her brand, or future in politics. Rather than coming up with a practical exit strategy, and disciplining herself to see it through, Palin's overconfidence appears to have gotten the best of her.

Power has a way of leading people astray. "Success plays strange tricks on the mind. It makes you feel invulnerable, while also making you more hostile and emotional when people challenge your power. It makes you less able to adapt to circumstances. You come to believe your character is more responsible for your success than your strategizing and planning."[1219] Rather than stepping back to assess the landscape and evaluate their options, rather than taking the time to test their assumptions with trusted advisors; people often make the mistake of attempting to repeat what worked in the past. Intoxicated with their own success, they march ahead in the same direction with little regard for how much things have changed.[1220] Napoleon Bonaparte—who himself fell into this trap with his invasion of Russia—said, "The greatest danger occurs at the moment of victory."[1221] After becoming the darling of the Tea Party, Palin apparently believed she could abandon her responsibilities as Governor and everyone would understand. After all, she reasoned, this was in the best interests of the voters. "Many just accept that lame-duck status, hit the road, draw the paycheck and milk it. I'm not putting Alaska through that—I promised efficiencies and effectiveness," she said.[1222] "I love my job, and I love Alaska. It hurts to make this choice, but I am doing what's best for Alaska."[1223]

Apparently, in Palin's mind, this was a solid rationale. Besides, she seems to have reasoned, quitting had worked for her once before.[1224] When Palin resigned in protest from the Alaska Oil and Gas Conservation Commission (AOGCC), in response to a conflict of interest of fellow board member Randy Ruedrich—who was also the chairman of Alaska's Republican Party—she was widely hailed as whistle-blower, with the courage to call out her own party. The bold move quickly catapulted Palin into the political limelight, opening up a shot at the top job in Alaska, which she won less than two years later. As governor, however, Palin's surprising and controversial step of resigning the governor's office was under an entirely different set of circumstances. Rather than once again emerging as a hero, standing up against corruption, and fighting for the good of Alaskans, Palin was seen as a quitter. To the voters in Alaska, her excuses for quitting were weak. Her rationale did not ring true.[1225] The widespread perception was that she was acting out of self-interest, striving to make herself even more famous and rich. Whatever her true motives, on a purely political level, the decision proved to be a major mistake, marking what now *seems* to be the end of Sarah Palin's political career.

Eliminate Weak Excuses.

It is, no doubt, not always easy to know when to quit. Every individual and situation is different. And there are often a number of important factors to take into account. And, yet, what is clear—particularly given the frequently stark consequences of quitting—is the importance of making rational and resourceful decisions about whether and when to quit, and how exactly to move ahead. There are a number of common, yet corrosive, excuses people use to quit, explanations that simply do not measure up. The following are some of the most common themes, rationalizations that may seem justifiable, but are far more often a clear-cut lack of grit:

1. *Your ambition is taking longer than you expected.* Success almost never comes as fast as we would like, or imagine that it should. In fact, *Hofstadter's Law* states that things always take longer than you expect, even when you take this law into account. Anecdotal evidence indicates that people often underestimate the time involved in a complex endeavor (known as the *planning fallacy*) by at least *half*.[1226] And, yet, quitting for the singular reason that something is taking longer than you imagined is weak and unwise. Recommendation: Set a timeline that's backed by evidence, and plan in advance to persevere.

2. *The work involved is harder than you imagined.* Most people tend to carry around romantic, idealized notions about what it's like to work in a particular field or pursue a specific interest. Initially, they see only the fun, interesting, or glamorous side of things without realizing just how challenging or unappealing it all is behind the scenes. What is most common in these situations is that people are not clear about the skills and abilities involved, or they underestimate the time and effort involved in developing the skills and abilities needed to succeed. The reality is that most everything of significance is harder than those on the outside imagine—not because everything in life is so hard, but because those who are really good (and who tend to gain our attention and stick in our minds) make it *appear* much easier than it is. But just because something is harder than you imagined does not mean you should quit. In fact, sticking it out long enough to overcome the difficulty may turn out to be the best thing you ever did. Remember *Engelbart's Law of Bootstrapping*: The better humans get at something, the better they get at getting even better. In other words, as you slowly start to develop the skills and abilities you need to succeed in your chosen domain, your performance will improve *exponentially*. Recommendation: Persist until *Engelbart's Law* begins to take effect.

3. *You don't think you have what it takes.* Quitting because you've decided you don't have whatever it is you *imagine* is required is another frequent mistake, based on a flawed set of beliefs. Quitting because you lack the connections, talent, skill, money, personality, appearance, support or whatever it is you think you're lacking now, is a mistake because not one of these things is fixed. To a lesser or greater degree, they can all change or be improved with sufficient time and effort. And, in fact, learning to grow, develop, strengthen, or enhance your prospects in one or more of these areas is usually a considerable part of the normal, predictable *work* of achieving your mission and goals.

4. *The rivalry from competitors, criticism from opponents, or ridicule from detractors is more intense than you anticipated.* Quitting as a *reaction* to others is almost always a mistake. Your decisions about how and when to advance must be guided by your own dreams and goals, not the will of your competitors or the personal interests of your critics. What's more, competition and criticism are perfectly normal. These things should be *expected*. And it is very often good for you in the end. Muscles are built only by enduring resistance. Moreover, the resistance you face is bound to change over time, particularly as you lean into it more, and start to improve, learn and grow.

5. *The odds are longer than you estimated.* Be careful about relying on odds. Statistics and data can be a powerful part of decision making. Yet, they can also be highly misleading and, therefore, should never be the sole basis of your decision. People tend to trust in numbers because they seem objective. But they rarely ever are. What numbers hide, for example, are the underlying assumptions of the research, the questions that influenced the answers, and the time and contextual factors that shaped the final results. Remember the adage: Statistics are like bikinis. What they show is revealing. But what they hide is vital. Recommendation: Collect quantitative data, but also interview experts, study the field, get input from your network of colleagues, family and friends (360 degrees). As Solomon said, "Plans fail for lack of counsel: but with many advisers they succeed."[1227]

6. *You're frustrated, angry, bored or upset.* Sometimes it's just the sheer monotony, repetition, or slow pace that is wearing you thin. Alas, this is often just the nature of the beast. Even the most exciting dreams and goals have their less appealing parts. Far better to find ways to make the work more engaging, agreeable or fulfilling than to surrender to your emotions and abandon it for a lack of grit.

A number of these excuses could have been eliminated, or significantly curtailed with adequate research and discovery *before* you started.[1228] But they are also all excellent reasons to stick it out. Why? Because these are precisely the things that make most people quit. If you can figure out a way to make yourself stick, you will set yourself apart from the pack. In the words of Seth Godin, "It's the incredibly difficult challenges…that give you the opportunity to pull ahead. In a competitive world, adversity is your ally. The harder it gets, the better chance you have of insulating yourself from the competition."[1229]

Delay the Decision, Take Time to Cool Off.

When billionaire Texan Ross Perot announced his campaign for president against Bill Clinton and George Bush in February, 1992, on CNN's *Larry King Live* show, he immediately captured the attention of the nation. Grassroots support for Perot erupted overnight, and he was soon on the ballot in all fifty states. By summer, Perot was leading both Clinton and Bush in the polls.

And that's when the pressure really started to mount. Citing alleged "character flaws," both the Clinton and Bush campaigns began to question Perot's temperament. The press likewise began to step up their attacks and use of, as Perot put it, "gotcha journalism," until Perot's poll numbers began a significant slide.[1230] When Perot's support fell to 20% in July, citing concerns about throwing the election to the House of Representatives if the electoral college was split, Perot abruptly returned to *Larry King Live* to announce that he was ending his campaign for president.

Perot's volunteers were outraged. One of his lieutenants in Boston abruptly fed Perot petitions into a paper shredder; fuming, he said, "I feel like I've been stood up by a hooker."[1231] Volunteers in Ventura, California ripped a large statute of Perot down, hung a noose around its neck, and dropped it into the dumpster with a forklift.[1232] Another young man faxed Perot saying, "'My parents taught me to respect my elders, but under this situation, if I was in a room with you, I would kick your ass.'"[1233]

When Perot then reentered the race on October 1, the damage was done. Even after winning the debates, Perot never again gained his previous standing in the election polls. "His chances of winning," wrote *The New York Times*, "are much less than when he quit in July. His only dim practical hope is to confuse and destabilize the contest."[1234] On Election Day, Perot ended up winning almost 19% of the vote, but failed to win a single state in the Electoral College.

No one knows for sure what was going through Perot's head when he quit, but the lesson was clear: Quitting only to reenter later spoiled his shot at the presidency. Making the decision to quit in the heat of the moment is almost always a mistake. Far better to delay the decision until you've had time to explore your options and think it through. The longer you can effectively delay the decision, the more useful data and greater perspective you will gain. Your delay may in fact allow time for the situation itself to change, which may make it easier to stick it out.

Making a wiser, more strategic decision does not necessarily mean waiting indefinitely. Sometimes delaying your decision until the next morning is enough time to get the distance you need to make the best choice. In fact, when you're thinking about a potential career-defining or life-altering move, patience can pay enormous dividends. As

Solomon wrote in Proverbs, "He that is patient is very wise and he that is impatient, very foolish."[1235]

Taking the time to think through your decision, however, should not be taken as a pretext to lessen your commitment or reduce your effort. As long as you're in, be in all the way. Double down and don't look back. Otherwise, it's better to admit to yourself that you've really already quit, *before* your weakened commitment and diminished results make the decision for you.

Put It Aside for Now with the Intent to Return to It Later.

Ross Perot's decision to end his campaign, only to begin again two and a half months later, proved to be a major political miscalculation. The time period was too short for Perot to argue that anything significant had changed. Rather his actions, and his previous argument about the Electoral College, now seemed self-serving and disingenuous, and, perhaps, a little too erratic for the Oval Office.

This is not to say, however, that abandoning a goal for the time-being is *never* a good idea. Sometimes it makes sense to let a particular pursuit go, knowing that the situation or circumstances may change later, enabling you to begin again with improved odds or greater hope. In fact, it is not uncommon for political candidates to drop out of races that are proving to be unwinnable at the time, only to return years later to steal the show. John McCain dropped out of the 2000 primary election for president against George W. Bush only to return and win the GOP nomination in 2008. George H.W. Bush dropped out of the 1980 primary election for president against Ronald Reagan, but won the presidency in 1988. Not surprisingly, this happens all the time in state and local races.

Naturally, this approach goes well beyond politics. Entrepreneurs, entertainers, athletes, are just a few of the groups of people that have employed this approach. Thomas Edison took this view with his own work, particularly his inventions. "In trying to perfect a thing," he said, "I sometimes run straight up against a granite wall a hundred feet high. If, after trying and trying and trying again, I can't get over it, I turn to something else."[1236] But Edison never fully abandoned the idea. In fact, Edison kept systematic records of his experiments,[1237] which allowed him to begin again right where he left off; just in case, as he said, "...some day, it may be months or it may be years later, something is discovered either by myself or someone else, or something happens in some part of the world, which I recognize may help me to scale at least part of that wall."[1238]

Be careful not to use this as a mental trick to lighten the load of the decision to quit after a few weak attempts. Even the decision to quit temporarily, with the hope of beginning again later, should not be taken lightly. As Edison also said, "It usually takes me from five to seven years to perfect a thing. Some things I have been working on for twenty-five years—and some of them are still unsolved."[1239] This includes experiments that he never put aside; including, for example, the first commercially viable incandescent light bulb which, he said, "was the hardest one of all; it took many years not only of concentrated thought but also of world-wide research."[1240]

Quit to Continue Your Advance

When Theodore Roosevelt was appointed to the post of Assistant Secretary of the Navy by President McKinley in 1897 he immediately began pushing to place the Navy on a war-time footing. Convinced that a strong Navy was the key to America's future on the world stage, as well as the peace and stability of the Western Hemisphere, Roosevelt worked hard to persuade Secretary of the Navy John D. Long, and the

President himself, of the need to radically increase the size and strength of the U.S. Navy.

Meanwhile, a mere 90 miles off the coast of Florida, Cuban revolutionaries had been engaged in a fight for independence from Spanish colonial rule since 1895. Like many Americans, Roosevelt longed to see the Cubans win their freedom. But he was equally eager to see Spain's colonial ambitions severely curtailed; and, preferably—as a champion of the Monroe Doctrine—eradicated from the Americas altogether.

Roosevelt never doubted that war was coming, whether President McKinley wanted it or not. Americans were sickened by the bloodshed and horrific conditions the Cubans were suffering under Spanish rule, and public opinion was beginning to favor some kind of intervention on behalf of the Cuban revolutionaries. As reports rolled in, Americans became increasingly alarmed by the toll of the economic depression, and stories of Cuban peasants being herded into concentration camps, many others to their deaths. "The revolt in Cuba," wrote Theodore Roosevelt, "had dragged its weary length until conditions in the island had become so dreadful as to be a standing disgrace to us for permitting them to exist."[1241] The "unspeakable horror, degradation, and misery," Roosevelt continued, "was not 'war' at all, but murderous oppression."[1242]

As Roosevelt effectively made his case for intervention (see the "Roosevelt Corollary")—and took independent initiative at every conceivable opportunity—the U.S. Navy was soon gearing up to face the impending war with Spain. Again and again, Spain repeatedly promised reform in Cuba, but repeatedly failed to deliver; until, finally, after the sinking of the *U.S.S. Maine*, McKinley was forced to send an ultimatum to Spain demanding they surrender control of the island nation. Within weeks, first Madrid and then Washington issued formal declarations of war.

Put Your Purpose Before Your Position.

Roosevelt knew this day would come, and when it did he knew he had no real choice but to leave his comfortable job in Washington to take his place as close as possible to the "flashing of the guns."[1243] Alas, when it looked as if the logistics were lining up for a smooth exit from his post in the Navy, personal matters began to complicate his plans. Roosevelt's wife, Edith, fell gravely ill with what was suspected to be typhoid fever.[1244] Roosevelt, moreover, had a newborn at home and other children who needed him, including little Ted who was suffering with anxiety. This was a dilemma for the loving father. As his friend, journalist Jacob Riis, writes, "I never had the good fortune to know a man who loves his children more devotedly and more sensibly than he."[1245] Certainly, TR might have found a number of reasons to stay back. "There was enough to keep him at home; there were plenty to plead with him. I did myself," Riis said, "for I hated to see him go."[1246]

The pressures were not just from the responsibilities at home, however. "The press implied that TR faced a difficult personal decision. It reported that Long wanted him to remain in Washington and that his continued presence in the Navy Department was regarded as essential."[1247] According to Riis, "They told him to stay, he was needed where he was."[1248]

But once Roosevelt had effectively prepared the Navy for war with Spain, he believed his work was done. "There is nothing more for me to do here," he said. "I've got to get into the fight myself."[1249] "He was right: His work *was* done. It was to prepare for war."[1250] But now the war had arrived and, as Riis said, "Merely to sit in an office and hold down a job, a title, or a salary, was not his way."[1251] The honorable Roosevelt also had a powerful sense of moral duty. "I have done all I could to bring on the war, because it is a just war," he said, "and the sooner we meet it the better. Now that it has come, I have no business to ask others to do the fighting and stay at home myself."[1252]

And so, despite the many objections, Roosevelt quit. He simply could not miss the opportunity to be at the heart of the action, serving his country, the Cuban revolutionaries, and the cause of freedom. This was getting to the core of his life's purpose. He was not quitting a job. He was advancing on his mission. For TR this was a nonnegotiable. Roosevelt wrote to his friend, "I made up my mind that I would not allow even a death to stand in my way; that it was my one chance to do something for my country and for my family and my one chance to cut my little notch on the stick that stands as a measuring-rod in every family."[1253]

TR's vision for America's future—and, of course, *his* role in that future—went well beyond any specific job or title. It was easy for Roosevelt to quit—even against the wishes of his wife, family, friends, or the President himself—because Roosevelt's commitment was to his vision, his grand aspiration, a purpose that was beyond the ups and downs of any individual move. Roosevelt understood, as the great Harvard psychologist William James once said, "The most important thing in life is to live your life for something more important than your life."[1254]

Quit When Your Dreams Demand It.

Sometimes quitting is the best, most practical way to move forward with your broader ambitions and goals. In fact, when what you are doing is no longer bringing you closer to your dreams and goals, then *it's time* to quit. Of course TR did not know he would become the "Hero of San Juan Hill," or that his heroism in Cuba would, just a few months later, lead to his successful bid for the governorship in New York. But he did know that his desk job in Washington was only a stepping stone to his real ambition, that there was no real value in staying any longer and, therefore, that his time there was now at an end. Roosevelt used action and progress as a means of judging when it was time to move on. In fact, Roosevelt often seemed to have a hankering to be where the action was and, whenever and wherever possible, initiating the actions himself. And that, not surprisingly, meant sometimes he had to abandon one track toward his purpose to move on to the next.

The great heroes of history were not afraid to quit once they realized they were no longer on track, advancing toward their goals. Harry Truman and Abraham Lincoln both abandoned the business world to run for office. Ronald Reagan and Arnold Schwarzenegger both quit their careers as successful actors to enter elective politics, both winning their respective campaigns for Governor of California. Jimmy Carter quit his successful business as a peanut farmer to run for local office. Benjamin Franklin, Thomas Edison, John D. Rockefeller, Walt Disney, Princess Diana, Richard Branson, and Bill Gates all dropped out of school to pursue their dreams.

Understand: The point is not to do whatever you feel like doing whenever you feel like doing it. Dropping out of school, for example, is very often a bad idea. But the point stands: As Seth Godin put it, "Winners quit all the time."[1255] But, he adds, "*They just quit the right stuff at the right time.*"[1256] Your life should be guided by your dreams and goals, not society's rules, cultural standards, or the expectations of your family and friends. Quit when your dreams demand it. Persistence, resilience and grit have little value if they are not geared toward achieving your life's purpose and goals.

Quit When Sticking Undermines True North.

Fortitude, perseverance, resilience, guts and grit—these are some of the most indispensable characteristics of success. However, just as they are worthless if they are not serving your ultimate dreams and goals, these characteristics must also be subservient to your core principles—to wit, in the hierarchy of timeless principles, grit will not always be at the top. In 458 B.C., the great Roman general Cincinnatus was living a humble retirement with his family, tending to his small farm. When the Roman Senate selected him to answer Rome's call to serve as dictator ("Master of the People") to face down the threat of invading tribes, Cincinnatus dutifully put down his plow and marched off to war. To the surprise and delight of Rome, Cincinnatus defeated the invading tribes in a mere sixteen days. He returned home to a hero's welcome. Suddenly, Cincinnatus, as the supreme elected official with absolute authority, then unexpectedly resigned his commission and returned to his modest farm, instantly becoming a legend in his own time.

When George Washington's second term as president was coming to an end in 1797, a great many influential citizens urged him to seek a third term. America was still in a precarious stage as a young country and, the argument was, it still needed Washington's strong and steady hand at the helm. Washington, however, was deeply committed to the Enlightenment principles at the heart of their new Republic, and wanted nothing more than to see America's great experiment succeed. Washington had stepped down from power before, when he resigned his position as the Commander-in-Chief of the Continental Army at the end of the war, and he had also roundly rejected the notion of an American monarchy, and the call for him to be America's first king. Now, at the end of his second term as President, he was just as eager to see the people choose a new leader from amongst themselves. If *the people* were to continue to be the true leaders of America, he believed, then it was time for him to return to his farm in Mount Vernon.

> *"Masters of the first rank are recognized by the fact that in matters great and small they know how to find an end perfectly, be it at the end of a melody or a thought; of a tragedy's fifth act or an act of state."*
> —Friedrich Nietzsche (1844—1900), German Philosopher

Plan Your Exit Strategy, Then See It All the Way Through.

When Theodore Roosevelt left his position as Assistant Secretary of the Navy at the start of the Spanish American War, he didn't merely get up and walk out. His departure was carefully planned. He made sure that the Navy was on a solid war-time footing before he resigned. In fact, from the moment he began his job, Roosevelt had been working to ensure the Navy was prepared for war. Shortly after Roosevelt took office, he set the tone for his tenure as the Assistant Secretary in a speech at the Naval War College in Rhode Island. "In public as in private life," Roosevelt said to his audience, "*a bold front tends to ensure peace* and not strife. If we possess a formidable navy, small is the chance indeed that we shall ever be dragged into a war to uphold the Monroe Doctrine. If we do not possess a navy, war may be forced on us at any time. It is certain, then, that we need a first-class navy." [1257]

There was nothing Roosevelt wanted to get done more during his time in Washington than this. But he also knew that he faced resistance within the administration, indeed from the President himself. "There are," he continued, "higher things in this life than the soft and easy enjoyment of material comfort. It is through strife, or the readiness for strife, that a nation must win greatness. We ask for a great navy," Roosevelt continued, determined to build his case, "partly because we feel that no national life is worth having if the nation is not willing, when the need shall arise, to stake everything on the supreme arbitrament of war, and to pour out its blood, its treasure, and its tears like water, rather than submit to the loss of honor and renown."[1258] It was clear from his speech that Roosevelt was intent on building a "great navy," and that the United States would be ready for war whenever the need might arise. Indeed, this was his purpose for the time he was there, and he fulfilled that mission before he left.

As Roosevelt clearly demonstrated, making the decision to quit does not mean suddenly walking away from your responsibilities and prior commitments. In fact, to effectively bring an end to one part of an endeavor or goal often requires some thoughtful planning well in advance. But it is well worth it, and can have lasting advantages in whatever you commit yourself to next. Part of what has proven so destructive to Sarah Palin's reputation is the way she ends things. Whether it was the way the McCain-Palin campaign unraveled at the end of the presidential election in 2008, or the way she abruptly resigned as the Governor of Alaska in 2009, her lack of a thoughtful exit strategy has further damaged her standing with people and, thus, has undermined her own future goals. The reality is, in the words of Robert Greene, "You are judged in this world by how well you bring things to an end. A messy or incomplete conclusion can reverberate for years to come, ruining your reputation in the process."[1259]

It is not so much that something ends, it is the way that it ends that is left lingering in the mind. Whatever it is—a business endeavor, a political campaign, a term of office, or even something as simple as a conversation—it is the ending that will resonate in people's minds. "The art of ending things well," writes Greene, "entails ending on the right note, with energy and flair."[1260] When George Washington peacefully relinquished the presidency to John Adams in 1797 he set a precedent that has served as an example to the citizens of this country—and many other republics around the world—for well over two centuries. Indeed, the smooth transfer of power between these two powerful political forces—the incoming and outgoing U.S. presidents, who are often from opposing parties—is one of Washington's greatest legacies. The lesson is clear: Never just finish or quit. Finish well. Plan not just to the end, but to the aftermath.[1261]

Never Merely Quit, Quit to Begin Something New.

Most people give up too often and quit too soon. They begin with a great flash of excitement and zeal, but when they fail to succeed right away their interest and enthusiasm quickly fades. Rather than seeking alternative strategies to make it work, they start imagining the many reasons it makes more sense to give up. People like this are perpetual casualties of the "shiny object syndrome." They lack staying power. In the beginning, they are usually convinced they made the right choice. But when the *inevitable* challenges and obstacles arise, they become increasingly open and vulnerable to the next new shiny object that comes along.

What makes this pattern so destructive is not just that it wastes energy, resources and time. What makes it so destructive is that every time you quit, it gets easier and easier to quit the next time around. The action of quitting becomes a habit which, as William James said, becomes part of their character and, ultimately, if the pattern is not interrupted and replaced, it becomes their destiny.[1262] The solution is to end the cycle of new pursuits. Set your sites on a star and stick. Theodore Roosevelt, writing for *The Outlook*, argues that, "perhaps there is no more important component of character than steadfast resolution. The boy who is going to make a great man," TR asserts, "or is going to count in any way in after life, must make up his mind not merely to overcome a thousand obstacles, but to win in spite of a thousand repulses or defeats."[1263] And, yet, TR also acknowledged that perseverance and grit are not always enough. There are times when *quitting* makes sense. There are times, however infrequent, when walking away is your best, most strategic way to move ahead with your life and dreams. You may indeed, through heroic determination and grit, find success in your original endeavor. Or you may, Roosevelt said, "have to try something entirely new."[1264]

The truth is success virtually never goes to those who are impulsive, capricious, irresolute and weak. On the other hand, if you've determined that quitting is your best move, you must not hesitate to begin something new. In fact, the critical factor in making a successful transition is to think in terms of a transition. Never merely quit. Instead, quit in order to begin something new. Like Janus, the Roman god of beginning and endings, who looked both backwards and forwards at the same time, learn all that you can from the past, while staying focused on the future. "There's a trick to the 'graceful exit,' writes Pulitzer Prize-winning American columnist Ellen Goodman.[1265] "It begins with the vision to recognize when a job, a life stage, or a relationship is over—and let it go. It means leaving what's over without denying its validity or its past importance to our lives. It involves a sense of future, a belief that every exit line is an entry, that we are moving up, rather than out."[1266]

Many of the great legends of history have, at one point or another, made the decision to abandon an endeavor or goal. But they quickly moved on to something else. They always seemed to know there was more beyond. "Grant did well as a boy and well as a young man," writes Roosevelt, "then came a period of trouble and failure, and then the Civil War and his opportunity; and he grasped it, and rose until his name is among the greatest in our history."[1267] Throughout his life, Grant grasped each new opportunity that he could, learning from the past, looking to the future, knowing that there was more beyond, until finally he was elected President of the United States. "Young Lincoln, struggling against incalculable odds, worked his way up, trying one thing and another until he, too, struck out boldly into the turbulent torrent of our national life."[1268] Like Grant, Lincoln always believed there was…more beyond.

Today, there is a statue of Christopher Columbus in Valladolid, Spain, where he died in 1506. Intended to commemorate the renowned discoverer, the statue also serves as a reminder of the importance of remembering that there is always something more to discover in the future. For centuries, the Spaniards, believing that they had reached the ultimate limits of the Earth, lived by the motto, "Ne Plus Ultra" (No More Beyond)—until, that is, the discoveries of Columbus. Today, the statue in Spain depicts a lion ripping off the word "Ne" (No) so that it now reads simply "Plus Ultra." Columbus had proven to the Spaniards that there was in fact always…"More Beyond."

Remember
to Get Your FREE
Companion Poster Guide
for *Mastering the Power of Grit* here:

www.ClassicInfluence.com/grit

ABOUT THE AUTHOR

 John C. Welch IV, Ed.D., M.T.S., M.B.A. is the National Campaign Manager for the movement to launch the new Progressive Bull Moose Party. Johnny's broad experience ranges from serving as the program manager for the Columbia Coaching Certification Program, to corporate training and consulting—with clients that have included Burke Rehabilitation Hospital, Kawasaki, International Boys' Schools Coalition, and New York Presbyterian Hospital, the University Hospital of Columbia and Cornell—to teaching undergraduate and graduate business courses in Southern California. He has coached leadership teams in large ministries, and served in the district offices of members of the California State Senate, the United States House of Representatives and the United States Senate. He currently teaches a course at Columbia University entitled, *Creating Revolutionary Change in a Democratic Society*, and works as a professional speaker on topics related to influence, leadership, hustle and grit. He earned a master's degree in business administration from San Diego State University and a master's degree from Harvard University where he split his time between the Divinity School and the Kennedy School of Government. He completed his doctorate in the department of Organization and Leadership at Columbia. Johnny currently lives in San Diego and, in his free time, enjoys weightlifting, running, traveling and, above all, surfing on some clean, hollow, *warm* water waves.

The following are a few ways you can connect with Johnny:
www.ClassicInfluence.com
www.ProgressiveBullMoose.Party

One Last Thing...

Thank you very much for investing the time in reading this book. If you enjoyed this book or found it useful I would be very grateful if you would post a short review on Amazon. Your support really does make a difference. I also read all of the reviews in an effort to improve and, hopefully, help more people.

Thanks for your support!

Works Cited & Notes

Please Note: The following references are available as a PDF at:
http://www.classicinfluence.com/grit-book-resources

"The ideas I stand for are not mine.
I borrowed them from Socrates.
I swiped them from Chesterfield.
I stole them from Jesus.
And I put them in a book.
If you don't like their rules, whose would you use?"

–Dale Carnegie (1888—1955)

1. Helferich, Gerard (2013). *Theodore Roosevelt and the Assassin: Madness, Vengeance, and The Campaign Of 1912.* Guilford, CT: Globe Pequot Press. Pg. 169.
2. Knokey, Jon (2015). *Theodore Roosevelt and the Making of American Leadership.* New York: Skyhorse Publishing. Pg. 406.
3. Knokey (2015), Pg. 406.
4. Klein, Christopher (2012, October 12). "Shot in the Chest 100 Years Ago, Teddy Roosevelt Kept on Talking." *History.com*, A&E Television Networks, LLC. http://www.history.com/news/shot-in-the-chest-100-years-ago-teddy-roosevelt-kept-on-talking
5. Morris, Edmund (2010). *Colonel Roosevelt.* NY: Random House. Pg. 244.
6. Wolraich, Michael (2014). *Unreasonable Men: Theodore Roosevelt and the Republican Rebels Who Created Progressive Politics.* New York: Palgrave Macmillan. Pg. 250.
7. Morris, Edmund (2010). *Colonel Roosevelt.* NY: Random House. Pg. 244.
8. Morris (2010), Pg. 244.
9. Dudek, Duane (2014, September 11). "'Maniac' shooting in Milwaukee part of Ken Burns' 'Roosevelts' miniseries." *Journal Sentinel.* http://www.jsonline.com/entertainment/tvradio/maniac-shooting-in-milwaukee-part-of-ken-burns-roosevelts-miniseries-b99349241z1-274832441.html
10. Morris, Edmund (2010). *Colonel Roosevelt.* New York: Random House. Pg. 245.
11. Bishop, Joseph Bucklin (1920). *Theodore Roosevelt and His Time: Shown in His Own Letters*, Vol. 2. New York: Scribner's Sons. Pg. 337.
12. Schwarzenegger, Arnold (2013). *Total Recall: My Unbelievably True Life Story.* New York: Simon and Schuster. Pg. 554.
13. Schwarzenegger (2013), Pg. 554.
14. Schwarzenegger (2013), Pg. 554.
15. Schwarzenegger (2013), Pg. 554.
16. Schwarzenegger (2013), Pg. 554.
17. Greene, Robert (1998). *The 48 Laws of Power.* New York: Penguin Books. Pg. 60.
18. Cronin, Thomas E. "All the World's a Stage..." Acting and the Art of Political Leadership." *Leadership Quarterly.* Volume 19. Pg. 462.

19. Burlingame, Michael (1994). *The Inner World of Abraham Lincoln.* Chicago: University of Illinois Press. Pg. 277.
20. Burlingame, Michael (2008). *Abraham Lincoln: A Life*, Volume 1. Baltimore: The Johns Hopkins University Press. Pg. 90.
21. Porter, Gen. Horace (1897). "Campaigning with Grant." *Century Illustrated Monthly Magazine*, Vol. LIV. NY: MacMillan & Co. Pg. 202.
22. Morris, Edmund (2010). *Colonel Roosevelt.* New York: Random House. Pg. 245.
23. Morris (2010), Pg. 245.
24. Morris (2010), Pg. 245.
25. James, William (1914). *The Energies of Men.* New York: Moffat, Yard and Company. [Copyright 1907 by The American Magazine.]
26. James (1914).
27. Bergland, Christopher (2007). *The Athlete's Way: Training Your Mind and Body to Experience the Joy of Exercise.* New York: St. Martin's Griffin. Pg. 202.
28. Roosevelt, Theodore (1899, April 10). "The Strenuous Life." Speech before the Hamilton Club, Chicago. In *The Strenuous Life; Essays and Addresses.* New York: The Century Co., 1900. http://www.bartleby.com/58/1.html
29. Shakespeare, William (1599). *The Tragedy of Julius Caesar.* (Act 4, Scene 3, Lines 218-224)
30. Oswald, Brad (2010, January 26). "Yes, she's Queen of all Media, but to Discovery, she's Life itself." Winnipeg Free Press. http://www.winnipegfreepress.com/arts-and-life/entertainment/TV/yes-shes-queen-of-all-media-but-to-discovery-shes-life-itself-82678662.html
31. Marden, Orison Swett (1901). *An Iron Will.* New York: Thomas Y. Crowell and Company. Pg. 26.
32. Marden, Orison Swett (1911). *Pushing to the Front.* Petersburg, NY: The Success Company's. Pg. 338.
33. Heath, Dan and Heath, Chip (2011, February 16). "Why True Grit Matters in the Face of Adversity." *Fast Company.* http://www.fastcompany.com/1722712/why-true-grit-matters-face-adversity
34. Heath & Heath (2011).

35. Duckworth, Angela Lee (2013). Grit: The Power of Passion and Persistence. *TED Talk*, TED.com. Transcript: https://www.ted.com/talks/angela_lee_duckworth_the_key_to_success_grit/transcript?language=en
36. Duckworth, Angela; Peterson, Christopher; Matthews, Michael & Kelly, Dennis (2007). "Grit: Perseverance and Passion for Long-Term Goals." *Journal of Personality and Social Psychology*, Volume 92, Number 6. Pg. 1087.
37. Morgan, Edmund S. (2003). *Benjamin Franklin.* New Haven: Yale University Press. Pg. 22.
38. Kohn, Alfie (2014, April 8). "Ten concerns about the 'let's teach them grit' fad." *The Washington Post.* https://www.washingtonpost.com/news/answer-sheet/wp/2014/04/08/ten-concerns-about-the-lets-teach-them-grit-fad/
39. Duckworth, Angela; Peterson, Christopher; Matthews, Michael & Kelly, Dennis (2007). "Grit: Perseverance and Passion for Long-Term Goals." *Journal of Personality and Social Psychology*, Volume 92, Number 6. Pg. 1088.
40. Duckworth et al (2007), Pg. 1088.
41. Duckworth et al (2007), Pg. 1088.
42. James, William (1914). *The Energies of Men.* New York: Moffat, Yard and Company. [Copyright 1907 by The American Magazine.] Pg. 15.
43. James (1914), Pg. 7.
44. James (1914), Pg. 7.
45. James (1914), Pg. 7.
46. James (1914), Pgs. 7-8.
47. James (1914), Pg. 14.
48. James (1914), Pg. 9.
49. Smiles, Samuel (1873). *Self-Help: With Illustrations of Character, Conduct, and Perseverance.* Nashville: A.H.Redford. 248.
50. Porter, Nancy (Producer, Director). (1996). *The Wright Stuff.* American Experience. PBS. [Documentary Film]. United States: WGBH Educational Foundation. Transcript: http://www.pbs.org/wgbh/amex/wright/transcript.html
51. Porter (1996).
52. Goddard, Stephen B. (2003). *Race to the Sky: The Wright Brothers Versus the*

United States Government. Jefferson, NC: McFarland & Company, Inc. Pg. 92.

53. Barber, James David (1992). *The Presidential Character: Predicting Performance in the White House.* New York: Prentice Hall.

54. Sheldon, Arthur F. (1903). *The Science of Successful Salesmanship.* Chicago: The Sheldon School. Pg. 25.

55. Butler-Bowdon, Tom (2004). *50 Success Classics: Winning Wisdom for Work and Life from 50 Landmark Books.* London: Nicholas Brealey Publishing. Pg. 249.

56. Godin, Seth (2007). *The Dip: A Little Book that Teaches You When to Quit (And When to Stick).* New York: Portfolio. Pg. 10.

57. Ash, Mary Kay (2003). *Miracles Happen: The Life and Timeless Principles of the Founder of Mary Kay Inc.* St. Louis: Turtleback Books.

58. Marden, Orison Swett (1901). *How They Succeeded: Life Stories of Successful Men Told by Themselves.* Boston: Lothrop Publishing Company. Pg. 207.

59. Marden, Orison Swett (1901). *An Iron Will.* New York: Thomas Y. Crowell and Company. Pg. 23.

60. Marden (1901), Pg. 23.

61. Marden (1901), Pg. 23.

62. Marden (1901), Pg. 23.

63. Strock, James M. (2001). *Theodore Roosevelt on Leadership: Executive Lessons form the Bully Pulpit.* Roseville: Prima Publishing. Pg. 52.

64. Morris, Edmund (1979). *The Rise of Theodore Roosevelt.* New York: Random House. Pg. 825.

65. Leuchtenburg, William E. (1988). "Franklin D. Roosevelt: The First Modern President." In Fred I. Greenstein (ed.) *Leadership in the Modern Presidency.* Cambridge, MA: Harvard University Press. Pg. 15.

66. Leuchtenburg (1988), Pg. 15.

67. Leuchtenburg (1988), Pg. 15.

68. Ziglar, Zig (2014). *How to Stay Motivated: Developing Qualities of Success.* Issaquah: Made for Success Publishing.

69. Ziglar (2014).

70. Machiavelli, Niccolo (1903 [1532]). *The Prince.* London: The World's Classics. Pg. 104.

71. Morris, Edmund (2010). *Colonel Roosevelt.* New York: Random House. Pg. 245.

72. Morris (2010), Pg. 245.

73. Howland, Harold (1921). *Theodore Roosevelt and His Times: A Chronicle of the Progressive Movement.* New Haven: Yale University Press. Pg. 229.

74. Morris, Edmund (2010). *Colonel Roosevelt.* New York: Random House. Pg. 245.

75. Morris (2010), Pg. 245.

76. Roosevelt, Theodore (1912, October 14). "Progressive Cause Greater Than Any Individual." *Newer Roosevelt Messages,* Volume 3 (1919). New York: The Current Literature: Publishing Company. Pg. 749.

77. Roosevelt (1912), Pg. 749.

78. Roosevelt (1912), Pg. 749.

79. Roosevelt (1912), Pg. 749.

80. Roosevelt (1912), Pg. 749.

81. Robbins, Anthony (2003). *Awaken the Giant Within: How to Take Immediate Control of Your Mental, Emotional, Physical and Financial Destiny!* New York: Free Press. Pg. 127.

82. Roosevelt, Theodore (1903, September 7). "A Square Deal." Address to Farmers at the New York State Agricultural Association, Syracuse, New York.

83. O'Toole, Patricia (2012, November). "The Speech that Saved Teddy Roosevelt's Life." *Smithsonian Magazine.* http://www.smithsonianmag.com/history/the-speech-that-saved-teddy-roosevelts-life-Godin, Seth (2007). *The Dip: A Little Book that Teaches You When to Quit (And When to Stick).* New York: Portfolio. Pg. 23.

84. Godin, Seth (2007). *The Dip: A Little Book that Teaches You When to Quit (And When to Stick).* New York: Portfolio. Pg. 23.

85. Clinton, William J. (2001). *Public Papers of the Presidents of the United States, William J. Clinton, 2000-2001.* Washington, D.C.: U.S. Government Publishing Office. Pg. 2913

86. Clinton (2001), Pg. 2913.

87. Clinton (2001), Pg. 2913.

88. Greene, Robert (2012). *Mastery.* New York: Viking.

89. Greene, Robert (2013). "The Key to Transforming Yourself." *TEDX Talks,* Brixton. https://www.youtube.com/watch?v=gLt_yDvdeLQ

90. Klein, Maury (2003). *The Change Makers: From Carnegie to Gates, How the Great Entrepreneurs Transformed Ideas into Industries.* New York: Times Books. Pg. 108.

91. Marden, Orison Swett (1911). Pushing to the Front. Petersburg, NY: The Success Company's. Pg. 324.

92. Mabie, Hamilton, et al (1896). *The Great American Book of Biography: Illustrious Americans, Their Lives and Great Achievements.* Philadelphia: International Publishing Company. Pg. 241.

93. Porter, Darwin (2005). *Howard Hughes: Hell's Angel.* New York: Blood Moon Productions, Ltd. Pg. 414.

94. "Christopher Columbus Biography." [Documentary Film]. Biography.com (Editors). United States: A&E Television Networks. http://www.biography.com/people/christopher-columbus-9254209/videos/christopher-columbus-full-episode-2073085807

95. Earhart, Amelia (1928). *20 Hrs. 40 Min: Our Flight in the Friendship.* New York: Arno Press. Pg. 110.

96. Earhart (1928), Pg. 110.

97. Marden, Orison Swett (1901). *An Iron Will.* New York: Thomas Y. Crowell and Company. Pg. 25.

98. Marden (1901), Pg. 25.

99. Marden (1901), Pg. 25.

100. Foster, John (1835). *Essays in a Series of Letters, The Eleventh Edition.* London: Holdsworth and Ball. Pg. 100.

101. Wheeler, Edward J. (Ed.) (1912, November). "A Review of the World." *Current Literature,* Volume 53, Number 5. New York: The Current Literature Publishing Company. Pg. 487.

102. Wheeler (1912), Pg. 487.

103. Strock, James M. (2001). *Theodore Roosevelt on Leadership: Executive Lessons form the Bully Pulpit.* Roseville: Prima Publishing. Pg. 50.

104. Wheeler, Edward J. (Ed.) (1912, November). "A Review of the World." *Current Literature,* Volume 53, Number 5. New York: The Current Literature Publishing Company. Pg. 488.

105. Strock, James M. (2001). *Theodore Roosevelt on Leadership: Executive Lessons form the Bully Pulpit.* Roseville: Prima Publishing. Pg. 50.

106. Strock (2001), Pg. 50.

107. Roosevelt, Theodore (1922). *Theodore Roosevelt: An Autobiography.* New York: Charles Scribner's Sons. Pg. 126.

108. Roosevelt (1922), Pg. 126.

109. Strock, James M. (2001). *Theodore Roosevelt on Leadership: Executive Lessons form the Bully Pulpit.* Roseville: Prima Publishing. Pg. 50.

110. Roosevelt, Theodore (1912, October 14). "Progressive Cause Greater Than Any Individual." *Newer Roosevelt Messages,* Volume 3 (1919). New York: The Current Literature: Publishing Company. Pg. 754.

111. Strock, James M. (2001). *Theodore Roosevelt on Leadership: Executive Lessons form the Bully Pulpit.* Roseville: Prima Publishing. Pg. 50.

112. Bishop, Joseph Bucklin (1920). *Theodore Roosevelt and His Time: Shown in His Own Letters,* Vol. 2. New York: Scribner's Sons. Pg. 344.

113. O'Toole, Patricia (2012, November). "The Speech that Saved Teddy Roosevelt's Life." *Smithsonian Magazine.* http://www.smithsonianmag.com/history/the-speech-that-saved-teddy-roosevelts-life-83479091/?all&no-ist

114. O'Toole (2012).

115. Bishop, Joseph Bucklin (1920). *Theodore Roosevelt and His Time: Shown in His Own Letters,* Vol. 2. New York: Scribner's Sons. Pg. 176.

116. Schwarzenegger, Arnold (2013). *Total Recall: My Unbelievably True Life Story.* New York: Simon and Schuster. Pg. 420.

117. Schwarzenegger (2013), Pg. 77.

118. Schwarzenegger (2013), Pg. 77.

119. Schwarzenegger (2013), Pg. 77.

120. Schwarzenegger (2013), Pg. 77.

121. Schwarzenegger (2013), Pg. 77.

122. Schwarzenegger (2013), Pg. 78.

123. Duhigg, Charles (2012). *The Power of Habit: Why We Do What We Do in Life and Business.* New York: Random House. Pg. 86.

124. Duhigg (2012), Pg. 86.

125. Duhigg (2012), Pg. 87.

126. Duhigg (2012), Pg. 87.

127. Phillips, Thomas R. (1985). *Roots of Strategy: The 5 Greatest Military Classics of All Time.* Mechanicsburg, PA: Stackpole Books. Pg. 75.

128. Amundsen, Roald (1913). *The South Pole: An Account of the Norwegian Antarctic Expedition in the "Fram," 1910—1912,* Volume 1. New York: Lee Keedick. Pg. 370.

129. Amundsen, Roald (1927). *My Life as an Explorer.* New York: Cambridge University Press. Pg. 259.

130. Amundsen (1927), Pg. 259.

131. Amundsen (1927), Pg. 259.

132. Amundsen (1927), Pg. 1.

133. Barrett, Emma; and Martin, Paul (2014). *Extreme: Why Some People Thrive at the Limits.* New York: Oxford University Press. Pg. 141.

134. Trump, Donald J. (2004). *Trump: How to Get Rich.* New York: Random House. Pg. 56.

135. Robbins, Anthony (1998). *The Ultimate Edge.* [CD]. Robbins Research International, Inc. New York: Simon & Schuster.

136. Trump, Donald J. (2007). *Trump 101: The Way to Success.* New York: John Wiley and Sons, Inc. Pg. 165.

137. Trump, Donald J. (2004). *Trump: How to Get Rich.* New York: Random House. Pg. 56.

138. Robbins, Anthony (1998). *The Ultimate Edge.* [CD]. Robbins Research International, Inc. New York: Simon & Schuster.

139. Trump, Donald J. (2007). *Trump 101: The Way to Success.* New York: John Wiley and Sons, Inc. Pg. 165.

140. Clinton, William J. (1998). *Public Papers of the Presidents of the United States, William J. Clinton, January 1 to June 30, 1998.* Washington, D.C.: U.S. Government Publishing Office. Pg. 129.

141. Trump, Donald J. (2007). *Trump 101: The Way to Success.* New York: John Wiley and Sons, Inc. Pg. 165.

142. Trump (2007), Pg. 165.

143. Chandler, Steve (2008). *Fearless: Creating the Courage to Change the Things You Can.* Anna Maria, FL: Maurice Bassett. Pg. 19.

144. Trump, Donald J. (2007). *Trump 101: The Way to Success.* New York: John Wiley and Sons, Inc. Pg. 165.

145. McClure, Colonel Alexander K. (1901). *"Abe" Lincoln's Yarns and Stories: A Complete Collection of the Funny and Witty Anecdotes that Made Lincoln Famous as America's Greatest Storyteller.* Henry Neil, Publisher. Pg. 412.

146. McClure (1901), Pg. 412.

147. Derfler, Leslie (2012). *Political Resurrection in the Twentieth Century: The Fall and Rise of Political Leaders.* New York: Palgrave MacMillan. Pg. vii.

148. Nixon, Richard (1982). *Leaders: Profiles and Reminiscences of Men Who Have Shaped the Modern World.* NY: Simon & Schuster. Pg. 26.

149. Jenkins, Roy (2001). *Churchill: A Biography.* New Yor: Farrar, Straus and Giroux. Pg. 49.

150. Nixon, Richard (1982). *Leaders: Profiles and Reminiscences of Men Who Have Shaped the Modern World.* NYC: Simon & Schuster. Pg. 26.

151. Nixon (1982), Pg. 26.

152. Nixon, Richard (1974, August 8). "President Nixon's Resignation Speech." *PBS.*

153. Nixon (1974).

154. Nixon (1974).

155. Nixon (1974).

156. Nixon, Richard (1974, August 8). "President Nixon's Resignation Speech." *PBS.*

157. Nixon (1974).

158. Nixon, Richard (1982). *Leaders: Profiles and Reminiscences of Men Who Have Shaped the Modern World.* NYC: Simon & Schuster. Pg. 26.

159. Nixon (1982), Pg. 26.

160. Nixon (1982), Pg. 26.

161. Rahall, Nick (2003, January 8). "Recognizing 50 Years of Tireless Work for West Virginia by Senator Robert C. Byrd." *Congressional Record: Proceedings and Debates of the 108th Congress First Session,* Volume 149, Part 1, January 7, 2003 to January 17, 2003. Washington, D.C.: United States Government Printing Office. Pg. 170.

162. Fadiman, Clifton and Bernard, Andre (eds.) (2000). *Bartlett's Book of Anecdotes.* New York: Little, Brown and Company. Pg. 20.

163. Plutarch (1894). Stewart, Aubrey (Translator). *Plutarch's Lives,* Volume I. New York: George Bell and Sons. Pg. 23.

164. Plutarch (1894), Pg. 23.

165. Plutarch (1894), Pg. 23.

166. Plutarch (1894), Pg. 23.

167. Leuchtenburg, William E. (2015). *The American President: From Teddy Roosevelt to Bill Clinton.* New York: Oxford University Press. Pg. 24.

168. Safire, William (2004). *Lend Me Your Ears: Great Speeches in History.* New York: W.W. Norton & Company. Pg. 929.

169. Safire (2004), Pg. 929.

170. Cialdini, Robert (2001). *Influence: Science and Practice,* 4th Edition. Boston: Allyn and Bacon. Pg. 73.

171. Wolraich, Michael (2014). *Unreasonable Men: Theodore Roosevelt and the Republican Rebels Who Created Progressive Politics.* New York: Palgrave Macmillan. Pg. 250.

172. Cialdini, Robert (2001). *Influence: Science and Practice,* 4th Edition. Boston: Allyn and Bacon. Pg. 96.

173. Baumeister, Roy F. and Tierney, John (2011). *Willpower: Why Self Control is the Secret to Success.* New York: Penguin. Pg. 87.

174. Morris, Edmund (2010). *Colonel Roosevelt.* New York: Random House. Pg. 232.

175. McFarland, Philip (2012). *Mark Twain and the Colonel: Samuel L. Clemens, Theodore Roosevelt, and the Arrival of a New Century.* Lanham, MD: Rowman & Littlefield Publishers, Inc. Pg. 414.

176. Morris, Edmund (2010). *Colonel Roosevelt.* New York: Random House. Pg. 231.

177. Safire, William (2004). *Lend Me Your Ears: Great Speeches in History.* New York: W.W. Norton & Company. Pg. 929.

178. O'Brien, Timohty L. (2005, October 23). "What's He Really Worth?" *The New York Times.* http://www.nytimes.com/2005/10/2 3/business/yourmoney/23trump.html ?pagewanted=all&_r=0

179. Kynaston, Nic (Editor). *Guinness World Records 2000: Millennium Edition (Guinness Book of Records)* (1999). Guinness World Records Ltd., 43rd Edition. Pg. 107. Listed as: "Greatest Personal Financial Recovery."

180. Robbins, Anthony (1991). *Awaken the Giant Within: How to Take Immediate Control of Your Mental, Emotional, Physical and Financial Destiny.* New York: Simon and Schuster. Pg. 132.

181. Kilpatrick, Carroll (1973, November 18). "Nixon Tells Editors, 'I'm Not a Crook.'" *Washington Post.* http://www.washingtonpost.com/wp-srv/national/longterm/watergate/arti cles/111873-1.htm

182. Kunhardt, Peter (Producer)(2014). *Nixon By Nixon: In His Own Words* [HBO Documentary Film]. United States: Kunhardt Films.

183. Isaacson, Walter (2005). *Kissinger.* York: Simon & Schuster. Pg. 598.

184. Black, Conrad (2008). *Richard M. Nixon: A Life in Full.* New York: PublicAffairs. Pg. 22.

185. Robbins, Anthony (1991). *Awaken the Giant Within: How to Take Immediate Control of Your Mental, Emotional, Physical and Financial Destiny.* New York: Simon and Schuster. Pg. 132.

186. Bochin, Hal (1990). *Richard Nixon: Rhetorical Strategist.* Westport, CT: Greenwood Publishing Group. Pg. 78.

187. Bochin (1990), Pg. 78.

188. Aitken, Jonathan (1993). *Nixon: A Life*. New York: Regnery History. Pg. 612.

189. Tomlinson, Gerald (1990). *Speaker's Treasury of Political Stories, Anecdotes and Humor*. New York: MJF Books. Pg. 179.

190. Tomlinson (1990), Pg. 179.

191. Tomlinson (1990), Pg. 179.

192. Tomlinson (1990), Pg. 179.

193. Covey, Stephen (1990). *The Seven Habits of Highly Effective People*. New York: Simon and Schuster. Pg. 56.

194. Shenkman, Richard (1999). *Presidential Ambition: How the Presidents Gained Power, Kept Power, and Got Things Done*. New York: HarperCollins. Pg. 149.

195. Covey, Stephen (2004). *The 8th Habit: From Effectiveness to Greatness*. New York: Free Press. Pg. 149

196. Robbins, Anthony (1991). *Awaken the Giant Within: How to Take Immediate Control of Your Mental, Emotional, Physical and Financial Destiny*. New York: Simon and Schuster. Pg. 133.

197. Greene, Robert (2006). *The 33 Strategies of War*. New York: Penguin Books. Pg. 34.

198. Persico, Joseph (2013). *Roosevelt's Centurions: FDR and the Commanders He Led to Victory in World War II*. NYC: Random House. Pg. 229.

199. Greene, Robert (2006). *The 33 Strategies of War*. New York: Penguin Books. Pg. 34.

200. Blumenson, Martin (1985). *Patton: The Man Behind the Legend, 1885-1945*. New York: William Morrow. Pg. 113.

201. Blumenson (1985), Pg. 113.

202. Axelrod, Alan (2009). *Patton's Drive: The Making of America's Greatest General*. Guilford, CT: The Lyons Press. Pg. 247.

203. Dolan, Samuel K. and Hense, Jim (2009). "Blood and Guts." *Patton 360* [Documentary Film]. History Channel.

204. Rice, Earle (2013). *George S. Patton: Great Military Leaders of the 20th Century*. New York: Chelsea House. Pg. 19.

205. Walker, Harold Blake (1962, April 23). "Living Faith." *Chicago Daily Tribune*, Part 1, Page 4. http://archives.chicagotribune.com/1962/04/23/page/4

206. D'Este, Carlo (1995). *Patton: A Genius for War*. New York: Harper Collins. Pg. 536.

207. D'Este (1995), Pg. 818.

208. Walker, Harold Blake (1962, April 23). "Living Faith." *Chicago Daily Tribune*, Part 1, Page 4. http://archives.chicagotribune.com/1962/04/23/page/4

209. Robbins, Anthony (2014). *Money: Master the Game. 7 Simple Steps to Financial Freedom*. New York: Simon and Schuster. Pg. 183.

210. Greene, Robert (2006). *The 33 Strategies of War*. New York: Penguin Books. Pg. 34.

211. Greene (2006), Pg. 34.

212. Yenne, Bill (2010). *Alexander the Great: Lessons from History's Undefeated General* (World Generals Series). NYC: St. Martin's. Pg. 195.

213. Schuhly, Thomas (Producer), Stone, Oliver (Director). (2004). *Alexander* [Film]. United States: Warner Bros. Pictures.

214. Schuhly (2004).

215. Arrian, Flavius (1884). *The Anabasis of Alexander; or, The history of the Wars and Conquests of Alexander the Great*. E.J. Chinnock (Translator). London: Hodder and Stoughton. Pg. 423.

216. Schuhly, Thomas (Producer), Stone, Oliver (Director). (2004). *Alexander* [Film]. United States: Warner Bros. Pictures.

217. Groom, Winston (2015). *The Generals: Patton, MacArthur, Marshall, and the Winning of World War II*. Washington, D.C.: National Geographic. Pg. 184.

218. Roosevelt, Eleanor (1960). *You Learn By Living: Eleven Keys for a More Fulfilling Life*. Louisville: Westminster John Knox Press. Pg. 29.

219. Idol, Billy (2014). *Dancing with Myself*. New York: Simon & Schuster. Pg. 27.

220. Greene, Robert (2006). *The 33 Strategies of War*. New York: Penguin Books. Pgs. 34-35.

221. Vietze, Andrew (2010). *Becoming Teddy Roosevelt: How a Maine Guide Inspired America's 26th President*. Rockport, Maine: Down East Books. Pg. 15.

222. Vietze (2010), Pg. 15.

223. Roosevelt, Theodore (1922). *Theodore Roosevelt: An Autobiography*. New York: Charles Scribner's Sons. Pg. 14.

224. Brands, H. W. (2003). *T.R.: The Last Romantic*. New York: Basic Books. Pg. 31.

225. Brands (2003), Pg. 31.

226. Roosevelt, Theodore (1922). *Theodore Roosevelt: An Autobiography*. New York: Charles Scribner's Sons. Pg. 14.

227. Brands, H. W. (2003). *T.R.: The Last Romantic*. New York: Basic Books. Pg. 31.

228. Morris, Edmund (1979). *The Rise of Theodore Roosevelt*. New York: Random House. Pg. 52.

229. Roosevelt, Theodore (1922). *Theodore Roosevelt: An Autobiography*. New York: Charles Scribner's Sons. Pg. 14.

230. Morris, Edmund (1979). *The Rise of Theodore Roosevelt*. New York: Random House. Pg. 35.

231. Morris (1979), Pg. 35.

232. Goodwin, Doris Kearns (2014). *The Bully Pulpit: Theodore Roosevelt, William Howard Taft, and the Golden Age of Journalism*. New York: Simon and Schuster. Pg. 39.

233. Roosevelt, Theodore (1922). *Theodore Roosevelt: An Autobiography*. New York: Charles Scribner's Sons. Pg. 25.

234. Roosevelt, Theodore (1922). *Theodore Roosevelt: An Autobiography*. New York: Charles Scribner's Sons. Pg. 14.

235. Roosevelt (1922), Pg. 52.

236. Roosevelt (1922), Pg. 52.

237. Roosevelt (1922), Pg. 52.

238. Roosevelt (1922), Pg. 52.

239. Roosevelt (1922), Pg. 52.

240. Peale, Norman Vincent (1996). *Treasury of Joy and Enthusiasm*. Southfield: Fawcett Columbine. Pg. 22.

241. Roosevelt, Theodore (1922). *Theodore Roosevelt: An Autobiography*. New York: Charles Scribner's Sons. Pg. 54.

242. Roosevelt (1922), Pg. 55.

243. Roosevelt (1922), Pg. 55.

244. Roosevelt (1922), Pg. 55.

245. Roosevelt (1922), Pg. 55.

246. Roosevelt (1922), Pg. 55.

247. Peterson, Christopher & Seligman, Martin E.P. (2004). *Character Strengths and Virtues: A Handbook and Classification*. Chapter 9: "Bravery [Valor]." New York: Oxford University Press. Pg. 223.

248. Palmisano, Donald J. (2012). *The Little Red Book of Leadership Lessons*. New York: Skyhorse Publishing. Pg. 66.

249. Snyder, C.R. et al (2011). *Positive Psychology: The Scientific and Practical Explorations of Human Strengths*, 2rd Edition. Los Angeles: Sage. Pg. 238.

250. Barnes, Paul; Baucom, Pam Tubridy; & Burns, Ken (Producers). Burns, Ken (Director). (2014). *The Roosevelts: An Intimate History* [Documentary Film]. United States: Florentine Films.

251. Peterson, Christopher & Seligman, Martin E.P. (2004). *Character Strengths and Virtues: A Handbook and Classification*. Chapter 9: "Bravery [Valor]." New York: Oxford University Press. Pg. 215.

252. Roosevelt, Eleanor (1960). *You Learn By Living: Eleven Keys for a More Fulfilling Life*. Louisville: Westminster John Knox Press. Pg. 29.

253. Roosevelt (1960), Pg. 29.

254. Roosevelt (1960), Pg. 30.

255. Barnes, Paul; Baucom, Pam Tubridy; & Burns, Ken (Producers). Burns, Ken (Director). (2014). *The Roosevelts: An Intimate History* [Documentary Film]. United States: Florentine Films.

256. Robbins, Anthony (2014). *Money: Master the Game. 7 Simple Steps to Financial Freedom*. New York: Simon and Schuster. Pg. 183.

257. Silver, Idora (1996). *The Chutzpah Connection: Blueprint for Success*. Reno: Chutzpress. Pg. 59.

258. Peale, Norman Vincent (1992). *You Can If You Think You Can*. New York: Fireside. Pg. 134.

259. Isaacson, Walter (2011). *Steve Jobs*. New York: Simon & Schuster. Pg. 55.

260. Silver, Idora (1996). *The Chutzpah Connection: Blueprint for Success*. Reno: Chutzpress. Pg. 59.

261. Moore, Robert W. (1919). "These Force Successes." *The Standard*, Volume 84. Boston. Pg. 581.

262. Dennis, Felix (2010). *The Narrow Road: A Brief Guide to the Getting of Money*. New York: Penguin. Pg. 44.

263. Goodwin, Doris Kearns (2014). *The Bully Pulpit: Theodore Roosevelt, William Howard Taft, and the Golden Age of Journalism*. New York: Simon and Schuster. Pg. 39-40.

264. Roosevelt, Theodore (1922). *Theodore Roosevelt: An Autobiography*. New York: Charles Scribner's Sons. Pg. 52.

265. Roosevelt (1922), Pgs. 52-53.

266. Emerson, Ralph Waldo (1850). *Representative Men: Seven Lectures*. London: John Chapman. Pg. 175.

267. Dwyer, Philip (2007). *Napoleon: The Path to Power, 1769—1799*. New Haven: Yale University Press. Pg. 171.

268. Englund, Steven (2004). *Napoleon: A Political Life*. New York: Scribner. Pg. 92.

269. Dwyer, Philip (2007). *Napoleon: The Path to Power, 1769—1799*. New Haven: Yale University Press. Pg. 215.

270. Asprey, Robert (2000). *The Rise of Napoleon Bonaparte*. New York: Basic Books. Pg. 144.

271. Englund, Steven (2004). *Napoleon: A Political Life*. New York: Scribner. Pg. 108.

272. Lockhart, John Gibson (1830). *The History of Napoleon Buonaparte*, Volume 1. New York: J & J Harper. Pg. 37.

273. Connelly, Owen (2006). *The Wars of the French Revolution and Napoleon, 1792-1815*. London: Routledge. Pg. 79.

274. Twain, Mark (1982). *Mississippi Writings*. New York: The Library of America. Pg. 985.

275. Langer, Ellen J. (1989). *Mindfulness*. Menlo Park: Addison-Wesley. Pg. 61.

276. Langer (1989), Pg. 61.

277. Tolstoy, Leo (1869). *War and Peace*. New York: Random House. Pg. 756. See also: Langer, Ellen J. (1989). *Mindfulness*. Menlo Park: Addison-Wesley. Pg. 61.

278. Markham, Felix (1963). *Napoleon*. New York: Penguin. Pg. 188.

279. Lepage, Jean-Denis G.G. (2010). *French Fortifications, 1715-1815: An Illustrated History*. Jefferson, NC: McFarland & Company, Inc. Pg. 39.

280. Langer, Ellen J. (1989). *Mindfulness*. Menlo Park: Addison-Wesley. Pg. 62.

281. Nietzsche, Friedrich (1990). *Beyond Good and Evil: Prelude to a Philosophy of the Future*. New York: Penguin Books. Pg. 269.

282. Chandler, David G. (1966). *The Campaigns of Napoleon*. New York: Scribner. Pg. 831.

283. Emerson, Ralph Waldo (1856). *Representative Men: Seven Lectures*. Boston: Phillips, Sampson and Company. Pg. 239.

284. Foster, John (1970, April). "The Bravest of the Brave." *Boys' Life*. Pg. 62.

285. Marden, Orison Swett (1896). *How to Succeed; or Stepping Stones to Fame and Fortune*. New York: The Christian Herald. Pg. 247.

286. Isaacson, Walter (2003). *Benjamin Franklin: An American Life*. New York: Simon & Schuster. Pg. 50.

287. Bonaparte, Napoleon (1916). *Napoleon in His Own Words*. (Herbert Edward Law, Translator). Chicago: A.C. McClurg & Co. Pg. 128.

288. Trump, Donald and Zanker, Bill (2007). *Think Big: Make it Happen in Business and Life*. New York: HarperCollins. Pg. 228.

289. Tully, Shawn (1996, July 22). "Donald Trump: An Ex-Loser is Back in the Money." *Fortune*. http://archive.fortune.com/magazine s/fortune/fortune_archive/1996/07/2 2/214724/index.htm

290. Trump, Donald J. (2009). *Never Give Up: How I Turned My Biggest Challenges into Success*. Hoboken, NJ: John Wiley and Sons, Inc. Pg. 2.

291. Trump (2009), Pg. 2.

292. O'Brien, Timothy L. (2005, October 23). "What's He Really Worth?" *The New York Times*. http://www.nytimes.com/2005/10/2 3/business/yourmoney/23trump.html ?pagewanted=all&_r=0

293. Trump, Donald J. (2009). *Never Give Up: How I Turned My Biggest Challenges into Success*. Hoboken, NJ: John Wiley and Sons, Inc. Pg. 2.

294. Trump (2009), Pg. 2.

295. Trump (2009), Pg. 2.

296. Trump (2009), Pg. 3.

297. Trump (2009), Pg. 3.

298. O'Brien, Timothy L. (2005, October 23). "What's He Really Worth?" *The New York Times*. http://www.nytimes.com/2005/10/2 3/business/yourmoney/23trump.html ?pagewanted=all&_r=0

299. O'Brien (2005).

300. Trump, Donald and Zanker, Bill (2007). *Think Big: Make it Happen in Business and Life*. New York: HarperCollins. Pg. 229.

301. Trump, Donald J. (2009). *Never Give Up: How I Turned My Biggest Challenges into Success*. Hoboken, NJ: John Wiley & Sons, Inc. Pg. 138.

302. Trump, Donald and Zanker, Bill (2007). *Think Big: Make it Happen in Business and Life*. New York: HarperCollins. Pg. 229.

303. Trump & Zanker (2007), Pg. 229.

304. Tully, Shawn (1996, July 22). "Donald Trump: An Ex-Loser is Back in the Money." *Fortune*.

http://archive.fortune.com/magazine s/fortune/fortune_archive/1996/07/2 2/214724/index.htm

305. Tully (1996).

306. Trump, Donald J. (2009). *Never Give Up: How I Turned My Biggest Challenges into Success*. Hoboken, NJ: John Wiley and Sons, Inc. Pg. 4.

307. Trump, Donald (2009). *Think Like a Champion: An Informal Education in Business and Life*. Philadelphia: Vanguard Press. Pg. 140.

308. Trump (2009), Pg. 140.

309. Seligman, Martin E. (2006). *Learned Optimism: How to Change Your Mind and Your Life*. New York: Random House. Pg. 213.

310. Seligman (2006), Pg. 213.

311. Byrne, Rhonda (2006). *The Secret*. New York: Atria Books. Pg. 30.

312. Trump, Donald and Zanker, Bill (2007). *Think Big: Make it Happen in Business and Life*. New York: HarperCollins. Pg. 229.

313. Byrne, Rhonda (2006). *The Secret*. New York: Atria Books. Pg. 32.

314. Trump, Donald and Zanker, Bill (2007). *Think Big: Make it Happen in Business and Life*. New York: HarperCollins. Pg. 229.

315. Byrne, Rhonda (2006). *The Secret*. New York: Atria Books. Pg. 30.

316. Byrne (2006), Pg. 52.

317. Trump, Donald and Zanker, Bill (2007). *Think Big: Make it Happen in Business and Life*. New York: HarperCollins. Pg. 229.

318. Trump & Zanker (2007), Pg. 229.

319. Trump & Zanker (2007), Pg. 229.

320. Trump & Zanker (2007), Pg. 230.

321. Barnum, Phineas Taylor (1880). *The Art of Money Getting*. Bedford, MA: Applewood. Synopsis.

322. Morrell, Margot (2001). *Shackleton's Way: Leadership Lessons from the Great Antarctic Explorer*. New York: Viking. Pg. 107.

323. Morrell & Capparell (2001), Pg. 107.

324. Worsley, Frank Arthur (1931). *Endurance: An Epic of Polar Adventure*. New York: W.W. Norton & Company, Inc. Pg. 53.

325. Worsley (1931), Pg. 1.

326. Worsley (1931), Pg. 1.

327. Worsley (1931), Pg. 2.

328. Worsley (1931), Pg. 2.

329. Worsley (1931), Pg. 2.

330. Worsley (1931), Pg. 2.

331. Ainsberg, Arthur (2010). *Shackleton: Leadership Lessons from Antarctica*. Bloomington, IN: iUniverse. Pg. 5.

332. Perkins, Dennis N.T. (2000). *Leading at the Edge: Leadership Lessons from the Extraordinary Saga of Shackleton's Antarctic Expedition*. New York: Amacom. Pg. xiii.

333. Perkins (2000), Pg. xiii.

334. Perkins (2000), Pg. xiii.

335. Morrell, Margot (2001). *Shackleton's Way: Leadership Lessons from the*

Great Antarctic Explorer. New York: Viking. Pg. 39.

336. Ainsberg, Arthur (2010). *Shackleton: Leadership Lessons from Antarctica*. Bloomington, IN: iUniverse. Pg. 5.

337. Morrell, Margot (2001). *Shackleton's Way: Leadership Lessons from the Great Antarctic Explorer*. New York: Viking. Pg. 5.

338. Ainsberg, Arthur (2010). *Shackleton: Leadership Lessons from Antarctica*. Bloomington, IN: iUniverse. Pg. 5.

339. Ainsberg (2010), Pg. 60.

340. Morrell, Margot (2001). *Shackleton's Way: Leadership Lessons from the Great Antarctic Explorer*. New York: Viking. Pg. 6.

341. Morrell and Capparell (2001), Pg. 6.

342. Worsley, Frank Arthur (1931). *Endurance: An Epic of Polar Adventure*. New York: W.W. Norton & Company, Inc. Pg. 50.

343. Worsley (1931), Pg. 50.

344. Worsley (1931), Pg. 49.

345. Morrell, Margot and Capparell, Stephanie (2001). *Shackleton's Way: Leadership Lessons from the Great Antarctic Explorer*. New York: Viking. Pg. 77.

346. Morrell and Capparell (2001), Pg. 77.

347. Perkins, Dennis N.T. (2000). *Leading at the Edge: Leadership Lessons from the Extraordinary Saga of Shackleton's Antarctic Expedition*. New York: Amacom. Pg. 81.

348. Butler, George (2000). "The Endurance: Shackleton's Legendary Antarctic Expedition" [Documentary Film]. United States: Discovery Channel Pictures.

349. Shackleton, Ernest Henry (2009 [1919]). *South: The Story of Shackleton's Last Expedition, 1914-1917*. Auckland, New Zealand: The Floating Press. Pg. 375.

350. Alexander, Caroline (1998). *The Endurance: Shackleton's Legendary Antarctic Expedition*. New York: Alfred A. Knopf. Pg. 171.

351. Alexander (1998), Pg. 171.

352. Worsley, Frank Arthur (1931). *Endurance: An Epic of Polar Adventure*. New York: W.W. Norton & Company, Inc. Pg. 100.

353. Worsley (1931), Pg. 88.

354. Worsley (1931), Pg. 97.

355. Butler, George (2000). "The Endurance: Shackleton's Legendary Antarctic Expedition" [Documentary Film]. United States: Discovery Channel Pictures.

356. Coonradt, Charles A. (2007). *The Better People Leader*. Layton, UT: Gibbs Smith Publisher. Pg. 11.

357. Alexander, Caroline (1998). *The Endurance: Shackleton's Legendary Antarctic Expedition*. New York: Alfred A. Knopf. Pg. 153.

358. Alexander (1998), Pg. 153.

359. Alexander (1998), Pg. 164.

360. Alexander (1998), Pg. 165.

361. Alexander (1998), Pg. 165.

362. Alexander (1998), Pg. 165.

363. Perkins, Dennis N.T. (2000). *Leading at the Edge: Leadership Lessons from the Extraordinary Saga of Shackleton's Antarctic Expedition*. New York: Amacom. Pg. 48.

364. Alexander, Caroline (1998). *The Endurance: Shackleton's Legendary Antarctic Expedition*. New York: Alfred A. Knopf. Pg. 182.

365. Alexander (1998), Pg. 182.

366. Alexander (1998), Pg. 183.

367. Worsley, Frank Arthur (1931). *Endurance: An Epic of Polar Adventure*. New York: W.W. Norton & Company, Inc. Pg. 183.

368. Coonradt, Charles A. (2007). *The Better People Leader*. Layton, UT: Gibbs Smith Publisher. Pg. 12.

369. Coonradt (2007), Pg. 12.

370. Alexander, Caroline (1998). *The Endurance: Shackleton's Legendary Antarctic Expedition*. New York: Alfred A. Knopf. Pg. 183.

371. Butler, George (2000). "The Endurance: Shackleton's Legendary Antarctic Expedition" [Documentary Film]. United States: Discovery Channel Pictures.

372. Perkins, Dennis N.T. (2000). *Leading at the Edge: Leadership Lessons from the Extraordinary Saga of Shackleton's Antarctic Expedition*. New York: Amacom. Pg. 41.

373. Perkins (2000), Pg. 41.

374. Frankl, Viktor (1984). *Man's Search for Meaning*. New York: Pocket Books. Pg. 86.

375. Morrell, Margot (2001). *Shackleton's Way: Leadership Lessons from the Great Antarctic Explorer*. New York: Viking. Pg. 215.

376. Worsley, Frank Arthur (1931). *Endurance: An Epic of Polar Adventure*. New York: W.W. Norton & Company, Inc. Pg. 49.

377. Perkins, Dennis N.T. (2000). *Leading at the Edge: Leadership Lessons from the Extraordinary Saga of Shackleton's Antarctic Expedition*. New York: Amacom. Pg. 42.

378. Perkins (2000), Pg. 42.

379. *The Holy Bible*, 1 Corinthians 15:33, International Standard Version.

380. Perkins, Dennis N.T. (2000). *Leading at the Edge: Leadership Lessons from the Extraordinary Saga of Shackleton's Antarctic Expedition*. New York: Amacom. Pg. 43.

381. Perkins (2000), Pg. 43.

382. Alexander, Caroline (1998). *The Endurance: Shackleton's Legendary Antarctic Expedition*. New York: Alfred A. Knopf. Pg. 54.

383. Ralling, Christopher (1983). *Shackleton: His Antarctic Writings Selected and Introduced by Christopher Ralling*. London: British Broadcasting Corporation. Pg. 162.

384. Alexander, Caroline (1998). *The Endurance: Shackleton's Legendary Antarctic Expedition*. New York: Alfred A. Knopf. Pg. 54.

385. Alexander (1998), Pg. 56.

386. Alexander (1998), Pg. 56.

387. Perkins, Dennis N.T. (2000). *Leading at the Edge: Leadership Lessons from the Extraordinary Saga of Shackleton's Antarctic Expedition*. New York: Amacom. Pg. 44.

388. Perkins (2000), Pg. 79.

389. Perkins (2000), Pg. 45.

390. Perkins (2000), Pg. 45.

391. Perkins (2000), Pg. 51.

392. Morrell, Margot (2001). *Shackleton's Way: Leadership Lessons from the Great Antarctic Explorer*. New York: Viking. Pg. 108.

393. Houck, Davis W. (2002). *FDR and Fear Itself: The First Inaugural Address*. College Station: Texas A&M University Press. Pg. 136.

394. Walsh, Kenneth T. (2009, February 12). "The First 100 Days: Franklin Roosevelt Pioneered the 100-Day Concept During FDR's first months in office, he pushed 15 major bills through Congress." *U.S. News & World Report*. http://www.usnews.com/news/history/articles/2009/02/12/the-first-100-days-franklin-roosevelt-pioneered-the-100-day-concept

395. Walsh (2009).

396. Rubenzer, Steven J. and Faschingbauer, Thomas R. (2004). *Personality, Character, and Leadership in the White House: Psychologists Assess the Presidents*. Washington, D.C.: Brassey's Inc. Pg. 254.

397. Rubenzer and Faschingbauer (2004), Pg. 254.

398. Wilson, Robert (Ed.) (1995). *Character Above All: Ten Presidents from FDR to George Bush*. New York: Simon & Schuster. Pg. 16.

399. Brands, H.W. (2015). *Reagan: The Life*. New York: Anchor Books. Pg. 27.

400. Reagan, Ronald (1982). *Public Papers of the Presidents of the United States: Ronald Reagan, 1982*. Washington, D.C.: Pgs. 88-89.

401. Roosevelt, Franklin D. (1941). *The Public Papers and Addresses of Franklin D. Roosevelt, 1939 Volume, War and Neutrality*. Book 1. United States. Pg. 197.

402. Leuchtenburg, William E. (1995). The FDR Years: On Roosevelt and His Legacy. New York: Columbia University Press. Pg. 9.

403. Leuchtenburg (1995), Pg. 9.

404. Leuchtenburg (1995), Pgs. 8-9.

405. Palmer, Russell E. (2008). *Ultimate Leadership: Winning Execution Strategies for Your Situation*. Upper

Saddle River, NJ: Wharton School Publishing. Pg. 183.

406. Palmer (2008), Pg. 183.

407. Plutarch (1894 [c. 1st century]). Stewart, Aubrey (Translator). *Plutarch's Lives*, Volume I. New York: George Bell and Sons. Pg. 470.

408. Pitney, John J.(2001) The Art of Political Warfare. University of Oklahoma Press. Pg. 51.

409. "Christopher Columbus Biography." [Documentary Film]. Biography.com (Editors). United States: A&E Television Networks. http://www.biography.com/people/christopher-columbus-9254209/videos/christopher-columbus-full-episode-2073085807

410. "Christopher Columbus Biography." [Documentary Film].

411. Gelb, Michael J. (2003). *Discover Your Genius: How to Think Like History's Ten Most Revolutionary Minds.* New York: Harper. Pg. 95.

412. Gelb (2003), Pg. 95.

413. Gelb (2003), Pg. 95.

414. Gelb (2003), Pg. 95.

415. Trump, Donald and Zanker, Bill (2007). *Think Big: Make it Happen in Business and Life.* New York: HarperCollins. Pg. 124.

416. Trump, Donald J. (2004). *Trump: How to Get Rich.* New York: Random House. Pg. 70.

417. Trump, Donald and Zanker, Bill (2007). *Think Big: Make it Happen in Business and Life.* New York: HarperCollins. Pg. 124.

418. Trump, Donald J. (2007). *Trump 101: The Way to Success.* New York: John Wiley and Sons, Inc. Pg. 76.

419. Trump, Donald (2009). *Think Like a Champion: An Informal Education in Business and Life.* Philadelphia: Vanguard Press. Pg. 139.

420. Trump (2009), Pg. 139.

421. Trump (2009), Pgs. 139-140.

422. Trump (2009), Pg. 140.

423. Trump (2009), Pg. 140.

424. Perkins, Dennis N.T. (2000). *Leading at the Edge: Leadership Lessons from the Extraordinary Saga of Shackleton's Antarctic Expedition.* New York: Amacom. Pg. 54.

425. Rauchway, Eric (2008). *The Great Depression and the New Deal: A Very Short Introduction* (Very Short Introductions). New York: Oxford. Pg. 23.

426. Brown, Vivienne (1993). Book Review: Capitalism as a Moral System: Adam Smith's Critique of the Free Market Economy by Spencer J. Pack. *The Economic Journal*, Vol. 103, No. 416. January 1993. Pgs. 230.

427. Alaska and Hawaii joined the U.S. in 1959.

428. Roosevelt, Franklin D. (1933, March 4). First Inaugural Address of Franklin D. Roosevelt. The Avalon Project, Yale Law School. http://avalon.law.yale.edu/20th_century/froos1.asp

429. Roosevelt (1933).

430. Roosevelt (1933).

431. Lincoln, Abraham (1858, September 8). "Speech at Clinton, Illinois." In *The Dearborn Independent* (1926), Volume 26, Issue 47, Pg. 18.

432. Perkins, Dennis N.T. (2000). *Leading at the Edge: Leadership Lessons from the Extraordinary Saga of Shackleton's Antarctic Expedition.* New York: Amacom. Pg. 2.

433. Read, Piers Paul (1975). *Alive: The Story of the Andes Survivors.* New York: HarperCollins. Pg. 85.

434. Read (1975), Pg. 85.

435. Read (1975), Pg. 85.

436. Read (1975), Pg. 85.

437. Read (1975), Pg. 85.

438. Read (1975), Pg. 86.

439. Read (1975), Pg. 86.

440. Faber, David (2008). *Munich: The 1938 Appeasement Crisis.* New York: Simon & Shuster. Pg. 417.

441. Martin, Benjamin F. (2006). *France in 1938.* Baton Rouge: Louisiana State University Press. Pg. 219.

442. Shawcross, William (2009). *The Queen Mother: The Official Biography.* New York: Random House. Pg. 507.

443. Safire, William (1997). *Lend Me Your Ears: Great Speeches in History.* New York: W.W. Norton & Company. Pg. 135.

444. Safire (1997), Pgs. 135-136.

445. "Winston Churchill." (1992). Contemporary Heroes and Heroines (Vol. 2). Gale Biography in Context.

446. Herman, Arthur (2008). *Gandhi and Churchill: The Epic Rivalry that Destroyed an Empire and Forged Our Age.* New York: Bantam. Pg. 47.

447. Churchill, Winston and Gilbert, Martin (2001). *The Churchill War Papers: The Ever-Widening War,* Volume 3, 1941. New York: W. W. Norton & Company. Pg. xlvii.

448. Goodwin, Doris Kearns (1994). *No Ordinary Time: Franklin and Eleanor Roosevelt: The Home Front.* New York: Simon & Schuster. Pg. 63.

449. Maxwell, John (2007). *Talent is Never Enough: No Matter How Gifted You Are, These 13 Choices Will Make You Better* (Workbook). Nashville, TN: Thomas Nelson, Inc. Pg. 135.

450. Maxwell (2007), Pg. 135.

451. Greene, Robert (2012). *Mastery.* New York: Viking. Pg. 115.

452. Greene (2012), Pg. 116.

453. Greene (2012), Pg. 116.

454. Collins, Jim (2001). *Good to Great: Why Some Companies Make the Leap...and Others Don't.* New York: Random House. Pg. 67.

455. Collins (2001), Pg. 70.

456. Marsh, Alan (1998). "POWs in American History: A Synopsis."

National Park Service. Andersonville, GA. Note: These are the official figures of the National Park Service of the United States, but they have been disputed.

457. Collins, Jim (2001). *Good to Great: Why Some Companies Make the Leap...and Others Don't.* New York: Random House. Pg. 85.

458. Southwick, Steven M. And Charney, Dennis S. (2012). *Resilience: The Science of Mastering Life's Greatest Challenges.* New York: Cambridge University Press. Pg. 31.

459. Collins, Jim (2001). *Good to Great: Why Some Companies Make the Leap...and Others Don't.* New York: Random House. Pg. 85.

460. Stockdale, James B. (1995). *Thoughts of a Philosophical Fighter Pilot.* Hoover Institution Press. Pg. 226.

461. Covey, Stephen (1990). *The Seven Habits of Highly Effective People: Powerful Lessons in Personal Change.* New York: Simon and Schuster. Pg. 49.

462. Collins, Jim (2001). *Good to Great: Why Some Companies Make the Leap...and Others Don't.* New York: Random House. Pg. 85.

463. Trump, Donald (2009). *Think Like a Champion: An Informal Education in Business and Life.* Philadelphia: Vanguard Press. Pg. 140.

464. Ziglar, Zig (2003). *Secrets of Closing the Sale.* Grand Rapids: Revell. Pg. 103.

465. Trump, Donald (2009). *Think Like a Champion: An Informal Education in Business and Life.* Philadelphia: Vanguard Press. Pg. 140.

466. Williams, Pat (2004). *How to Be Like Walt: Capturing the Disney Magic Every Day of Your Life.* Deerfield Beach, Florida: Health Communications, Inc. Pg. 28.

467. Stockdale, James B. (1995). *Thoughts of a Philosophical Fighter Pilot.* Hoover Institution Press. Pg. 226.

468. Covey, Stephen (1990). *The Seven Habits of Highly Effective People.* New York: Simon and Schuster. Pg. 49.

469. Gabler, Neal (2006). *Walt Disney: The Triumph of the American Imagination.* New York: Alfred A. Knopf. Pg. 68.

470. Gabler (2006), Pg. 67.

471. Williams, Pat (2004). *How to Be Like Walt: Capturing the Disney Magic Every Day of Your Life.* Deerfield Beach, Florida: Health Communications, Inc. Pg. 28.

472. Mosley, Leonard (1990). *Disney's World: A Biography.* Lanham, MD: Scarborough House. Pg. 70.

473. Mosley (1990), Pg. 70.

474. Mosley (1990), Pg. 70.

475. Gabler, Neal (2006). *Walt Disney: The Triumph of the American Imagination.* New York: Alfred A. Knopf. Pg. 65.

476. Gabler (2006), Pg. 65.

477. Gabler (2006), Pg. 67.

478. Williams, Pat (2004). *How to Be Like Walt: Capturing the Disney Magic Every Day of Your Life*. Deerfield Beach, Florida: Health Communications, Inc. Pg. 26.
479. Williams (2004), Pg. 26.
480. Williams (2004), Pg. 26.
481. Williams (2004), Pg. 28.
482. Williams (2004), Pg. 28.
483. Williams (2004), Pg. 28.
484. Williams (2004), Pg. 28.
485. Williams (2004), Pg. 28.
486. Williams (2004), Pg. 28.
487. Williams (2004), Pg. 28.
488. Gabler, Neal (2006). *Walt Disney: The Triumph of the American Imagination*. New York: Alfred A. Knopf. Pg. 70.
489. Gabler (2006), Pg. 70.
490. Gabler, Neal (2006). *Walt Disney: The Triumph of the American Imagination*. New York: Alfred A. Knopf. Pg. 69.
491. Gabler (2006), Pg. 69.
492. Williams, Pat (2004). *How to Be Like Walt: Capturing the Disney Magic Every Day of Your Life*. Deerfield Beach, Florida: Health Communications, Inc. Pg. 28.
493. Gabler, Neal (2006). *Walt Disney: The Triumph of the American Imagination*. New York: Alfred A. Knopf. Pg. 67.
494. Gabler (2006), Pg. 67.
495. Gabler (2006), Pg. 67.
496. Beck, Melinda (2008, April 29). "If at First You Don't Succeed, You're in Excellent Company." *The Wall Street Journal*. http://www.wsj.com/articles/SB1209 40892966150319
497. George, Bill (2015). *Discover Your True North: Becoming an Authentic Leader*. New York: Wiley. Pg. 80.
498. Klein, Maury (2003). *The Change Makers: From Carnegie to Gates, How the Great Entrepreneurs Transformed Ideas into Industries*. New York: Times Books. Pg. 102.
499. Rowling, J. K. (2008, June 5). "The Fringe Benefits of Failure, and the Importance of Imagination." *Harvard University Commencement Address*. Harvard University, Cambridge, MA. https://vimeo.com/1711302
500. Keller, Helen (1957). *The Open Door*. New York: Doubleday. Pg. 17.
501. Jones, W. Randall (2009). *The Richest Man in Town: The Twelve Commandments of Wealth*. New York: Business Plus. Pg. 106.
502. North, Jack (1995). *Arnold Schwarzenegger*. Dillon Press. Pg. 40.
503. Marden, Orison Swett (1901). *An Iron Will*. New York: Thomas Y. Crowell and Company. Pg. 27.
504. Isquith, Elisas (2015, March 22). "'He is already a winner': Why Paul Krugman's attacks on Bernie Sanders miss the mark." *Salon*.
505. Bennis, Warren & Nanus Burt (1985). *Leaders: The Strategies for Taking

Charge*. New York: Harper and Row, Publishers, Inc. Pg. 76.
506. Covey, Stephen (2006). *The Speed of Trust: The One Thing that Changes Everything*. New York: Free Press. Pg. 183.
507. Deutsch, Donny (2009). *The Big Idea: How to Make Your Entrepreneurial Dreams Come True, from the Aha Moment to Your First Million*. New York: Hyperion. Pgs. 116-117.
508. Klein, Maury (2003). *The Change Makers; From Carnegie to Gates, How the Great Entrepreneurs Transformed Ideas into Industries*. New York: Times Books. Pg. 151.
509. Friends, An Association of (1877). *Friends' Intelligencer*, Volume XXXIII. Philadelphia: John Comly, Publishing Agent. Pg. 150.
510. Friends (1877), Pg. 150.
511. Friends (1877), Pg. 150.
512. Jones, Francis Arthur (1908). *Thomas Alva Edison: Sixty Years of an Inventor's Life*. New York: Thomas Y. Crowell & Co. Pg. 94.
513. Jones (1908), Pg. 94.
514. Jones (1908), Pg. 94.
515. Dyer, Frank Lewis (1910). *Edison: His Life and Inventions*, Volume 1. New York: Harper and Brothers Publishers. Pg. 248.
516. Forbes, B.C. (1921). "Why Do So Many Men Never Amount to Anything? Thomas A. Edison, the Great Inventor, Answers this Pointed Question." *American Magazine*, Volume 91. Pg. 86.
517. Forbes (1921), Pg. 89.
518. Forbes (1921), Pg. 89.
519. Forbes (1921), Pg. 89.
520. Dyer, Frank Lewis (1910). *Edison: His Life and Inventions*, Volume 1. New York: Harper and Brothers Publishers. Pg. 263.
521. O'Connell, Bill (2005). *Solution-Focused Therapy*, Second Edition. Thousand Oaks: Sage Publications. Pg. 15.
522. Furr, Nathan (2011, June 9). "How Failure Taught Edison to Repeatedly Innovate." *Forbes*. http://www.forbes.com/sites/nathanf urr/2011/06/09/how-failure-taught-edison-to-repeatedly-innovate/
523. Jones, Francis Arthur (1908). *Thomas Alva Edison: Sixty Years of an Inventor's Life*. New York: Thomas Y. Crowell & Co. Pg. 97.
524. Jones (1908), Pg. 96.
525. Munson, Richard (2005). *From Edison to Enron: The Business of Power and What It Means for the Future of Electricity*. Westport, CT: Praeger Publishers. Pg. 15.
526. Forbes, B.C. (1922, September). "Buying Education with Sweat and Sacrifice." *Association Men*, Volume 48. Pg. 5.

527. Baldwin, Neil (2001). *Edison: Inventing the Century*. Chicago: The University of Chicago Press. Pg. 74.
528. Luntz, Frank (2011). *Win: The Key Principles to Take Your Business from Ordinary to Extraordinary*. New York: Hyperion. Pg. 244.
529. Gelb, Michael & Caldicott, Sarah Miller (2007). *Innovate Like Edison: The Success System of America's Greatest Inventor*. New York: Penguin. Pg. 53.
530. Dyer, Frank Lewis (1910). *Edison: His Life and Inventions*, Volume 1. New York: Harper and Brothers Publishers. Pg. 719.
531. Marden, Orison Swett (1911). *Pushing to the Front*. Petersburg, NY: The Success Company's. Pg. 329.
532. Marden (1911), Pg. 329.
533. Greene, Robert (2012). *Mastery*. New York: Viking. Pg. 84.
534. Maxwell, John (2000). *Failing Forward: Turning Mistakes into Stepping Stones for Success*. Nashville: Thomas Nelson. Pg. 21.
535. Dyer, Frank Lewis (1910). *Edison: His Life and Inventions*, Volume 1. New York: Harper and Brothers Publishers. Pg. 124.
536. Safire, William & Safir, Leonard (2000). *Leadership: A Treasury of Great Quotations for Those Who Aspire to Lead*. New York: Sterling Publishing Company. Pg. 89.
537. Hann, Christopher (2013, January 23). "How Your Failures Can Help You Succeed." *Entrepreneur*. http://www.entrepreneur.com/article /225199
538. Murray, Derik; Farley, Kevin; Gertz, Paul (Producers). Hodge, Brent; Murray, Derik (Directors). (2015). *I Am Chris Farley*. [Documentary Film]. United States: Network Entertainment.
539. Murray (2015).
540. Roosevelt, Franklin D. (1932, May 22). "Address at Oglethorpe University." Atlanta Georgia. Online by Gerhard Peters and John T. Woolley, *The American Presidency Project*. http://www.presidency.ucsb.edu/ws/ ?pid=88410
541. Fallows, James (2012, March). "Obama, Explained." *The Atlantic*. http://www.theatlantic.com/magazin e/archive/2012/03/obama-explained/308874/
542. Jones, W. Randall (2009). *The Richest Man in Town: The Twelve Commandments of Wealth*. New York: Business Plus. Pg. 104.
543. Dickerson, John (2012, September 27). "How to Measure for a President." *Slate*.
544. Dickerson (2012).
545. Dickerson (2012).
546. Gergen, David (2001). *Eyewitness to Power: The Essence of Leadership

193

Nixon to Clinton. New York: Simon & Schuster. Pg. 138.

547. Dickerson, John (2012, September 27). "How to Measure for a President." *Slate*.

548. Roosevelt, Franklin D. (1933, May 7). "Radio Address on the Banking Crisis." The Fireside Chats. The White House, Washington, D.C.

549. Idol, Billy (2014). *Dancing with Myself*. New York: Simon & Schuster. Pg. 61.

550. Krass, Peter (2002). *Carnegie*. New York: John Wiley & Sons, Inc. Pg. 101.

551. Krass (2002), Pg. 101.

552. Charlson, Carl (Producer)(2000). Secrets of a Master Builder: How James Eads Tamed the Mighty Mississippi [Documentary Film]. *American Experience*. United States: WGBH Educational Foundation. http://www.pbs.org/wgbh/amex/eads/index.html http://www.pbs.org/wgbh/amex/eads/peopleevents/p_carnegie.html

553. Charlson (2000).

554. Reams, Patrick & Magan, Ruan (Directors), (2012). The Men Who Built America, Season 1, Episode 3, "A Rivalry is Born." [Documentary]. *The History Channel*. United States.

555. Reams (2012).

556. Gelb, Michael J. (2003). *Discover Your Genius: How to Think Like History's Ten Most Revolutionary Minds*. New York: Harper. Pg. 91.

557. Gelb (2003), Pg. 91.

558. Bostaph, Samuel (2015). *Andrew Carnegie: An Economic Biography*. Lanham: Lexington Books. Pg. 33.

559. Krass, Peter (2002). *Carnegie*. New York: John Wiley & Sons, Inc. Pg. 116.

560. MacArthur, Douglas (1951, April 19). "Farewell Address to Congress." Washington, D.C.

561. Fay, Scott M. (2014). *Discover Your Sweet Spot: The 7 Steps to Create a Life of Success and Significance*. New York: Morgan James Publishing. Pg. 49.

562. Senge, Peter M. (1990). *The Fifth Discipline: The Art & Practice of The Learning Organization*. New York: Doubleday. Pg. 209.

563. Nanus, Burt (1992). *Visionary Leadership*. San Francisco: Jossey-Bass. Pg. 27.

564. Maxwell, John (2003). *Leadership Promises for Everyday: A Daily Devotional*. Nashville, TN: Thomas Nelson, Inc. Pg. 219.

565. Nixon, Richard (1982). *Leaders: Profiles and Reminiscences of Men Who Have Shaped the Modern World*. NYC: Simon and Schuster. Pg. 5.

566. Charlson, Carl (Producer)(2000). Secrets of a Master Builder: How James Eads Tamed the Mighty Mississippi [Documentary Film]. *American Experience*. United States: WGBH Educational Foundation.

http://www.pbs.org/wgbh/amex/eads/index.html http://www.pbs.org/wgbh/amex/eads/peopleevents/p_carnegie.html

567. Charlson (2000).

568. Voltaire (1764). "Dramatic Art." *Philosophical Dictionary*.

569. Woodward, C.M. (1881). *A History of the St. Louis Bridge*. St. Louis: G.I. Jones and Company. Pg. 71.

570. Jackson, Robert Wendell (2001). *Rails Across the Mississippi: A History of the St. Louis Bridge*. Chicago: University of Illinois Press. Pg. 125.

571. Jackson (2001), Pg. 125.

572. Charlson, Carl (Producer)(2000). Secrets of a Master Builder: How James Eads Tamed the Mighty Mississippi [Documentary Film]. *American Experience*. United States: WGBH Educational Foundation.

573. "James B. Eads and His Amazing Bridge at St. Louis." In the *Museum Gazette*, National Park Service, U.S. Department of the Interior. http://www.nps.gov/jeff/learn/historyculture/upload/eads.pdf

574. "James B. Eads and His Amazing Bridge at St. Louis." In the *Museum Gazette*, National Park Service, U.S. Department of the Interior.

575. Charlson (2000).

576. Charlson (2000).

577. Barry, John M. (1997). *Rising Tide: The Great Mississippi Flood of 1927 and How it Changed America*. New York: Simon & Schuster. Pg. 28.

578. Charlson (2000).

579. Krass, Peter (2002). *Carnegie*. New York: John Wiley & Sons, Inc. Pg. 52.

580. Fridson, Martin S. (2000). *How to Be a Billionaire: Proven Strategies from the Titans of Wealth*. New York: John Wiley & Sons, Inc. Pg. 53.

581. Brandon, John (2014, October 14). "35 Quotes on Turning Setbacks Into Successes: Don't let failure stop you. Let it be the jolt you need to succeed." *Inc. Magazine*. http://www.inc.com/john-brandon/35-quotes-on-turning-setbacks-into-successes.html

582. Lindbergh, Charles Augustus (1970). *The Wartime Journals of Charles A. Lindbergh*. New York: Harcourt, Brace, Jovanovich. Pg. 60.

583. Lindbergh, Charles and Lindbergh, Reeve (2003). *The Spirit of St. Louis*. New York: Scribner. Pg. 244.

584. Reams, Patrick & Magan, Ruan (Directors), (2012). The Men Who Built America, Season 1, Episode 3, "A Rivalry is Born." [Documentary]. *The History Channel*. United States.

585. Ainsworth, William H. (Editor) (1867). "Beautiful Thoughts." *The New Monthly Magazine*, Vol. 139. London: Chapman & Hall. Pg. 73.

586. Ferriss, Timothy (2012). *The 4-Hour Chef: The Simple Path to Cooking Like a Pro, Learning Anything, and Living the Good Life*. Boston: Houghton Mifflin Harcourt. Pg. 68.

587. Trump, Donald (2015). *The Art of the Deal*. New York: Ballantine Books. Pg. 1.

588. Trump (2015), Pg. 1.

589. Viser, Matt (2016, May 27). "Donald Trump's airline went from opulence in the air to crash landing." *Boston Globe*. https://www.bostonglobe.com/news/politics/2016/05/27/donald-trump-airline-went-from-opulence-air-crash-landing/zEf1Er2Hok2dPTVVmZT6NP/story.html

590. Reed, Ted (2001, May 5). "Trump: I Ran a Great Airline." *The Globe and Mail*. http://www.theglobeandmail.com/globe-investor/trump-i-ran-a-great-airline/article600873/?page=all

591. Reed (2001).

592. Reed (2001).

593. Reed (2001).

594. Snyder, Benjamin (2015, July 6). "Donald Trump's Business Fumbles." *Fortune*. http://fortune.com/2015/07/06/failed-trump-businesses/

595. Snyder (2015).

596. Trump, Donald J. (2009). *Never Give Up: How I Turned My Biggest Challenges into Success*. Hoboken, NJ: John Wiley and Sons, Inc. Pg. 6.

597. Trump (2009), Pg. 6.

598. Luntz, Frank (2011). *Win: The Key Principles to Take Your Business from Ordinary to Extraordinary*. New York: Hyperion. Pg. 177.

599. Hughes, Ivy (2012, January 16). "Profiles in Greatness: Walt Disney. One Mans' Will and a 'Wonderful World.'" *Success.com*. http://www.success.com/article/profiles-in-greatness-walt-disney

600. Dill, Kathryn (2016, February 18). "Disney Tops Global Ranking Of The Most Powerful Brands In 2016." *Forbes*. http://www.forbes.com/sites/kathryndill/2016/02/18/disney-tops-global-ranking-of-the-most-powerful-brands-in-2016/#618a63b07181

601. "Quarterly Earnings Reports." *The Walt Disney Company*. Fiscal Year 2015. https://thewaltdisneycompany.com/investors/financial-information/earnings

602. Van Gogh, Vincent (1995). *Dear Theo: The Autobiography of Vincent Van Gogh*. Stone & Stone (Editors). New York: Penguin. Pg. 83.

603. Cuban, Mark (2011). *How to Win at the Sport of Business: If I Can Do It, You Can Do It*. New York: Diversion Books. Pg. 31.

604. Cuban (2011). Pg. 73.

194

605. Culhane, John (1990). *The American Circus: An Illustrated History*. New York: Henry Holt and Company, Inc. Pg. 128.
606. Vitale, Joe (2006). *There's a Customer Born Every Minute: P.T. Barnum's Amazing 10 "Rings of Power" for Creating Fame, Fortune, and a Business Empire Today—Guaranteed!* Hoboken, NJ: John Wiley & Sons, Inc. Pg. 103.
607. Kunhardt Jr., Philip B.; Kunhardt III, Philip B.; and Kunhardt, Peter W. (1995). *P.T. Barnum: America's Greatest Showman*. New York: Alfred A. Knopf. Pg. 280.
608. Kunhardt (1995), Pg. 280.
609. Langer, Ellen J. (2009). *Counterclockwise: Mindful Health and the Power of Possibility*. New York: Random House. Pg. 33.
610. McClellan, Andrew (2014, September 22). "Jumbo: Marvel, Myth and Mascot." *Tufts University YouTube Channel*, Tuftsu. https://www.youtube.com/watch?v=vmRmD1GPpvg
611. Wilson, Susan (2002). "An Elephant's Tale: An Unadulterated and Relatively True Story Chronicling the Life, Death and Afterlife of Jumbo, Tufts' Illustrious Mascot." *Tufts Magazine*. http://www.tufts.edu/alumni/magazine/spring2002/jumbo.html
612. McClellan, Andrew (2014, September 22). "Jumbo: Marvel, Myth and Mascot." *Tufts University. YouTube Channel*, Tuftsu. https://www.youtube.com/watch?v=vmRmD1GPpvg
613. McClellan (2014).
614. Kunhardt Jr., Philip B.; Kunhardt III, Philip B.; and Kunhardt, Peter W. (1995). *P.T. Barnum: America's Greatest Showman*. New York: Alfred A. Knopf. Pg. 298.
615. Vitale, Joe (2006). *There's a Customer Born Every Minute: P.T. Barnum's Amazing 10 "Rings of Power" for Creating Fame, Fortune, and a Business Empire Today—Guaranteed!* Hoboken, NJ: John Wiley & Sons, Inc. Pg. 143.
616. Kunhardt Jr., Philip B.; Kunhardt III, Philip B.; and Kunhardt, Peter W. (1995). *P.T. Barnum: America's Greatest Showman*. New York: Alfred A. Knopf.
617. McClellan, Andrew (2014, September 22). "Jumbo: Marvel, Myth and Mascot." *Tufts University. YouTube Channel*, Tuftsu. https://www.youtube.com/watch?v=vmRmD1GPpvg
618. Wilson, Susan (2002). "An Elephant's Tale: An Unadulterated and Relatively True Story Chronicling the Life, Death and Afterlife of Jumbo, Tufts' Illustrious Mascot." *Tufts Magazine*.

http://www.tufts.edu/alumni/magazine/spring2002/jumbo.html
619. Wilson, Susan (2002). "An Elephant's Tale: An Unadulterated and Relatively True Story Chronicling the Life, Death and Afterlife of Jumbo, Tufts' Illustrious Mascot." *Tufts Magazine*. http://www.tufts.edu/alumni/magazine/spring2002/jumbo.html
620. "The Brightest Brains." (1904). *Printer's Ink: A Journal for Advertisers*, Volume 48, Number 2. Pg. 5.
621. Duening, Thomas N. (2016). *Leading The Positive Organization: Actions, Tools, and Processes*. New York: Business Expert Press.
622. Aurelius, Marcus (2002 [Circa 170-180 A.D.). *The Meditations*. New York: Random House, Inc. Pg. 60.
623. Aurelius (2002), Pg. 60.
624. Joyce, James (1922). *Ulysses*. Mineola, New York: Dover Publications, Inc. Pg. 182.
625. Joyce (1922), Pg. 182.
626. Jordan, William George (1907). *The Majesty of Calmness: Individual Problems and Possibilities*. New York: Fleming H. Revell Co. Pg. 16.
627. Nietzsche, Friedrich (1968). *The Will to Power*. New York: Random House. Pg. 200.
628. Lincoln, Abraham (1832). "Communication to the People of Sangamo County." *Collected Works of Abraham Lincoln*, Volume 1. http://quod.lib.umich.edu/l/lincoln/lincoln1/1:8?rgn=div1;view=toc;q1=disappointments
629. Lincoln (1832).
630. Branson, Richard (2007). *Losing My Virginity: How I Survived, Had Fun, and Made a Fortune Doing Business My Way*. New York: Random House. Pg. 62.
631. Branson (2007), Pg. 62.
632. Branson (2007), Pg. 62.
633. Coleman, Alison (2015, March 15). "Why Richard Branson Thinks Failure Should Be An Option For All Entrepreneurs." Forbes. http://www.forbes.com/sites/alisoncoleman/2015/03/15/why-richard-branson-thinks-failure-should-be-an-option-for-all-entrepreneurs/
634. Coleman (2015).
635. Branson, Richard (2012). *Like a Virgin: Secrets They Won't Teach You at Business School*. New York: Penguin. Pg. 162.
636. Drogin, Bog (1994, May 11). "'Let Freedom Reign': Mandela: South Africa: The new president appeals for peace, reconciliation and healing at his inauguration." *Los Angeles Times*. http://articles.latimes.com/1994-05-11/news/mn-56345_1_south-africa
637. Drogin (1994).
638. King, Larry (2000, May 16). "President Nelson Mandela One-on-One." *Larry King Live*. CNN.

http://www.cnn.com/TRANSCRIPTS/0005/16/lkl.00.html
639. King (2000).
640. Marden, Orison Swett (1901). *An Iron Will*. New York: Thomas Y. Crowell and Company. Pg. 27.
641. Marden (1901), Pg. 27.
642. Marden (1901), Pg. 27.
643. Marden (1901), Pg. 27.
644. Marden (1901), Pg. 27.
645. Marden (1901), Pg. 27.
646. Lacey, Michael James (Editor) (1991). *The Truman Presidency*. Cambridge: Cambridge University Press. Pg. 57.
647. Lacey (1991), Pg. 57.
648. McCullough, David (1992). *Truman*. New York: Simon and Schuster. Pg. 436.
649. Whitman, Alden (2010). "Harry S. Truman: Decisive President." On This Day. *The New York Times*. http://www.nytimes.com/learning/general/onthisday/bday/0508.html
650. Whitman (2010).
651. Sidey, Hugh (2004), *Hugh Sidey's Portraits of the Presidents: Power and Personality in the Oval Office*. TIME, Special Collector's Edition. Des Moines, IA: Time Books. Pg. 21.
652. Miller, Merle (1974). *Plain Speaking: An Oral Biography of Harry S. Truman*. New York: Berkley Publishing Corp. Pg. 203.
653. Miller (1974), Pg. 226.
654. Miller (1974), Pg. 226.
655. Miller (1974), Pg. 198.
656. Miller (1974), Pg. 198.
657. Miller, Merle (1974). *Plain Speaking: An Oral Biography of Harry S. Truman*. New York: Berkley Publishing Corp. Pg. 215.
658. McClure, Colonel Alexander K. (1901). *"Abe" Lincoln's Yarns and Stories: A Complete Collection of the Funny and Witty Anecdotes that Made Lincoln Famous as America's Greatest Storyteller*. Henry Neil, Publisher. Pg. 96.
659. McClure (1901), Pg. 96.
660. Marden, Orison Swett (1911). *Pushing to the Front*. Petersburg, NY: The Success Company's. Pg. 325.
661. Marden (1911), Pg. 326.
662. McClure, Colonel Alexander K. (1901). *"Abe" Lincoln's Yarns and Stories: A Complete Collection of the Funny and Witty Anecdotes that Made Lincoln Famous as America's Greatest Storyteller*. Henry Neil, Publisher. Pg. 97.
663. Boller, Paul F. (1996). *Presidential Anecdotes*. New York: Oxford University Press. Pg. 281.
664. Hamby, Alonzo L. (Ed.)(2015). "Harry S. Truman: Impact and Legacy." Miller Center of Public Affairs, University of Virginia. http://millercenter.org/president/biography/truman-impact-and-legacy

665. Dallek, Robert (2007). *Nixon and Kissinger: Partners in Power*. New York: Harper Collins. Pg. 90.

666. Dallek (2007), Pg. 90.

667. Matthews, Chris (2009). *The Hardball Handbook: How to Win at Life*. New York: Random House. Pg. 12.

668. Goodwin, Doris Kearns (2012, October 25). "A.L. Confidential: To really understand Abraham Lincoln, you've got to know what he hid in his desk." *Time*. http://nation.time.com/2012/10/25/abraham-lincoln-confidential/

669. McCullough, David (1992). *Truman*. New York: Simon and Schuster. Pg. 988.

670. McCullough (1992), Pg. 989.

671. McCullough (1992), Pg. 989.

672. Safire, William (2008). *Safire's Political Dictionary*. Oxford: Oxford University Press. Pg. 142.

673. McCullough, David (1992). *Truman*. New York: Simon and Schuster. Pg. 989.

674. Dallek, Robert (2008). *Harry S. Truman. The American Presidents*. New York: Times Books. Pg. 114.

675. McCullough, David (1992). *Truman*. New York: Simon and Schuster. Pg. 989.

676. McCullough (1992), Pg. 989.

677. Mieder, Wolfgang (1997). *The Politics of Proverbs: From Traditional Wisdom to Proverbial Stereotypes*. Madison: The University of Wisconsin. Pg. 94.

678. Hamby, Alonzo L. (Ed.)(2015). "Harry S. Truman: Impact and Legacy." Miller Center of Public Affairs, University of Virginia. http://millercenter.org/president/biography/truman-impact-and-legacy

679. Bush, George (1990). *Public Papers of the Presidents of the United States: George Bush, 1990*. Washington, D.C.: Office of the Federal Register. Pg. 1388.

680. Hamby, Alonzo L. (Ed.)(2015). "Harry S. Truman: Impact and Legacy." Miller Center of Public Affairs, University of Virginia. http://millercenter.org/president/biography/truman-impact-and-legacy

681. Bent, Samuel Arthur (1887). *Familiar Short Sayings of Great Men with Historical and Explanatory Notes*. Boston: Ticknor & Co. Pg. 10.

682. Hugo, Victor (1893). *Things Seen*. Boston: Estes and Lauriat. Pg. 78.

683. Hugo (1893), Pg. 79.

684. Smarandache, Florentin and Yuhua, Fu (2011). *Neutrosophic Interpretation of Tao Te Ching*. Glendale, AZ: Kappa & Omega. Pg. 78.

685. White, Richard D. (2006). *Kingfish: The Reign of Huey P. Long*. New York: Random House. Pg. 23.

686. White (2006), Pg. 23.

687. White (2006), Pg. 23.

688. Hewett, James S. (Editor)(1988). *Illustrations Unlimited*. Wheaton, IL: Tyndale House Publishers, Inc. Pg. 134.

689. Marden, Orison Swett (1911). *Pushing to the Front*. Petersburg, NY: The Success Company's. Pg. 336.

690. Marden (1911), Pg. 336.

691. Williams, Pat and Williams, Karyn (2009). *The Takeaway: 20 Unforgettable Life Lessons Every Father Should Pass On to His Child*. Deerfield Beach: Health Communications, Inc. Pg. 110.

692. Colvin, Geoff (2008). *Talent is Overrated: What Really Separates World-Class Performers from Everybody Else*. New York: Penguin. Pg. 65.

693. Janis, Irving (1983). *Groupthink: Psychological Studies of Policy Decisions and Fiascoes*, 2nd Edition. Boston: Houghton Mifflin Company. Pg. 14.

694. Janis (1983), Pg. 16.

695. Wicker, Tom; Finney, John W.; Frankel, Max; and Kenworthy, E.W. (1966, April 25). "C.I.A.: Maker of Policy, or Tool?" *The New York Times*. Pg. 20.

696. Burns, James MacGregor (2006). *Running Alone: Presidential Leadership from JFK to Bush II: Why It Has Failed and How We Can Fix It*. New York: Basic Books. Pg. 49.

697. Burns (2006), Pg. 49.

698. Janis, Irving (1983). *Groupthink: Psychological Studies of Policy Decisions and Fiascoes*, 2nd Edition. Boston: Houghton Mifflin Company. Pg. 47.

699. Kennedy, Robert F. (1969). *Thirteen Days: A Memoir of the Cuban Missile Crisis*. New York: Penguin Books. Pg. 112.

700. Hilsman, Roger (1996). *The Cuban Missile Crisis: The Struggle Over Policy*. Westport, CT: Praeger Publishers. Pg. 111.

701. Janis, Irving (1983). *Groupthink: Psychological Studies of Policy Decisions and Fiascoes*, 2nd Ed. Boston: Houghton Mifflin. Pg. 138.

702. Mosettig, Michael D. (2012, October 22). "Cuban Missile Crisis: Memories of a Young Reporter." *PBS Newshour*. http://www.pbs.org/newshour/rundown/cuban-missile-crisis/

703. Burns, Richard D. and Siracusa, Joseph M. (2015). *Historical Dictionary of the Kennedy-Johnson Era*, Second Edition. Lanham: Rowman & Littlefield. Pg. 377.

704. Burns (2015), Pg. 378.

705. Burns (2015), Pg. 378.

706. Burns (2015), Pg. 378.

707. Chapman, Lionel (Producer) Wiley, Foster (Director)(1992). *The Missiles of October: What the World Didn't Know*. [Documentary Film]. United States: Washington Media Associates.

708. Nye, Joseph S. (1989, March 13). "Where Were You in 62?: Cuban Graffiti." *The New Republic*. Pg. 16.

709. Chomsky, Noam (2012, October 15). "Cuban missile crisis: how the US played Russian roulette with nuclear war." *The Guardian*. http://www.theguardian.com/commentisfree/2012/oct/15/cuban-missile-crisis-russian-roulette

710. Kennedy, Robert F. (1969). *Thirteen Days: A Memoir of the Cuban Missile Crisis*. New York: Penguin Books. Pg. 49.

711. Kennedy (1969), Pg. 28.

712. Millard, Candice (2005). *The River of Doubt: Theodore Roosevelt's Darkest Journey*. New York: Random House. Pg. 202.

713. Kennedy, Robert F. (1969). *Thirteen Days: A Memoir of the Cuban Missile Crisis*. New York: Penguin Books. Pg. 49.

714. Kennedy (1969), Pg. 49.

715. Klein, Christopher (2012, October 26). "The Cuban Missile Crisis Pilot Whose Death May Have Saved Millions." *The History Channel*. http://www.history.com/news/the-cuban-missile-crisis-pilot-whose-death-may-have-saved-millions

716. Klein (2012).

717. Klein (2012).

718. Klein (2012).

719. Covey, Stephen R. (2004). *The 7 Habits of Highly Effective People: Powerful Lessons in Personal Change*. NYC: Simon & Schuster. Pg. 79.

720. Rangel, Charles B. (2007, April 18). *Congressional Record: Proceedings and Debates of the 110th Congress, First Session*, Volume 153, Part 7. Washington, D.C.: United States Government Printing Office. Pg. 9295.

721. Rangel (2007), Pg. 9295.

722. "Jackie Robinson Biography." [Documentary Film]. *Biography.com*. United States: A&E Television Networks. http://www.biography.com/people/jackie-robinson-9460813 (Robinson)

723. May, Ernest R. And Zelikow, Philip D. (Editors)(2002). *The Kennedy Tapes: Inside the White House During The Cuban Missile Crisis*. New York: W. W. Norton & Company. Pg. 232.

724. Frankel, Max (2002, October). "Learning from the Missile Crisis: What Really Happened on Those Thirteen Fateful Days in October." *Smithsonian Magazine*. http://www.smithsonianmag.com/history/learning-from-the-missile-crisis-68901679/?no-ist

725. Chomsky, Noam (2012, October 15). "Cuban missile crisis: how the US played Russian roulette with nuclear war." *The Guardian*. http://www.theguardian.com/comm

entisfree/2012/oct/15/cuban-missile-crisis-russian-roulette

726. Chomsky (2012).

727. Chomsky (2012).

728. Frankel, Max (2002, October). "Learning from the Missile Crisis: What Really Happened on Those Thirteen Fateful Days in October." *Smithsonian Magazine*. http://www.smithsonianmag.com/history/learning-from-the-missile-crisis-68901679/?no-ist

729. White, Ronald C. (2009). *A. Lincoln: A Biography*. New York: Random House. Pg. 621.

730. Thomas, Helen and Crawford, Craig (2009). *Listen Up, Mr. President: Everything You Always Wanted Your President to Know and Do*. New York: Simon and Schuster. Pg. 190.

731. Dobbs, Michael (2012, October 15). "The Price of a 50-Year Myth." *The New York Times*. http://www.nytimes.com/2012/10/16/opinion/the-eyeball-to-eyeball-myth-and-the-cuban-missile-crisiss-legacy.html?_r=0

732. Schlesinger, Arthur M. (2002). *A Thousand Days: John F. Kennedy in the White House*. New York: Houghton Mifflin Company. Pg. 841.

733. Dobbs, Michael (2008). *One Minute to Midnight: Kennedy, Khrushchev, and Castro on the Brink of Nuclear War*. New York: Vintage Books. Pg. 353.

734. Aurelius, Marcus (2002 [Circa 170-180 A.D.). *The Meditations*. New York: Random House, Inc.

735. Aurelius (2002).

736. Greene, Robert (2006). *The 33 Strategies of War*. New York: Penguin Books. Pg. 33.

737. Dick, Bernard F. (2016). *The Screen is Red: Hollywood, Communism, and the Cold War*. Jackson: University Press of Mississippi. Pg. 242.

738. Jamieson, Kathleen Hall (1996). *Packaging the Presidency: A History and Criticism of Presidential Campaign Advertising*. New York: Oxford University Press. Pg. 238.

739. Harper, Jennifer (2016, March 29). "Facing an enemy? Take a a cue from Gen. Curtis LeMay." *The Washington Times*.

740. Rhodes, Richard (1995, June 19). "The General and World War III" *The New Yorker*. Pg. 58. http://www.newyorker.com/magazine/1995/06/19/the-general-and-world-war-iii

741. Douglass, James W. (2008). *JFK and the Unspeakable: Why He Died and Why It Matters*. New York: Simon and Schuster. Pg. 30.

742. Chomsky, Noam (2012, October 15). "Cuban missile crisis: how the US played Russian roulette with nuclear war." *The Guardian*. http://www.theguardian.com/comm

entisfree/2012/oct/15/cuban-missile-crisis-russian-roulette

743. Hargrove, Erwin C. (2014). *The Effective Presidency: Lessons on Leadership from John F. Kennedy to Barack Obama, Second Edition*. New York: Routledge.

744. Roberts, Gary L. (2006). *Doc Holliday: The Life and Legend*. New York: John Wiley & Sons, Inc. Pg. 186.

745. O'Reilly, Bill & Fisher, David (Producers). (2015). "Doc Holliday." Season 1, Episode 2. *Legends and Lies: The Real West*. United States: Henry Holt and Company.

746. Roberts, Gary L. (2006). *Doc Holliday: The Life and Legend*. New York: John Wiley & Sons, Inc. Pg. 186.

747. Roberts (2006), Pg. 187.

748. Schacter, Daniel; Gilbert, Daniel; and Wegner, Daniel (2009). *Psychology*. NY: Worth Publishers. Pg. 377. "Because emotions are reactions to the appraisals of an event and not to the event itself, changes in appraisal bring about changes in emotional experience" (p. 377).

749. Ricard, Serge (Editor)(2011). *A Companion to Theodore Roosevelt*. Blackwell Companions to American History. Malden, MA: Wiley-Blackwell. Pg. 29.

750. McCullough, David (2001). *Mornings on Horseback: The Story of an Extraordinary Family, a Vanished Way of Life, and the Unique Child Who Became Theodore Roosevelt*. New York: Simon and Schuster. Pg. 274.

751. Morris, Edmund (1979). *The Rise of Theodore Roosevelt*. New York: Random House. Pg. 147.

752. Morris (1979), Pg. 153.

753. Morris (1979), Pg. 163.

754. Hagedorn, Hermann (1918, March). "A Boy's Life of Roosevelt." *Boy's Life*, Vol. VIII, No. 3. Pg. 81.

755. Morris, Edmund (1979). *The Rise of Theodore Roosevelt*. New York: Random House. Pg. 175.

756. Knokey, Jon (2015). *Theodore Roosevelt and the Making of American Leadership*. New York: Skyhorse Publishing. Pg. 116.

757. Morris, Edmund (1979). *The Rise of Theodore Roosevelt*. New York: Random House. Pg. 163.

758. Knokey, Jon (2015). *Theodore Roosevelt and the Making of American Leadership*. New York: Skyhorse Publishing. Pg. 117.

759. Hagedorn, Hermann (1918, March). "A Boy's Life of Roosevelt." *Boy's Life*, Vol. VIII, No. 3. Pg. 81.

760. Hagedorn (1918), Pg. 81.

761. Knokey, Jon (2015). *Theodore Roosevelt and the Making of American Leadership*. New York: Skyhorse Publishing. Pg. 117.

762. Morris, Edmund (1979). *The Rise of Theodore Roosevelt*. New York: Random House. Pg. 177.

763. Morris (1979), Pg. 177.

764. Knokey, Jon (2015). *Theodore Roosevelt and the Making of American Leadership*. New York: Skyhorse Publishing. Pg. 120.

765. Morris, Edmund (1979). *The Rise of Theodore Roosevelt*. New York: Random House. Pg. 176.

766. Morris (1979), Pg. 178.

767. Knokey, Jon (2015). *Theodore Roosevelt and the Making of American Leadership*. New York: Skyhorse Publishing. Pg. 120.

768. McCullough, David (2001). *Mornings on Horseback: The Story of an Extraordinary Family, a Vanished Way of Life, and the Unique Child Who Became Theodore Roosevelt*. New York: Simon and Schuster. Pg. 270.

769. McCullough (2001), Pg. 270.

770. Knokey, Jon (2015). *Theodore Roosevelt and the Making of American Leadership*. New York: Skyhorse Publishing. Pg. 120.

771. Knokey (2015), Pg. 118.

772. Knokey, Jon (2015). *Theodore Roosevelt and the Making of American Leadership*. New York: Skyhorse Publishing. Pg. 121.

773. McCullough, David (2001). *Mornings on Horseback: The Story of an Extraordinary Family, a Vanished Way of Life, and the Unique Child Who Became Theodore Roosevelt*. New York: Simon and Schuster. Pg. 271.

774. McCullough (2001), Pg. 271.

775. Knokey, Jon (2015). *Theodore Roosevelt and the Making of American Leadership*. New York: Skyhorse Publishing. Pg. 117.

776. Knokey (2015), Pg. 117.

777. Chisholm, Hugh (1911). "Roosevelt, Theodore." *The Encyclopedia Britannica: A Dictionary of Arts, Sciences, Literature and General Information*, Eleventh Edition. New York: The Encyclopedia Britannica Company.

778. Morris, Edmund (1979). *The Rise of Theodore Roosevelt*. New York: Random House. Pg. 180.

779. Roosevelt, Theodore (1922). *Theodore Roosevelt: An Autobiography*. New York: Charles Scribner's Sons. Pg. 85.

780. Morris, Edmund (1979). *The Rise of Theodore Roosevelt*. New York: Random House. Pg. 153.

781. Morris (1979), Pg. 153.

782. Frankel, Max (2002, October). "Learning from the Missile Crisis: What Really Happened on Those Thirteen Fateful Days in October." *Smithsonian Magazine*. http://www.smithsonianmag.com/history/learning-from-the-missile-crisis-68901679/?no-ist

783. Janis, Irving (1983). *Groupthink: Psychological Studies of Policy Decisions and Fiascoes*, 2nd Edition. Boston: Houghton Mifflin Company.

784. Sharlet, Jeff (2016, April 12). "Donald Trump, American Preacher: Building a congregation for his prosperity gospel, one chaotic rally at a time." *The New York Times*. http://www.nytimes.com/2016/04/17/magazine/donald-trump-american-preacher.html

785. Marans, Daniel (2016, March 19). "Donald Trump's Wife And Daughter Tell Him To 'Act Presidential,' He Claims: But the Republican front-runner says he just can't help himself." *Huffington Post*. http://www.huffingtonpost.com/entry/donald-trump-wife-daughter-act-presidential_us_56edd87be4b084c6722075b4

786. Edsall, Thomas B. (2015, December 2). "Donald Trump's Appeal." *The New York Times*. http://www.nytimes.com/2015/12/02/opinion/campaign-stops/donald-trumps-appeal.html?_r=0

787. Confessore, Nicholas and Yourish, Karen (2016, March 15). "Measuring Donald Trump's Mammoth Advantage in Free Media." *The New York Times*. http://www.nytimes.com/2016/03/16/upshot/measuring-donald-trumps-mammoth-advantage-in-free-media.html

788. Roberts, David (2015, December 1). "The real reason the media is rising up against Donald Trump." *Vox*. http://www.vox.com/2015/12/1/9828086/donald-trump-media

789. O'Brien, Michael (2005). *John F. Kennedy: A Biography*. New York: St. Martin's Press. Pg. 805.

790. O'Brien (2005), Pg. 805.

791. Bellows, Susan (Producer & Director) (2013). *JFK*. [Documentary Film]. United States: PBS: American Experience Films. http://www.pbs.org/wgbh/americanexperience/features/transcript/jfk-transcript/

792. O'Brien, Michael (2005). *John F. Kennedy: A Biography*. New York: St. Martin's Press. Pg. 804.

793. O'Brien (2005), Pg. 805.

794. O'Brien (2005), Pg. 805.

795. O'Brien (2005), Pg. 805.

796. Clifford, Clark M. (1992). *Counsel to the President*. New York: Random House. Pg. 304.

797. O'Brien, Michael (2005). *John F. Kennedy: A Biography*. New York: St. Martin's Press. Pg. 805.

798. Ury, William (1993). *Getting Past No: Negotiating Your Way from Confrontation to Cooperation*. New York: Bantam Books. Pg. 38.

799. Ury (1993), Pg. 38.

800. Ury (1993), Pg. 38.

801. O'Brien, Michael (2005). *John F. Kennedy: A Biography*. New York: St. Martin's Press. Pg. 805.

802. O'Brien (2005), Pg. 805.

803. Kaiser, David E. (2000). *American Tragedy: Kennedy, Johnson, and the Origins of the Vietnam War*. Cambridge: Harvard University Press. Pgs. 265-266.

804. O'Brien, Michael (2005). *John F. Kennedy: A Biography*. New York: St. Martin's Press. Pg. 805.

805. Butler-Bowdon, Tom (2003). *50 Self-Help Classics: 50 Inspirational Books to Transform Your Life from Timeless Sages to Contemporary Gurus*. London: Nicholas Brealey Publishing. Pg. 16.

806. O'Brien, Michael (2005). *John F. Kennedy: A Biography*. New York: St. Martin's Press. Pg. 802.

807. Dallek, Robert (2003). *An Unfinished Life: John F. Kennedy, 1917—1963*. Boston: Little, Brown and Company. Pg. 470.

808. Dallek (2003), Pg. 470.

809. Olasky, Marvin (1999). *The American Leadership Tradition: The Inevitable Impact of a Leader's Faith on a Nation's Destiny*. New York: Simon and Schuster. Pg. 246.

810. Nixon, Richard (1974, February 12). "Remarks at a Ceremony Commemorating the Birth of Abraham Lincoln." Gerhard Peters and John T. Woolley, *The American Presidency Project*. http://www.presidency.ucsb.edu/ws/?pid=4348

811. Nixon (1974).

812. Nixon (1974).

813. Nixon (1974).

814. Nixon (1974).

815. Nixon (1974).

816. Nixon (1974).

817. Gallwey, W. Timothy (1997). *The Inner Game of Tennis: The Classic Guide to the Mental Side of Peak Performance*. New York: Random House. Pg. 32.

818. Chopra, Deepak (2010). *The Soul of Leadership: Unlocking Your Potential for Greatness*. New York: Random House. Pg. 132.

819. Gallwey, W. Timothy (1997). *The Inner Game of Tennis: The Classic Guide to the Mental Side of Peak Performance*. New York: Random House. Pg. 12.

820. Butler-Bowdon, Tom (2003). *50 Self-Help Classics: 50 Inspirational Books to Transform Your Life from Timeless Sages to Contemporary Gurus*. London: Nicholas Brealey Publishing. Pg. 33.

821. Chopra, Deepak (1994). *The Seven Spiritual Laws of Success: A Practical Guide to the Fulfillment of Your Dreams*. San Rafael, CA: Amber-Allen Publishing. Pg. 83.

822. Chopra (1994), Pg. 83.

823. Butler-Bowden, Tom (2013). *The Literature of Possibility*. London: Nicholas Brealey Publishing. Pg. 272.

824. *The Holy Bible*. Proverbs, 16:32, New International Version (NIV)

825. Heifetz, Ronald A. (1994). *Leadership Without Easy Answers*. Cambridge, MA: Harvard University Press. Pg. 252.

826. Gergen, David (2001). *Eyewitness to Power: The Essence of Leadership Nixon to Clinton*. New York: Simon & Schuster. Pg. 42.

827. Heifetz, Ronald A. (1994). *Leadership Without Easy Answers*. Cambridge, MA: Harvard University Press. Pg. 252.

828. Heifetz (1994), Pg. 252.

829. Kennedy, Robert F. (1969). *Thirteen Days: A Memoir of the Cuban Missile Crisis*. New York: Penguin Books. Pg. 66.

830. Schlesinger, Arthur M. (2002). *Robert Kennedy and His Times*. Boston: Houghton Mifflin Company. Pg. 213.

831. Schlesinger (2002), Pg. 213.

832. Schlesinger (2002), Pg. 213.

833. Barr, Robert (1988, June 5). "Remembering A Kennedy A Passionate, Ruthless Man." *Philly.com*. http://articles.philly.com/1988-06-05/news/26265819_1_campaign-manager-bobby-kennedy-robert-f-kennedy

834. Barr (1988).

835. Rothstein, Mervyn (1997). "King of the Q & A: What Do Clint Eastwood, Jack Kemp, Richard Nixon and the Beatles have in Common? They Were all Interviewed by David Frost." *Cigar Aficionado*. March/April 1997. http://www.cigaraficionado.com/webfeatures/show/id/King-of-the-Q--A_6050

836. Rothstein (1997).

837. Rothstein (1997).

838. Rothstein (1997).

839. Rothstein (1997).

840. Geier, Ben (2016, April 18). "Donald Trump Has a New Nickname for Hillary Clinton." *Fortune*. http://fortune.com/2016/04/18/trump-clinton-nickname/

841. Schleifer, Theodore (2016, May 30). "Rubio says he apologized to Trump for 'small hands' jest." *CNN*. http://www.cnn.com/2016/05/29/politics/marco-rubio-jake-tapper-interview/

842. Voorhees, Josh (2016, March 3). "The Fox News Debate Was Ugly, Rowdy, and Immature. Of Course Trump Won. *Slate*. http://www.slate.com/blogs/the_slatest/2016/03/03/the_fox_new_debate_in_detroit_was_ugly_and_immature_of_course_trump_won.html

843. Zimmerman, Neetzan (2015, September 9). "Trump mocks Fiorina's physical appearance: 'Look at that face!'" *The Hill*. http://thehill.com/blogs/blog-briefing-

room/253178-trump-insults-fiorinas-physical-appearance-look-at-that-face

844. Ruta, Garance Franke (2015, September 16). "Carly Fiorina to Donald Trump's face: 'I think women ... heard very clearly what Mr. Trump said.'" *Yahoo News*. https://www.yahoo.com/news/carly-fiorina-to-donald-trumps-face-i-think-129254505186.html

845. Keneally, Meghan (2015, September 18). "Donald Trump's History of Raising Birther Questions About President Obama." *ABC News*. http://abcnews.go.com/Politics/donald-trumps-history-raising-birther-questions-president-obama/story?id=33861832

846. Beckwith, Ryan Teague (2015, August 10). "Watch President Obama Troll Donald Trump in 2011." *Time*. http://time.com/3991301/donald-trump-barack-obama/

847. Eisenhower, Dwight D. (1954, April 23). "Remarks at the Birthplace of Abraham Lincoln, Hodgenville, Kentucky" Gerhard Peters and John T. Woolley, *The American Presidency Project*. http://www.presidency.ucsb.edu/ws/?pid=10218

848. Eisenhower (1954).

849. Eisenhower (1954).

850. Eisenhower (1954).

851. Carnegie, Dale (1958). *How to Win Friends and Influence People*. New York: Pocket Books. Pgs. 24-27.

852. Eisenhower, Dwight D. (1954, April 23). "Remarks at the Birthplace of Abraham Lincoln, Hodgenville, Kentucky" Gerhard Peters and John T. Woolley, *The American Presidency Project*. http://www.presidency.ucsb.edu/ws/?pid=10218

853. Eisenhower (1954).

854. Eisenhower (1954).

855. Eisenhower (1954).

856. Parry, Jos. Hyrum (1886). "Anecdotes of President Lincoln." *Parry's Literary Journal: A Monthly Magazine of the Best Reading*, Volume 2. Salt Lake City: Jos. Hyrum Parry & Co., Publishers. Pg. 94.

857. Parlette, Ralph Albert (1922, June). "The Spotlight." *The Lyceum Magazine*, Volume 32, Number 1. Pg. 21.

858. Sandburg, Carl (1929). *Abraham Lincoln: The Prairie Years*. New York: Harcourt. Pg. 485.

859. Sandburg (1929), Pg. 485.

860. Eisenhower, Dwight D. (1954, April 23). "Remarks at the Birthplace of Abraham Lincoln, Hodgenville, Kentucky" Gerhard Peters and John T. Woolley, *The American Presidency Project*. http://www.presidency.ucsb.edu/ws/?pid=10218

861. Eisenhower (1954).

862. Dallek, Robert (2003). *An Unfinished Life: John F. Kennedy, 1917—1963*. Boston: Little, Brown and Company. Pg. 470.

863. Dallek (2003), Pg. 470.

864. Goodwin, Doris Kearns (2014). *The Bully Pulpit: Theodore Roosevelt, William Howard Taft, and the Golden Age of Journalism*. New York: Simon and Schuster. Pg. 209.

865. Goodwin (2014), Pg. 209.

866. Goodwin (2014), Pg. 209.

867. Barnes, Paul; Baucom, Pam Tubridy; & Burns, Ken (Producers). Burns, Ken (Director). (2014). *The Roosevelts: An Intimate History* [Documentary Film]. United States: Florentine Films.

868. Goodwin, Doris Kearns (2014). *The Bully Pulpit: Theodore Roosevelt, William Howard Taft, and the Golden Age of Journalism*. New York: Simon and Schuster. Pg. 209.

869. Goodwin (2014), Pg. 209.

870. Goodwin (2014), Pg. 210.

871. Brands, H. W. (Editor) (2001). *The Selected Letters of Theodore Roosevelt*. Lanham, MD: Rowman & Littlefield Publishers, Inc. Pg. 106.

872. Goodwin, Doris Kearns (2014). *The Bully Pulpit: Theodore Roosevelt, William Howard Taft, and the Golden Age of Journalism*. New York: Simon and Schuster. Pg. 210.

873. Goodwin (2014), Pg. 210.

874. Stratemeyer, Edward and Copeland, Charles (1904). *American Boys' Life of Theodore Roosevelt*. Boston: Lee and Shepard. Pgs. 100-101.

875. Bishop, Joseph Bucklin (1920). *Theodore Roosevelt and His Time Shown in His Own Letters*, Volume 1. New York: Charles Scribner's Sons. Pg. 59.

876. Barnes, Paul; Baucom, Pam Tubridy; & Burns, Ken (Producers). Burns, Ken (Director). (2014). *The Roosevelts: An Intimate History* [Documentary Film]. United States: Florentine Films.

877. Goodwin, Doris Kearns (2014). *The Bully Pulpit: Theodore Roosevelt, William Howard Taft, and the Golden Age of Journalism*. New York: Simon and Schuster. Pg. 210.

878. Barnes, Paul; Baucom, Pam Tubridy; & Burns, Ken (Producers). Burns, Ken (Director). (2014). *The Roosevelts: An Intimate History* [Documentary Film]. United States: Florentine Films.

879. Goodwin, Doris Kearns (2014). *The Bully Pulpit: Theodore Roosevelt, William Howard Taft, and the Golden Age of Journalism*. New York: Simon and Schuster. Pg. 210.

880. Goodwin (2014), Pg. 210.

881. Goodwin (2014), Pg. 210.

882. Goodwin (2014), Pg. 210.

883. Lewis, Alfred Henry (1905, March). "Mr. Roosevelt's New Policies."

Success Magazine, Volume 8. NY: The Success Company. Pg. 170.

884. Lewis (1905), Pg. 170.

885. Lewis (1905), Pg. 170.

886. Lewis, Alfred Henry (Ed.) (1906). A Compilation of the Messages and Speeches of Theodore Roosevelt (1901—1905). Washington, D.C.: Bureau of National Literature and Art. Pg. viii.

887. Lewis (1906). Pg. viii.

888. Goodwin, Doris Kearns (2014). *The Bully Pulpit: Theodore Roosevelt, William Howard Taft, and the Golden Age of Journalism*. New York: Simon and Schuster. Pg. 211.

889. Goodwin (2014), Pg. 211.

890. Leupp, Francis Ellington (1904). *The Man Roosevelt: A Portrait Sketch*. New York: D. Appleton and Company. Pg. 188.

891. Goodwin, Doris Kearns (2014). *The Bully Pulpit: Theodore Roosevelt, William Howard Taft, and the Golden Age of Journalism*. New York: Simon and Schuster. Pg. 211.

892. Lewis, Alfred Henry (Ed.) (1906). A Compilation of the Messages and Speeches of Theodore Roosevelt (1901—1905). Washington, D.C.: Bureau of National Literature and Art. Pg. viii.

893. Goodwin, Doris Kearns (2014). *The Bully Pulpit: Theodore Roosevelt, William Howard Taft, and the Golden Age of Journalism*. New York: Simon and Schuster. Pg. 211.

894. Greene, Robert (1998). *The 48 Laws of Power*. New York: Penguin Books. Pg. 167.

895. Plutarch (1960 [100 A.D.]). *Plutarch's Moralia*. Cambridge: Harvard University Press. Pg. 7.

896. Plutarch (1960), Pg. 7.

897. Plutarch (1960), Pg. 7.

898. Griffith, Samuel B. (1963). *Sun Tzu: The Art of War*. New York: Oxford University Press. Pg. vii.

899. Dweck, Carol (2008). *Mindset: The New Psychology of Success. How We Can Learn to Fulfill Our Potential*. New York: Random House. Pg. 122.

900. Gracian, Baltasar (1892). Jacobs, Joseph (Translator). *The Art of Worldly Wisdom*. London: MacMillan and Co. Pg. 29.

901. Plutarch (1960 [100 A.D.]). *Plutarch's Moralia*. Cambridge: Harvard University Press. Pg. 8.

902. Nixon, Richard (2008). *Richard Nixon: Speeches, Writings, Documents*. Perlstein, Rick (Editor). Princeton, NJ: Princeton University Press. Pg. 76.

903. Morris, Roger (1990). *Richard Milhous Nixon: The Rise of an American Politician*. New York: Henry Holt and Company. Pg. 852.

904. Black, Conrad (2008). *Richard M. Nixon: A Life in Full*. New York: PublicAffairs. Pg. 259.

905. McCullough, David (1992). *Truman*. New York: Simon and Schuster. Pg. 989.

906. Isaacson, Walter (2003). *Benjamin Franklin: An American Life*. New York: Simon & Schuster. Pg. 65.

907. Isaacson (2003), Pg. 65.

908. Isaacson (2003), Pg. 65.

909. Greene, Robert (1998). *The 48 Laws of Power*. New York: Penguin Books. Pg. 46.

910. Vitale, Joe (2006). *There's a Customer Born Every Minute: P.T. Barnum's Amazing 10 "Rings of Power" for Creating Fame, Fortune, and a Business Empire Today—Guaranteed!* Hoboken, NJ: John Wiley & Sons, Inc. Pg. 152.

911. Kunhardt Jr., Philip B.; Kunhardt III, Philip B.; and Kunhardt, Peter W. (1995). *P.T. Barnum: America's Greatest Showman*. New York: Alfred A. Knopf. Pg. 20.

912. Kunhardt (1995), Pg. 22.

913. Cole, Henry (1835, August 20). "Joice Heth." [Letter to the Editor] *New York Sun*. http://lostmuseum.cuny.edu/archive/exhibit/heth/

914. Kunhardt Jr., Philip B.; Kunhardt III, Philip B.; and Kunhardt, Peter W. (1995). *P.T. Barnum: America's Greatest Showman*. New York: Alfred A. Knopf. Pg. 22.

915. Vitale, Joe (2006). *There's a Customer Born Every Minute: P.T. Barnum's Amazing 10 "Rings of Power" for Creating Fame, Fortune, and a Business Empire Today—Guaranteed!* Hoboken, NJ: John Wiley & Sons, Inc. Pg. 70.

916. Vitale (2006), Pg. 70.

917. Kunhardt Jr., Philip B.; Kunhardt III, Philip B.; and Kunhardt, Peter W. (1995). *P.T. Barnum: America's Greatest Showman*. New York: Alfred A. Knopf. Pg. 22.

918. Jeansonne, Glen (1993). *Messiah of the Masses: Huey P. Long and the Great Depression*. New York: Longman. Pg. 35.

919. Jeansonne (1993), Pg. 35.

920. Jeansonne (1993), Pg. 35.

921. Jeansonne (1993), Pg. 35.

922. Parini, Jay (2004). *The Oxford Encyclopedia of American Literature*. New York: Oxford University Press. Pg. 58.

923. Plutarch (1960 [100 A.D.]). *Plutarch's Moralia*. Cambridge: Harvard University Press. Pg. 9.

924. Gracian, Baltasar (1892). Jacobs, Joseph (Translator). *The Art of Worldly Wisdom*. London: MacMillan and Co. Pg. 29.

925. Pederson, William D. (2006). *Presidential Profiles: The FDR Years*. New York: Facts on File, Inc. Pg. 356.

926. Pederson (2006), Pg. 356.

927. Roosevelt, Franklin D. (1932, September 21). "Campaign Address in Portland, Oregon on Public Utilities and Development of Hydro-Electric Power." *The American Presidency Project*, Peters, Gerhard and Woolley, John T. http://www.presidency.ucsb.edu/ws/?pid=88390

928. Hagedorn, Hermann (1922). *The Boys' Life of Theodore Roosevelt*. New York: Harper & Brothers Publishers. Pg. 67.

929. Hagedorn (1922), Pg. 67.

930. Ferris, Tim (2015, December 22). "Amelia Boone on Beating 99% of Men and Suffering for High Performance." *The Tim Ferris Show*. http://fourhourworkweek.com/2015/12/22/amelia-boone/

931. Freeley, Austin J. and Steinberg, David L. (2014). *Argumentation and Debate: Critical Thinking for Reasoned Decision Making*, Thirteenth Edition. Boston: Wadsworth. Pg. 380.

932. Freeley (2014), Pg. 380.

933. Boller, Paul F. (1996). *Presidential Anecdotes*. New York: Oxford University Press. Pg. 291.

934. White, Richard D. (2006). *Kingfish: The Reign of Huey P. Long*. New York: Random House. Pg. 122.

935. Schlesinger, Arthur M. (2003). *The Age of Roosevelt: The Politics of Upheaval: 1935-1936*. New York: Houghton Mifflin Company. Pg. 50.

936. Long, Huey P. (1996 [1933]). *Every Man a King: The Autobiography of Huey P. Long*. Jackson, TN: Da Capo Press. Pg. 278.

937. Long (1996), Pg. 278.

938. Sabato, Larry J. (2013). *The Kennedy Half-Century: The Presidency, Assassination, and Lasting Legacy of John F. Kennedy*. New York: Bloomsbury. Pg. 46.

939. Sabato (2013), Pg. 46.

940. Watson, Robert P.; Pederson, William D.; and Williams, Frank J. (2011). *Lincoln's Enduring Legacy: Perspective from Great Thinkers, Great Leaders, and the American Experiment*. Lanham, MD: Lexington Books. Pg. 94.

941. Benioff, David and Weiss, D.B. (Writers), & Van Patten, Tim (Director) "Winter is Coming" [Season 1, Episode 1]. In George R.R. Martin's (Producer) *Game of Thrones*. HBO. Belfast, Northern Ireland: Paint Hall Studios.

942. Barrier, Michael (2008). *The Animated Man: A Life of Walt Disney*. Berkeley: University of California Press. Pg. 243.

943. Landrum, Gene N. (1999). *Eight Keys to Greatness: How to Unlock Your Hidden Potential*. Amherst, NY: Prometheus Books. Pg. 203.

944. Gabler, Neal (2006). *Walt Disney: The Triumph of the American Imagination*. New York: Alfred A. Knopf. Pg. 430.

945. Landrum, Gene N. (1999). *Eight Keys to Greatness: How to Unlock Your Hidden Potential*. Amherst, NY: Prometheus Books. Pg. 203.

946. Landrum (1999), Pg. 203.

947. Gabler, Neal (2006). *Walt Disney: The Triumph of the American Imagination*. New York: Alfred A. Knopf. Pg. 433.

948. Robbins, Anthony (1995). *Notes from a Friend: A Quick and Simple Guide to Taking Charge of Your Life*. NYC: Simon & Schuster. Pg. 30.

949. Robbins (1995), Pg. 30.

950. Faulk, Matthew and Skeet, Mark (Writers); Bazalgette, Edward (Director). (2006). Hannibal: Rome's Worst Nightmare [Television Movie]. *British Broadcasting Corporation* (BBC).

951. Knox, James Samuel (1917). *Salesmanship and Personal Efficiency*. Cleveland, OH: The Knox School of Salesmanship and Business Efficiency. Pg. 21.

952. Williams, Pat (2004). *How to Be Like Walt: Capturing the Disney Magic Every Day of Your Life*. Deerfield Beach, Florida: Health Communications, Inc. Pg. 21.

953. Williams (2004), Pg. 21.

954. Williams (2004), Pg. 21.

955. Landrum, Gene N. (1999). *Eight Keys to Greatness: How to Unlock Your Hidden Potential*. Amherst, NY: Prometheus Books. Pg. 203.

956. Robbins, Anthony (1995). *Notes from a Friend: A Quick and Simple Guide to Taking Charge of Your Life*. NYC: Simon & Schuster. Pg. 30.

957. Williams, Pat (2004). *How to Be Like Walt: Capturing the Disney Magic Every Day of Your Life*. Deerfield Beach, Florida: Health Communications, Inc. Pg. 41.

958. Williams (2004), Pg. 41.

959. Gabler, Neal (2006). *Walt Disney: The Triumph of the American Imagination*. New York: Alfred A. Knopf. Pg. 443.

960. Covey, Stephen (1990). *The Seven Habits of Highly Effective People*. NYC: Simon and Schuster. Pg. 107.

961. Robbins, Anthony (1995). *Notes from a Friend: A Quick and Simple Guide to Taking Charge of Your Life*. NYC: Simon & Schuster. Pg. 30.

962. Nixon, Richard (1982). *Leaders: Profiles and Reminiscences of Men Who Have Shaped the Modern World*. NY: Simon & Schuster. Pg. 7.

963. Nixon (1982), Pg. 7.

964. Churchill, Winston (1940, June 4). "We Shall Fight on the Beaches" [Speech]. House of Commons of the Parliament of the United Kingdom. http://www.winstonchurchill.org/resources/speeches/128-we-shall-fight-on-thebeaches

965. James, Robert Rhode (1967). *Chips: The Diaries of Sir Henry Channon*. Channon's diary entry on June 4, 1940. London: Littlehampton Book Services Ltd. Pg. 256.

966. Churchill, Winston (1940, June 4). "We Shall Fight on the Beaches" [Speech]. House of Commons of the Parliament of the United Kingdom. http://www.winstonchurchill.org/resources/speeches/128-we-shall-fight-on-thebeaches

967. Gartner, John (2008). In Search of Bill Clinton: A Psychological Biography. New York: St. Martin's Press. Pg. 120.

968. Gartner (2008), Pg. 120.

969. Gartner (2008), Pg. 120.

970. Clinton, William J. (2001). Public Papers of the Presidents of the United States, William J. Clinton, 2000-2001. Washington, D.C.: U.S. Government Publishing Office. Pg. 2913.

971. Clinton (2001), Pg. 2913.

972. Heilemann, John & Halperin, Mark (2010). Game Change: Obama and the Clintons, McCain and Palin, and the Race of a Lifetime. New York: HarperCollins. Pg. 254.

973. Trump, Donald J. (2009). Never Give Up: How I Turned My Biggest Challenges into Success. Hoboken, NJ: John Wiley and Sons, Inc. Pg. 2.

974. Trump (2009), Pg. 2.

975. Trump (2009), Pg. 2.

976. Trump (2009), Pg. 2.

977. Trump, Donald and Zanker, Bill (2007). Think Big: Make it Happen in Business and Life. New York: HarperCollins. Pg. 27.

978. Trump & Zanker (2007), Pg. 27.

979. Trump & Zanker (2007), Pg. 28.

980. Trump & Zanker (2007), Pg. 28.

981. Matthews, Chris (2009). The Hardball Handbook: How to Win at Life. New York: Random House. Pg. 14.

982. Matthews (2009), Pg. 14.

983. Loftus, Geoff (2012, May 9). "If You're Going Through Hell, Keep Going—Winston Churchill." Forbes. http://www.forbes.com/sites/geoffloftus/2012/05/09/if-youre-going-through-hell-keep-going-winston-churchill/#3c3c46ff3a3b

984. Leamer, Laurence (2005). Fantastic: The Life of Arnold Schwarzenegger. New York: St. Martin's Press. Pg. 175.

985. Leamer (2005), Pg. 336.

986. Stahl, Lesley (2012, September 30). "Arnold Schwarzenegger: Success and Secrets." 60 Minutes. http://www.cbsnews.com/8301-18560_162-57523140/arnold-schwarzenegger-success-and-secrets/

987. Gallo, Carmine (2006). "The Governator's Charisma." Business Week. http://www.businessweek.com/smallbiz/content/nov2006/sb20061108_048096.htm

988. Schwarzenegger, Arnold (2013). Total Recall: My Unbelievably True Life Story. New York: Simon and Schuster. Pg. 421.

989. Schwarzenegger (2013), Pg. 421.

990. Leamer, Laurence (2005). Fantastic: The Life of Arnold Schwarzenegger. New York: St. Martin's Press. Pg. 251.

991. Schwarzenegger, Arnold (2013). Total Recall: My Unbelievably True Life Story. New York: Simon and Schuster. Pg. 421.

992. Nasaw, David (2006). Andrew Carnegie. New York: Penguin.

993. Nasaw (2006).

994. Klein, Maury (2003). The Change Makers: From Carnegie to Gates, How the Great Entrepreneurs Transformed Ideas into Industries. New York: Times Books. Pg. 108.

995. Grubin, David (Producer). (1994). FDR. American Experience. PBS. [Documentary Film]. United States: David Grubin Productions, Inc. Transcript: http://www.pbs.org/wgbh/americanexperience/features/transcript/fdr-transcript/

996. Grubin (1994).

997. Grubin (1994).

998. Pitney, John J.(2001) The Art of Political Warfare. University of Oklahoma Press. Pg. 51.

999. Marden, Orison Swett (1911). Pushing to the Front. Petersburg, NY: The Success Company's. Pg. 329.

1000. Marden (1911), Pg. 329.

1001. Branson, Richard (2012). Like a Virgin: Secrets They Won't Teach You at Business School. New York: Penguin. Pg. 37.

1002. Marden, Orison Swett (1911). Pushing to the Front. Petersburg, NY: The Success Company's. Pg. 554.

1003. Peale, Norman Vincent (1985). Have a Great Day: Daily Affirmations for Positive Living. New York: Ballantine Books.

1004. Marden, Orison Swett (1911). Pushing to the Front. Petersburg, NY: The Success Company's. Pg. 554.

1005. Branson, Richard (2012). Like a Virgin: Secrets They Won't Teach You at Business School. New York: Penguin. Pg. 21.

1006. Konnikova, Maria (2016, February 11). "How People Learn to Become Resilient." The New Yorker. http://www.newyorker.com/science/maria-konnikova/the-secret-formula-for-resilience?intcid=mod-most-popular

1007. Loder, Vanessa (2015, June 3). "Can Stress Kill You? Research Says Only If You Believe It Can." Forbes. http://www.forbes.com/sites/vanessaloder/2015/06/03/can-stress-kill-you-research-says-only-if-you-believe-it-can/#3f0deae672d6 See also: McGonigal, Kelly (2013, June). "Kelly McGonigal: How to make stress your friend." TED. https://www.ted.com/talks/kelly_mcgonigal_how_to_make_stress_your_friend?language=en

1008. Konnikova, Maria (2016, February 11). "How People Learn to Become Resilient." The New Yorker. http://www.newyorker.com/science/maria-konnikova/the-secret-formula-for-resilience?intcid=mod-most-popular

1009. Robbins, Anthony (1991). Awaken the Giant Within: How to Take Immediate Control of Your Mental, Emotional, Physical and Financial Destiny. New York: Simon and Schuster. Pg. 36.

1010. Robbins (1991), Pgs. 32-33.

1011. Grubin, David (Producer). (1994). FDR. American Experience. PBS. [Documentary Film]. United States: David Grubin Productions, Inc. Transcript: http://www.pbs.org/wgbh/americanexperience/features/transcript/fdr-transcript/

1012. Grubin (1994).

1013. Grubin (1994).

1014. Bardhan-Quallen, Sudipta (2007). Franklin D. Roosevelt: A National Hero. New York: Sterling Publishing. Pg. 39.

1015. Grubin, David (Producer). (1994). FDR. American Experience. PBS. [Documentary Film]. United States: David Grubin Productions, Inc. Transcript: http://www.pbs.org/wgbh/americanexperience/features/transcript/fdr-transcript/

1016. Gallagher, Hugh (1999). FDR's Splendid Deception: The Moving Story of Roosevelt's Massive Disability—and the Intense Efforts to Conceal It from the Public. St. Petersburg, FL: Vandamere Press.

1017. Golway, Terry (2009). Together We Cannot Fail: FDR and the American Presidency in Years of Crisis. Naperville, IL: Sourcebooks. Pg. 8.

1018. Grubin, David (Producer). (1994). FDR. American Experience. PBS. [Documentary Film]. United States: David Grubin Productions, Inc. Transcript: http://www.pbs.org/wgbh/americanexperience/features/transcript/fdr-transcript/

1019. Grubin (1994).

1020. Golway, Terry (2009). Together We Cannot Fail: FDR and the American Presidency in Years of Crisis. Naperville, IL: Sourcebooks, Inc. Pg. 8.

1021. Grubin, David (Producer). (1994). FDR. American Experience. PBS. [Documentary Film]. United States: David Grubin Productions, Inc. Transcript: http://www.pbs.org/wgbh/americanexperience/features/transcript/fdr-transcript/

1022. Marden, Orison Swett (1911). Pushing to the Front. Petersburg, NY: The Success Company's. Pg. 329.

1023. Grubin, David (Producer). (1994). FDR. American Experience. PBS.

[Documentary Film]. United States: David Grubin Productions, Inc.

1024. Grubin (1994).

1025. Gaffney, Peter and Gaffney, Dennis (2012). *The Seven-Day Scholar: The Presidents: Exploring History One Week at a Time*. History.com. New York: Hyperion. Pg. 187.

1026. Grubin (1994).

1027. Aitken, Jonathan (1993). *Nixon: A Life*. New York: Regnery History. Pg. 359.

1028. Pitney, John J.(2001) *The Art of Political Warfare*. University of Oklahoma Press. Pg. 51.

1029. Waldman, Michael (2010). *My Fellow Americans: The Most Important Speeches of America's Presidents*. Pg. 224.

1030. Woodward, Bob (1999). *Shadow: Five Presidents and The Legacy Of Watergate*. New York: Simon & Schuster.

1031. Knokey, Jon (2015). *Theodore Roosevelt and the Making of American Leadership*. New York: Skyhorse Publishing. Pg. 106.

1032. Morris, Edmund (1979). *The Rise of Theodore Roosevelt*. New York: Random House. Pg. 278.

1033. Morris (1979), Pg. 277.

1034. Nixon, Richard (1974, August 8). "Remarks on Departure From the White House." Miller Center, University of Virginia. http://millercenter.org/president/nixo n/speeches/speech-3891

1035. Nixon (1974).

1036. Nixon (1974).

1037. Nixon (1974).

1038. Black, Conrad (2008). *Richard M. Nixon: A Life in Full*. New York: PublicAffairs. Pg. 983.

1039. Black (2008), Pg. 983.

1040. Pitney, John J.(2001) *The Art of Political Warfare*. University of Oklahoma Press. Pg. 161.

1041. Branson, Richard (2014). *The Virgin Way: If It's Not Fun, It's Not Worth Doing*. New York: Portfolio. Pg. 86.

1042. Hughes, Ken (2016, January 19). "Richard Nixon: Life After the Presidency." Miller Center of Public Affairs, University of Virginia. http://millercenter.org/president/biog raphy/nixon-life-after-the-presidency

1043. Hughes (2016).

1044. Hughes (2016).

1045. Clinton, William J. (1994, April 27). "Remarks at the Funeral Service for President Richard Nixon in Yorba Linda, California." *The American Presidency Project*. Peters, Gerhard and Woolley, John T. http://www.presidency.ucsb.edu/ws/ ?pid=50052

1046. *The Holy Bible*, 2 Corinthians 15:17, English Standard Version.

1047. Clinton, William J. (1994, April 27). "Remarks at the Funeral Service for President Richard Nixon in Yorba

Linda, California." *The American Presidency Project*. Peters, Gerhard and Woolley, John T. http://www.presidency.ucsb.edu/ws/ ?pid=50052

1048. Rahall, Nick (2003, January 8). "Recognizing 50 Years of Tireless Work for West Virginia by Senator Robert C. Byrd." Congressional Record: Proceedings and Debates of the 108th Congress First Session, Volume 149, Part 1, January 7, 2003 to January 17, 2003. Washington, D.C.: United States Government Printing Office. Pg. 170.

1049. Gardner, Howard (1997). *Extraordinary Minds: Portraits Of 4 Exceptional Individuals And An Examination Of Our Own Extraordinariness*. New York: Basic Books. Pg. 121.

1050. Greenblatt, Miriam (1989). *Franklin D. Roosevelt: 32nd President fo the United States*. Ada, OK: Garrett Educational Corporation. Pg. 35.

1051. Rowling, J.K. (2008, June 5). "The Fringe Benefits of Failure, and the Importance of Imagination." *Harvard Commencement Address*, Cambridge, MA. http://news.harvard.edu/gazette/stor y/2008/06/text-of-j-k-rowling-speech/

1052. Bennis, Warren (1999). *Managing People is Like Herding Cats: Warren Bennis on Leadership*. Provo, UT: Executive Excellence Publishing. Pg. 97.

1053. Mezirow, Jack (1990). *Fostering Critical Reflection in Adulthood: A Guide to Transformative and Emancipatory Learning*. San Francisco: Jossey-Bass. Pg. 13.

1054. Goodwin, Doris Kearns (2013, November 27). "The Bully Pulpit (Part 2 of 5)." [Video] Abraham Lincoln Book Shop, Chicago. https://www.youtube.com/watch?v=i 7rgaNFiDpQ

1055. Goodwin (2013).

1056. Goodwin (2013).

1057. Hamilton, Edith (1930). *The Greek Way*. New York: W. W. Norton & Company. Pg. 61.

1058. Morris, Edmund (1979). *The Rise of Theodore Roosevelt*. New York: Random House. Pg. 248.

1059. Nixon, Richard (1974, August 8). "Remarks on Departure From the White House." Miller Center, University of Virginia. http://millercenter.org/president/nixo n/speeches/speech-3891

1060. Markham, Felix (1966). *Napoleon*. New York: Mentor. Pg. 204.

1061. Markham (1966), Pg. 218.

1062. Greene, Robert (1998). *The 48 Laws of Power*. New York: Penguin Books. Pg. 63.

1063. Greene (1998), Pg. 63.

1064. Markham, Felix (1966). *Napoleon*. New York: Mentor. Pg. 218.

1065. Thomas, Helen and Crawford, Craig (2009). *Listen Up, Mr. President: Everything You Always Wanted Your President to Know and Do*. New York: Scribner. Pg. 74.

1066. Burlingame, Michael (1994). *The Inner World of Abraham Lincoln*. Chicago: University of Illinois Press. Pg. 4.

1067. Burlingame (1994), Pg. 3.

1068. Burlingame (1994), Pg. 3.

1069. Burlingame (1994), Pg. 4.

1070. Cronin, Vincent (1988). *Napoleon*. New York: Penguin. Pg. 478.

1071. Cronin (1988), Pg. 478.

1072. Andrew, Roberts (2014). *Napoleon: A Life*. New York: Viking. Pg. 724.

1073. Headley, Phineas Camp (1858). *The Life of Napoleon Bonaparte*. New York: Derby & Jackson. Pg. 333.

1074. MacKenzie, Norman (2007). *The Escape From Elba: The Fall & Flight of Napoleon 1814-1815*. South Yorkshire: Pen & Sword. Pg. 202.

1075. Smith, Timothy Wilson (2007). *Napoleon*. London: Haus Publishing Limited. Pg. 125.

1076. Pooley, Eric (1996). "Who is Dick Morris? How a Rogue Genius in the Game of Political Strategy Became the Most Influential Private Citizen in America." *Time Magazine*, Volume 148, Issue 11. http://www.cnn.com/ALLPOLITICS/19 96/analysis/time/9609/02/morris.sht ml

1077. Pooley (1996).

1078. DeMarco, MJ (2011). *The Millionaire Fastlane: Crack the Code to Wealth and Live for a Lifetime*. Phoenix, AZ: Viperion Publishing Corporation. Pg. 59.

1079. Trump, Donald (2009). *Think Like a Champion: An Informal Education in Business and Life*. Philadelphia: Vanguard Press. Pg. 66.

1080. Trump (2009), Pg. 66.

1081. Jensen, Keld (2012, August 8). "Rock Bottom: How Great Leaders Triumph Over Failure." *Forbes*. http://www.forbes.com/sites/keldjen sen/2012/08/08/rock-bottom-how- great-leaders-triumph-over- failure/#1ed9699842cb

1082. Trump, Donald and Zanker, Bill (2007). *Think Big: Make it Happen in Business and Life*. New York: HarperCollins. Pg. 26.

1083. Trump and Zanker (2007), Pg. 26.

1084. Trump and Zanker (2007), Pg. 26.

1085. Foster, John (1970, April). "The Bravest of the Brave." *Boys' Life*. Pg. 62.

1086. Scott, Sir Walter (1836). *The Life of Napoleon Buonaparte, Emperor of the French*. Exeter: J&B Williams. Pg. 302.

1087. Esdaile, Charles (2007). *Napoleon's Wars: An International History*. New York: Viking. Pg. 461.

1088. Klein, Christopher (2014, November 18). "Napoleon's Hat Fetches $2.4

Million at Auction." History in the Headlines, *The History Channel*. http://www.history.com/news/napol eons-hat-fetches-2-4-million-at-auction

1089. Englund, Steven (2004). *Napoleon: A Political Life*. New York: Scribner. Pg. 428.

1090. Englund (2004), Pg. 428.

1091. Englund (2004), Pg. 428.

1092. Markham, Felix (1966). *Napoleon*. New York: Mentor. Pg. 226.

1093. Markham (1966), Pg. 226.

1094. Greene, Robert (1998). *The 48 Laws of Power*. New York: Penguin Books. Pg. 63.

1095. Markham, Felix (1966). *Napoleon*. New York: Mentor. Pg. 227.

1096. Markham (1966), Pg. 227.

1097. Markham (1966), Pg. 227.

1098. Markham (1966), Pg. 227.

1099. Read, Piers Paul (1975). *Alive: The Story of the Andes Survivors*. New York: HarperCollins. Pg. 86.

1100. Trump, Donald and Zanker, Bill (2007). *Think Big: Make it Happen in Business and Life*. New York: HarperCollins. Pg. 26.

1101. "The Charles Goodyear Story: Charles Goodyear, and the accidental discovery that lead to the vulcanization process." (1958, January). *Reader's Digest*. The Reader's Digest Association, Inc. Pleasantville, NY. https://corporate.goodyear.com/en-US/about/history/charles-goodyear-story.html

1102. "The Charles Goodyear Story" (1958).

1103. Edwards, Tryon (1891). *A Dictionary of Thoughts Being a Cyclopedia of Laconic Quotations*. New York: Cassell Publishing Co. Pg. 157.

1104. Schwartz, David J. (2010). *The Magic of Thinking Big*. New York: Simon and Schuster. Pg. 26.

1105. Gartner, John (2008). *In Search of Bill Clinton: A Psychological Biography*. New York: St. Martin's Press. Pg. 336.

1106. Lehrer, Jim (1998, January 26). "The Big Speech: Clinton's State of the Union Address." *PBS News Hour*. http://www.pbs.org/newshour/bb/w hite_house-jan-june98-historians_1-26/

1107. Lehrer (1998).

1108. Lehrer (1998).

1109. Waldman, Michael (2000). *POTUS Speaks: Finding the Words that Defined the Clinton Presidency*. New York: Simon & Schuster. Pg. 215.

1110. Waldman (2000), Pg. 215.

1111. Waldman (2000), Pg. 216.

1112. Waldman (2000), Pg. 216.

1113. Gartner, John (2008). *In Search of Bill Clinton: A Psychological Biography*. New York: St. Martin's Press. Pg. 336.

1114. Maraniss, David (1998, January 25). "In Clinton, a Past That's Ever Prologue." *Washington Post*, Page

A01. http://www.washingtonpost.com/wp -srv/politics/special/clinton/stories/clin ton012598.htm

1115. Maraniss (1988).

1116. "Poll: Clinton's Approval Rating Up in the Wake of Impeachment." (1998, December 20). *CNN*. http://www.cnn.com/ALLPOLITICS/st ories/1998/12/20/impeachment.poll/

1117. Matthews, Chris (2011). *Jack Kennedy: Elusive Hero*. New York: Simon and Schuster. Pg. 59.

1118. Matthews (2011), Pg. 59.

1119. Trump, Donald and Zanker, Bill (2007). *Think Big: Make it Happen in Business and Life*. New York: HarperCollins. Pg. 26.

1120. Andersen, Erika (2013, May 31). "21 Quotes From Henry Ford On Business, Leadership And Life." *Forbes*. http://www.forbes.com/sites/erikaan dersen/2013/05/31/21-quotes-from-henry-ford-on-business-leadership-and-life/#63e2ba6b3700

1121. McCullough, David (2006), *1776*. New York: Simon and Schuster. Pg. 180.

1122. McCullough (2006), Pg. 179.

1123. Stockwell, Mary (Retrieved: 2016, February 10). "Battle of Long Island." George Washington's Mount Vernon. [Video: "Washington and the New York Campaign of 1776."] http://www.mountvernon.org/digital-encyclopedia/article/battle-of-long-island/

1124. Stockwell (2016).

1125. Stockwell (2016).

1126. Chernow, Ron (2010). *Washington: A Life*. New York: The Penguin Press. Pg. 254.

1127. Stockwell, Mary (Retrieved: 2016, February 10). "Battle of Long Island." George Washington's Mount Vernon. [Video: "Washington and the New York Campaign of 1776."] http://www.mountvernon.org/digital-encyclopedia/article/battle-of-long-island/

1128. Stockwell (2016).

1129. Stockwell (2016).

1130. Chernow, Ron (2010). *Washington: A Life*. New York: The Penguin Press. Pg. 254.

1131. Chernow (2010), Pg. 254.

1132. Chernow (2010), Pg. 254.

1133. Rees, James C. (2007). *George Washington's Leadership Lessons: What the Father of Our Country Can Teach Us About Effective Leadership and Character*. New York: John Wiley & Sons, Inc. Pg. 69.

1134. Rees (2007), Pg. 69.

1135. Rees (2007), Pg. 69.

1136. Carrington, Henry B. (1898). *Washington the Soldier*. New York: Lamson, Wolffe and Company. Pg. 117.

1137. Carrington (1898), Pg. 117.

1138. Ellis, Joseph (2004). *His Excellency George Washington*. New York: Random House. Pg.101.

1139. Ellis (2004). Pg.101.

1140. Carrington, Henry B. (1898). *Washington the Soldier*. New York: Lamson, Wolffe and Company. Pg. 117.

1141. Carrington (1898), Pg. 117.

1142. Rees, James C. (2007). George Washington's Leadership Lessons: What the Father of Our Country Can Teach Us About Effective Leadership and Character. New York: John Wiley & Sons, Inc. Pg. 72.

1143. Brookhiser, Richard (1996). *Founding Father: Rediscovering George Washington*. New York: The Free Press. Pg. 34.

1144. Ferling, John (2000). *Setting the World Ablaze: Washington, Adams, Jefferson, and the American Revolution*. New York: Oxford University Press. Pg. 147.

1145. McCullough, David (2006), *1776*. New York: Simon and Schuster. Pg. 291.

1146. Brookhiser, Richard (1996). *Founding Father: Rediscovering George Washington*. New York: The Free Press. Pg. 33.

1147. Grizzard, Frank E. (2002). *George Washington: A Biographical Companion*. Santa Barbara: ABC-CLIO, Inc. Pg. 270.

1148. Rees, James C. (2007). *George Washington's Leadership Lessons: What the Father of Our Country Can Teach Us About Effective Leadership and Character*. New York: John Wiley & Sons, Inc. Pg. 70.

1149. Rees (2007), Pg. 70.

1150. Rees (2007), Pg. 70.

1151. Ferling, John (2000). *Setting the World Ablaze: Washington, Adams, Jefferson, and the American Revolution*. New York: Oxford University Press. Pgs. 147-148.

1152. Levin, Robert E. and Landres, J. Shawn (1992). *Bill Clinton: The Inside Story*. New York: Shapolsky Publishers, Inc. Pg. 148.

1153. Levin and Landres (1992), Pg. 148.

1154. Greenstein, Fred I. (1994). "The Two Leadership Styles of William Jefferson Clinton." *Political Psychology*, Volume 15, Number 2. Pg. 357.

1155. Greenstein (1994), Pg. 357.

1156. Greenstein (1994), Pg. 357.

1157. Branson, Richard (2012). *Like a Virgin: Secrets They Won't Teach You at Business School*. New York: Penguin. Pg. 38.

1158. Finn, Christine A. (2002). *Artifacts: An Archaeologist's Year in Silicon Valley*. Cambridge: MIT Press. Pg. 90.

1159. Branson, Richard (2012). *Like a Virgin: Secrets They Won't Teach You at Business School*. New York: Penguin. Pg. 38.

1160. Branson (2012), Pg. 38.

1161. Branson (2012), Pg. 38.
1162. Schwarzenegger, Arnold (2013). *Total Recall: My Unbelievably True Life Story*. New York: Simon and Schuster. Pg. 23.
1163. Schwarzenegger (2013), Pg. 23.
1164. Schwarzenegger (2013), Pg. 23.
1165. Schwarzenegger (2013), Pg. 23.
1166. Marden, Orison Swett (1901). *An Iron Will*. New York: Thomas Y. Crowell and Company. Pg. 26.
1167. Gabler, Neal (2006). *Walt Disney: The Triumph of the American Imagination*. New York: Alfred A. Knopf. Pg. 381.
1168. "Notes." (1916, July 6). *The Nation*, Volume 103, Number 2662. Pg. 206.
1169. Levin, Robert E. and Landres, J. Shawn (1992). *Bill Clinton: The Inside Story*. New York: Shapolsky Publishers, Inc. Pg. 148.
1170. Levin (1992), Pg. 149.
1171. Levin (1992), Pg. 149.
1172. Levin (1992), Pg. 149.
1173. Peck, M. Scott (2002). *The Road Less Traveled: A New Psychology of Love, Traditional Values and Spiritual Growth*, 25th Anniversary Edition. New York: Simon & Schuster. Pg. 16.
1174. Greenstein, Fred I. (1994). "The Two Leadership Styles of William Jefferson Clinton." *Political Psychology*, Volume 15, Number 2. Pg. 352.
1175. Robbins, Anthony (2014). *Money: Master the Game. 7 Simple Steps to Financial Freedom*. New York: Simon and Schuster. Pg. 199.
1176. Robbins (2014), Pg. 199.
1177. Brinkley, Alan (1982). *Voices of Protest: Huey Long, Father Coughlin, and the Great Depression*. New York: Vintage Books. Pg. 25.
1178. Brinkley (1982), Pg. 25.
1179. Brinkley (1982), Pg. 25.
1180. Brinkley (1982), Pg. 25.
1181. Burns, Ken & Killberg, Richard (Producers). Burns, Ken (Director). (1986). *Huey Long*. [Documentary Film]. United States: Florentine Films.
1182. Chopra, Deepak (1991). *Unconditional Life: Discovering the Power to Fulfill Your Dreams*. New York: Bantam Books. Pg. 233.
1183. Schwarzenegger, Arnold (2013). *Total Recall: My Unbelievably True Life Story*. New York: Simon and Schuster. Pg. 425.
1184. Schwarzenegger (2013), Pg. 425.
1185. Schwarzenegger (2013), Pg. 425.
1186. Smith, Timothy Wilson (2007). *Napoleon*. London: Haus Publishing Limited. Pg. 25.
1187. Bosch, Adriana (Director). (1988). *American Experience: Jimmy Carter*. [Documentary Film]. United States: PBS. Transcript: http://www.pbs.org/wgbh/americanxperience/features/transcript/carter-transcript
1188. Bosch (1988).
1189. Bosch (1988).
1190. George, Alexander L. & George, Juliette L. (1998). *Presidential Personality and Performance*. Boulder, CO: Westview Press. Pg. 219.
1191. Bosch, Adriana (Director). (1988). *American Experience: Jimmy Carter*. [Documentary Film]. United States: PBS. Transcript: http://www.pbs.org/wgbh/americanxperience/features/transcript/carter-transcript
1192. Johnson, Steve (2002, November 11). "Ch. 11 gives us Carter in a nutshell." *Chicago Tribune*. http://articles.chicagotribune.com/2002-11-11/features/0211110025_1_jimmy-carter-rosalynn-american-people
1193. Wehner, Peter (2015, October 15). "Advice to the Next President." *The Miller Center*. http://eppc.org/publications/advice-to-the-next-president/
1194. Smith, Hedrick (1977, February 18). "Congress and Carter: An Uneasy Adjustment." *The New York Times*. http://www.nytimes.com/1977/02/18/archives/congress-and-carter-an-uneasy-adjustment.html?_r=0
1195. *Note*: The following are the eighteen presidents who did not serve in either the House or Senate prior to being elected President of the United States: George Washington, John Adams, Thomas Jefferson, Zachary Taylor, Ulysses Grant, Chester Arthur, Grover Cleveland, Theodore Roosevelt, William Taft, Woodrow Wilson, Calvin Coolidge, Herbert Hoover, Franklin Roosevelt, Dwight Eisenhower, Jimmy Carter, Ronald Reagan, Bill Clinton, and George W. Bush.
1196. Neustadt, Richard E. (1990). *Presidential Power and the Modern Presidents: The Politics of Leadership from Roosevelt to Reagan*. New York: The Free Press. Pg. 233.
1197. Evans, Mike (2009). *Jimmy Carter: The Liberal Left and World Chaos*. Phoenix: Time Worthy Books. Pg. 31.
1198. Holtzclaw, Eric (2012, June 21). "Power of Consistency: 5 Rules." *Inc. Magazine*. http://www.inc.com/eric-v-holtzclaw/consistency-power-success-rules.html
1199. Tomlinson, Gerald (1990). *Speaker's Treasury of Political Stories, Anecdotes and Humor*. New York: MJF Books. Pg. 37.
1200. Califano, Joseph A. (2015). *The Triumph & Tragedy of Lyndon Johnson: The White House Years*. New York: Touchstone. Pg. 312.
1201. Carville, James and Begala, Paul (2002). *Buck Up, Suck Up and Come Back When You Foul Up: 12 Winning Secrets from the War Room*. New York: Simon and Schuster. Pg. 162.
1202. Carville and Begala (2002), Pg. 162.
1203. Clinton, Bill (2006, August 22). "How We Ended Welfare, Together." *The New York Times*. http://www.nytimes.com/2006/08/22/opinion/22clinton.html?_r=0
1204. Clinton (2006).
1205. Carville, James and Begala, Paul (2002). *Buck Up, Suck Up and Come Back When You Foul Up: 12 Winning Secrets from the War Room*. New York: Simon and Schuster. Pg. 162.
1206. Carville and Begala (2002), Pg. 173.
1207. Collins, Jim & Porras, Jerry I. (1996, September-October). "Building Your Company's Vision." *Harvard Business Review*. Pg. 21. https://hbr.org/1996/09/building-your-companys-vision
1208. Vasan, Nina and Przybylo, Jennifer (2013). *Do Good Well: Your Guide to Leadership, Action, and Social Innovation*. San Francisco: Jossey-Bass. Pg. 226.
1209. Clausewitz, Carl Von (1989). *On War*. Howard, Michael & Paret, Peter (Eds., Trans.). Princeton: Princeton University Press. Pg. 119.
1210. Moltke, Helmuth Von (1993). *Moltke on the Art of War: Selected Writings*. Hughes, Daniel (Editor). New York: Random House. Pg. 92.
1211. Clausewitz, Carl Von (1989). *On War*. Howard, Michael & Paret, Peter (Eds., Trans.). Princeton: Princeton University Press. Pg. 101.
1212. "Flexibility." (2011, November). *British Defence Doctrine, Joint Doctrine Publication 0-01*, (JDP-0-01). 4th Edition. Pgs. 2-7. https://www.gov.uk/government/uploads/system/uploads/attachment_data/file/33697/20111130jdp001_bdd_Ed4.pdf
1213. Carville, James and Begala, Paul (2002). *Buck Up, Suck Up and Come Back When You Foul Up: 12 Winning Secrets from the War Room*. New York: Simon and Schuster. Pg. 160.
1214. Nye, Joseph (2013). *Presidential Leadership and the Creation of the American Era*. Princeton: Princeton University Press. Pg. 87.
1215. Machiavelli, Niccolo (1903 [1532]). *The Prince*. London: The World's Classics. Pg. 59.
1216. Axelrod, Alan (1999). *Patton on Leadership: Strategic Lessons for Corporate Warfare*. New York: Prentice Hall. Pg. 57.
1217. Carville, James and Begala, Paul (2002). *Buck Up, Suck Up and Come Back When You Foul Up: 12 Winning Secrets from the War Room*. New York: Simon and Schuster. Pg. 93.
1218. Sun Tzu (1910 [c. 5th century]). *The Art of War: The Oldest Military Treatise in the World*. Giles, Lionel (Translator). London.

1219. Greene, Robert (1998). *The 48 Laws of Power*. New York: Penguin Books. Pgs. 414-415.

1220. Greene (1998), Pg. 415.

1221. Greene (1998), Pg. 415.

1222. Millstone, Ken (2009, July 7). "Sarah Palin's Lame Duck Defense." *CBS News*. http://www.cbsnews.com/news/sarah-palins-lame-duck-defense/

1223. Millstone (2009).

1224. Newton-Small, Jay (2009, July 6). "Why Palin Quit: The Five Best Explanations." *Time*. http://content.time.com/time/politics/article/0,8599,1908800,00.html

1225. Newton-Small (2009).

1226. Note: Estimates of the time involved vary widely, depending on the project or endeavor. However, researchers such as Daniel Kahneman and Amos Tversky have shown that most people have a significant *optimism bias* when it comes to planning (they underestimate the time needed to complete a project), which can lead to both time and cost overruns. Source: Kahneman, Daniel and Tversky, Amos (1979). "Intuitive prediction: biases and corrective procedures". *TIMS Studies in Management Science* Volume 12. Pgs. 313–327.

1227. *The Holy Bible*, Book of Proverbs 15:22, New International Version (NIV).

1228. See the *Principle of the Hiding Hand* (i.e. people often begin projects because they are unaware of the challenges involved, but then, once the endeavor has begun, they will creatively overcome the obstacles, finding that they did in fact have the creativity and resources needed to succeed).

1229. Godin, Seth (2007). *The Dip: A Little Book that Teaches You When to Quit (And When to Stick)*. New York: Portfolio. Pg. 22.

1230. Sack, Kevin (1992, October 21). "THE 1992 CAMPAIGN: The Independent; Perot Scores in 3d Debate, Then Opens Fire on the Press." *The New York Times*. http://www.nytimes.com/1992/10/21/us/1992-campaign-independent-perot-scores-3d-debate-then-opens-fire-press.html

1231. "Superhero." (1992, October 31). *Newsweek*.

1232. "Superhero" (1992).

1233. "Superhero" (1992).

1234. "The Uses of Ross Perot." (1992, October 2). *The New York Times*. http://www.nytimes.com/1992/10/02/opinion/the-uses-of-ross-perot.html

1235. *The Holy Bible*, Proverbs 14:29, Aramaic Bible in Plain English

1236. Forbes, B.C. (1921). "Why Do So Many Men Never Amount to Anything? Thomas A. Edison, the Great Inventor, Answers this Pointed Question." *American Magazine*, Volume 91. Pg. 89.

1237. Israel, Paul (Editor) (2012). "Thomas Edison and His Papers." *The Thomas Edison Papers*, Rutgers University. http://edison.rutgers.edu/papers.htm In his own words, Edison said at age twenty-three: "All new inventions I will here after keep a full record."

1238. Forbes, B.C. (1921). "Why Do So Many Men Never Amount to Anything? Thomas A. Edison, the Great Inventor, Answers this Pointed Question." *American Magazine*, Volume 91. Pg. 89.

1239. Forbes (1921), Pg. 86.

1240. Forbes (1921), Pg. 86.

1241. Roosevelt, Theodore (1922). *Theodore Roosevelt: An Autobiography*. New York: Charles Scribner's Sons. Pg. 91.

1242. Roosevelt (1922), Pg. 92.

1243. Morris, Edmund (1979). *The Rise of Theodore Roosevelt*. New York: Random House. Pg. 445.

1244. Morris (1979), Pg. 449.

1245. Riis, Jacob A. (1904). *Theodore Roosevelt: The Citizen*. Washington, D.C.: Johnson, Wynne Company. Pg. 166.

1246. Riis (1904), Pg. 166.

1247. Smith, Joseph (2011). "The Assistant Secretary of the Navy and the Spanish-American War Hero." In Ricard, Serge (Editor) *A Companion to Theodore Roosevelt*. Blackwell Companions to American History. Malden, MA: Wiley-Blackwell. Pg. 49.

1248. Riis, Jacob A. (1904). *Theodore Roosevelt: The Citizen*. Washington, D.C.: Johnson, Wynne Company. Pg. 166.

1249. Halstead, Murat (1902). *The Life of Theodore Roosevelt*. Chicago: The Saalfield Publishing Co. Pg. 144.

1250. Riis, Jacob A. (1904). *Theodore Roosevelt: The Citizen*. Washington, D.C.: Johnson, Wynne Company. Pg. 166.

1251. Riis (1904), Pg. 166.

1252. Barber, James David (2007). *The Pulse of Politics: Electing Presidents in the Media Age*. New Brunswick: Transaction Publishers. Pg. 41.

1253. Goodwin, Doris Kearns (2014). *The Bully Pulpit: Theodore Roosevelt, William Howard Taft, and the Golden Age of Journalism*. New York: Simon and Schuster. Pg. 171.

1254. Schuller, Robert H. (1987). *The Be Happy Attitudes: 8 Positive Attitudes that Can Transform Your Life*. New York: Bantam. Pg. 109.

1255. Godin, Seth (2007). *The Dip: A Little Book that Teaches You When to Quit (And When to Stick)*. New York: Portfolio. Pg. 3.

1256. Godin (2007), Pg. 3.

1257. Roosevelt, Theodore (1897). *The Works of Theodore Roosevelt: American Ideals, with a Biographical Sketch by Gen. Francis Vinton Greene*. New York: P. F. Collier & Son, Publishers. Pg. 281.

1258. Roosevelt (1897), Pgs. 287-288.

1259. Greene, Robert (2006). *The 33 Strategies of War*. New York: Penguin Books. Pg. 283.

1260. Greene (2006), Pg. 283.

1261. Greene (2006), Pg. 292.

1262. Cotkin, George (1994). *William James: Public Philosopher*. Chicago: University of Illinois Press. Pg. 69. Actual quote: "Sow an action, and you reap a habit; sow a habit and you reap a character; sow a character and you reap a destiny."

1263. Roosevelt, Theodore (1900, March 31). "Character and Success." *The Outlook*, 64. Pg. 727. See also: http://www.foundationsmag.com/tr-character.html

1264. Roosevelt (1900), Pg. 727.

1265. Goodman, Ellen (2010, January 1). "Ellen Goodman Writes of Letting Go in Her Final Column." *The Washington Post*. http://www.washingtonpost.com/wp-dyn/content/article/2009/12/31/AR2009123101743_2.html

1266. Goodman (2010).

1267. Roosevelt, Theodore (1900, March 31). "Character and Success." *The Outlook*, 64. Pg. 727.

1268. Roosevelt (1900), Pg. 727.

Made in the USA
San Bernardino, CA
15 August 2016